John G.R McElroy

The Structure of English Prose

a manual of composition and rhetoric

John G.R McElroy

The Structure of English Prose

a manual of composition and rhetoric

ISBN/EAN: 9783337373962

Printed in Europe, USA, Canada, Australia, Japan

Cover: Foto ©Paul-Georg Meister /pixelio.de

More available books at **www.hansebooks.com**

THE
STRUCTURE OF ENGLISH PROSE

A MANUAL

OF

COMPOSITION AND RHETORIC

BY

JOHN G. R. McELROY, A. M.

Professor of Rhetoric and the English Language in the University of Pennsylvania,
Member of the Modern Language Association of America, Author of
"Essential Lessons in English Etymology," etc. etc.

"If, therefore, Plato had reason for writing over the door of his Academy, 'let no one who is not a geometrician enter here,' the Rhetorician has equal reason for inscribing upon the rostrum, 'let no one ascend here who is not a scholar and a thinker.'"

FIFTH EDITION, WITH COMPLETE ANALYSIS.

NEW YORK
A. C. ARMSTRONG & SON
No. 714 Broadway
TORONTO: ROSE PUBLISHING COMPANY
1889.

COPYRIGHT BY
JOHN G. R. McELROY
1885

PHILADELPHIA:
COLLINS, PRINTER, 705 JAYNE STREET.

PREFACE TO THE THIRD EDITION.

THE gratifying success of my book has led me, in preparing this new edition, to add a complete Analysis of the entire work. (See pp. ix. to xxviii.)

This Analysis, it will be observed, is not only by paragraphs, but also by the larger sections of the book. First, the main divisions are set forth; then, under each of these main divisions in turn, the several chapters of that main division, the sub-divisions of these chapters, and even the sections of these sub-divisions. Finally, the subject of each paragraph is given, and thus the last analysis of the work is reached. Complete tabular views of all classifications, and occasionally of the contents of more difficult paragraphs, are included in the Analysis, in the hope that, serving as "*maps*" of important parts of the subject, they may help materially to fix in the student's memory the sometimes perplexing minutiæ of the subject.

If properly used, the Analysis can hardly fail to promote topical recitations. No student of seventeen or eighteen ought to need severe, or even close, questioning to enable him to state concisely the contents of a paragraph; but he will very often need such help as is here offered, if only to show him how to analyze a paragraph for himself. The Analysis will, therefore, promote a second useful purpose; it will indicate clearly a method of studying, not only this, but all kindred subjects.

The best results in the use of the Analysis will be obtained, I think, if the student will first read over a paragraph, then, with the help of the Analysis, learn what that paragraph contains, and last, in re-reading the paragraph, verify and store away in his memory every detail. After each paragraph has been acquired thus, he can memorize the topics treated in his whole lesson, and then go into recitation fully armed and equipped. Even a final examination will lose its terrors to one who has prepared the subject thus.

A few slips in the book, not observed in the previous editions, are now corrected.

J. G. R. McE.

UNIVERSITY OF PENNSYLVANIA,
August, 1889.

PREFACE.

The teacher of Rhetoric has a double office. First, and chiefly, he must make writers; secondly, he must so exhibit the laws of his art as to promote mental discipline. In other words, he must be practical, without being a mere empiricist; he must be rational, without for an instant losing sight of skill in composition.

With these views in mind, I have tried to fill what seemed to me an empty place among books on Rhetoric. None of them, I thought, aimed at practical results, without sacrificing too far the principles of the art; none of them taught these principles in their fullness, without sacrificing in part or in whole the practical side of the work. I have aimed to strike the happy medium,—to make a book that shall teach composition while it forces the student to think, and shall exhibit the principles of the art at the same time that it keeps uppermost the problem *How to Write*. I have adopted Dr. Shedd's words quoted on my title-page, accepting fully the doctrine that Thought is more than Style, and modifying this doctrine by only one other truth—a truth to which Dr. Shedd would doubtless equally assent—that worthy thought deserves, as it promotes, an excellent form. In other words, while, with Herbert Spencer, I extol practice, I also accept, with him, the doctrine that "some practical result may be expected from a familiarity with the principles of style. . . . If in no other way, yet, as facilitating revision, a knowledge of the thing to be achieved—a clear idea of what constitutes a beauty, and what a blemish—can not fail to be of service."

I have also tried to exhibit the laws of Rhetoric in their entirety, —not the laws of Style alone, but also those of Invention. However we may quibble about that word *Invention* in its rhetorical sense, Rhetoric does teach other laws than those of Form; and these laws must be exhibited, if the art is to be taught fully. I admit freely that, in a book whose chief aim is skill in composition, Invention will occupy a considerably less number of pages than Style; and, hence, even after saying what I have said of the superior importance of Invention [§ 32], I have given by far the greater portion of my whole space to Style. The questions discussed under the head of Invention are largely theoretical; and their full exposition belongs either to a distinctively theoretical treatise on Rhetoric or to the several sciences that furnish the theory of the art. Were Rhetoric now, as it once was, a purely disciplinary study of Senior year, my book would have taken an entirely different form; but, in view of the wholesome change in our college work which assumes, not that the men know their mother-tongue because they speak it, but that, sadly ignorant of this mother-tongue, they need lessons in English, even more than they need the discipline of foreign languages, ancient or modern,—in view of this change, I have tried to make a book that shall start our younger college students and the older students in high schools and academies on the only road, difficult as it is, to a mastery of English composition.

The limitation of the book to Prose has been adopted, because I believe that every one who will apply himself can acquire appreciable skill in this kind of writing; while Poetry and Romance are products of exceptionally endowed minds. But I have not scrupled to quote examples from either poets or novelists. In many cases, such examples are of superior interest; while, not infrequently, they illustrate the laws of composition even better than examples in prose.

The work is the product of my own teaching. Circumstances led me about eight years ago to write a course of lectures for my class, with which to replace the text-book then in use. Later I printed an abstract of these lectures; and now this abstract has grown into an entire work. I do not wish to boast, much less to anticipate criticism; but the course has never yet failed to yield in large measure the fruit expected of it.

From the many works on Rhetoric, acknowledged and obscure, ancient and modern, I have sought both light and help. I am indebted, therefore, to all these writers: indeed, although I have in the main sought new examples and illustrations for the rules, yet I must adopt Dr. Austin Phelps's words;—"I have not scrupled to use any material which has seemed to me adapted to my purpose. I have appropriated principles of which no one knows the origin; I have employed illustrations, some of which belong to the common stock of rhetorical discussion." With him, too, I can excuse myself for not always noting the sources whence I drew my material, on the ground that even "to name them would be in part commonplace, and in part pedantic." To one writer, however, I must make especial acknowledgments. Early in my professorship, *The Art of Discourse*, by Prof. Henry N. Day, taught me the outline of a systematic Rhetoric, and so gave my studies a direction they have never since lost. Prof. Day will doubtless smile, should he ever honor me by turning my pages, to think that he could have stimulated the production of a work so unlike his as is mine: yet I hold to my confession. I believe there is nothing extant even purporting to have been written by Timothy; but, if there were, it would doubtless be as little Pauline as are the epistles of James or Peter. Yet Timothy was "son in the faith" to Paul, and evidently his particular disciple.

Many friends—more than I could readily mention here—have helped me in my work. Besides the names that appear in several foot-notes, the name of my colleague, Professor ALBERT S. BOLLES, must be specially recorded. To him I owe what is worth more than help,—continual and hearty encouragement, even when I was most discouraged.

J. G. R. McE.

UNIVERSITY OF PENNSYLVANIA,
February 26, 1885.

SUGGESTION.

The author's own experience with his book leads him to suggest to his fellow teachers that the best results with it may be obtained by omitting until review nearly all paragraphs in the smaller type. Then these paragraphs, which, as a rule, are theoretical rather than practical, will be the more easily understood. Of course, examples and illustrative extracts must be excepted; but these are not commonly numbered as separate paragraphs. The judicious teacher, however, will modify this plan at his discretion.

The Appendix is intended almost exclusively for the teacher.

CONTENTS.

INTRODUCTION, ... Page 9

> Rhetoric Defined, 9; Rhetoric Proper and Composition, 12; Sciences that give Laws to Rhetoric, 14; Fundamental Maxims, 16; Departments of Rhetoric, 19; Kinds of Discourse, 23.

PART FIRST.—STYLE, ... 50

> GRAMMATICAL PURITY, 53: Standard of Purity, 55; The Characteristics of Good Use, 64; Offences against Purity, 69; Exceptions, 114; Divided Use, 125.
>
> THE ELEMENTS OF STYLE, 132: Vocabulary, 133; The Sentence, 160; The Paragraph, 196; The Whole Composition, 223; Figures of Speech, 235.
>
> THE QUALITIES OF STYLE, 247: Significance, 248; Continuousness, 250; Naturalness, 250; Simplicity, 252; Clearness, 254; Force, 262; Pathos, 268; Humor, Satire, Wit, 271; Melody, Harmony, 275; Variety, 278; Elegance, 278.

PART SECOND.—INVENTION, ... 281

> THE THEME, 282.
>
> THE DISCUSSION, 287: General Rules, 288; Modes of Discussion, 290; Explanation, 291; Definition, 292; Narration, 296; Description, 299; Division, 306; Partition, 307; Exemplification, 307; Comparison and Contrast, 308; Argument, 309; Excitation, 320; Persuasion, 324.

APPENDIX, ... 329

> The Definition of Rhetoric, 329; Science, Art, Criticism, 331; Pure and Applied Science, 331; Theory, 332; True Method of Studying Rhetoric, 334; Technical Terms 336; The Latin Word *Tropus*, 336.

INDEX, ... 337

ANALYSIS.

MAIN DIVISIONS.

INTRODUCTION. PART SECOND.—INVENTION.
PART FIRST.—STYLE. APPENDIX.

INTRODUCTION.

I. RHETORIC DEFINED.
II. RHETORIC PROPER AND COMPOSITION.
III. THE SCIENCES THAT GIVE LAWS TO RHETORIC.
IV. FUNDAMENTAL MAXIMS.
V. THE DEPARTMENTS OF RHETORIC.
VI. THE KINDS OF DISCOURSE.

I. Rhetoric Defined.

1.* What Rhetoric is; 'Discourse' defined.
2. What Rhetoric is not; why.
3. 'Discourse' and 'Composition'; the former term in the definition.
4. 'Thought' as used here; Campbell's definition of Rhetoric.
5. The Mental Faculties:—
    1. Intellect, or Cognition;—
        (1) The Presentative Faculties,—
            (a) Intuition,
            (b) Perception;
        (2) The Representative Faculties,—
            (a) Memory,
            (b) Imagination;
        (3) The Elaborative Faculties,—
            (a) Conception,
            (b) Judgment,
            (c) Reasoning;
    2. Sensibility, or Feeling;
    3. Will.
6. 'Terms' defined; 'Judgment' defined.
7. Primary meaning of 'Language'; scope of the laws of Rhetoric.
8, 9. Why this statement is true; examples.

* Initial numbers refer to paragraphs.

II. Rhetoric Proper and Composition.

10. Kinds of study included in Rhetoric.
11. Authorities for this view;—J. Q. Adams, Prof. H. N. Day.
12. Sources of the distinction; illustrations.
13. Further reason for distinguishing Rhetoric and Composition.
14. Limitations of the distinction; relations of Rhetoric and Composition.
15. More technical statement of this truth.

III. The Sciences that give Laws to Rhetoric.

16. Whence Rhetoric derives its underlying principles.
17, 18. Relations of Rhetoric to its nomothetical sciences:—
 (A) Discourse involves
  1. Matter, or Content.   (Logic.)
  2. Form, or Style,
   (a) Outward and bodily. (Grammar.)
   (b) Inward and Spiritual. (Æsthetics.)
  3. Purpose, or End in View. (Ethics.)

 (B) These sciences independent of Rhetoric.

IV. Fundamental Maxims.

19. The four *Dicta* of Rhetoric.
20. 'Genuine thought' defined; examples; false use of 'rhetorical.'
21. Variation in the standard of taste.
22. Meaning of the dictum of Ethics; examples.

V. The Departments of Rhetoric.

23. Names of the departments of Rhetoric; what each includes.
24. Why two departments, not three.
25. Why Disposition, or Arrangement, is not a department of Rhetoric.
26. The argument against a department of Invention.
27, 28. Reasons for conceding such a department;—
 (a) The reasoning against it an evasion of the point at issue;
 (b) Rules for the matter of discourse exist; they belong to Rhetoric; they are not laws of form.
29. The real question raised here.
30. Why 'invention' may imply too much; if so, what?
31. Bad effects of limiting Rhetoric to Style.
32. Relative importance of Invention and Style; preparatory topic in next chapter.
33. Why this topic must be treated here.

VI. The Kinds of Discourse.

34. Compositions are divided
   1. With respect to Form, into
      (a) Prose,
      (b) Verse;
   2. With respect to Intrinsic Character, into
      (a) Oratory,
      (b) Representative Discourse,
      (c) Romance,
      (d) Poetry;
   3. With respect to Purpose, into
      (a) Explanatory Discourse,
      (b) Argumentative Discourse,
      (c) Excitatory Discourse,
      (d) Persuasive Discourse.
35. Caution.
36. Verse; rhythm; metre; a verse.
37. Example in § 36 explained.
38. Remark.
39. Prose defined.
40. The rhythm of fine prose; examples.
41. Metric Prose; a better name for it; examples.
42, 43. Other examples, increasingly rhythmical.
44. Example of blank verse.
45. Oratory defined; example.
46. Another form of the same example.
47. Essential characteristic of the Oration.
48. Narrower meaning of 'oration.'
49, 50. Specific cases of the oration.
51. The Letter, oratorical form.
52. Difference between this form of letter and the oration.
53. Other examples.
54. The letter, ordinary form.
55. Representative Discourse defined.
56. 'We' and 'I' in representative discourse.
57. Sub-divisions of Representative Discourse;—
   1. Those in which the subject is a *fact*,—
      (a) History,
      (b) Biography,
      (c) Travels;
   2. Those in which the subject is a *truth*,—
      (a) Scientific Treatises,
      (b) Essays,
      (c) Theses.
58. Combined Oratory and Representative Discourse; example.
59. Other examples.
60. Representative Discourse in the Letter; example.
61. Other examples.

62. Most usual form of the Letter.
63. Romance defined; two sub-divisions.
64. Hawthorne's definition of Romance.
65. Examples of (1) the Romance proper, (2) the Novel.
66. 'Romance,' 'the Novel,' and 'Fiction' as synonyms.
67. In what sense the Romance is true; example.
68. The definition of Poetry; two particulars widely agreed on.
69. Examples of definitions of Poetry.
70. Sub-divisions of Poetry;—
    (1) Lyric Poetry,—
        Song,
        Ode,
        Elegy,
        Sonnet,
        Simple Lyric;
    (2) Epic Poetry,—
        Great Epic,
        Romance,
        Ballad,
        Pastoral, or Idyll;
    (3) Dramatic Poetry,—
        Tragedy,
        Comedy.
71, 72. Remark; examples.
73. The word 'Prose' to mean Oratory and Representative Discourse.
74. Romance and Poetry as opposed to Prose.
75. Why the third class of compositions is not treated here.

PART FIRST.—STYLE.

DEFINITIONS.
(A) GRAMMATICAL PURITY.
(B) THE ELEMENTS OF STYLE.
(C) THE QUALITIES OF STYLE.

Definitions.

76. Style defined; examples.
76a. The study of Style—what it is.
77. Three distinctions of Style; what they are not; example.
78. Sub-divisions of Part First.

(A) GRAMMATICAL PURITY.

  I. ITS IMPORTANCE.
  II. THE STANDARD OF PURITY.
  III. THE CHARACTERISTICS OF GOOD USE.

IV. Offences against Purity.
V. Varieties of Diction. Exceptions to the Laws of Purity.
VI. Divided Use.

I. The Importance of Grammatical Purity.

79. Grammatical Purity and correctness of drawing in painting; examples.

II. The Standard of Purity.

80. Necessity for a standard; its proper character.
81. Explanation of the violations of Purity by good writers.
82. Two opinions as to what the Standard of Purity is.
83. Authority for the first opinion.
84. The opposite opinion; by whom held.
85-94. Reasons for preferring this opposite opinion;—
   1st. Principles anterior to Use, and, therefore, superior to it;
   2d. Man's use of language bound by definite laws;
   3d. Monstrosity a violation of the laws of Nature;
   4th. The facts of Usage all point this way;—
      (1) The case of settled usage;
      (2) The case of unsettled ('divided') use;
      (3) Changes in good use;
   5th. Exceptions to the laws of Purity not inconsistent with the doctrine here maintained;
   6th. The Good Use theory inconsistent with itself;—
      (1) Not all Good Use, it says, is binding, but only such as has certain characteristics;
      (2) In cases of 'divided use,' even this theory falls back on principle.
95. How Grammatical Purity is best studied; why.

III. The Characteristics of Good Use.

96. What use is 'good'?
97. The answer to this question; examples.
98. Reputable Use defined.
99. National Use defined; dialecticism; the 'literary' dialect.
100. Illustrations from the history of English and of French.
101. How a common dialect is chosen; examples.
102. Why Present Use is not easily defined;—
   (a) Most languages spoken by several generations at once;
   (b) A vocabulary ebbs and flows;
   (c) The fate of words varies as regards both adoption and disuse; examples;
      Principles of judgment; Polonius's advice to Laertes; Quintillian's rule.
103. Rhetorical praxis.

IV. Offences against Purity.

104. Two classifications of Errors in Diction;—
    (I.) As opposed to Good Use;—
        To 1. Reputable, 2. National, 3. Present, Use;
    (II.) With reference to the several Departments of Grammar;—
        1. Etymology, 2. Syntax, 3. Lexicography.
105. Relation of the two classifications to each other.
    (I.) Violations of Purity as opposed to Good Use;—
        1. Violations of Reputable Use,—
            (1) Vulgarisms,
            (2) Idiotisms;
        2. Violations of National Use,—
            (1) Provincialisms,
            (2) Technicalities,
            (3) Alienisms;
        3. Violations of Present Use,—
            (1) Archaisms,
            (2) Neologisms.
106. Violations of Reputable Use;—(1) Vulgarisms, (2) Idiotisms; examples.
107. The "slovenly" use of words.
108. Vulgarism and coarseness.
109. Slang; when vulgarism; when technicality.
110. Vulgarisms among educated people; price of Purity in this respect.
111. Means to Purity; Purity and Purism.
112. "Fine writing"; three grades of it.
113. *First*, that of imperfectly educated professional men.
114. *Second*, the language of "Mrs. Viney" and her class, etc.
115. *Third*, the "penny-a-liner's" diction, "newspaper English."
116. Criticism of "newspaper English" by a newspaper.
117. Violations of National Use;—(1) Provincialisms, (2) Technicalities, (3) Alienisms; examples.
118. When the Alienism is most objectionable.
119. Limitations of the rule against the Alienism; examples.
120. When a word may be considered naturalized; three cases.
121. Necessary and admissible alienisms.
122. Mr. Oliphant's view of the subject.
123-126. Tests of Alienism;—
    1st. Italicization,
    2d. Inflection and syntax,
    3d. Intelligibility.
127. How to pronounce foreign words; again three cases.
127a. Influence of the study of foreign languages; works of reference.
128. Provincialisms and archaisms.
129. When technical terms are preferable; Whately's view.

130. Fred Viney's argument in "Middlemarch."
131. Violations of Present Use;—(1) Archaisms, (2) Neologisms; examples.
132. Neologism and Vulgarism.
133. Unobjectionable archaisms.

(II.) Violations of Purity with reference to the Departments of Grammar;—
    1. Offences against Etymology, called Barbarisms.
        (1) Radical words and phrases,
        (2) Inflections,
        (3) Derivatives,
        (4) Compounds;
    2. Offences against Syntax, called Solecisms,—in
        (1) Concord,
        (2) Grammatical Arrangement,
        (3) Grammatical Propriety,
        (4) Grammatical Precision;
    3. Offences against Lexicography, called Improprieties,—
        (1) Single words,
        (2) Phrases.

134. How Etymology, etc. treat of words; meaning of Barbarism, etc.
135. Campbell's statement of all this for English.
136. Sub-divisions of the Barbarism; examples.
137. Campbell's sub-divisions; why Prof. Day's are better.
138. Mispronunciations and misspellings.
139. Compounds in English; their history.
140. Mr. Oliphant's opinion, and the reply to it.
141. Hybridism defined; how accounted in most languages; in English; examples.
142. Abbreviated forms; when justifiable; examples.
143. Objectionable abbreviations; examples.
144. Kinds of abbreviated forms.
145. Sub-divisions of the solecism; examples.
146. Proposed rule for (1) *who* and *which*, (2) *that*.
147. Reasons for the rule;—
    1st. It promotes clearness;
    2d. It gains more than it loses; the relative a troublesome word.
148. History of the words.
149. Possible explanation of the distinction.
150. Exceptions to the rule.
151. Optional use of *that* or of *who* or *which*.
152. Distinction between *shall* and *will*; Sir E. W. Head's rules.
153. Exceptions.
154. Improprieties;—

(1) Single words,—
    (*a*) Alike in sound or appearance,
    (*b*) Alike in sense,
    (*c*) Alike in both sound or appearance and sense,
    (*d*) Resembling in meaning their foreign equivalents or etymological primitives,
    (*e*) Misused for each other though not alike,
    (*f*) Blunder-words;
(2) Phrases,—
    (*a*) Absurd, inconsistent, or contradictory in meaning,
    (*b*) Apparent only,
    (*c*) Rhetorical.

V. Varieties of Diction. Exceptions to the Laws of Purity.

155. How diction and the laws of Purity vary; illustrations.
156. These statements true of style in general.
157. Characteristics of the diction of Prose and of Poetry;
    1st. Prose like speech; but is
        (*a*) more exact,
        (*b*) less brief,
        (*c*) more varied in construction;
    2d. Poetic diction
        (*a*) is archaic,
        (*b*) is picturesque,
        (*c*) substitutes epithets for the things denoted,
        (*d*) avoids lengthiness and is euphonious;—
            (α) omits connectives,
            (β) avoids length without force, etc.,
            (γ) seeks euphony, but
            (δ) is long to give added pleasure.
158. Exceptional forms of Prose;—
    (1) Intentional archaism; examples;
    (2) Impassioned Prose; examples;
    (3) Poetic Prose; examples.
159. The diction of Romance; examples.
160. The diction of dramatic writings; examples.
161. Literal quotation; quotations in foreign languages.
162. Colloquialisms; why admissible; limitations of the privilege.

VI. Divided Usage.

163. Divided Use defined; necessity of an appeal to principles.
164. When an alternative form does not divide usage; examples.
165. The law of correctness in cases of divided usage.
166. When a form is preferable; Campbell's canons; other laws.
167. Campbell's canons in tabular form.
168. Examples under each canon.
169. Relative value of the five canons; the controlling principle.

ANALYSIS. xvii

(B) THE ELEMENTS OF STYLE.

SUB-DIVISIONS.
I. VOCABULARY.
II. THE SENTENCE.
III. THE PARAGRAPH.
IV. THE WHOLE COMPOSITION.
V. FIGURES OF SPEECH.

Sub-Divisions.

170. Mechanical components of language; sub-divisions of (B).
171. How these sub-divisions are determined; the law of unity.

I. Vocabulary.

1. *The Choice of Words.*
2. *The Number of Words.*

I. THE CHOICE OF WORDS.

172. Probable number of English words; comparison with German.
173. More exact statements on these points.
174. Part of this vocabulary used by single writers; instances.
175. Mr. Marsh's explanation of these facts.
176. But command of language most important; why; price one may well pay for it; the English speaker's special obligation.
177. What is implied by command of language.
178. Evil consequences of poverty or monotony of language.
179. Results of the unskilful selection of words.
180. Kinds of reading that promote command of language; reasons for each specification.
181. Value of works of reference; examples.
182. How practice in composition extends one's vocabulary.
183. Principles of choice in words; three especially in place here;
    (1) Native *vs.* foreign words;
    (2) Short *vs.* long words;
    (3) " Proper words in proper places."
184. Why native words are preferable;—
    (*a*) They are "to the manner born";
    (*b*) In English, they are simple and brief.
185. Etymological analysis of English,—(*a*) in bulk, (*b*) in our best writers.
186. Limitations of the rule in favor of Anglo-Saxon English;—
    (*a*) Other English also good; the rule often over-stated;
    (*b*) Many cases do not admit a choice.
187. Summary of §§ 184-186.

188. Anglo-Saxon 'hobby-riding'; examples.
189. Advantages of short words;—
    (*a*) Economy of space and time;
    (*b*) Compactness of structure;
    (*c*) Simplicity and clearness.
  Opposing considerations;—
    (*a*) Difficulty of understanding a series of short words;
    (*b*) Compactness of structure not always desirable; why;
    (*c*) Short words not always simple, nor long ones always abstruse; examples; length of word a mere accident; the true rule.
190. Other considerations that vary vocabulary; Swift's statement.

2. The Number of Words.

191. The law of "judicious" Brevity; Brevity the resultant of many opposing considerations.
192, 193. Examples; variations in a single writer.
194. Sources of violations of Brevity; their evil effects.
195. Violations of Brevity on the side of Excess;—
    (1) Tautology;
    (2) Pleonasm, or Redundancy;
    (3) Verbosity,—
        (*a*) Circumlocution, or Periphrasis,
        (*b*) Paraphrase,
        (*c*) Prolixity.
196. Exceptions to the law of Brevity.
197. Violations of Brevity on the side of Deficiency.
198. The means to Brevity.

II. The Sentence.

1. *The Order of Words and Clauses in the Sentence.*
2. *The Period and the Loose Sentence.*
3. *Explicit Reference.*
4. *Long and Short Sentences.*
5. *The Balanced Sentence.*
6. *The Condensed Sentence.*
7. *Unity.*
8. *Due Proportion.*

199. Importance of correct sentence-structure; over-estimate of it.

1. The Order of Words and Clauses in the Sentence.

200. Rules for ordering words and clauses;—
    (1) The Law of Proximity,
    (2) The Law of Modifiers,
    (3) The Principle of Emphasis,
    (4) The Law of Modifying Clauses.

201. The Law of Proximity; examples.
202. Special importance of Position in English.
203. The Law of Modifiers; examples; exceptions.
204. The Principle of Emphasis; (*a*) unusual arrangement; (*b*) emphatic places; examples.
205. Minto's estimate of the importance of the law.
206. Difficulty in obeying it; examples.
207. How to succeed in applying the rule; spoken and written sentences in this respect; examples.
208. The Law of Modifying Clauses; their two positions.
209. Limitations of 'natural' and 'inverted' in this use; both positions good; ill effects of excess in either; examples.
210. Reason for the direct order; for inversion; examples.
211. Opposite tendency of these reasons in many cases.
212. The case of two or more dependent clauses, with one principal clause.

2. The Period and the Loose Sentence.

213. Periodic and loose sentences defined; periodic and loose style.
214. Essential character of the Period; Campbell's definition; its erroneousness.
215. True meaning of the word *suspense* in this use; its common use.
216. Effect of the periodic structure; examples.
217. Why neither structure is always better.

3. Explicit Reference.

218, 219. Law of explicit reference; reasons for it; how it is effected; special devices for securing it;—
  1. Connectives,—
      (*a*) Conjunctions, including adverbs, etc.;
      (*b*) Pronouns, etc.;
  2. Intentional Repetitions.
      Examples of inserted or omitted connectives.
220. Evil effects of (1) the excessive use, (2) the undue omission, of connectives; examples.
221. Excessive use of the Relative Pronoun; equivalents for the relative.
222. Law of intentional repetition; examples.

4. Long and Short Sentences.

223. How length of sentence is determined; sentences too short; too long; examples.
224. Care to avoid extremes; early English prose; "asthmatic" sentences; recent examples.
225. Effects of short and of long sentences; advantages of each; other distinctions; examples.
226. Unobjectionable, though very long, sentences.

227. Length of sentence and periodicity.
228. Devices for making a long sentence clear.

5. The Balanced Sentence.

229. Definition of the balanced sentence; examples.
230. The common definition; in what respects erroneous; examples.
231. Nature and effect of the peculiar structure.
232. Advantages and disadvantages of the balanced sentence.
233. Balance by the "splitting" of two allied constructions.
234. Balance with antithesis, epigram, or climax; the "pointed" style.

6. The Condensed Sentence.

235. 'Zeugma' in English; its chief use at present; an exception.

7. Unity.

236. The law of Unity; examples, and comments on them.
237. Sentences that violate Unity.
238. Overstatements of the law; opposite considerations; Blair's rules.
239. Criticism of Blair's first rule.
240. Blair's second rule; how far true.
241. Blair's third rule; when parentheses destroy Unity; examples.
242. Blair's fourth rule; a necessary limitation of it.
243. The relative "tag" and Unity.
244. Intentional violations of Unity; their purpose; examples.

8. Due Proportion.

245. The Law of Due Proportion; the reason for it; examples.

III. The Paragraph.

1. *Initial Theme, or Topic, Sentences.*
2. *Explicit Reference.*
3. *Parallel Construction.*
4. *Method.*
5. *Unity.*
6. *Due Proportion.*
7. *Climax. Bathos.*

246. Nature of the Paragraph; importance of its laws.
247. Neglect of paragraph-arrangement by even the best writers; silence of rhetoricians on the subject.
248. Rules for the paragraph.

1. Initial Theme, or Topic, Sentences.

249. Office of the opening sentence of a paragraph; examples.

ANALYSIS. xxi

2. EXPLICIT REFERENCE.

250. The law of Explicit Reference; reasons for it; example.
251. When neglect of explicit reference is especially bad; example.
252. How explicit reference in the paragraph is produced.
253. Special Devices for Explicit Reference:—
  1. Connective Particles;—
    (a) Conjunctions,
    (b) Adverbs, etc., used conjunctively,
    (c) Pronouns so used;
  2. Repetitions;—
    (a) Literal,
    (b) In substance;
  3. Inversions, etc.
254. Kinds of sentences that need no connectives.
255. Older use of the relative pronoun as connective; examples.
256. Reasons against this use.
257. Rule for all other English connectives.
258. Objections to initial *and, but, for, however;* Prof. A. S. Hill's view.
259. General reply to these objections.
259a. Possible grounds of some of the objections.
260–267. Detailed reply to Prof. Hill;—
  1st. Objections to *and* or *but* as connectives hold to all connectives;
  2d. Most English connectives too insignificant to attract attention;
  3d. The folly of crippling ourselves by giving up any weapon we may properly use;
  4th. The two grounds of Prof. Hill's statement; their untenability; facts to prove their untenability; summary of his argument;
  5th. The testimony of competent authorities—(a) rhetoricians, (b) good authors.

3. PARALLEL CONSTRUCTION.

268. The Law of Parallel Construction; its reason; examples.
269. The effect of joining Balance, etc., to assimilation.
270. The means to Parallel Construction; examples.
271. Opposing laws; examples with comments on them.
272. Emphasis by parallel construction.

4. METHOD.

273. The law of Method in the paragraph; reasons for orderly arrangement; examples with comments.

5. UNITY.

274. The law of Unity in the paragraph; where the "principal affirmation" is made; examples with explanations.

275. Limitations of the rule; danger of giving undue prominence to unimportant matter.
276. Why the rule is more stringent for the paragraph than for the sentence.

6. Due Proportion.

277. The law of Due Proportion in the paragraph; examples.

7. Climax. Bathos.

278. Definition of Climax, of Bathos; kinds of each and their character; aim of intentional Bathos; examples.

IV. The Whole Composition.

1. *The Parts of a Composition.*
2. *Canons of the Composition as a Whole.*

279. Laws of the composition as a whole; which of them belong here.

1. The Parts of a Composition.

280. The four parts of a composition; the essential parts; the non-essential parts; definition of each part.
281. Analysis of Matthew Arnold's essay *On Translating Homer*.
282. Law of the introduction and the conclusion; example.
283. Limitations of the rule; example.
284. Less methodical structure of many compositions; what is always necessary; example.
285. Danger of this plan; possible evil results.
285*a*. A fair test of the doctrine.
285*b*. Apparent exceptions to the principle.
286. The *mechanical* in this use of method; why better than confusion; formality not necessarily a result.
287. The value of a synopsis, or 'skeleton,' in writing; how to use such a synopsis; how to work without one.
288. Forms of the Proposition; need of variety; danger of including the proposition in the title.
288*a*. When the Proposition is, when it is not, a judgment.

2. Canons of the Composition as a Whole.

289. Four rules obeyed by the composition as a whole;—
 (1) Unity; necessity of excluding interesting matter, even from extended works;
 (2) Method; reason for this rule;
 (3) Selection; when the rule is most binding; its high importance; influence of method on selection;
 (4) Completeness; meaning of the rule; judicious brevity and incompleteness.

V. The Figures of Speech.

290. Figure of speech defined; examples.
291. Classification of the figures of speech; how far possible.
292.—(1) Figures in the 'use of single words,' or '*tropes.*'
293.—(2) Figures 'stated at length,' or '*schemata.*'
294.—(3) 'Figures of diction' and 'figures of thought'; the distinction between them; value of the phrase 'figures of thought.'
295. Table of the Figures of Speech; the principal figures defined.
296. Why a longer list is not given.
297–302. Another arrangement of the figures of speech;—
    (1) Figures that compare objects much alike;—Metaphor, Simile;
    (2) Figures that compare objects remotely alike;—Allegory, Personification;
    (3) Figures that substitute one thing for another;—Metonymy, Synecdoche;
    (4) Figures that present the unexpected;—Antithesis, Epigram, Irony, Hyperbole, Euphemism.
    (5) The Figures of Thought;—(see § 295.)
303. Further (but not essential) details.
304. When comparison is figurative; when literal.
305. Rules for the use of Figures;—
    (1) The Law of Keeping; examples;
    (2) The Law of Moderation; examples;
    (3) The Law of Clearness; examples;
    (4) The Law of Congruity; examples.

(C) THE QUALITIES OF STYLE.
Definition and Sub-Divisions.
I. The Subjective Qualities.
II. The Objective Qualities.

Definition and Sub-Divisions.

306. Meaning of the phrase, 'subtler properties of language'; distinctions between these properties and the grammatical and the mechanical properties of language; to what part of man's nature the qualities of style appeal.
307. Classification of the Qualities of Style; meaning of 'subjective' and 'objective.'

I. The Subjective Qualities of Style.

308. The names of the subjective qualities of style.
309. What is implied by Significance; 'spurious oratory'; 'the Nonsensical.'
310. The Humorous and the Nonsensical.
311. What is implied by Continuousness; the sources of true Sententiousness; 'talking in a circle.'
312. Naturalness defined; grounds for the quality; imitation.
313. Modifications of Naturalness in discourse; examples.

II. The Objective Qualities of Style.

314. Classification:—
   1. The Intellectual Qualities;—
      (1) Simplicity,
      (2) Clearness,
         (a) Perspicuity,
         (b) Precision;
   2. The Emotional Qualities;—
      (1) Force,
      (2) Pathos,
      (3) The Ludicrous,—
         (a') Satire,
         (a'') Humor,
         (b) Wit;
   3. The Æsthetic Qualities;—
      (1) Melody,
      (2) Harmony,
      (3) Variety,
      (4) Elegance.

1. THE INTELLECTUAL FACULTIES.

315. Simplicity defined; contrasted with clearness; examples.
316. Abstruseness only relatively a fault; examples.
317. Means to Simplicity;—(1) Familiar terms, (2) Particular terms; examples.
318. Clearness defined; not a relative quality, but "of obligation."
319. Relations of clear thinking to clear writing.
320. Clearness as produced by correctness of form in general.
321. Special rules for Clearness;—
   (a) Indicate the particular meaning intended;
   (b) Avoid two meanings of the same word in the same context;
   (c) Use every word in its exact sense, and always express that sense by that word;
   (d), (e), (f) Avoid ambiguous pronouns, ambiguous negatives, obscure sentence-structure;
322. Mutual relations of simplicity, perspicuity, and precision.
323. Absurdity of Blair's rule about clear thinking and clear writing.

2. THE EMOTIONAL QUALITIES.

324. Error in their classification before Bain.
325. Force defined; other terms for it.
326. The chief source of Force in composition; examples.
327. Restraint of language and true force; Bombast; examples.
328. Further conditions to Force; examples.
329. Pathos defined; relations of Pathos and Force; examples
330. Feeling and true Pathos; Sentimentality.

331. The Ludicrous defined; its several forms;—
(a) Degradation of an object ordinarily dignified;
(a') Satire, (a'') Humor;
(b) Unexpected and ingenious association of objects not usually connected,—Wit.
332. Criticism of another use of the terms Humor and Wit.
333. Humor and Pathos united in the same composition.
334. Other terms to denote the Ludicrous.

3. The Æsthetic Qualities.

335. Æsthetic qualities defined; how refinement of style is produced.
336. Melody and Harmony in Music, in Style; euphony; rhythm; further distinctions; examples.
337. Law of the rhythmic in Prose.
338. Variety defined; its opposite.
339. Elegance defined; Taste; examples.
340. The permanent and the variable element of Taste.

PART SECOND.—INVENTION.

Sub-Divisions.
(A) The Theme.
(B) The Discussion.

Sub-Divisions.

341. Definition of Invention; the sub-divisions of Part II.
342. The word "discussion" as used here and in § 280.

(A) The Theme.

343. Source of the Theme; three cases; examples.
344. The exercise of judgment in each case; examples.
345. Three things to be determined when the subject is not given;—
(a) occasion of speaking, (b) character of audience, (c) purpose in writing; work done in ignorance of (a) and (b).
346. Relation of the writer to his subject.
347. The danger of choosing "fertile" subjects.
348. Development of the theme; (a) preparatory reading; (b) determining the Proposition; (c) mapping the outline; avoidance of formality; example.
349. Probable results of working without method.

(B) The Discussion.

I. General Rules.
II. The Modes of Discussion.

350. Collection of matter for the composition; how guided; resulting sub-divisions of this section.
350a. Why Rhetoric cannot teach the discussion of separate themes; earnest writing and earnest reading; plagiarism.

I. GENERAL RULES.

Three modes of treating a theme;—
    (1) Exhaustive treatment,
    (2) Treatment within limited portions of a subject;
    (3) Treatment for specific purposes.
351. Exhaustive treatment of a subject; examples.
352. Writing within limited portions of a subject; examples.
353. When partial knowledge is enough; example.
354. Rule for all cases; examples.

II. THE MODES OF DISCUSSION.

355. The matter of a composition as determined by the Purpose of the writer; this always to communicate thought; hence, four Modes of Discussion;—
    (a) Discourse addressed to the Understanding,—
        (I.) Explanation, which presents a Term,
        (II.) Argument, which presents a Judgment
    (b) Discourse addressed to the Feelings,—
        (III.) Excitation;
    (c) Discourse addressed to the Will,—
        (IV.) Persuasion.
356. Mutual relations of the modes of discussion.
357. Inclusion of the corresponding negative processes.
358. Why Explanation, etc., involve each other.

(I.) EXPLANATION.

359. Explanation defined; a synonym for it.
360. What the theme in Explanation is; when it is presented intelligibly.
361. Clear and distinct presentation—their difference illustrated.
362. Means to the intelligible presentation of an object.
363. The most exact definition.
364. Substitutes for logical definition.
365. The general principles that control Definition.
366. The six processes involved in Explanation Proper.
367. The distinction between Division and Partition.
368. The six processes viewed as three pairs of processes.
369. Mutual relations of Narration and Description;—
    (a) What each presents; fitness of language to the function of each;
    (b) Details involved in each; capacity of language to express these details;
    (c) Which is especially the work of the writer, which of the painter or sculptor.
370. Division and Partition distinguished.
371. In what Exemplification and Comparison and Contrast agree; the last really a single process; why.
372. Kinds of Narration; their names; their interdependence; the order of their occurrence in time; examples.

ANALYSIS. xxvii

373-378. Laws of Method in Narration;—
 (*a*) Adherence to the order chosen, except
  (α) A familiar state of things,
  (β) Concurring streams;
 (*b*) Value of summaries;
 (*c*) Use of cross-sections.
379. Forms of Description; their mutual relations.
380. Laws of Method in Description;—
 (*a*) When addressed to the understanding;
 (*b*) When addressed to the imagination;
 (*c*) How illusion is produced;
 (*d*) How illusion may be dispelled;
 (*e*) Reason of the failure of many descriptions.
386. Example of self-restraint in this matter.
387. When descriptions of the "inventory" kind are available.
388. Description from "the traveller's point of view."
389. Description involved in other modes of composition.
390. The laws that control Division.
391. The laws of Partition.
392. The rules that control Exemplification.
393. When examples may precede principles.
394. Methods of Comparison and Contrast; examples.

II. ARGUMENT.

395. What the theme in Argument always is.
396. This judgment and the subject of composition; examples.
397. Means to determining the theme in Argument; examples.
398. 'Hypothesis' and 'Theory'; examples.
399. On what Argument proceeds; proofs defined; relations of the process to Logic, to Rhetoric.
400. Reasoning of two kinds;—(α) Immediate, (β) Mediate; examples.
401. Proof of two kinds;—(α) Direct, (β) Indirect (=Refutation); examples.
402. Proofs are—
 (*a*) Analytic, given in the terms of the judgment;
 (*b*) Synthetic, derived from outside the judgment;
  (*b'*) Intuitive, furnished by the mind itself;
  (*b''*) Empirical, furnished by experience;—
   (α) *A priori*, from whole to part (Antecedent Probability);
   (β) *A posteriori*, from part to whole (Signs);
   (γ) Examples, resting on—
    (γ') a common property, Induction;
    (γ'') a common relation, Analogy.
403. 'Cause' and 'Effect' defined.
404. Value of the several classes of arguments.
405. Other conditions to success in Argument.

406. State of the mind addressed; degrees of belief; method of argumentation in each case.
407. Difference between written and spoken argument; examples.
408. Place of the proposition in Argument; exceptions; examples.
409. Order of the several proofs; determined by
 (α) State of the mind addressed,
  (a′) Without belief, or in weak faith,
  (a″) In positive disbelief;
 (β) Relative value of the proofs,—
  (β′) Analytic proofs,
  (β″) *A priori* proofs, signs, examples.
410. 'Burden of Proof' explained; the 'Presumption'; 'Apology.'
411. Importance of determining which side has the Burden of Proof.
412. On which side the Presumption always is; examples.
413. Opposed and shifting presumptions; examples.
414. Explanation in Argument; where explanations "come in."
415. Other considerations in Argument; example.
416. Conclusion of an argumentative composition; what it may contain.

III. Excitation.

417. What the theme in Excitation is; how expressed.
418. Means to the arousing of passion; their mutual relation.
419. Possible state of mind of the persons addressed; rule for each case; examples.
420. Place of the Proposition in Excitation; Whately's view; Day's criticism of Whately.
421. When gradual approach is necessary; examples.
422–425. Rules for Pathetic Explanation;—
 (a) Narrow Selection; examples;
 (b) Particular Views; examples;
 (c) Appeal to the imagination; examples.
426. Modes of Expressing Emotion; examples.

IV. Persuasion.

427. The theme in Persuasion; what it is; examples.
428. Means to Persuasion; examples.
429. Motives defined; their classification; general truths concerning them;
 (α) Their different power;
 (β) Pure motives preferable to lower ones; examples;
 (γ) Must be adapted to the mind addressed; examples;
 (δ) Higher motives most successful in large audiences.
430. Necessity of observing state of the mind addressed.
431. Rules for the proposition in Persuasion.
432. Arrangement in persuasive discourse; rules for it; caution.

APPENDIX.

THE STRUCTURE OF ENGLISH PROSE.

INTRODUCTION.

I.

RHETORIC DEFINED.

1. RHETORIC IS THE ART OF DISCOURSE[1],—*the Art of Communicating Thought in Language.*

2. In no proper sense, is Rhetoric a *science;* nor should it be defined as the art of *effective* discourse. It discovers nothing; it is like all other arts in aiming at efficient work; and its full definition, therefore, is that just given. The discussion of these questions, however, belongs elsewhere.[2]

3. A more familiar word for Discourse is COMPOSITION,—a synonym that will be used freely in these pages. The more technical term seems necessary in the definition, however, if only for clearness' sake; since *Composition* also denotes *Practical Rhetoric* as opposed to the *Theory* of the art.[3]

4. THOUGHT[4] is here intended in its widest signification. In a certain sense, the mind *thinks* whenever it *acts;* and in this sense, Thought is the product of any mental action. Hence, Dr. Campbell speaks of Rhetoric

---

[1] H. N. Day, *The Art of Discourse,* § 1.
[2] Appendix, pp. 329 ff.
[3] § 10, *below.*
[4] § 1, *above.*

as "*the grand art of communication, not of ideas only, but of sentiments, passions, dispositions, and purposes*[1]," —in a word, the art of communicating *any product of the mental faculties.* Exactly how much is intended by the term will appear from the following analysis.

5. The human mind acts in three ways;—it *knows*, it *feels*, it *wills.* Hence, three modes of mental activity, or (as they are otherwise called) *mental faculties*,—1. INTELLECT, or COGNITION; 2. SENSIBILITY, or FEELING; 3. WILL. The Intellectual, or Cognitive Faculties may (for present purposes) be distinguished as (1) *Presentative*, (2) *Re-presentative*, (3) *Elaborative.* The Presentative Faculties include (*a*) *Intuition*, or *Self-consciousness*, the power of knowing *what is going on in one's own mind;* (*b*) *Perception*, the power of knowing *through the senses.* The Re-presentative Faculties are (*a*) *Memory*, which re-presents objects as *real;* (*b*) *Imagination*, which re-presents them as *ideal.* The Elaborative Faculties are (*a*) *Conception*, or *Generalization*, the power of forming *class-ideas;* (*b*) *Judgment*, the power of *comparing conceptions* (or *one·conception* with *an intuition* or *a perception*) *and affirming their agreement or disagreement;* (*c*) *Reasoning*, the power of *comparing judgments.*

6. Words that either present or re-present intuitions, perceptions, or conceptions, are called *Terms.* Hence, Judgment is the power of comparing terms.

7. LANGUAGE[2] primarily and chiefly means articulate speech or alphabetic writing ; but many principles of Rhetoric apply equally well to the communication of thought by other means. Signs, symbols, pictures, statues,—all express thought, and in so far are amenable to the laws of Rhetoric. Indeed, both picture-writing and symbolism are older than the alphabet,—are the sources from which the alphabet took its rise.

8. The truth of this statement will hardly be challenged by any one who reflects that the *medium* of communication is of secondary importance, – that the essential characteristic of

---

[1] *The Philosophy of Rhetoric*, Introduction.   [2] § 1, above.

discourse is its communicating thought. The mode of communication may vary; but, so long as thought is communicated, so long must the process be governed in certain particulars by the same rules. For example, the artist, who has this end at least partly in view, is directed in his work by certain laws that are equally binding upon the writer. The laws of unity, of definiteness and continuousness, of proper resolution of the subject into its several parts, as well as many other rules, direct both workers alike,—and for the same reason, that both seek to communicate thought. Lessing[1] has actually asserted that Painting can express some kinds of thought better than Poetry.

9. Further, (if further discussion is necessary,) the case of the deaf-mute is strongly in point. Until he acquires his signlanguage, his mind lies dormant, failing of its office because it lacks a means of communication. But, this once furnished, even if he does not learn to articulate, his mind develops and admits of the highest education. The idiot, on the other hand, can never be relieved because he cannot receive thought, however it is addressed to him. Midway stands the feebleminded child, who is capable of training exactly in proportion to his degree of mental endowment. An extreme case of a mind aroused to the exercise of all its faculties, simply by receiving a medium of communication, and this not language in the ordinary sense, is that of Miss Laura Bridgman, who, though born deaf and dumb and blind, was taught through the sense of touch. Moreover, gestures and facial signs not only add to the effectiveness of spoken discourse, but, it is said, were the only means by which the famous conspiracy of the Sicilian Vespers was inaugurated and carried to a successful issue.[2] So, the Greek sculptor *carved* motion by setting one foot of his statue in front of the other.

[1] *Laocoön*, xx., xxi.—Of course, he concedes, too, the limitations of Painting and its cognate arts. (See §§ 369 ff., *below*.)

[2] Geo. P. Marsh, *Lectures on the English Language*, p. 34.

II.

RHETORIC PROPER AND COMPOSITION.

10. As thus broadly defined, Rhetoric includes studies of two widely different kinds ;—(1) *Theoretical Discussions of Rhetorical Rules and Principles,*—RHETORIC PROPER, or simply RHETORIC; (2) *Practice in the actual work of Constructing Discourse,*—COMPOSITION.

11. "Rhetoric and Oratory," says John Quincy Adams,[1] "are to be distinguished as properly applying, the former to the *theory*, and the latter to the *practice* of the art." By *oratory*, Mr. Adams meant composition[2]; so that his statement fully supports that made in § 10. Prof. Day, too, calls his theoretical treatise *The Art of Discourse* (that is, *Rhetoric*), but his more practical (as well as more elementary) work *The Art of English Composition*.

12. The distinction results from the fact that, in every art, there may be distinguished three elements ;—(1) *Rules*, which guide and control the practice of the art; (2) *Scientific Principles*, which underlie the rules, and explain or justify them; (3) *Practice*, the application of both rules and principles to actual work. Thus, in Drawing, the pupil is not simply given a copy or a model, and told to reproduce it on his paper: he is taught, also, rules for his guidance while at work, and principles—of form, of light and shade, of perspective—for the elucidation of his rules. So, in Engineering, in Analytical Chemistry, in every art, rules and principles at every step direct the practical work, and throw light upon it. Indeed, if, in any art, one of these three elements is wanting, the art is yet in embryo, or the missing element undeveloped.[3] In the Art of Discourse, (1) and (2) constitute Rhetoric Proper; (3) is Composition.

13. Further, rules and principles, as true in all cases to which they apply, are in this respect essentially opposed to the practical application of rules or principles to special examples.

---

[1] *Lectures*, I. p. 34.   [2] Appendix, p. 336.   [3] Appendix, p. 333.

The methods of study in each case must, therefore, be different, and a distinction between the two departments be inevitable. Not to concede this is only to create confusion and to place obstacles in the way of the student. Of course, rhetorical rules may be studied simply as rules, and not in the light of their underlying principles, just as the principles may be studied as such, and not with a view to formulating rules that are to be based upon them; but, in either case,—and neither is usual or likely to occur,—the study is still Theoretical Rhetoric, and is opposed in the sense stated to the practice of Composition, or Practical Rhetoric. This is true, too, whether the practical work proceeds only by "rules of thumb," (that is, by unexplained rules, rules without their underlying scientific truths—their *rationale*,) or whether this *rationale* is in every case carefully given with the rule.

14. But the distinction must not be carried too far. Rhetoric and Composition are not wholly separable. Each implies the other; each contributes to the other's improvement. Of course, either can be conceived of separately; either can at any time command the chief attention; but the two studies are in fact only one,—a single object approached from different sides.

15. To speak more technically, Theory and Practice are *correlatives*, implying each other, and having their common ground of relation in the nature of Art as art. Practice unfailingly tends to develop theory; theoretical discussion as inevitably makes practice more perfect. Certain art-practice, it is true, seems to be wholly unguided by either rule or principle; but, in fact, it is not so. Every one who practices an art, though in ever so unintelligent a way, acquires by his experience both rules and principles; and these, though he never formulates them, really control and direct his work.[1]

[1] Appendix, p. 335.

III.

THE SCIENCES THAT GIVE LAWS TO RHETORIC.

16. The scientific principles that underlie the rules of Rhetoric come from (1) *Grammar*, the Science of the Sentence, (2) *Logic*, the Science of Thought, (3) *Æsthetics*, the Science of Beauty, and (4) *Ethics*, the Science of Morals;—the four sciences *nomothetical*, or *law-giving*, to Rhetoric.[1] The first two contribute most largely to the theory of the art; but the principles furnished by the others are of no less value, and cannot properly be left out of sight. Though in no sense a part of Rhetoric, these sciences stand in such close relations to it, that at least some knowledge of them is essential to any one who would comprehend the subject on its theoretical side. Exactly what these relations are will appear from the following considerations.

17. (A) The writing of a composition involves (1) the finding of something to say—the *Matter*, or *Content*, of Discourse—*Thought;* (2) the embodying of this "something to say" in a correct *Form*, or *Style;* and (3) the adapting of the whole work (and its every part) to its *Purpose*, or *End in View*. But, (1) the science of Thought is Logic. (2) Form is either (*a*) *outward and bodily*—in Discourse, the *language* used to convey thought—or (*b*) *inward and spiritual*—that something which appeals to our sense of *Beauty*.[2] The principles of language are taught by Grammar: the science of the Beautiful is Æsthetics. (3) "Discourse is more than mere thought, more than mere

---

[1] The Greek *nomothetes* was not only a proposer of a law, but also (and primarily) a law-giver, like Solon or Lycurgus. Hence, *nomothetical* may properly be used in the sense of *law-giving*.

[2] Compare Spenser, *An Hymne in Honour of Beautie*, ll. 89 and 132:—

"Confesse it then,
That Beautie is not, as fond men misdeeme,
An *outward* shew of thinges that only seeme.
For of the *soule* the bodie forme doth take;
For *soule is forme*, and doth the bodie make."

So, Robert Browning, *Old Pictures in Florence*, 11:—

thought uttered or formed; it is thought *communicated*, implying a mind *addressed* in the communication."[1] Hence, in every rhetorical process, a mutually related speaker and hearer,[2]—a speaker and a hearer, whose relations to each other are, of course, moral. The science of Morals is Ethics.

18. (B) These underlying principles are not discovered or discoverable by Rhetoric; nor can their truth or falsity be determined by it. They form parts of four great systems of truths, constructed each by itself and for its own sake, and brought into relation to Rhetoric, only when the latter, having formulated its rules for art-work, presents these rules to the sciences for explanation or justification.[3] Further, the evidence by which the laws of Rhetoric are established is peculiar in each case to the science from which the underlying principle comes; and with this evidence, therefore, Rhetoric has nothing whatever to do.

> "When Greek Art ran and reached the goal,
> Thus much had the world to boast *in fructu*—
> The truth of Man, as by God first spoken
> Which the actual generations garble
> Was re-uttered,—and Soul (which Limbs betoken)
> And Limbs (Soul informs) were made new in marble."[*]

---

[*] For this confirmation of Spenser the author is indebted to Mr. Mark Wilks Collet, of Germantown, who was already a reader of Browning in his Sophomore year.

[1] Day, *The Art of Discourse*, § 4.—The italics are inserted here.

[2] Or writer and reader. For brevity's sake, only one pair of these terms (which must occur incessantly) will commonly be written.

[3] Appendix, p. 333.

IV.
FUNDAMENTAL MAXIMS.

19. The sciences nomothetical to Rhetoric furnish it with four *Dicta*, or fundamental maxims, which serve as guides throughout the course. They set forth *in miniature* the whole body of scientific truths on which the rules of Rhetoric depend. They are,—

I. THE DICTUM OF GRAMMAR.—*The writer must conform to the usage of the language he employs.*

II. THE DICTUM OF LOGIC.—*The thought communicated must be genuine.*

III. THE DICTUM OF ÆSTHETICS.—*The Composition must appeal to and stimulate the sense of Beauty.*

IV. THE DICTUM OF ETHICS.—*Discourse must proceed upon moral principles,—those which control the relation of man to man.*

The full meaning of these rules will appear hereafter. Dicta II., III., and IV., however, need a few words here, by way of special explanation.

20. *First,* "genuine thought," like genuine money, is exactly what it seems to be. Spurious thought, on the contrary, has all the forms of genuine thought, but as little as may be of its matter. The mind of man, by virtue of its own constitution, acts normally in certain ways, according to certain laws. These laws have been discovered and codified by Logic; so that normal mental action is also logical. Hence, when the writer, for whatever reason;—whether because he is fundamentally incapable of thinking clearly, or because, in his anxiety to express himself well, he forgets to have something worthy to say, or even, perhaps, because he actually desires to deceive his reader;—when, from whatever cause, he violates the laws of Logic, he becomes a mere counterfeiter, a companion (in some sense) of the coiner of spurious gold. For example, he may use language that seems to convey thought, while, in fact, it only covers with a cloud of words the mere pretence of thinking,—a pretence that, if exposed nakedly to other minds, would be at once detected; and he may do this consciously or

unconsciously. Or he may maliciously choose such forms or such matter of discourse as shall deceive the unwary reader. In any case, he is dealing unfairly both by himself and by his reader as rational beings; he is violating both his own and his reader's mental constitution. This method of discourse is sometimes contemptuously spoken of as "rhetorical," in opposition (expressed or implied) to the "logical" method; but as here defined,—truly rhetorical discourse is logical, and the shrewdest logician (as does every thinker) finds discourse impossible, except in conscious or unconscious obedience to the laws of Rhetoric. The question whether such an illogician[1] errs wittingly or not, belongs to Ethics, is one with which the Dictum of Logic does not and cannot concern itself. Its business is only with the genuineness or the spuriousness of thought; its duty, only to remind the writer that, in the same sense in which noble birth or good breeding puts a man under special bonds to discharge his whole duty in every walk of life, so the rationality that constitutes man's distinctive mark among animals demands from him special fidelity to the laws of his intellectual nature.

21. *Secondly,* "beauty" is a relative term, and the standard of taste has varied in different ages and different lands. Hence, though it cannot be true that "there is no disputing about tastes,"—in the sense, at least, in which this proverb is commonly quoted,—yet it *is* true that the beauty of plainness or even of ruggedness, as well as the beauty of grace, of polish, or of inherent loveliness, is intended by the term as used in the dictum, and that, for certain purposes in Composition, conformity to the dictum may lie in the acceptance of a standard of taste different from that of either our own day or our own nation.[2]

22. *Thirdly,* the meaning of the Dictum of Ethics is not that, in order to success in Composition, the writer must teach only what is true, but that, in every communication of thought, no matter what its subject or its purpose, he must proceed upon principles discovered by Ethics to be laws of the moral nature of man. The rhetorical methods are unfortunately, as applicable to apologizing for wrong as to championing the right, to

---

[1] If this word is "made to order," it is certainly no worse a term than *unfriend*, and is certainly quite as useful. The phrase *ill logician* expresses a far different thought.

[2] § 340 *below.*

lying as to truth-telling; but, in whatever application, they are powerless when used in forgetfulness or in contradiction of the fundamental relations of men to each other. The dictum is not a table of the Ten Commandments, but a warning that all attempts to address men in violation of the fundamental principles of their nature must fail. For example, it is a well-known truth that ruthlessly to assail the prejudices of men is not commonly successful as a means to persuasion. Hence, should an orator wish to influence the voters of a certain election-district, or to induce men to abandon certain bad habits, Rhetoric will warn him that he must approach his subject warily, carefully finding his way through his listeners' prejudices, and opening his battery of arguments against the favorite candidate or the allowed bad habit, only when he feels the ground thus made firm under his feet.[1] No *Morey Letter*, even when issued as a "Last Card to the Voter," ever, perhaps, changed the vote of a fair-minded man; no *Counterblast to Tobacco*, even though from a royal pen, ever cured excessive smoking; no unsympathetic denunciation of intemperance ever won the drunkard from his evil ways. Discourse is a communication of thought from man to man; and hence, if it is to achieve its purpose, it must be guided at all points by those ethical truths which unfold the nature of the relations of men to each other.

[1] § 430, *below*.

V.
THE DEPARTMENTS OF RHETORIC.

23. The rules of Rhetoric fall naturally into two DEPARTMENTS, long known by the Latin names INVENTION[1] and STYLE.[2] Invention states the rules that direct and control the discovery of *matter* for the composition; Style exhibits the laws of its *form*.

24. As already stated,[3] the writing of a composition involves (1) the finding of something to say, (2) the expression of this something in a suitable form, (3) the adapting of the whole work and its every part to its purpose. But the composition can be adapted to its purpose only by means of modifications in either its matter or its form; and hence there are but two departments of Rhetoric, not three.

25. For a similar reason, the ancient view that *Disposition*, or *Arrangement*, constitutes a separate department of the art, must be set aside. So far as the arrangement of the *matter* of a composition is concerned, the rules that control it belong to Invention; so far as arrangement is a question of *form*, it belongs under Style. Besides, since every rational process implies decency and order, Arrangement can not be a department of Rhetoric, but must be assumed throughout.

26. Many writers deny the possibility of such a department of Rhetoric as Invention. They aver that men can not be taught how to find something to say; since, if they could, Rhetoric would be the encyclopædic art dreamed of by Quintilian,—an art under obligations to give lessons in all the known branches of learning. On the contrary, they say, it is only the art of *communication, originating* nothing, and prescribing merely the *forms* of expression, not the *matter* that is to wear these forms.

27. But this mode of reasoning is simply an evasion of the point at issue. The question is not, Can Rhetoric teach men *what* to say on every conceivable subject? but, Can Rhetoric

---

[1] *Inventio*, a finding.

[2] *Stilus*, an instrument used for writing on wax. Often, but improperly, spelled *stylus*, as if from Greek στῦλος, a pillar. [Skeat, *Etymological Dictionary*, s. v. The Greek word for *style* was λέξις.]

[3] § 17, *above*.

teach men *how to find* something to say on any subject? In other words, can it teach men the *methods* by which they must proceed in their search after the matter of a composition? No one pretends to-day that Rhetoric ought to make a man a *Johannes Factotum* (Greene's phrase for a *Jack of all Trades*), any more than that Rhetoric ought to furnish the words, constructions, and other instruments of speech needed by a writer. The assertion is only that, just as, in Style, Rhetoric teaches rules that determine the Form of a composition, so, in Invention, it teaches rules that determine its Content. In each department, of course, it leaves the writer to apply the rules to the special cases that arise in the course of his work; the art being no more under obligations to supply the matter of discourse than to supply the needed forms of expression. It is quite a different thing, however, to say that Rhetoric has for the thought to be expressed rules quite analogous to those which it has for the expression of the thought.

28. That Rhetoric *can* determine such rules, and that it has, therefore, a department of Invention, is best shown by the fact that such rules exist. The very books which declare most positively that Rhetoric teaches only Style, contain rules that are certainly not laws of Style, and which must therefore belong to a second department of the art, by whatever name it may be known. Further, while Rhetoric is, indeed, the art of communication, and goes to its nomothetical sciences for underlying principles, yet its *laws* are its own, and would never have been determined by the sciences. The truths of Logic, *etc.*, are as true in one mind as in two; but there can be no communication, unless there are a speaker and a hearer. Thus, Logic classifies arguments, but Rhetoric lays down laws that direct the writer in his choice of both the class of arguments and the particular arguments of their class that will best work conviction under certain varying circumstances. Yet these laws are not laws of Form: they are laws by which Persuasion may be the more easily accomplished.

29. The question raised here is not merely one of name. The point is not, Shall Rhetoric have one department or two? but, shall the office of Rhetoric be limited to the giving of form to thought already discovered? The rules of Rhetoric may, indeed, be all included under one head; but, in that case, either the definition of Style must be materially modified, or both names, Style and Invention, must be abandoned. By

either plan a valuable distinction will be lost, and nothing be gained but an apparent simplification, which, however, is, in fact, a complication of things that are better kept distinct.

30. The term *invention*, even in its rhetorical sense of *finding*, may, perhaps, imply too much, and, therefore, be an unfortunate name for the department; but then it were surely the part of wisdom to choose a better name, not to ignore the department. The history of the controversy makes it highly probable (to say no more) that a rather stupid misunderstanding of the word has given undue plausibility to the arguments against such a department of Rhetoric.

31. Further, the very method of studying Rhetoric is affected by the decision of this question. A complete Rhetoric rests on all the sciences nomothetical to the art.[1] But a Rhetoric that restricts itself to questions of Style, can not consistently do this: it must confine its attention to questions of Form, and tend, accordingly, to mere showiness in composition—to a shallowness of thought that only makes a beautiful style the more hideous—like a grinning skull, which can not laugh because its brains are out. Since Whately, indeed, Blair's emphasizing of Æsthetics has been the less dangerous; but even Whately does not give a complete view of the department of Invention, and Blair's influence is by no means spent. Besides, man seems as totally depraved in intellect as (in the view of some theologians) he is in his moral nature; and he needs, therefore, to fight as earnestly against the temptation to play the fool as against that to do wrong. Rhetoric can ill afford, then, to teach him respecting the communication of thought a doctrine that even seems unduly to exalt the merely external consideration of form.

32. The two Departments of Rhetoric, then, are *I. Invention, II. Style.* This order, too, is that, not only of their development, but also of their importance; since *it is always better to have something to say, however rudely one says it, than merely to bring together elegant expressions that mean nothing.* A correct form, it is true, renders worthy thought the more attractive; but mere excellence of form can never recommend a composition to an intelligent reader. "When you have noth-

[1] Appendix, p. 334.

ing to say," runs the epigram, "say it." At the same time, the laws of Form are simpler than those of thought; and, for this reason, they may properly be presented first. Part I. of this volume will therefore treat of *Style*, Part II. of *Invention*. A preparatory topic, *the Kinds of Discourse*, will occupy a concluding chapter of this Introduction.

33. The full analysis and classification of the kinds of compositions belongs, perhaps, to Literature rather than to Rhetoric; but the instructor in Rhetoric can not assume that his students are conversant with it: he may rather assume that they know nothing about it; and, hence, since some knowledge of it is essential for them, he must supply at least an outline. Nor can there be any serious impropriety in his doing so. At several points in the exhibition of his subject, brief summaries or classifications that properly belong to other branches of knowledge must be inserted for the information of his readers. Of course, such summaries should be given only when they are plainly necessary, and should be kept within narrow bounds; but they can not be wholly excluded. Indeed, many works of Rhetoric contain nearly complete systems of Grammar, Logic, *etc.;* while other works make these systems nearly the whole of Rhetoric, carrying them to an illogical extreme.

VI.

THE KINDS OF DISCOURSE.

34. Compositions may be distinguished,—

1. With respect to *Form*,[1] as (*a*) VERSE, (*b*) PROSE;
2. With respect to *Intrinsic Character*, as (*a*) ORATORY, (*b*) REPRESENTATIVE DISCOURSE, (*c*) ROMANCE, (*d*) POETRY;
3. With respect to *Purpose*, or *End in View*, as (*a*) EXPLANATORY, (*b*) ARGUMENTATIVE, (*c*) EXCITATORY, and (*d*) PERSUASIVE DISCOURSE.

35. These divisions, it will be observed, are not branches of a single classification, but three distinct classifications each with its own *principle of division* (*fundamentum divisionis*). The same composition, therefore, may be assigned a place under each classification, or even belong in part to one, in part to another head of the same classification. Thus, Macaulay's *England* or Motley's *Dutch Republic* is plainly of classes 1 (*b*), 2 (*b*), and 3 (*a*); Webster's *Argument in the Dartmouth College Case*, 1 (*b*), 2 (*a*), and 3 (*d*), except in certain passages, in which Mr. Webster now turns historian, 3 (*a*), now argues his points, 3 (*b*), and again advocates his cause by an appeal to the feelings, 3 (*c*).

1. COMPOSITIONS WITH RESPECT TO FORM.

36. (*a*) VERSE is distinguished from PROSE by having (1) *Rhythm*, (2) *Metre*. RHYTHM is the regular recurrence of accented and unaccented syllables, any prescribed combination of these syllables constituting a *Foot*. METRE is the arrangement of feet into *lines* or *verses*, each of which has a given number of feet of a certain rhythm. A VERSE, therefore, is any fixed number of accented and unaccented syllables. It is generally printed or written in the middle of the page, and with a

[1] I. e., rhythm and metre. The word is used here in a narrow sense.

capital initial letter; but it would still be a verse, no matter how arranged. For example,

> "Come, sir,
> I would you would make use of that good wisdom
> Whereof I know you are fraught; and put away
> These dispositions which of late transform you
> From what you rightly are."[1]

37. Here the *foot* is the *iambus*—an unaccented followed by an accented syllable; and there are five feet in each line. The rhythm, therefore, is *iambic*, the metre *pentameter*, and the verse *iambic pentameter*. The exceptional feet, "Come, sir," and "you are fraught," like the further licenses of the broken line (v. 239) and the added, "grace-note" syllables at the end of vv. 240 and 242, in no way disturb this general description. The lines are unquestionably verses, since they have both rhythm and metre; but they would no less be verses—no less have both rhythm and metre—were they printed, as in the Quarto editions of Shakspere, in prose form:—

"Come, sir, I would you would make use of that good wisdom whereof I know you are fraught; and put away these dispositions which of late transform you from what you rightly are."[2]

38. The precise intention of some of the terms used in §§ 36, 37 is not settled even among technical writers; but there is abundant authority for the meanings here given—so far at least as English verse is concerned—and the use of the words in these significations is certainly convenient. The full discussion of the subject hardly finds place in a work limited to Prose Composition.

39. (*b*) PROSE has no *regular* rhythm, and, except so far as grammatical structure or a proper distribution of the several thoughts or divisions of thought expressed may require, is printed continuously from one margin of the page to the other.

[1] Shakspere, *King Lear*, I. iv. 239-243. (Lines by the *Globe Edition*.)
[2] See the Cambridge Edition, *in loc.*

40. But fine Prose has a rhythm,—a rhythm of its own, to be sure, irregular, but perceptible to a good ear. It is thus described by Mrs. Browning:[1]—

"Then we talked—oh, how we talked! her voice, *so cadenced*
  in the talking,
Made another singing—of the soul! *a music without bars.*"[2]

Melody, Euphony, Harmony,[3] are qualities, not of Verse only, but of Style; and a Prose that lacked them in a marked degree would be both bald and harsh. The further illustration of this truth belongs elsewhere;[4] but a few quotations by way of example will not be improper here:—

(1) "After a pause, Charles rose to address a few parting words to his subjects. He stood with apparent difficulty, and rested his right hand on the shoulder of the prince of Orange,—intimating, by this preference on so distinguished an occasion, the high favor in which he held the young nobleman. In the other hand he held a paper, containing some hints for his discourse, and occasionally cast his eyes upon it, to refresh his memory. He spoke in the French language. He begged them to believe that this, and no other motive, induced him to resign the sceptre which he had so long swayed. They had been to him dutiful and loving subjects; and such, he doubted not, they would prove to his successor. Above all things, he besought them to maintain the purity of the faith. If any one, in these licentious times, had admitted doubts into his bosom, let such doubts be extirpated at once. 'I know well,' he concluded, 'that in my long administration, I have fallen into many errors, and committed some wrongs. But it was from ignorance; and, if there be any here whom I have wronged, they will believe that it was not intended, and grant me their forgiveness.'"[5]

[1] *Lady Geraldine's Courtship.*
[2] Cf. the previous lines;—
  "Oh, to see or hear her singing! scarce I know which is divinest—
   For her looks sing, too—she *modulates her gestures on the tune.*"
This, of course, is *music with bars*—the music of verse.
[3] §§ 336 ff, below.   [4] § 337 *below.*   [5] Prescott, *Philip II.*, ch. I.

(2) "Whether or no Beatrice possessed those terrible attributes, that fatal breath, the affinity with those so beautiful and deadly flowers, which were indicated by what Giovanni had witnessed, she had at least instilled a fierce and subtle poison into his system. It was not love, although her rich beauty was a madness to him; nor horror, even while he fancied her spirit to be imbued with the same baneful essence that seemed to pervade her physical frame; but a wild offspring of both love and horror that had each parent in it, and burned like one and shivered like the other. Giovanni knew not what to dread; still less did he know what to hope; yet hope and dread kept a continual warfare in his breast, alternately vanquishing one another and starting up afresh to renew the contest. Blessed are all simple emotions, be they dark or bright! It is the lurid intermixture of the two that produces the illuminating blaze of the infernal regions."[1]

(3) "Nature has no kindness, no hospitality, during a rain. In the fiercest heat of sunny days she retains a secret mercy, and welcomes the wayfarer to shady nooks of the woods whither the sun can not penetrate; but she provides no shelter against her storms. It makes us shiver to think of those deep, umbrageous recesses, those overshadowing banks, where we found such enjoyment during the sultry afternoons. Not a twig of foliage there but would dash a little shower into our faces. Looking reproachfully towards the impenetrable sky,—if sky there be above that dismal uniformity of cloud,—we are apt to murmur against the whole system of the universe, since it involves the extinction of so many summer days in so short a life by the hissing and spluttering rain. In such spells of weather,—and it is to be supposed such weather came,—Eve's bower in Paradise must have been but a cheerless and aguish kind of shelter, nowise comparable to the old parsonage, which had resources of its own to beguile the week's imprisonment. The idea of sleeping on a couch of wet roses!"[2]

41. Some writers use a form of composition generally called METRIC PROSE. As its name would indicate, it is a compromise between Prose and Verse, having the Prose features but the Verse character. Like Prose, it is written from margin to margin; but it adopts a per-

---
[1] Hawthorne, *Mosses from an Old Manse*, I. p. 115. (Little Classics Edition.)
[2] Id. ib. I. 21.

ceptible rhythm,—though a rhythm commonly less regular than that of Verse; while in some places it admits of being roughly marked off into metres. An apter name for it, perhaps, would be *Rhythmic Prose;* for its essential characteristic is its rhythmic construction, not its accidentally being metrical.

A few examples may be appended:—

(1) "On the back of a huge wave rose for the last time the unfortunate *Aliwal*. Stem on, as if with strong men steering, she rushed through the foam and the white whirl, like a hearse run away with in snowdrifts. Then she crashed on the stones, and the raging sea swept her from taffrail to bowsprit, rolled her over, pitched her across, and broke her back in two moments. The shock rang through the roar of billows, as if a nerve of the earth were thrilling. Another mountain-wave came marching to the roll of the tempest-drum. It curled disdainfully over the side, like a fog sweeping over a hedge-grow; swoop—it broke the timbers away, as a child strews the quills of a daffodil."[1]

(2) "The storm was now at its height; and of more than a hundred people gathered on the crown of the shore, and above the reach of the billows, not one durst stand upright. Nearer the water the wind had less power, for the wall of waves broke the full brunt of it. But there no man, unless he were most quick of eye and foot, might stand without great peril. For scarcely a single billow broke, but what, in the first rebound and toss, two churning hummocks of surf met, and flashed up the strand like a mad white horse, far in advance of the rest. Then a hissing ensued, and a roll of shingle, and the water poured huddling and lappeting back from the chine itself had crannied."[1]

(3) "The moment they got to the kennel, which they did by a way of their own, avoiding all grooms and young lumbermen, fourteen dogs, of different faces and a dozen languages, thundered, yelled, and yelped at the guns, some leaping madly and cracking their staples, some sitting up and begging dearly, with the muscles of their chests all quivering, some drawing along on their stomachs, as if they were thoroughly callous, and yawning for a bit of activity; but each in his several way entreating to be the chosen one, each protesting that he was

[1] R. D. Blackmore, *Cradock Nowell*, ch. xxxii.

truly the best dog for the purpose—whatever that might be—and swearing stoutly that he would 'down-charge' without a hand being lifted, never run in upon any temptation, never bolt after a hare. All the while Caldo sat grimly apart; having trust in human nature, he knew that merit must make its way, and needed no self-assertion. As his master came to him he stood upon his hindlegs calmly, balanced by the chainstretch, and bent his forearms as a mermaid or a kangaroo does. Then, suddenly, Cradock Nowell dropped the butt of his gun on his boot, and said, with his voice quite altered,—"[1]

42. In these passages, the rhythm is detected, not so much by marking off the several feet formed by the words, as by reading the paragraphs aloud with the emphases necessary to bring out the sense. In the following extracts, the rhythm may not only be heard by the ear, but even be marked off with greater or less regularity.

(4) "Go, go; you are a counterfeit cowardly knave. Will you mock at an ancient tradition, begun upon an honourable respect, and worn as a memorable trophy of predeceased valour, and dare not avouch in your deeds any of your words? I have seen you gleeking and galling at this gentleman twice or thrice. You thought, because he could not speak English in the native garb, he could not therefore handle an English cudgel: you find it otherwise; and henceforth let a Welsh correction teach you a good English condition. Fare ye well!"[2]

43. In a fifth example the structure is much more verse-like :—

(5) "Thus says my king: Say thou to Harry of England: Though we seemed dead, we did but sleep: advantage is a better soldier than rashness. Tell him we could have rebuked him at Harfleur, but that we thought not good to bruise an injury till it were full ripe; now we speak upon our cue, and our voice is imperial: England shall repent his folly, see his weakness, and admire our sufferance. Bid him therefore consider of his ransom; which must proportion the losses we have borne; the subjects we have lost, the disgrace we have digested; which in weight to re-answer, his pettiness would

---

[1] R. D. Blackmore, *Cradock Nowell*, ch. xviii.

[2] Shakspere, *Henry V.*, V. i. 73-84.—The rhythm is in the main anapaestic; but it is by no means regular.

THE KINDS OF DISCOURSE.   29

bow under. For our losses, his exchequer is too poor; for the effusion of our blood, the muster of his kingdom too faint a number; and for our disgrace, his own person, kneeling at our feet, but a weak and worthless satisfaction. To this add defiance: and tell him, for conclusion, he hath betrayed his followers, whose condemnation is pronounced. So far my king and master; so much my office."[1]

44. A short step brings the writer from prose like this to downright blank verse :—

(6) "Thou dost thy office fairly. Turn thee back,
    And tell thy king I do not seek him now;
    But could be willing to march on to Calais
    Without impeachment; for, to say the sooth,
    Though 'tis no wisdom to confess so much
    Unto an enemy of craft and vantage,
    My people are with sickness much enfeebled;
    My numbers lessened, and those few I have
    Almost no better than so many French;
    Who when they were in health, I tell thee, herald,
    I thought upon one pair of English legs
    Did march three Frenchmen. Yet, forgive me, God,
    That I do brag thus! This your air of France
    Hath blown that vice in me; I must repent.
    Go therefore, tell thy master here I am;
    My ransom is this frail and worthless trunk,
    My army but a weak and sickly guard;
    Yet, God before, tell him we will come on,
    Though France himself and such another neighbour
    Stand in our way. There's for thy labour, Montjoy.
    Go, bid thy master well advise himself:
    If we may pass, we will; if we be hinder'd,
    We shall your tawny ground with your red blood
    Discolour: and so, Montjoy, fare you well.
    The sum of all our answer is but this:
    We would not seek a battle, as we are;
    Nor, as we are, we say we will not shun it:
    So tell your master."[2]

---

[1] Shakspere, *Henry V.*, III. vi. 125-145.—This passage can actually be arranged in blank verse, and is so arranged in the surreptitious Quartos and by Pope in his Edition. (See the Cambridge Edition.)

[2] Id. ib., III. vi. 148-175.—A fuller discussion of rhythm in Prose will be found in §§ 158 (2), (3), *below*.

2. Compositions with Respect to Intrinsic Character.

45. (*a*) Oratory is the personal address of a speaker to a hearer, for the purpose of producing upon the mind of the latter a certain effect. For example, Webster's *Argument in the Dartmouth College Case* was designed to secure a decision by the Supreme Court of the United States that certain acts of the Legislature of New Hampshire were "unconstitutional and invalid." To this end, (1) it recites the history of the creation and establishment of the corporation under a royal charter to certain trustees ; (2) it describes the acts passed by the Legislature ; (3) it shows that, if these acts are valid, the old corporation is abolished, and a new corporation created, and that thereby the legal rights of the trustees are violated ; and (4) it contends that the acts are not valid, (*a*) because they are against common right and the constitution of New Hampshire, (*b*) because they are repugnant to the constitution of the United States. Each of these four points is carefully elaborated ; but, without going into details, one can readily see that the purpose of the speaker throughout is to impress upon the judges the conviction that the acts in question ought not to be allowed to stand. This Mr. Webster's conclusion shows so fully, that it may be quoted at length as a more definite specimen of this sort of composition :—

"The case before the court is not of ordinary importance, nor of every day occurrence. It affects not this college only, but every college, and all the literary institutions of the country. They have flourished hitherto, and have become in a high degree respectable and useful to the community. They have all a common principle of existence, the inviolability of their charters. It will be a dangerous, a most dangerous experiment, to hold these institutions subject to the rise and fall of popular parties, and the fluctuations of political opinions. If the franchise may be at any time taken away, or impaired, the property also may be taken away, or its use perverted. Benefactors will have no certainty of effecting the object of their bounty ; and learned men will be deterred from devoting themselves to the service of such institutions, from the precarious title of their offices. Colleges and halls will be deserted by all better spirits, and become a theatre for the contention of politics. Party and faction will be cherished in the places consecrated to piety and learning. These consequences are neither remote nor possible only. They are certain and immediate. * * * It was for many and obvious reasons most anxiously desired, that the question of the power of the legislature over this charter should have been finally decided in the state court. An earnest hope was entertained that the judges of that court might have viewed the case in the light favorable to the rights of the trustees. That hope has failed. It is here, that those rights are now to be maintained, or they are prostrated forever. *Omnia alia perfugia bonorum, subsidia, consilia, auxilia, jura ceciderunt. Quem enim alium appellem? quem obtester? quem implorem? Nisi hoc loco, nisi apud vos, nisi per vos, judices, salutem nostram, quae spe exigua extremaque pendet, tenuerimus; nihil est præterea quo confugere possimus.*"

46. In another form—that given by Prof. Chauncey A. Goodrich to Rufus Choate—this extract is even more oratorical. Mr. Choate quotes it in his *Discourse Commemorative of Daniel Webster*, before the Dartmouth College Alumni Society, July 27, 1853 :—[1]

"The argument ended. Mr. Webster stood for some moments silent before the Court, while every eye was fixed intently upon him. At length, addressing the Chief Justice, Marshall, he proceeded thus :—

"' *This, sir, is my case !* It is the case, not merely of that humble institution, it is the case of every college in our land. It is more. It is the case of every Eleemosynary Institution throughout our country—of all those great charities founded by the piety of our ancestors to alleviate human misery, and scatter blessings along the pathway of life. It is more. It is, in some sense, the case of every man among us who has property

---

[1] The author's attention was called to this varying form of Webster's peroration by his friend and colleague Prof. Francis A. Jackson, who also loaned him an original copy of Choate's *Discourse*.

of which he may be stripped, for the question is simply this: Shall our State Legislatures be allowed to take *that* which is not their own, to turn it from its original use, and apply it to such ends or purposes as they, in their discretion, shall see fit?

"'Sir, you may destroy this little Institution; it is weak; it is in your hands! I know it is one of the lesser lights in the literary horizon of our country. You may put it out. But if you do so, you must carry through your work! You must extinguish, one after another, all those great lights of science which, for more than a century, have thrown their radiance over our land!

"'It is, sir, as I have said, a small college. And yet, *there are those who love it* ——.'

"Here the feelings which he had thus far succeeded in keeping down, broke forth. His lips quivered; his firm cheeks trembled with emotion; his eyes were filled with tears, his voice choked, and he seemed struggling to the utmost simply to gain that mastery over himself which might save him from an unmanly burst of feeling. I will not attempt to give you the few broken words of tenderness in which he went on to speak of his attachment to the college. The whole seemed to be mingled throughout with the recollections of father, mother, brother, and all the trials and privations through which he had made his way into life. Every one saw that it was wholly unpremeditated, a pressure on his heart, which sought relief in words and tears.

"The court room during these two or three minutes presented an extraordinary spectacle. Chief Justice Marshall, with his tall and gaunt figure bent over as if to catch the slightest whisper, the deep furrows of his cheek expanded with emotion, and eyes suffused with tears; Mr. Justice Washington at his side, with his small and emaciated frame and countenance more like marble than I ever saw on any other human being—leaning forward with an eager, troubled look; and the remainder of the Court, at the two extremities, pressing, as it were, toward a single point, while the audience below were wrapping themselves round in closer folds beneath the bench to catch each look, and every movement of the speaker's face. If a painter could give us the scene on canvas—those forms and countenances, and Daniel Webster as he then stood in the midst, it would be one of the most touching pictures in the history of eloquence. One thing it taught me, that the *pathetic* depends not merely on the words uttered, but still more on the estimate we put upon him who utters them. There was not one among the strong-minded men of that assembly who could think it unmanly to weep when he saw standing before him the man who had made such an argument, melted into the tenderness of a child.

"Mr. Webster had now recovered his composure, and fixing his keen eye on the Chief Justice, said, in that deep tone with which he sometimes thrilled the heart of an audience :—

"'Sir, I know not how others may feel,' (glancing at the opponents of the college before him,) 'but, for myself, when I see my alma mater surrounded, like Cæsar in the Senate house, by those who are reiterating stab upon stab, I would not, for this right hand, have her turn to me and say, *Et tu quoque, mi fili!* And thou too, my son!'

"He sat down. There was a deathlike stillness throughout the room for some moments; every one seemed to be slowly recovering himself, and coming gradually back to his ordinary range of thought and feeling."

47. The *essential characteristic* of the oration is the *opposition* it implies between speaker and hearer,—the *resistance* made (or supposed to be made) by the hearer to the speaker, and which the speaker seeks to overcome by exerting an influence. The moment the composition drops this personal address to a present listener, or no longer aims at producing its specific effect, it ceases to be an oration, and becomes an essay[1] or some other form of discourse. The delivery is oral; but this is an accident, not an essential attribute, of the oration. An essay or a poem does not become an oration by being addressed to an audience; nor does an oration lose its specific difference by being read by the eye or aloud.

48. The term *oration*, however, is often used in a narrower sense, to denote only "an *elaborate* and *prepared* speech upon an important subject treated in a dignified manner,"—"especially, a discourse having refer-

[1] § 57, below.

ence to some occasion, as a funeral, an anniversary, a celebration, or the like."[1] In this meaning, it is to be "distinguished from an argument or plea delivered in court, from a speech made off-hand, from a sermon delivered at a religious service, from a lecture designed to convey knowledge, and the like."[1] But this signification of the term,—which is, in fact, only a specific sense to which the broader meaning is generic,—would be far too narrow for use here. The same laws that control the oration in the narrower sense of the word,—so far, at least, as it is a personal address designed to exert an influence on a hearer,—control, also, all similar speeches; and the limitation of the term would, therefore, be unscientific and unwise.

49. The opposition between speaker and hearer implied by the oration is assumed to exist, and the orator must address himself to overcome it, even when both hearer and speaker are fully agreed. Otherwise, the composition at once becomes representative discourse[2] or something else not oratory. For example, the aim of a Christian preacher may be to impress upon his hearers their duty in view of the death or the resurrection of Christ. Every soul in the church may be of the preacher's mind; and yet, if the sermon is not to be a mere essay, it will be written and delivered as if the assent of the listeners were still to be won.[3]

50. Further, the opposition between speaker and hearer may be simply that of ignorance or indifference, the aim of the orator being either to enlighten this ignorance or to place before his hearers in the most attractive form facts or truths already sufficiently well known. Indeed, his aim may be only to give pleasure by pre-

---

[1] Webster's *Dictionary*, 1864, s. vv. *Harangue* and *Oration*.

[2] § 55, *below*.

[3] Many a good sermon is, indeed, only an essay or other form of representative discourse; the occasion demanding nothing more. But such sermons can not be classed as *orations*.

senting thoughts so worthy of consideration that their mere exhibition will please. But, in all these cases, if the discourse is to attain the rank of oratory, the effect must be secured, not by a mere exhibition of the facts or truths, but by placing these truths or facts in such a personal relation to the hearer, that they will exert an influence upon him.

51. Akin to the Oration is the LETTER, an address to an *absent reader*. It often, though not commonly,[1] has the same design as the oration, to produce an effect by exerting a personal influence ; and, in this form, is, of course, most nearly like the oration. For example, Charles Lamb, stung by Southey's criticism of his *Essays of Elia*, writes to Southey in the vein of a pulpit orator haranguing his congregation :—

"Sir,—You have done me an unfriendly office, without perhaps much considering what you were doing. You have given an ill name to my poor lucubrations. In a recent paper on Infidelity, you usher in a conditional commendation of them with an exception : which, preceding the encomium, and taking up nearly the same space with it, must impress your readers with the notion that the objectionable parts in them are at least equal in quantity to the pardonable. The censure is in fact the criticism ; the praise—a concession merely. Exceptions usually follow, to qualify praise or blame. But there stands your reproof, in the very front of your notice, in ugly characters, like some bugbear, to frighten all good Christians from purchasing. Through you I become an object of suspicion to preceptors of youth and fathers of families. 'A book, which wants only a sounder religious feeling to be as delightful as it is original.' With no further explanation, what must your readers conjecture but that my little volume is some vehicle for heresy or infidelity? The quotation, which you honour me by subjoining, oddly enough, is of a character which bespeaks a temperament in the writer the very reverse of that your reproof goes to insinuate. Had you been taxing me with superstition, the passage would have been pertinent to the censure. Was it worth your while

---

[1] § 54, *below*.

to go so far out of your way to affront the feelings of an old friend, and commit yourself by an irrelevant quotation, for the pleasure of reflecting upon a poor child, an exile at Genoa!"[1]

52. The difference between a letter-writer of this sort and an orator is wholly in the fact that the writer is absent from the person he addresses, while the orator is present (as well as personal) in his address. The writer, however, though absent in body, is present in spirit,[2] and, by the exercise of even an ordinary imagination, may easily feel all the incentives to oratory that are lent to the public speaker by the knowledge that what he is writing will be addressed to a present audience. Of course, when the orator relies upon the moment for the language he will use, or still more, when his speech is strictly "off-hand," his audience exerts upon him an influence more powerful than that which an absent or a prospective audience can exert, but still an influence not different from this.

53. Other examples of the Letter in this sense of the word may be found in St. Paul's Epistles,—1 Corinthians, ch. vi.; Romans, xiv.; Hebrews, xii. Verses 18–29 of this last-named chapter exhibit a lofty oratorical eloquence, even when tried by Theremin's severe definition of this term.[3]

54. Ordinarily, however, the Letter is more like a *conversation* than it is like a formal address, and may lose its oratorical character entirely. The forms it then takes can best be described in subsequent paragraphs.[4]

55. (*b*) In REPRESENTATIVE DISCOURSE thought is communicated for its own sake. The speaker or writer appears, not as seeking to exert an influence upon his

---

[1] Letter lxxix., 1st Paragraph. *Works of Charles Lamb*, Moxon Edition Vol. I. pp. 208-209.

[2] 1 Cor. v. 3.—St. Paul tells the Corinthians that he "*has judged already, as though he were present;*" and his declamation could not be more real or effective than in the chapter cited, were the words excerpts from an oration instead of from a letter.

[3] Appendix, p. 336.   [4] ¶¶ 58 ff, *below*.

audience, but as "the mere mouthpiece" of that audience or of his profession or of some other body of men whose "common convictions and sentiments"[1] he expresses.

56. Hence, the usual (and eminently proper) *we* of the essayist, the editor, and other such writers, as opposed to the equally proper (but, perhaps, less usual) *I* of the orator. The essayist uses *I*, only when he speaks in his own person, individually; the orator uses *we* in two cases;—(1) when he is expressing truths that he believes to be as well known to his hearers, and as fully accepted by them, as they are known to himself and accepted by him; (2) when, in any other way, he includes his hearers with himself in a class all members of which are equally affected or concerned by what he is saying. In pure discourse of either sort, however, if the personal form is used at all, the distinction between the pronouns holds sharply, and should be strictly observed.

57. Sub-divisions of Representative Discourse (which may also serve as examples) are,—

(1) *History*, "a methodical record of the important events which concern a community of men";[1] *Biography*, a similar record of the events in the life of one man; *Travels*, "accounts of occurrences and observations"[2] during personal visits by the writer to particular places or localities;

(2) *Scientific Treatises; Essays*, which are less pretentious efforts; *Theses*, treatises or essays intended to demonstrate or to maintain particular propositions.

In (1), the subject is always a *fact;* in (2), it is a *truth.*

58. Oratory and Representative Discourse are often combined in the same composition. For example, Macaulay, in his famous speech *The People's Charter*, often stops to insert matter that is purely explanatory, and which would, of course, be out of place but for its value in making the speaker's position clearer, and in thus promoting his aim, the rejection of the petition under discussion. In the following extract, the passages

[1] Day, pp. 27, 28.   [2] Webster, *Dictionary*, s. v.

printed in italics are of this explanatory character, though they are woven closely with the purely oratorical parts of the work:—

"I am far from wishing to throw any blame on the ignorant crowds which have flocked to the tables where this petition was exhibited. *Nothing is more natural than that the labouring people should be deceived by the arts of such men as the author of this absurd and wicked composition. We ourselves, with all our advantages of education, are often very credulous, very impatient, very short-sighted, when we are tried by pecuniary distress or bodily pain. We often resort to means of immediate relief which, as Reason tells us, if we would listen to her, are certain to aggravate our sufferings. Men of great abilities and knowledge have ruined their estates and their constitutions in this way.* How, then, can we wonder that men less instructed than ourselves, and tried by privations such as we have never known, should be easily misled by mountebanks who promise impossibilities? Imagine a well meaning laborious mechanic fondly attached to his wife and children. Bad times come. He sees the wife whom he loves grow thinner and paler every day. His little ones cry for bread; and he has none to give them. Then come the professional agitators, the tempters, and tell him that there is enough and more than enough for everybody, and that he has too little only because landed gentlemen, fund-holders, bankers, manufacturers, railway proprietors, shopkeepers, have too much. Is it strange that the poor man should be deluded, and should eagerly sign such a petition as this? *The inequality with which wealth is distributed forces itself on everybody's notice. It is at once perceived by the eye. The reasons which irrefragably prove this inequality to be necessary to the well being of all classes are not equally obvious. Our honest workingman has not received such an education as enables him to understand that the utmost distress that he has ever known is prosperity, when compared with the distress which he would have to endure if there were a single month of general anarchy and plunder.* But you say, It is not the fault of the labourer that he is not well educated. Most true. It is not his fault. But, though he has no share in the fault, he will, if you are foolish enough to give him supreme power in the state, have a very large share of the punishment. You say that, if the Government had not culpably omitted to establish a good system of public instruction, the petitioners would have been fit for the elective franchise. But is that a reason for giving them the franchise when their own petition proves that they are not fit for it, when they give us fair notice that, if we let them have it they will use it to our ruin and their own? It is not necessary now to inquire whether, with universal education, we could safely have universal suffrage? What we are asked to do is to give universal suffrage before there is universal education. Have I any unkind feeling towards these poor people? No more than I have to a sick friend who implores me to give him a glass of iced water which the physician has forbidden. No more than a humane collector in India has to those poor peasants who in a season of scarcity crowd round the granaries and beg with tears and piteous gestures that the doors may be opened and the rice distributed. I would not give the draught of water, because I know that it would be poison. I would not give up the keys of the granary, because I know that, by doing so, I should turn a scarcity into a famine. And in the same way I would not yield to the importunity of multitudes who, exasperated by suffering and blinded by ignorance, demand with wild vehemence the liberty to destroy themselves."[1]

59. Other examples of combined Oratory and Representative Discourse may be found in nearly any specimen of forensic oratory;[2] long passages by way of explanation are neither unusual nor improper. Webster's first two points in the argument analyzed above[3] are both of this character; and the orations of any period in the world's history are not infrequently a prolific source of information concerning the history, (especially the manners and customs) of the people among whom they were produced.

60. Similarly, in the Letter, any form of Representative Discourse may be joined with proper epistolary matter. Thus, Mr. Philip Gilbert Hamerton, in his *Intellectual*

[1] *Speeches of the Rt. Hon. T. B. Macaulay, M. P.* Tauchnitz Ed., I. pp. 314-316.

[2] Oratory of the *forum;* political and deliberative oratory, including that of the law courts.

[3] § 45.

Life, a series of *letter-essays*, each one of which was addressed to a real person, though it was never actually sent to him, writes,[1]—

"When I had the pleasure of staying at your father's house, you told me, rather to my surprise, that it was impossible for you to go to balls and dinner-parties because you did not possess such a thing as a dress-coat. The reason struck me as being scarcely a valid one, considering the rather high scale of expenditure adopted in the paternal mansion. It seemed clear that the eldest son of a family which lived after the liberal fashion of Yorkshire country gentlemen could afford himself a dress-coat if he liked. Then I wondered whether you disliked dress-coats from a belief that they were unbecoming to your person; but a very little observation of your character quite satisfactorily convinced me that, whatever might be your weaknesses (for everybody has some weaknesses,) anxiety about personal appearance was not one of them.

"The truth is, that you secretly enjoy this little piece of disobedience to custom, and all the disabilities which result from it. This little rebellion is connected with a larger rebellion, and it is agreeable to you to demonstrate the unreasonableness of society by incurring a very severe penalty for a very trifling offence. You are always dressed decently, you offend against no moral rule, you have cultivated your mind by study and reflection, and it rather pleases you to think that a young gentleman so well qualified for society in everything of real importance should be excluded from it because he has not purchased a permission from his tailor.

"The penalties imposed by society for the infraction of very trifling details of custom are often, as it seems, out of all proportion to the offence; but so are the penalties of nature. Only three days before the date of this letter, an intimate friend of mine was coming home from a day's shooting. His nephew, a fine young man in the full enjoyment of existence, was walking ten paces in advance. A covey of partridges suddenly cross the road; my friend in shouldering his gun touches the trigger just a second too soon, and kills his nephew. Now, think of the long years of mental misery that will be the punishment of that very trifling piece of carelessness! My poor friend has

---

[1] *Letter to a Young Gentleman who had Firmly Resolved Never to Wear Anything but a Grey Coat.* (Am. Ed. pp. 193 ff.)

passed, in the space of a single instant, from a joyous life to a life that is permanently and irremediably saddened. It is as if he had left the summer sunshine to enter a gloomy dungeon and begin a perpetual imprisonment. And for what? For having touched a trigger, without evil intention, a little too precipitately. It seems harder still for the victim, who is sent out of the world in the bloom of perfect manhood because his uncle was not quite so cool as he ought to have been. Again, not far from where I live, thirty-five men were killed last week in a coal-pit from an explosion of fire-damp. One of their number had struck a lucifer to light his pipe; for doing this in a place where he ought not to have done it, the man suffers the penalty of death, and thirty-four others with him. The fact is simply that Nature *will* be obeyed, and makes no attempt to proportion punishments to offences; indeed, what in our human way we call punishments are not punishments, but simple consequences. So it is with the great social penalties. Society *will be obeyed;* if you refuse obedience, you must take the consequences. Society has only one law, and that is custom. Even religion itself is socially powerful only just so far as it has custom on its side."

61. So, too, St. Paul, addressing the Corinthian Church on the abuses they had allowed in the celebration of the Lord's Supper, (1 Cor. xi. 17-22,) turns aside from his strictly personal address to recite the manner of the institution of that Supper (vv. 23-26), and then returns to his denunciation of their errors (vv. 27-34). In like manner, Hebrews, ch. xi., is simply an essay on Faith interjected between the strict letter-matter of ch. x. 19-39 and ch. xii. In all these cases, there is a mixture of Oratory and Representative Discourse; and the letters are to be distinguished, not only from the purely oratorical class, but also from those to be described in the next paragraph.

62. The most usual form of Letter is that in which the whole work consists of narrative, description, *etc.*,[1] with but the merest trace, or with no trace at all, of a personal relation on the part of the writer either to what he writes or to his reader. Of such sort are many letters between friends, (in which, however, the personal element is a chief charm, even when the oratorical element—the

---

[1] §§ 366 ff. *below.*

seeking to exert an influence—is wanting), many letters of travel, and (especially) the *"news-letters"* of the periodicals. One often fails to find a difference between the last-named kind of letters and the despatches by "Associated Press."

63. (*c*) ROMANCE in its widest acceptation (and in the sense intended here), includes all *narrative* compositions the details of which are not *historically* true.[1] It is commonly in prose form; though the oldest works of the kind, as well as some modern examples, are in verse. Two sub-divisions may be noted;—(1) *Romance Proper*, which introduces "the marvellous or the supernatural,"[2] surprising events usually befalling a hero or a heroine,—extravagant adventures of love and the like;[3] and (2) the *Novel*, a story of real life "intended to exhibit the operations of the passions, and particularly of love,"[4]—a work that describes character, and minutely and subtly analyzes motives and results.[5]

64. "When a writer calls his work a Romance," says Hawthorne,[6] "it need hardly be observed that he wishes to claim a certain latitude, both as to its fashion and material, which he would not have felt himself entitled to assume had he professed to be writing a novel. The latter form of composition is presumed to aim at a very minute fidelity, not merely to the possible, but to the probable and ordinary course of man's experience. The former—while, as a work of art, it must rigidly subject itself to laws, and while it sins unpardonably so far as it may swerve aside from the truth of the human heart—has fairly a right to present that truth under circumstances, to a great extent, of the writer's own choosing or creation. If he think fit, also, he may so manage his atmospherical medium as

---

[1] But see § 67, *below*. [2] Baldwin's *English Literature*, II. 135.

[3] Webster's *Dictionary*, s. v. *Romance*.—Hallam (*Literature of Europe*, Pt. I. ch. ii. § 50,) says that the mediæval romances rest upon the three "columns" of "chivalry, gallantry, and religion." His words not inaptly describe all romances of this first sub-division.

[4] Webster, s. v. *Novel*. [5] Baldwin, p. 189.

[6] *The House of the Seven Gables*, Preface.

to bring out or mellow the lights and deepen and enrich the shadows of the picture. He will be wise, no doubt, to make a very moderate use of the privileges here stated, and, especially, to mingle the marvellous rather as a slight, delicate, and evanescent flavor, than as any portion of the actual substance of the dish offered to the public. He can hardly be said, however, to commit a literary crime even if he disregard this caution."

65. Examples of Romance and the Novel can be given here only by name. Of Romances, Sir Philip Sidney's *Arcadia*, Sir Walter Scott's *Ivanhoe*, Charles Kingsley's *Hypatia*, Moore's *Lalla Rookh*, the *Arthurian Legends*, (constituting, in a modern form, Tennyson's *Idylls of the King*,) Scott's *Lay of the Last Minstrel*, Byron's *Bride of Abydos*, may be taken;[1] of Novels, many works by Bulwer, Dickens, Thackeray, George Eliot, and Hawthorne, with such stories in verse as Chaucer's *Canterbury Tales*, Scott's *Rokeby*, Mrs. Browning's *Lady Geraldine's Courtship*, William Morris's *Earthly Paradise*, and Longfellow's *Evangeline* and *Miles Standish*.

66. But this distinction is not always made. Both terms—*Romance* and *the Novel*—as well as a third word, *Fiction*, are constantly used as synonyms. Yet *Romance* is fairly treated as generic, since the Novel is simply an outgrowth from the earlier Romance Proper, and the distinction between Romance Proper and the Novel is inconsiderable, as compared with the characteristic quality that unites both in a single class. *Fiction* is too broad a term to include only Romance and the Novel; for in the same sense in which these are fictions, the Poem, also is fiction, and this last term must therefore include Poetry as well as Romance and the Novel.

67. In a certain sense, Romance, though not historically true, is Truth itself. In the Novel, at least, (as Fielding says,) "everything is true but the names and dates;"[2] and even in the Romance Proper the under-

---

[1] The *Arcadia* and *Lalla Rookh* are partly in prose, partly in verse; *Ivanhoe* and *Hypatia* are in prose; the others in verse.

[2] Fielding's antithesis is, happily, a less trustworthy statement,—"In the historians' productions nothing is true but the names and dates."

lying allegory or moral is unquestionably true.[1] The story (or at least its meaning) is *real*, though not *actual:* it *might* have occurred, though, exactly as told, it never *did* occur.[2] It is the *type* of numerous cases, for all of which (in a certain sense) it stands. For example, Dickens's *Nicholas Nickleby* provoked one Yorkshire schoolmaster to take legal advice upon the propriety of suing Mr. Dickens for libel, another to meditating assault and battery upon the author, and a third to a remarkable confidence that *he* was intended, because he "perfectly remembered being waited on, last January twelve month, by two gentlemen, one of whom held him in conversation while the other took his likeness." Mr. Dickens suggests "that these contentions may arise from the fact that Mr. Squeers is *the representative of a class*, and not *an individual.*" "Where imposture, ignorance, and brutal cupidity," continues Mr. Dickens, "are the stock in trade of a small body of men, and one is described by these characteristics, all his fellows will recognize something belonging to themselves, and each will have a misgiving that the portrait is his own."[3]

68. (*d*) Of POETRY no universally accepted definition has ever been secured. Ingenious metaphors, long catalogues of attributes, and not a few definitions in the ordinary way, have been offered, but all without the desired result. The following particulars, however, are widely agreed upon. (1) The essential character of

---

[1] § 64, *above*.

[2] Whately says, "Writers of fiction are allowed to assume any hypothesis they please, provided they represent the personages of the fiction as acting, and the events as resulting, in the same manner as might have been expected, supposing the assumed circumstances to have been real [actual]. And, hence, Aristotle establishes his paradoxical maxim, that impossibilities which appear probable, are to be preferred to possibilities which appear improbable."—Bk. I. ch. ii. § 2. (condensed.)

[3] Preface to the *Household Edition*, p. lx.

Poetry is in its *matter*, not in its *form;*[1] and, hence, the proper antithesis to Poetry is not Prose, but Oratory and Representative Discourse.[2] A true poem may take the form of prose; and the correct form of verse has varied in different lands and different ages.[3] (2) The thought in Poetry is (*a*) ideal, (*b*) emotional; that is, it is addressed to the imagination and the feelings. Yet even these criteria often leave the student perplexed. The question whether a certain composition is or is not truly a poem, frequently divides the critics; and in many cases the poet unquestionably becomes novelist, instructor, preacher, writing in the form of verse, only because he is thereby more apt to secure a patient hearing.

69. The following will serve as examples of the many definitions of Poetry. "Poetry is simple, sensuous, passionate."[4] "Poetry is 'the stuff of which our life is made.'"[5] "Poetry is the protest of genius against the unreality of actual life."[6] "The creation of new beauty, the manifestation of the real by the ideal, in 'words that move in metrical array.'"[7] "Poetry is a Fine Art, operating by means

---

[1] "Poetry is not the proper antithesis to prose, but to science."—Coleridge, *Lit. Remains*, p. 19 (N. Y., 1853). Bayard Taylor, on the other hand, valiantly contends (and cites weighty authority) for the opposite opinion. "Poetry," he says, "may be distinguished from Prose by the single circumstance, that it is the utterance of whatever in man cannot be perfectly uttered in any other than a rhythmical form." (*Faust*, I., p. v.)

[2] For the place of Romance, in relation to Poetry, and for a use of the term *Prose* in a sense to which *Poetry is* antithetical, see § 73, *below*.

[3] For example, Sir Philip Sidney's *Arcadia*, usually classified as a romance, is, even in places that have the prose form, a sustained poem. (Cf. Tom Moore's *Lalla Rookh*.) So the Psalms, the Prophets, and others of the sacred books have lost nothing of their poetical character by translation into a prose form. As to the correct form of verse, the Greeks and Romans found it in *quantity;* the Hebrews, in a very artificial system (described in *The Sunday Magazine*, Vol. III. n. s.); the Anglo-Saxons, in *alliteration;* the modern English and other nations in rhythm and metre, with or without rhyme.

[4] Milton, approved by Coleridge, *Lit. Remains*, p. 21.

[5] Hazlitt, *English Poets*, p. 3.

[6] E. P. Whipple, *English Poets of the Nineteenth Century*. (In *Essays and Reviews*, I. 300.)

[7] Quoted by Whipple, in *Poets and Poetry of America*. (*Essays and Reviews*, I. 32.)

of thought conveyed in language."[1] "Poetry is that kind of discourse in which the idea is expressed for the sake of the form. It is one of the arts of Free Beauty."[2] "Poetry is the spontaneous outburst of the nobler feelings of the soul. It appeals mainly to our imaginative faculties and to our sense of the beautiful, the true, the sublime. In its aim and tendency, it is a fine art, entertaining and teaching us by awakening our minds into sympathy with the higher and diviner side of things."[3] "Poetry may be defined as that division of literature which addresses itself to the imagination and the passions, and whose primary object is to please."[4] "Modes of expressing thought and feeling which are suitable to the imagination when excited or elevated, and characterized usually by a measured form of one sort or another. Imaginative composition, whether in prose or verse."[5]

70. Poetry has been variously sub-divided into classes. The following arrangement will perhaps prove most useful to the student :—[6]

(1) LYRIC POETRY, including the *Song*, the *Ode*, the *Elegy*, the *Sonnet*, and "the *simple* or *nondescript Lyric*." All Lyrics express "intense feeling, passion, emotion, or sentiment," and are usually short and concentrated. In form, they "deviate farthest from prose." The Song explains itself. The Ode, though originally intended to be sung, is not, in its English specimens, usually so intended. The Elegy is "a mournful or plaintive poem."[6] The Sonnet expresses a single thought or "phrase of feeling," must always be contained in fourteen lines, and must have its rhymes arranged according to a fixed rule. It has two parts,—the *Octave*, two stanzas of four lines each, and the *Sestette*, one stanza of six lines; but the rule for its rhymes has varied in all literature. The (so-called) perfect Sonnet

---

[1] Bain, *Rhetoric*, p. 257. (Am. Ed.)
[2] Baldwin, *English Literature*, Vol. I., p. 4.
[3] *Webster's Dictionary* (1864), s. v.
[6] Substantially borrowed from Bain, §§ 130 ff.

[2] H. N. Day, § 26.
[4] Id. ib. I., p. 8

has four rhymes, arranged thus,—1, 4, 5, 8+2, 3, 6, 7+9, 11,13+10, 12, 14;[1] but it would be most unjust to condemn as imperfect many sonnets that do not obey this rule; while still another form, which comprises three stanzas of four lines each and a concluding couplet, has no little or unworthy authority.

(2) EPIC POETRY, or narratives containing "plot or story, scenery, characters," and many other peculiarities of History or the Novel. "The author appears in his own person, lays the scenes, introduces the actors, and narrates the events." The Epic is necessarily long, and allows many a digression or other departure from the direct line of the story. Its chief divisions are *the Great Epic*, into which supernatural agents are admitted; *the Romance; the Ballad*, a short and simple poem in which incidents succeed each other rapidly; and *the Pastoral* or *Idyll*, "distinguished by the prominence of poetic description," whether "of external nature or of manners." Originally affecting to be written by shepherds or to be concerned with their lives and manners and customs, this class of poems received the name *pastoral*. Virgil's name, *Eclogues*, and Theocritus's, *Idylls*, have both survived, but often name verses little concerned with pastoral matters.

(3) DRAMATIC POETRY, intended for acting on the stage, and, hence, cast in the form of *dialogue*. The author nowhere appears in his own person, the whole story being told by the actors (the *dramatis personæ*). Dramas are (1) *Tragedies*, in which the emotions to be aroused are chiefly Pity and Fear; (2) *Comedies*, in which the appeal is to the sense of the Ludicrous.

71. Numerous other specifying terms applied to Poetry, either explain themselves, or can easily be found in the dictionaries.

72. Examples of these several divisions of Poetry can not, of course, be quoted at length. Well known Lyrics (in the order

---

[1] These figures indicate lines.

defined above) are Burns's *Scots, wha hæ*, the *Dies Iræ*, Milton's *Hymn on the Nativity*, Tennyson's *In Memoriam*, Shakspere's, Wordsworth's, Mrs. Browning's *Sonnets*, Burns's *Mountain Daisy*, Milton's *Paradise Lost*, Dante's *Divine Comedy*, the *Original Ballad of Chevy Chase*, Tennyson's *Idylls of the King ;* and Shakspere's *Lear, Macbeth, Hamlet, Comedy of Errors* and *Merry Wives of Windsor*.

73. By some writers,[1] the division of compositions with respect to Intrinsic Character is triple, into *Prose, Romance*, and *Poetry*, instead of quadruple, as above.[2] The term *Prose* has then, of course, no reference to the *form* of the composition, and is opposed, not to *Verse*, but to *Romance* and *Poetry*. In brief, when so used, it unites the first two sub-divisions of Class 2, and itself requires separation into those sub-divisions. The use of the term in this sense is convenient, though it may sometimes be ambiguous.

74. Romance and Poetry differ from Oratory and Representative Discourse, (that is, from Prose, as just defined,) rather in the *kind of thought expressed* than in *the mode of expressing it*. Both address the imagination and the feelings ; both are designed to give pleasure rather than to convey instruction. But here their *necessary* likeness ends. The Romance must tell a story ; the Poem *may* do this, but *need* not. The Romance generally takes the prose form ; the Poem is generally in verse. In the Romance, as in the Drama, (which is, in fact, little more than a romance *wholly* in dialogue,) the author stays behind the scenes ; the characters of the story or the actors representing them (the *dramatis personæ*) appearing in their own persons and speaking

---

[1] Notably by Minto,—*Manual of English Prose Literature*, Preface. Mr. Minto adopts " a division suggested by the late Professor George Moir, in his treatises on Poetry, Romance, and Rhetoric," originally contributed to the Eighth Edition of the *Encyclopædia Britannica*. So, Prof. Baldwin speaks of "matter of fact prose," as opposed to " prose-fiction-or story-telling prose."

[2] § 31, *above*.

with their own lips. In the Romance, the author now and then comes forward to make a critical or other observation on a character or an event of the story, or even (by way of change) to take the narrative out of his characters' mouths and carry it on; but he soon slips out again, and the dramatic form is resumed. The Poem (except the Drama) has not this character. The author is himself present: he may, indeed, harangue his readers like an orator; though he may also be only an essayist or a narrator. In this, perhaps, is the essential difference between Romance and Poetry. The former is dramatic; the latter is not. The essential difference between the Romance and the Poem, on the one hand, and Prose (as last defined[1]), on the other, has been thus expressed by Minto:—"Romance has a closer affinity with Poetry than with Prose: it is cousin to Prose, but sister to Poetry; it has the Prose features, but the Poetical spirit."

3. Compositions with Respect to Purpose, or End in View.

75. The four classes into which compositions are divided with respect to Purpose, or End in View, are, in fact, four *modes of discussion* applicable to any composition, no matter what its form or intrinsic character. Hence, the detailed consideration of this branch of the subject belongs under the head of Invention.[2]

[1] § 73, *above*.   [2] Part Second, §§ 341 ff.

PART FIRST.

STYLE.

DEFINITIONS.

76. **STYLE IS THE FORM OF DISCOURSE ;**—*the Form of Thought Expressed in Language.*[1] Thus, the following versions of a familiar passage of Scripture all express the same or nearly the same thought; yet each has a form in some respects its own;—

(1) "Then shall be brought to pass the saying that is written, Death is swallowed up in victory. O death, where is thy sting; O grave, where is thy victory? The sting of death is sin; and the strength of sin is the law."[2]

(2) "Then shall come to pass the saying that is written, Death is swallowed up in victory. O death, where is thy victory? O death, where is thy sting? The sting of death is sin; and the power of sin is the law."[3]

(3) "Then will be brought to pass that which is written: 'Death is swallowed up in victory.' 'Where, O death is thy sting? Where, O death, is thy victory?' The sting of death is sin; and the strength of sin is the Law."[4]

The special form of each version constitutes its Style; and the differences of form between the versions are differences of Style.[5] The province of this department of Rhetoric is to set forth and illustrate the several particulars by which the form of discourse is characterized.

---

[1] § 17, above.   [2] Version of 1611.   [3] Revision of 1881.

[4] George R. Noyes, *The New Testament Translated from the Greek Text of Tischendorf.*

[5] Another reading, "suggested by Dr. Robinson," and cited for this work by Roswell Smith, Esq., of New York, is, "O grave, where is thy victory? Where, O death, thy sting?"—The differences are in some particulars due to variations in the Greek text.

76 *a*. Hence, the study of Style is the study either of the Qualities of Thought as expressed in Speech or of the Properties of Language as expressing Thought. The two phrases are in fact, identical in meaning. Thought and Speech, no matter how they may be conceived, are inseparable. Each implies the other: neither is possible without the other. Thought, of course, is of primary importance; but the task were idle to quibble upon the words in defining Style. The composition necessarily takes a body; and this body is Language. As necessarily, the language used expresses the matter or substance of the composition; and this matter or substance is Thought. The properties of language, therefore, are the correlatives of the qualities of thought; and, the student once understanding that what he deals with is *Thought Expressed in Language*, and not mere *Words*, time is simply wasted by overmuch discussion of the relations of thought and speech, or of the question whether this or that is more particularly referred to in the word Style.

77. Style may be distinguished as—

(A) DICTION, or mere Expression,—the form of discourse with respect to the *grammatical* properties of language;

(B) PHRASEOLOGY, or Mechanical Structure, the form of discourse with respect to the *mechanical* properties of language;—for example, the order of words in a sentence, emphasis, modes of connecting words and sentences, *etc.*

(C) STYLE PROPER, "the niceties, the elegancies, the peculiarities, and the beauties of composition,"—the form of discourse with respect to the *subtler* properties of language.[1]

These distinctions are not sub-divisions of Style, but rather particulars in which, or points of view from which, the form of a composition may be examined and criticized. Thus, in the passage,—

"Enter ye in by the narrow gate: for wide is the gate, and broad is the way, that leadeth to destruction, and many be they that enter in thereby. For narrow is the gate, and straitened the way, that leadeth unto life, and few be they that find it,"—[2]

---

[1] ¶ 306, *below*.   [2] Revised Version of Matt. vii. 13, 14.

exceptions might be taken to *ye*, *leadeth* and *be* as out of present use, to *by* as over-precise for *at*, to *straitened* as having a sense not common in connection with roads or ways, to *thereby* as old-fashioned and formal, to *be they* as an unnecessary inversion,[1] and to the whole passage as artificial in structure and lacking in clearness and force. The first four exceptions are points of Diction, the fifth a point of Phraseology, and the sixth a point of Style Proper.[2]

78. The mechanical properties of language have been aptly named *the Elements of Style;*[3] the subtler properties are commonly spoken of as *the Qualities of Style;* and correctness in Diction is called *Grammatical Purity.* Hence, three sub-divisions of Part First,—(A) GRAMMATICAL PURITY, (B) THE ELEMENTS OF STYLE, (C) THE QUALITIES OF STYLE.

[1] Cf. the version of 1611, which uses the expletive *there*.

[2] The older version naturally has the archaisms mentioned, but it has none of the other faults specified. The Revisers of 1881 may have Englished the Greek Testament, but have they not un-Englished the Testament of 1611?

[3] Minto, *Manual*, p. 1.

(A) GRAMMATICAL PURITY.

I.

ITS IMPORTANCE.

79. GRAMMATICAL PURITY has been aptly compared to correctness of drawing in Painting. Not only is it a pre-requisite to success;[1] it often of itself constitutes success. The chief end of all rational discourse is to be understood; and nothing contributes more largely to this end than correct diction. Even the man whose own practice is in this respect faulty, both understands correct language and appreciates its use by others. The vulgar or provincial speaker who not only can not understand but condemns as "bad English" the vulgar or provincial speech of his neighbor, both understands and applauds the "good English" of the cultivated orator. "The common people like to be addressed in sound old English which has the centuries behind it. . . . Marines do not like to be preached to in the dialect of the forecastle. When one preacher of distinction . . . endeavored to preach thus on a man-of-war in Boston harbor, his hearers said, when his back was turned, that 'there were two things which he did not understand,— religion and navigation.'[2] A rabble in the street will often hoot if they are addressed in bad grammar. Patrick Henry thought to win the favor of the backwoodsmen of Virginia by imitating their colloquial

---

[1] "The beginning of Style," says Aristotle, "is correctness in diction" [ἑλληνίζειν].

[2] But compare: "Did you ever hear of Boatswain Smith? He is a preacher to sailors in London; himself a sailor, and a man of great eloquence and strange, quaint power. While *he does not stud his discourses with sea-phrases, neither does he avoid them*, and when he introduces them *he does so with great effect*. Sailors *have contempt for a landlubber's preaching*. But Boatswain Smith takes them on a true tack."—W. B. Hodgson, in a letter, an. 1843.

dialect . . . But his hearers, backwoodsmen though they were, knew better than that; and they knew that a statesman of the Old Dominion ought to speak good English. They were his severest critics."[1] Besides, correct language has a beauty of its own, and in many cases lends a charm to work not otherwise noteworthy. On the other hand, even a slip in grammar is a blot; while errors that are plainly "constitutional"—that spring from a fundamental ignorance—are fatal to the writer. "It is not so much a merit to know English as it is a shame not to know it; and I look upon this knowledge as essential for an Englishman, and not merely for a fine speaker."[2] Hence, at whatever expense of time and labor, the student of Rhetoric must perfect himself in Grammar; just as the student of Art must give himself without reserve to Anatomy and other studies of Outline.

[1] Austin Phelps, *English Style in Public Discourse*, pp. 17, 18.

[2] Adapted from Cicero by Abbott and Seeley, *English Lessons for English People*, Title-page.

II.

THE STANDARD OF PURITY.

80. What, then, constitutes Grammatical Purity? How shall a writer know whether his work is correct in Diction, or not? Plainly, there must be set up a *Standard of Purity*, to which reference can readily be made, and by which the correctness of work can easily be gauged. If such a standard exists, and access to it is quite unimpeded, little or no excuse can remain for violations of Purity; while, if there is a doubt what the standard truly is, or if the standard is inaccessible, violations of Purity will be inevitable, and can not be so severely censured.

81. It is this truth, perhaps, that best explains the continual violations of Purity by writers as well as speakers of English. The standard usually insisted upon is Good Use—a standard to which reference is difficult, and which is not a single, unfluctuating measure, but a cumulate authority, the binding force of which may be loosened by any writer, however heretical in this respect, who may be lucky enough to secure a wide reading. Of course, life in language, as in all other organisms, implies its putting forth new growths, sloughing off dead members, changing by many processes; of course, too, in the operation of this growth and decay, varying forms of many sorts will come into existence, so that a rigid conformity to any standard will be impossible; but it does not follow hence that, because there must be variation, there need be chaos,—that, because Liberty in speaking and writing is possible and desirable, there must be License.

82. Two opinions are held by rhetoricians as to what the STANDARD OF PURITY is. One side contends that it is USAGE, or GOOD USE, *the custom of the best writers and speakers;* the other side, that, while the Standard of Purity may be *inferred* from Good Use, yet, *ultimately*, it lies in THE LAWS OF THOUGHT AND SPEECH, *the*

principles to which Language conforms as one of man's faculties. The two views, it will be seen, are radically different. The former puts Usage forward as the only and absolute Law of Speech: whatever IS (in worthy speech and writing), it declares, is RIGHT.[1] The latter holds that Usage is an *exponent* of the standard, but not the standard itself. The theories differ as would two theories of Morals, one of which held that the standard of right and wrong was the character and mode of life of good men; the other, that, while correct moral principles can undoubtedly be learned from examples of good character and right living, yet there are absolute laws of right and wrong, apart from any or all illustrations of them. The former doctrine has certainly the weight of authority both ancient and modern; but the latter would seem the more reasonable.

83. Horace first stated the doctrine of Good Use,—"Use is the Law and Rule of Speech." Quintilian confirmed Horace,—"Custom is the surest guide [*magistra*] in speaking: our language, like our money, must bear the public stamp." Campbell says, "Every tongue whatever is founded in use or custom,

'Whose arbitrary sway
Words and the forms of language must obey.'"

And most other modern critics have accepted the rule unquestioningly. Moreover, were the statement intended to mean only that Use is *proximately* the standard of Purity, that it sets forth "the law and rule of speech" in a form convenient for study,—no one could cavil at it.

84. But such is plainly not the intention of the *dictum*;[2] and a few writers, foremost among whom is Prof. H. N. Day,[3] have, therefore, called the doctrine in question. They teach that, however accurately Usage may express "the law and rule of speech," it is not that law; that ultimate principles, broad general truths, give law to language; and, therefore, that the

---

[1] "Authority is *everything* in language; it is the want of it alone that constitutes" grammatical impurity.—Campbell, II. ii.

[2] § 94, below.   [3] *The Art of Discourse*, §§ 246, 284.

Standard of Purity lies in these truths. It is noticeable, too, that the *popular* feeling,—the *instinctive* judgment of all men, perhaps, before they *acquire* the belief that diction is controlled by Usage,—the popular feeling is that, whatever this or that great writer may do, whatever may be the passing fashion of speech even among the people themselves, nevertheless law, and not precedent, ultimately settles all questions of Grammar. The grounds for preferring this latter view of the question may be briefly stated as follows.

85. *First*, since the rules and the theory of an art are only systematic statements of principles that must have been active in nature before any practical art-work could have been done, —that is, before a usage of any kind, good or bad, could have existed,[1] it follows that these principles are superior, as well as anterior, to use. Else, practical work is but a blind groping in the dark, a wild beating of the air, which, by the grace of God or the fatuitous combination of atoms,[2] accomplishes its results, —results that not only were not foreseen, but positively could not have been foreseen. But does any one believe that mental action—and all art-work pre-supposes an intelligent, reasoning artist—is thus at hit or miss? In some cases, to be sure, the underlying and controlling principle can not easily, or even with difficulty, be detected; but it surely does not follow, hence, that no such principle exists; that, because, in these cases, man seems to act without reason, he acts so in all cases, even in those in which the reason can be discovered. On the contrary, the presumption is fair that, since in so many cases, a reasonable explanation of Usage can be found, such explanation must exist for those cases, also, in which it has not been detected.

86. *Secondly*, as a matter of fact, man, though apparently free to use his language as he will, is, in truth, bound by definite laws. These he may no more transcend, than he may digest his food in his lungs, or walk in steps of seven leagues each. For language is the product, not of man's mental faculties only, but of his physical organism as well; and this physical organism, developed in the very years of his life in which he is acquiring his mother tongue or the other language he may learn in child-

---

[1] Appendix, p. 333.

[2] And what odds does it make, if man is such an irrational creature as the Good Use theory pre-supposes?

hood, on this account takes the form (especially, the mutual relations of its parts) that is necessary to the full and perfect enunciation of this particular language. Later in life, therefore, when the organs of speech are settled into their due relationships, and have lost (in great measure, at least) their capacity to re-adjust themselves,—later in life, man is bound by this physical condition, and, while he can, of course, still acquire foreign tongues well enough to make them in a high sense valuable, he meets, in perhaps every case, certain sounds for the making of which *his* physical organism is incompetent. The children of Ephraim could not say *Shibboleth*,[1] as the Greeks could not say *Shem;* the Sandwich Islanders, importing English *steel*, both thing and name, were obliged, in order to pronounce even so simple a combination, to transform it into *Kila*.[2] The German, whose *th* is *t*, stumbles painfully over the delicately shaded sounds of this digraph in English; the Englishman, though on the rack of supreme effort, never pronounces like a native the German *œ* or the French *u*. So throughout the coasts of human speech, of the many sounds and combinations of sounds *ideally* possible, only a small part are *actually* pronounced by any one people. Some languages have but *eight* consonants; others as many as *forty-eight:* in every nation, certain ideally possible sounds can at best be only approximated by even the ablest speakers, while others must simply be despaired of.[2]

87. *Thirdly*, if these things are not so, why is any form *monstrous?* A child with six toes on one foot or with his heart on the right side of his body, is not simply an offence against correct Taste: such a creation violates the laws of Nature, and is *therefore* monstrous. So, in Art, monstrosities are forms that contradict well-ascertained principles,—principles true in the nature of man or of the work proposed or in some other necessary circumstance. Surely, no amount of authority could succeed in foisting such forms permanently upon any art. Fashion might make them temporarily popular, and, indeed,

---

[1] Judges xii. 6.

[2] Müller, *The Science of Language*, II. Lect. IV.; where may be found many other curious examples of the working of this law. The opposite view of the case is taken by Prof. Whitney, *Language and the Study of Language*, pp. 35 ff. But which opinion is preferable,—that man is simply a self-willed child, or that he is intelligent, law-governed, and law-abiding in this as in other respects?

has done so; but the good sense of the nation has ultimately asserted itself. For example, Anglo-Saxon *hw* gave Modern English the initial *wh* in such words as *whale, who*, etc. In the 16th century, a fashion arose of prefixing *w* to many words beginning with *h* that by their etymology had no right to it; as, *whot* for *hot, whome* for *home, wrapt* for *rapt*. But, the impropriety once remarked, the superfluous letter was soon dropped, and the correct forms resumed their place. So, under the false impression that the *'s* of the English possessive case was a contraction of the word *his*, such constructions as *the king his crown, the queen her robe*, had their day; but they ceased to be, as soon as the fact was remembered that Anglo-Saxon is an inflected language, and that English *'s* simply represents an older genitive case-ending. Like everything unnatural, such forms survive or perish in direct ratio to their approximation to what is natural. Often they exist only in the imagination of the poets, like the single eye of the Cyclops or the fan-like wings of Satan.

88. *Fourthly*, the facts of Usage itself all point the same way.

89. (1) When Usage is settled, a *sufficient reason* can generally be given for it (*a*); although sometimes this reason only *accounts for* the usage, without establishing its propriety or even its expediency (*b*). Thus, (*a*) the rule that requires the objective case after a transitive verb, rests upon a necessary law of thought. For, although, in many instances, (especially in English and other slightly inflected languages,) the nominative and objective cases are alike in form,—in other words, the case *distinction* has disappeared,—yet their *function* in the sentence is never the same, and they themselves are as radically distinguished by function as by case-ending. (*b*) The spelling of *number* with a *b*, or of *sound* with a *d*, while it can be accounted for, can not be shown to be necessary. Derived respectively from the Latin *numerus* and *sonus*, the words take *b* or *d* by "*eduction*," the prolonging of *m* or *n* with the lips tightly closed. This prolongation may at first have been a mere drawl or otherwise lazy pronunciation, the voice *staying* on *m* or *n* until the result followed;[1] but this, of course, is not

---

[1] Compare *p* from *m* and *t* from *d*; as, *presumption* from Lat. sumo, sumptum; *serpent* from Lat. serpens, serpentis. (That the Romans were "lazy" two thousand years ago does not injure the examples. *l'armint*, for *vermin*, (a French word, as if from the Latin *verminus*), and *sarmint*, for *sermon* (Latin sermo, sermonis), belong entirely at home.)

a necessary principle. For, in *numb* and *limb* (Anglo-Saxon *numen* and *lim*), though the *b* is written, it is not pronounced; in *slim* (old Dutch *slim*), it is neither written nor pronounced,— that is, eduction has not taken place; while in *clime* (Greek *klima*) and *climb* (Anglo-Saxon *climban* or *clymmian*), though heard in neither, it is written in one. So, too, in *gown*, (probably a Celtic word), *d* is added only in provincial utterance; but in *bound*, whether it mean *a limit* or *ready to go* eduction has taken place.[1]

90. The "sufficient reason" may even rest on (*c*) a misapprehension, or (*d*) a statement absolutely false, and yet may both account for the usage and seem to justify it. Thus, (*c*) if the phrases *it is I*, *it is he*, *etc.*, ever become the *only* good use for *it is me*, *etc.*, the controlling reason will undoubtedly be the erroneous belief that the English predicate after the verb *to be necessarily* takes the same case as its subject;[2] whereas the truth is that *it is me*, *etc.*, are peculiar, idiomatic expressions, and take, not the nominative, but the dative case in the predicate. *Me*, *etc.*, in this idiom are not accusatives—the case of the direct object—but old datives—the case of the indirect object—adopted, doubtless, under the influence of the French *c' est moi*,[3] and preserved in the popular speech despite the grammarians. (*d*) At a time when *contráry* was still in reputable use, Walker[4] wrote, "The accent of this word is invariably placed on the first syllable by all correct speakers, and as constantly removed to the second by the illiterate and vulgar,"—"rather hard terms," adds Mr. Earle,[5] "to apply to the really time-honored and classical pronunciation of *contráry*." But see what came of it. The accent of this word was, indeed, on its way back,—as in a host of English words, which seem more easily pronounced so than with the accent on the penult; but two other words, of like formation, then retained their penultimate accent, *vagáry* and *quandáry*.[6] Under Walker's lead,

---

[1] Skeat, *Etymo. Dict.*, s. vv.

[2] A. J. Ellis, *Letter to The Reader* (English newspaper), cited in Alford's *Queen's English*, note F., pp. 285-7. (See § 168 (5), *below*.)

[3] The dative in this construction is not unknown, however, to other Teutonic languages.

[4] *Pronouncing Dictionary*, s. v.

[5] *The Philology of the English Tongue*, p. 155.

[6] *Vagary* is still so pronounced according to all authorities; in regard to *quandary* there is a difference of usage.

however, it soon seemed as "vulgar and illiterate" not to say *vágary* and *quándary* as not to say *cóntrary;* and popular usage soon changed the accent of both words.

91. (2) When Usage is unsettled ("divided"[1]), an appeal to fundamental principles becomes necessary.[2] This appeal would undoubtedly both be made the sooner and be the more binding, were it not that the general acceptance of Good Use as the Standard of Purity delays a settlement in such cases, and that men are not always—perhaps not commonly—either able to be convinced by what is reasonable, or willing to be controlled by it. For example, in that curious case of *attraction, these kind of books*, the moment it is shown that agreement by attraction is not an English mode of thought, but simply (as, perhaps, it was in Latin and Greek) a blunder, all ground for the solecism is swept away.

92. (3) That usage is most easily unsettled which does not rest upon necessary truth,—in other words, that usage which can be accounted for, but can not be shown to be binding. In this case, either of three results may follow;—(*a*) the usage may change, (*b*) it may become obsolete, or (*c*) two forms may grow up side by side in the language. For example, (*a*) the termination *-or* has long contended with *-our* in such words as *honor, parlour, etc.* Chaucer wrote *-ure* (for French *-eur*), and Shakspere *-our;* but, before 1750, Latin influences had cast the weight for *-or.* Accordingly, in 1755, Dr. Johnson "restored the ancient usage" by replacing the *u;* in 1828, Webster professed to do the same thing by leaving it out; and to-day, oddly enough, the *u* is pronounced (*on-ur*) but the *o* is written.[3] (*b*) In Shakspere and other older writers *a many* takes the place of *many a.* In a word *many* was a noun. But, in English, "speech-part-ship"[4] depends, not upon termination, but upon the function of the word in the sentence; and hence, it can change almost at will. For this reason, *many* easily became a pronoun and adjective; while *a many* fell into disuse. (*c*) In certain strong verbs, English has two forms for the preterite, and holds them both with remarkable tenacity; for example, *sang* or *sung, drank* or *drunk.* The explanation of this double

---

[1] § 163, *below.* [2] See Campbell's Canons, § 167, *below.*

[3] Cf. *neighbor* for *neighbour,* the Anglo-Saxon *nehgebur.*

[4] This useful, if thoroughly un-English compound is borrowed from Earle's *Philology of the English Tongue,* ch. iv.

form is easy enough. Anglo-Saxon strong verbs used two stem-vowels in the preterite, one for the 1st and 3d persons singular, another for the 2d person singular and the plural. English in some cases borrowed them both, and, having no controlling reason for keeping either exclusively, kept both, with perhaps no care which was used, or whether usage ever settled on either to the exclusion of the other.

93. *Once more*, though many exceptions exist to the laws of Purity, as to all rules that rest on general principles, these exceptions are not in any way inconsistent with the view that principles, and not mere use, give the Standard of Purity. For, however clear it may be that both the regular and the exceptional form can not rest upon the same underlying truth, yet it is equally clear, of course, that the exception may rest (as, in fact, it always does rest) on another truth equally valid in itself and equally nomothetical. This is peculiarly true in those exceptional cases that are always treated under the head of Divided Usage,—the cases that *must* be judged by an appeal to fundamental law;[1] while, in the exceptional cases for which no explanation has been found, there is, of course, no necessity for concluding that no explanation exists.

94. *Finally*, the Good Use theory is inconsistent with itself. (1) Though it accepts as the final arbiter in language the fashion or custom of the speakers of that language, it nevertheless at once proceeds to define *what* fashion or custom it intends, and to appeal to *reason* to confirm this definition. "Language," says Campbell,[2] "is purely a species of *fashion*, in which, by the general but tacit consent of the people of a particular state or country, certain sounds come to be appropriated to certain things, as their signs, and certain ways of inflecting and combining these sounds come to be established, as denoting the relations which subsist among the things signified. *It is not the business of grammar*, as some critics seem preposterously to imagine, *to give law* to the fashions which regulate our speech. On the contrary, from its[3] *conformity to these*, and from *that alone, it*[3] *derives all its*[3] *authority and value.*" Yet in the very same chapter[4] Campbell defines Good Use as reputable, national, and present, and assigns *reasons* why it must have these characteristics.[5] More than this, the heading

---

[1] § 163, *below*.   [2] Bk I. ch. I.—Cf. § 83, *above*.

[3] § 321 (*d*), *below*.   [4] Sections 1–3.   [5] Cf. §§ 96 ff, *below*.

of a section in Campbell's very next chapter[1] reads, "Everything favoured by Good Use, not on that account worthy to be retained;" and the burden of the section is that "in some instances *custom* may very properly be checked by *criticism;*" in other words, that, though *custom*, and custom *alone* declares what is right in language, yet, when custom *goes astray*, criticism, appealing to fundamental principles, may *set it right!* The guide is *infallible*, to be sure, but this other guide is necessary now and then *to show him the road!* (2) In cases of Divided Use, Campbell lays down, and all later writers have accepted five "canons," which are simply appeals to one or more of the sciences exhibited above as nomothetical to Rhetoric.[2] Campbell, indeed, goes further and states four additional rules for cases in which even the *best* authority must be set aside;[3]—(α) "words and phrases remarkably harsh and inharmonious, and not absolutely necessary;" (β) words whose meanings are at war with their own etymologies; (γ) words obsolete except in certain phrases; and (δ) "phrases, which, when analyzed *grammatically*, include a solecism, and those to which use hath affixed a particular sense" contradictory of "the *general* and *established rules* of the language."[4]

95. The Standard of Purity, then, is ultimately to be found in the Laws of Thought and Speech; though, proximately, it may be inferred from Good Use as the exponent of those laws. Hence, it is both convenient and proper to study the laws of Grammatical Purity, rather as set forth in Good Use, than as abstract truths of the sciences nomothetical to Rhetoric; for this plan is practical rather than theoretical, and most surely promotes skill in composition. It will therefore be followed in this volume.

[1] II. ii. 2.   [2] See §§ 166 ff, *below.*   [3] *Ut cit.*

[4] Rule (α) is clearly a principle of Æsthetics; rules (β), (γ) and (δ), principles of Logic. Coming from an author who denies the right of Grammar to give laws to language, rule (δ) is absolutely refreshing.

III.

THE CHARACTERISTICS OF GOOD USE.

96. The first question that arises is, what use *is* Good? who *are* the best writers and speakers,—*those* writers and speakers, in other words, *whose usage so generally conforms to the laws of thought and speech, that it may be accepted as the proximate Standard of Purity?*

97. The answer to this question has been unanimous: The best writers and speakers are those who *now* enjoy a *national reputation*. In other words, Good Use is (1) *Reputable*, (2) *National*, (3) *Present*. Many writers who *have enjoyed* such a reputation; many who are now held in *local* repute; many who, though they live now and are widely read, yet confessedly use a diction not that of reputable writers;—many writers of these classes are models of style in other particulars, but they can not be cited as authorities for Good Use. For example, Bacon's *Essays* and *the Bible of 1611* are to-day as valuable exponents of certain qualities of style as are any modern books, but they are in many cases archaic in diction. *Hans Breitmann* talks English that makes no pretence to good repute. To be cited as authoritative in Diction, a work must have *all three* characteristics of Good Use.

98. REPUTABLE USE is the custom in speech of cultivated people, the people "who have had a liberal education, and are therefore presumed to be best acquainted with men and things."[1] Words are but signs of the things they name; and it is only natural "to believe, that those are the best judges of the proper signs, and of the proper application of them, who understand best the things which they represent."[1] For convenience of

[1] Campbell, II. i. 1.

reference, however, celebrated *authors* are taken in place of the whole class of liberally educated people; and reputable use includes, therefore, "whatever modes of speech are authorized as good by the writings of a great number, if not the majority,[1] of celebrated authors."[2]

99. NATIONAL USE is the custom of writers and speakers readily understood by people that use the language anywhere. From the earliest ages to which the existence of human speech can be traced, a tendency to *dialecticism*, the divergence of language from a common form towards several or many different forms, has been observed. A common dialect has never been maintained except by constant intercourse or (among cultivated peoples) by a literature. Not only do the languages of savage tribes vary to a degree, and change with a rapidity, that seems almost incredible,[3] but even literary tongues, now apparently settled beyond the danger of serious modifications, not only have passed through the dialectical stage before attaining uniformity, but show themselves now to be liable at any moment,

---

[1] *I. e.*, a respectable minority may protect a usage. (See § 321 (*c*), *below*.)

[2] Campbell, II. i. 1.

[3] Max Müller, Lectures on the Science of Language, Vol. I. Lect. II., (pp. 61-65, Am. Ed.) gives the following remarkable cases. (1) "Gabriel Sagard, who was sent as a missionary to the Hurons in 1626, . . . states that . . . hardly one village speaks the same language as another; nay, that two families of the same village do not speak exactly the same language. And he adds . . . that their language is changing every day." (2) Certain "missionaries in Central America . . . compiled with great care a dictionary of all the words they could lay hold of. Returning to the same tribe after a lapse of only ten years, they found that this dictionary had become antiquated and useless." (3) "Robert Moffat," missionary to Southern Africa, writes "The purity and harmony of language is kept up by . . . pitchos, or public meetings, by their festivals and ceremonies, as well as by their songs and their constant intercourse. With the isolated villagers of the desert it is far otherwise; they have no such meetings; they are compelled to traverse the wilds, often to a great distance from their native village. On such occasions the children are left for weeks at a time to the care of two or three infirm old people. The infant progeny . . . *become habituated to a language of their own*. . . . and *in the course of one generation the entire character of the language is changed*."

upon the breaking down of a standard of purity among them, to fly off at many different tangents into dialecticism again. Hence, the necessity, if a language is to be widely understood, of its conforming to the national, rather than to a narrower use.

100. The history of the English language and of its immediate predecessor on the island of Britain illustrates both these statements. The speech of the Teutonic tribes who won Britain from the Celts contained as many dialects as there were tribes. In the ninth century, a literature arose; and at once a common dialect was formed, the Anglo-Saxon of the books. Upon the Norman-French invasion, however, this standard was broken down, and a second Babel, which lasted for upwards of two centuries, was the result. In the fourteenth century, the English of Chaucer and Gower again gave the nation a literary tongue, and fixed (in great part) its modern peculiarities. The same story is true of modern French. The Teutonic invaders of the Romanized Gaul settled in at least two camps, one to the north and one to the south of the Loire. In each a literature sprang up; but the political events that finally welded these nations into a single people, at first involved the whole land in dialecticism, until further political changes, combined with other causes, produced a new standard speech about the second half of the seventeenth century.

101. The choice of a common dialect is generally made unconsciously. One or more great writers appear; and the form of speech they adopt is followed by all subsequent writers that aim at more than a local reputation. For example, in an era of unquestionable dialecticism in each land, Chaucer wrote *The Canterbury Tales* and so settled the literary form of modern English; Dante, *The Divine Comedy*, and fixed modern Italian; Luther, his *Translation of the Bible*, and determined modern High German. When a non-literary dialect is used for literary purposes, (as in Mr. Charles Leland's *Hans Breitmann* and the Rev. William Barnes's *Poems in the Dorset Dialect*,) or when several forms of the same language become literary together, (as in ancient Greece and mediæval Gaul,) the rule is not affected. Such writers as Mr. Leland and Mr. Barnes do not pretend (in works like those just named) to write the literary dialect; and the several forms of Greek, like Provençal

and French, were really the national tongues of independent states.[1]

102. PRESENT USE is not so easily defined. To say exactly when a word has passed out of current into archaic diction, or how long a new word must wait for recognition, is impossible; since, if there were no other difficulty in the way, there would be the fact that a language is commonly spoken by several generations at once, and that words still fresh in the memory of a Longfellow, may be obsolescent in the view of a Howells, or even obsolete in that of a Miss Woolson. Besides, words are in current speech as men in society: they come and go almost without observation; they disappear for a while, as if gone on a journey, and then, as suddenly as returned travellers, take their places again in Good Use. So, too, one word springs almost unheralded into full reputation; for example, *telegram*, which was deliberately *proposed* in the Albany *Evening Journal*, April 6, 1852, as a substitute for *telegraph* or *telegraphic dispatch* or *message*,[2] and was soon unanimously accepted as a valuable addition. Others wait long for recognition; as, *standpoint* and *scientist*, still (perhaps) unused by the most conservative writers. Others again, though long since cast out of the literary language, survive in the *natural* speech[3] of both educated and uneducated alike. For example, *the double negative*, used for emphasis, in our older literature, driven out by the philosophizing grammarians, and utterly indefensible to-day, is nevertheless still heard, as a slip, in the hurried speech of many people

[1] See Goodwin's *Greek Grammar*, pp. xix., xx.; Freeman's *General Sketch of History*, chap's ii. 11, v. 8, 9, vii. 6, xi. 6, xii. 6; Craik's *English Literature*, I. pp. 121 ff.; Miss H. W. Preston's translation of Frédéric Mistral's *Mirèio*, Introduction.

[2] Webster's Dict. (1864), *s. v.* Cf. *anagram, monogram, etc.*

[3] That is, speech, not so much *unguarded* or *ignorant*, as *instinctive, untrammelled* by present use or the philosophizings of the men who have (and often successfully) put their own ideas of right and wrong in language in place of the broad, general laws of the human mind and human speech.

who not only know better but would not think of justifying themselves in the blunder.[1] Two principles of judgment, however, are clearly applicable,—(1) intelligibility, (2) moderation. If a word has ceased to be generally understood,—especially, if a newer word has largely replaced it,—a careful writer will doubtless not use it, or, if at all, only in cases in which he feels sure of making his meaning clear: he will commonly prefer the newer word. On the other hand, accepting Polonius's advice, though he be "familiar," he will not be "vulgar:" his maxim will be,—

> "Those friends thou hast, and their adoption tried,
> Grapple them to thy soul with hoops of steel;
> But do not dull thy palm with entertainment
> Of each new-hatch'd, unfledged comrade."

Or, in the form long ago used by Quintilian, "As of new words the best are the very oldest, so of old words the best are the very newest."

103. Examples illustrative of these characteristics of Good Use would be but hindrances to the student, unless they were whole works, or (at least) lengthy excerpts from the works of many celebrated authors. One who would know with certainty what pure English is, who would cultivate his taste—acquire *the literary sense*—should read consecutively a series of good English writers and criticize them minutely. This work can be done best, after the study of Rhetoric has been completed; and it forms then, as does the writing of compositions, an important part of Rhetorical Praxis.[2] Meanwhile the most that can be done is to classify the offences against Purity and give examples of them. These examples will at least serve to warn the student against making similar errors, and so will enhance his appreciation of a really good diction.

---

[1] Such constructions, by way of emphasis,—the double comparative and the double superlative are other examples common enough in older English literature,—are justifiable upon many grounds, and have been sacrificed in English at the dictation of men usually least competent to judge.

[2] A valuable guide to such criticism is Minto's *Manual of English Prose Literature*, a detailed study of the style of De Quincey, Macaulay and Carlyle, with a less extended summary and criticism of the works of English prose writers from Mandeville to Landor and Lamb and Hazlitt.

IV.
OFFENCES AGAINST PURITY.

104. Errors in Diction have long been classified in two ways ;—
(I.) As opposed to 1. *Reputable*, 2. *National*, 3. *Present Use;*[1]
(II.) With reference to the *Departments of Grammar under which they fall*,—1. *Etymology*, 2. *Syntax*, 3. *Lexicography*.[2]

105. The two classifications are entirely distinct ; each has its own *principle of division ;* each includes all possible offences against Purity. Every violation of Purity, therefore, can be classified in both ways ; first, as opposed to Good Use, and, secondly, as offending against a principle of Grammar. Naturally, however, the fuller discussion and exemplification of the subject will be reserved for the second division of the subject.

(1.) Violations of Purity as Opposed to Good Use.
1. Violations of Reputable Use.

106. Violations of Reputable Use are, (1) Vulgarisms,[3] modes of speech *used chiefly by the illiterate ;* (2) Idiotisms,[4] *the affectations* and *the mannerisms* of single writers or groups of writers. For example ;—

(1) Vulgarisms : *Ain't*,[5] *don't* (for *does n't*),[5] *walkist, to wire, you was, to you and I, lay* (for *lie* or *laid*), *laid* (for *lay*)

---

[1] Day, § 285. (See § 97, *above*.) The distinctions had, of course, been made long before Day wrote ; but he was the first to state them formally. Curiously enough, he does not name either the *vulgarism* or the *neologism*. (§§ 106 and 131, *below*.)

[2] Quintilian, *Inst. Oral.*, I. v. 5.

[3] Latin *vulgus*, the many, and, hence, the illiterate, since the correct use of language has ever been the acquisition of but comparatively few people.

[4] Greek ἰδιώτης (idiótes), a citizen of peculiar political habits.

[5] Many such contractions, *don't* (for *do not*), *isn't, aren't, shan't, etc.*, are actually preferable in informal speech or writing ; but no valid excuse (one would think) can be found for *ain't*, unless, indeed, its nearly universal use warrants it. *I am not* is easily shortened into *I'm not ;* and *ain't* for *isn't* or *aren't* or *have n't* is, of course, unnecessary.

leave (for *let*), *female* (for *woman, lady*), *individual* (for *person, man, woman*), *less* (for *fewer*), *fewest* (for *smallest*),[1] *gums*, or *rubbers* (for *overshoes*), *gentleman* or *lady* (for *man* or *woman*), *man* or *woman* (for *gentleman* or *lady*).

"Tact and a sense of the fitness of things," says Alfred Ayres,[2] "decide when a man is a *man* or when he is a *gentleman*." Each word is good in its place; each is vulgar when out of its place. *Gentleman* and *lady* are, of course, far more frequently misused than *man* or *woman;* and it is no doubt true "that the terms *lady* and *gentleman* are least used by those who are most worthy of being designated by them."[2] But it is no cure for the misuse of either pair of words to exclude it from the vocabulary. "With a nice discrimination worthy of special notice, one of our daily papers recently said, 'Miss Jennie Halstead, daughter of the proprietor of the *Cincinnati Commercial*, is one of the most brilliant young *women* in Ohio;'"[2] but, surely, Mrs. So and So ought not to speak of her friends invited to a german as so many *men* and *women*.[3] Mr. So and So may ask a few *men* to the Club, or even to his own house; but both *men* and *women*, when spoken of as holding a certain social position, should be mentioned with courtesy and deference. In this view they are *gentlemen* or *ladies*, and should be called so.

Quite common, but often verbose as well as wrong in sense, is the phrase *a Boston lady* or *a Philadelphia gentleman* for *a Bostonian, a Philadelphian*, or equivalents.

(2) IDIOTISMS: *Tipsify*,[4] *toxophilite*,[4] *divagation*,[4] *Thukydidês*,[5] *Herodotos*,[5] *Senlac*,[6] *Elsass*,[6] *Regensburg*,[6] *neither* . . . . *or*,[7] *egoism, egoist* (for *egotism, egotist*).[8]

---

[1] As in *less people, the fewest number*, etc. The construction may be explained as *attraction* or *ad intellectum* (to the thought *in the writer's mind*, as opposed to the thought *expressed*); but this is only apologizing for error with high-sounding names.

[2] *The Verbalist*, s. v. *Lady*.

[3] A recent (and, doubtless, a passing) fashion.

[4] Thackeray, *Vanity Fair*.

[5] A purism imitated from the German, and practised by its few supporters with a refreshing disregard for either consistency or uniformity.

[6] Another purism, originated (apparently) by Dr. E. A. Freeman.

[7] In Shakspere, two cases are plain slips or misprints (*Meas.*, IV. ii. 108; I Henry VI., v. i. 59), and in a third (*Cor.*, II. ii. 13) *neither* is not correlative, but stands for *not*. (Cf. l. 18 of the same scene.)

[8] George Eliot and her imitators.

OFFENCES AGAINST PURITY. 71

107. Many vulgarisms spring from what has been aptly termed the "slovenly" use of words,—their use, that is, in a sense either grossly exaggerated or else vague and indefinite. Thus, *awfully*, *dreadfully*, *terribly*, etc., are used for *very* or *quite;* *very* or *quite*, when no qualifying word is needed; *nice*, without any definite meaning; *beastly*, *nasty*, for *ugly*, *uncomfortable;* and so on *ad nauseam*. Whether it records an actual occurrence, or not, the story of the witty American girl's reply to an overpunctilious [!] Englishman points the moral here intended. "Why do you say 'nice'?" he asked: "I think 'nice' is a nasty word." "And why do you say 'nasty'?" she rejoined: "do you think 'nasty' a nice word?" For a correct use of *nice* in the phrase "a nice discrimination," see the quotation from Mr. Ayres, § 106.

108. Vulgarisms *may* be coarse or indelicate expressions, but they *need* not be. Indeed, some of the deepest-dyed offences of this class result from the effort to *avoid* indelicacy or coarseness. Older English allowed a freedom of speech quite as great as that allowed to-day by certain foreign languages. Sex-names for the domestic animals, *dog*, *bitch*, *horse*, *mare*, *fox*, *vixen*, *he-wolf*, *she-wolf*, were never censured. Modest women —ladies of the highest rank—spoke in a way that is to-day condemned as coarse even on the part of men. Thoughts now considered incommunicable except under the strictest guard, were then freely interchanged. To-day all this is altered: many persons "shrink from plain words, and fear to call things by their names."[1] "Shade of Cobbet! we are now forbidden to call a spade a spade; our speech, like Bottom the weaver, is indeed translated."[2] Doubtless, the feeling that prompts to this squeamishness is delicacy, but it is a mistaken delicacy,

---
[1] Grant White, *Words and their Uses*, ch. v.
[2] T. L. Kington Oliphant, *Standard English*, ch. vi.

and it has betrayed many a speaker into gross vulgarism.[1] Surely, the English tongue is not so defective, that its speakers must choose between real indelicacies and actual vulgarities.

109. "Slang," in the sense of low, vulgar language, belongs under this head; but, meaning the language of a class, it is rather Technicality,[2] an offence against national use.

110. It ought to be true that vulgarisms are used *only* by the illiterate; but who will declare himself sinless, save in downright indelicacies? Bad habits of speech, contracted like an epidemic disease—no one knows how —cling to many otherwise cultured people, and defy all but the most strenuous efforts to dislodge them. That these efforts are worth making has already been seen; that they can be successful, let the exquisite purity of many a writer and speaker bear witness. But the student must keep one truth always before him. The price of freedom from blemishes of this sort is the price of liberty, eternal vigilance: indifference and the Will Honeycomb doctrine that to be able to spell correctly ill befits the character of a gentleman,[3] are the surest roads to impurity and literary incapacity.

111. At the same time, it is undoubtedly true that the surest road to grammatical purity is not a reckless striving after that virtue, but the cultivation of a refined literary feeling, a taste that, like an instinct, prompts to the use of language simple yet elegant, adorned or unadorned as the case may demand, but always unaffected and true. Purism is not Purity. In its very determination to be right at all costs, it either promotes an icy coldness of style, and so removes a writer to such a distance from

---

[1] For example, what of *lady-dog* as a polite (!) equivalent for *bitch;* and this, though the adjective *female* or the prefix *she* could have been used, if the special sex-word seemed indelicate?

[2] § 117, *below*.

[3] *Spectator*, No. 105. Cf. *Love's Labours Lost*, I., ii. 42.

his readers that he cannot influence them, or else betrays him into substituting for really pure speech a stilted, pretentious language that is certainly a most vulgar form of the Vulgarism.

112. The latter style of composition, known as "fine writing," especially besets the half-educated, whether those whose education is as yet only begun, or those who for any reason have not (as the phrase goes) "completed their education." Several grades of the bad practice may be noted.

113. *First*, among imperfectly educated professional men—especially those who, whatever their special knowledge, have no general culture, and who seek to cover their ignorance with a cloud of words—many abominations of this sort may be heard. The doctor of medicine who asks permission to *percute* his patient's chest; the lawyer whose "small Latin and less Greek" leads him to write *fecit per alium* instead of *act by another*, or whose mistaken idea of what constitutes "good English" sets him on to say *the heterogeneous masses with whom our profession brings us into daily contact* instead of *the common people whom I must meet every day;* the clergyman who exhorts his hearers to add "one more blossom to the millennial consummation," or who can not say that *plenty of soap and water have a healthy bracing effect upon the body*, but must talk of *habits of cleanliness* and *daily ablutions*—are sad examples; for they are "sinners above all the Galileans," their place among highly cultivated men demanding better things of them.

"Her Majesty's Diplomatic and Consular servants have been officially reminded that whatever may be the forms and habits of speech in the countries where they reside, they are expected to communicate with the Foreign Office in English pure and undefiled. Lord Granville has issued a circular containing examples of grotesque words and slovenly phrases taken from the department files of correspondence received during the current year. Virtually this is a warning to the entire Diplomatic and Consular body that the Queen's servants must speak and write the Queen's English. Many of the literary offences of which complaint is made are so flagrant as to create the suspicion that British Consuls are *barely more than half educated*. Lord Granville's *index expurgatorius* contains such distorted and senseless forms as these: *Disrecommended, unmotived, spiritiste, increasement, demission* (for *dismissal*), *arrestation* (for *arrest*), *suscitated* (for *raised*), and *veridical* (for *true*). There are many additional instances of correct words that are incorrectly used. *Transaction* takes the place of *compromise, incessantly* of *immediately, took act* of *took note, prorogation* of *prolongation*, and *destitution* of *dismissal*. Johnsonese is also a popular jargon in the Diplomatic service. *Signalize* is used in place of *point out, minimal* is a substitute for *very small*, and *category* for *class:* and instead of *returning to a previous understanding* the diplomatists or consuls consider it more dignified to *rally themselves to an antecedent solidarity.* Lord Granville seems to regard it as discreditable to the service that so many correspondents are taking such unwarrantable liberties with their mother tongue. He would have them speak and write with a reasonable degree of purity the language of the country they represent. The Queen's English first, as a matter of loyalty and common sense; Spanish or Bengalee afterward, if there be leisure or wit to acquire familiarity with the language of the country where they reside."[1]

114. *Secondly*, much that is high-sounding without a corresponding elevation of thought finds its way into the language of that large class of worthy people who, like Mrs. Vincy,[2] freely confess that they "never were good speakers," who find "the *best* young men of Middlemarch" "just as plain and common" as "the *pick* of them," and who, if they had "time to think," would say " the *most superior* young men." In the language of these good souls, a *school* (if it is to be especially commended) is an *academy*, an *educational establishment*, or even a *polite seminary; a college* must be a *university;*

---

[1] *The New York Tribune*, July 30, 1883. (See, also, ¿ 116, *below*.)
[2] George Eliot, *Middlemarch*, I. xi.

OFFENCES AGAINST PURITY. 75

fair lady is too mean praise for a *female possessing considerable personal attractions;* a *farmer,* grown rich, is an *eminent agriculturalist;* *healing* waters are not even *medicinal,* but *therapeutic;* and immigrants no longer *settle* in a country, but *locate* therein.¹

115. *Finally,* the penny-a-liner's average diction comes under this head, and at the bottom of the list. He it is who calls the *yellow fever* the *saffron scourge,*² the *season of fashionable society* the *socialistic era,*² and *a strike of cigar-makers in Chicago Chicago's*³ *Nicotine Strike;*² who heads his account of *a fire in a pork-packing house, Swine Flesh Incinerated;*² who speaks of children of *the school-age* as children of *schoolable ages.*² He always *vituperates* his enemies, never *abuses* or *reviles, rates* or *miscalls* them;⁴ his *brethren* in his really honorable vocation (if he would only exalt it to its true place)⁵ are his *confrères;*⁴ his *dancers* all *trip the light fantastic toe*⁴ or even *the light fantastic* (without *toe); threats* are *minatory expressions;*⁴ and *fire* is *the devouring element.*⁴ The men of Verdun, says one of these scribes, *ingurgitated spirituous stimulus.*⁴ "What," adds Mr. Oliphant, "will a penny paper of 1973 be like? What would become of our unhappy tongue, had we not the Bible and the Prayer Book to keep us fairly steady in the good old paths?" And yet, with both of these read daily in his church, an Irish Church of England man, at a convention in his land of "ornate phraseology," actually objected to the word *Ghost* in the name of the Third Person of the Trinity.⁴

116. The debt of the modern world to the newspapers is certainly great, perhaps incalculable. Yet "the penny-a-liner's help is often sought by an editor who knows what good English is,"⁴ but who pays tribute

---
¹ Oliphant, *Standard English,* ch. vi.
² Recent Philadelphia newspapers.   ³ § 145 (3) (*a*), *below.*
⁴ Oliphant, *ut cit.*   ⁵ § 116, *below.*

(perhaps unwillingly) to the vulgar demand for veneering instead of solid wood. To read the following criticism of "newspaper English" in a *New York Tribune* editorial, is, therefore, comforting, though it confirms the charges just made;—

"If the truth were laid bare, the amateur diplomatists of the press would be held responsible for a majority of the literary offences of the professional diplomatists. Slovenliness of style, distortions of plain and honest words, a pretentious use of incongruous phrases, are bad habits which the regulars acquire in their literary recreations, when the files of the London journals are received and the work of the volunteers comes under their eyes. The newspaper correspondents and leader-writers introduced such words as *veridical, signalize, franchise of duties* and *category,* and the consuls and secretaries of legation speedily adopted them. The Paris correspondent of *The London Times,* who fills up the gaps in his acquaintance whenever a sovereign out of employment happens to stroll along the Boulevards in search of a dinner, would keep a diary and store up reminiscences for posthumous fame, if he were not allowed to produce his own and his guest's conversation precisely as it occurs. If the use of such phrases as *antecedent* and *penultimate solidarity* were interdicted, he could not discuss any phase of European diplomacy. It is the volunteer ambassador of the London press who takes the mother tongue between his teeth and bites it until it bleeds. He knows that the English people wish to have public affairs discussed with the utmost seriousness, and accordingly he fashions high-sounding phrases and portentous words for general use. They have a doubtful ring at first, but they soon pass current even in Parliament. The diplomatists in the regular service have no wish to be archaic in matters of literary style. Accordingly they adopt the diplomatic jargon of the day." (See § 113, *above.*)

2. Violations of National Use.

117. Violations of National Use are, (1) *Provincialisms,* or *local* forms; (2) *Technicalities, professional* forms; (3) *Alienisms, foreign* forms *not yet naturalized.* For example;—

OFFENCES AGAINST PURITY. 77

(1) PROVINCIALISMS: *folks* (for *family*), *parts* (for *region*), *poke, gowned,*[1] *like* (for *as*), *while* (for *until*), *without* (for *unless*), *guess* (for *believe, suppose,* etc.), *right* (for *very*), *directly* (for *as soon as*), *nicely* (in answer to the question, *How do you do?*), *aggravate* (for *provoke*), *stop* (for *stay*).

(2) TECHNICALITIES: *To make good* (a check, a deficiency, etc.), *to soar* (of stocks), *to dovetail* (for *to fit accurately*), *governor* (for *equalizer, regulator*), *to credit* (for *ascribe to*), *to boss,*[2] *to clerk,*[2] [3] *get left* (for *fail*),[2] *figurines.*[4]

(3) ALIENISMS: *salon,* on the *tapis, Geistlicher,* (capital G and all),[5] *genialisch,*[5] *plastik,*[5] a volume where (?) a *vide supra* could serve instead of repetitions,[5] the word was *subauditum* in the King's mind,[5] *chaussure,*[6] *sehnsucht nach der Liebe,*[6] *sospiri,*[6] beggar-brats singing a dismal chorus of *Dateci qualche cosi,*[7] two or three *half-baiocchi,*[7] *contadino,*[8] *carretta,*[8] *poledri,*[8] *pecoraro,*[8] *osterias,*[9] *pergole,*[9] *fogliette,*[9] *lascia passare,*[9] *retortis littore Etrusco violenter undis,*[9] *maladie du pays,*[10] *gêne,*[10] *ex vi termini,*[10] *tiffin,*[11] the *caposetta* of a certain movement in the history of Poetry,[12] sunlight which invites to an *idlesse.*[13]

Glaring instances of the Alienism pervading the very structure of a book can be found in Mr. Story's *Roba di Roma,* already cited. Even the title needs explanation (it can not be translated); and whole lines are sometimes written in Italian.[14] Valuable and interesting as the work is, its usefulness is much impaired by this fault.

Even the professed critics of language sometimes err in this respect. Mr. Oliphant, whose strictures on other writers have already been quoted,[15] introduces Theocritus without translation; calls the contemporaries of George III. and Dr. Johnson "*prisca gens mortalium;*" exclaims, "O that they would learn '*deductum ducere carmen!*'" and "*Haec ego non*

---

[1] See § 89, *above.*
[2] These words are vulgarisms and neologisms as well as technicalities.
[3] "I don't like figures well enough *to clerk.*"—*The Bread Winners,* p. 13.
[4] *The Bread Winners,* p. 6. The word is more correctly written *figulines.* It is a technical term of ceramics, and means figures in pottery or pottery with figures on it. This connection with *figure* has, doubtless, changed its *l* to *r*. Longfellow uses *figuline* in *Keramos,* st. 8.
[5] George Eliot, *Middlemarch, passim.* [6] *Vanity Fair, passim.*
[7] W. W. Story, *Roba di Roma,* p. 1. [8] Id., p. 2. [9] Id., p. 4.
[10] Greg, *Enigmas of Life.* [11] Imported from India.
[12] Arthur Hallam, in a Review of Tennyson's Poems (1830).
[13] George Eliot, *Romola,* ch. xvi. [14] For example, on pp. 56–58.
[15] §§ 114 ff, *above.*

agilem?;" contrasts Horace's *meretrix* and *matrona, scurra* and *amicus;* remarks as to a certain group of synonyms "*haua equidem invideo; miror magis;*" speaks of "a London journal or two that might well stand for the *Cloaca Maxima;*" and all this on pages that lash the penny-a-liner's alienisms, and "cry up" Anglo-Saxon English. Nor does Mr. Oliphant mend the matter by his deprecatory remark, "I must apologize to those of my readers who are unlearned for the Latin [and Greek?] in my text; the truth is, that there are so many shades of meaning in our words, that I can not thoroughly explain myself without falling back upon the foreign tongue." Shade of the myriad-minded Shakspere, who *could* explain himself in English—and that Elizabethan English, far poorer in vocabulary than the English of to-day!

118. The Alienism is most objectionable, of course, when the foreign words are many, when they form whole sentences, or when they are woven into the very structure of the native speech. One can often guess at the meaning of a strange word or even a phrase, the context giving light enough; but a knowledge of French is required to understand the following;—

"I did not tell you Mr. Lydgate was haughty; but *il y en a pour tous les goûts,* as little Mamselle used to say."[1]

"Or suppose we adopt the genteel rose-water style. 'The Marquis of Osborne has just despatched his *petit tigre* with a *billet doux* to the Lady Amelia. The dear creature has received it from the hand of her *femme de chambre,* Mademoiselle Anastasie. "Dear Marquis! what amiable politeness! His lordship's note contains the wished-for invitation to Devonshire House." "Who is that monstrous fine girl," said the *Semillant* Prince G . . . rge of C . . . mbr . . . dge, at a mansion in Piccadilly the same evening . . . "Her name, Monseigneur, is Sedley." "*Vous avez alors un bien beau nom,*"said the young prince, turning . . . , and treading on the foot of an old gentleman . . . " *Trente mille tonnerres!* " shouted the victim, writhing under the *agonie du moment.*'"[2]

---

[1] George Eliot, *Middlemarch.* For *Mamselle,* see § 119, *below.*

[2] Thackeray, *Vanity Fair,* ch. vi., *The Night Attack.*—The passage, of course, satirizes the practice it exemplifies. (In late English editions it is omitted, and a rather dull, meaningless paragraph substituted.)

OFFENCES AGAINST PURITY. 79

119. Yet rhetoricians have, perhaps, been too dogmatic in stating the rule against the Alienism. Neither Good Use nor Good Sense sustains an absolute standard. There is surely a difference (at least in degree of offence) between *naïve* or even *naïveté*, in an English book or speech, and Mr. Cassaubon's *parergon*,[1] between an occasional slip into alienism and the completely debauched style of the example ridiculed by Thackeray. English, in particular, can not be subjected to a rigid rule. Not only is it a composite tongue, but it has, of all languages, most enriched itself, and is still enriching itself, by drawing synonyms from foreign sources. Mr. Earle's dictum,[2] "*That a French family settled in England, and edited the English language,*" describes only the English of Chaucer. Accretions have since been made from Latin (at several periods), from Greek, literary French, Celtic, and many other sources. Haldeman[3] gives lists of words from twenty-eight languages that have become English; and foreign names for foreign things are almost numberless in English; for example, *tea, coffee, alcohol, calico, muslin, cologne, (cologne-water, Eau-de-cologne), barége.* Even English syntax is not wholly native. The Anglo-Saxon relative pronoun was commonly *that; who, which* and *what* were usually interrogatives; but, with the coming of Norman French into England, the Romance custom was added to the Teutonic, and modern English made the richer thereby. So, English syntax is "flat"—that is, non-inflectional—chiefly because the French conquest shook the tree of Anglo-Saxon inflections so rudely as to bring them nearly all to the ground. Emphasis must be placed on the words "not yet naturalized" in the definition of Alienism; or not only will the law of Good Use, with its underlying principle of "life in language," be contradicted, but the vocabulary of the language will be sadly impoverished.

[1] *Middlemarch.* [2] *Philology*, p. 99. [3] *Etymology*, pp. 105 ff.

120. When, then, shall a form be considered naturalized? when shall such words as *boulevard* (a broad, handsome avenue), *cuisine*, *résumé*, *kaiser* (emperor), *gymnasium* (the English and American *college*), be admitted to thoughtful, careful writing,—writing that aims at purity without purism? Three cases may, perhaps, be distinguished;—(*a*) forms that have not even "declared their intention" of becoming citizens; (*b*) such as have so declared, and will, therefore, in all likelihood, soon be admitted to the language; (*c*) naturalized forms. The last case needs no discussion:[1] doubt arises only in cases (*a*) and (*b*). Wholly foreign forms can easily be recognized, and should commonly be avoided:[2] the difficulty begins with forms of class (*b*), as in the examples given above. Even here, neither Use nor underlying principles give positive laws, and the prudent teacher will hardly dogmatize. The beginner in Composition, however, had better err on the side of Purity, waiting for that best guide, a mature judgment chastened by experience.

121. But even unqualified aliens *must* be admitted sometimes, and in certain cases *may* be admitted without serious loss. (*a*) Necessary alienisms are (*a*) such as have no English equivalents; *ennui, bric-a-brac, bohemian;* (*β*) Proper names; as, *Rue d' Enghien, Boulevard St. Antoine, Friederichs Strasse*. (*b*) Admissible alienisms are (*a*) Forms superior in *brevity* to the English equivalents; *symposium, coup d'état, per contra, a priori;* (*β*) words or phrases added by way of explanation, and which, by calling up an additional notion, serve, in fact, as illustrations. Thus, the French term *cul-de-sac* is better known than the Latin *cauda vermiformis;* and an anatomist explaining the singular appendage called by the Latin name, may well use the French word by way of illustration. In all such cases, however, care must be taken that the alienism used in illustration is better known than the term to be explained.

[1] § 119, *above*.   [2] But see § 121, *below*.

122. "No man of sense," says Mr. Oliphant,[1] "can object to foreign words coming into English of late years, if they unmistakably fill up[2] a gap. Our hard-working fathers had no need of the word *ennui;* our wealth, ever waxing, has brought the state of mind; so France has given us the name for it. The importer who 'introduced' the French *prestige*, is worthy of all honour, for this word supplied a real want. Our ships sail over all seas; English is the language of commerce; we borrow, and rightly so, from the uttermost shores of the earth; from the Australians we took *kangaroo;* and the great Burke uses *taboo*, which came to him from Otaheite." *Plunder* belongs to the Thirty Years' War; *loot* to the Indian Mutiny; *bummer* (formerly *marauder*) to the War of the Rebellion;[3] *assassin* to the Crusades.

123. The following tests, if not too rigidly applied, will guide the student in forming safe opinions on this subject.

124. (1) Careful editors commonly print undoubted alienisms *in italics*. Hence, if a foreign word is not so printed in a well-edited book, the presumption is that it has been naturalized. For example, *apropos* and *connoisseur* are both in ordinary type ("Roman") in a fine edition of *Middlemarch;* and no one need be surprised, therefore, to learn that *apropos* is as old as Dryden. But the test not infrequently fails. The same edition of *Middlemarch* prints *connoscenti* (Italian for *connoisseurs*) in Roman; but this is probably an oversight. On the other hand, though *aquarium* is familiar enough as an English word, both Webster and Worcester print it in italics, as they do the less familiar *aqua vitæ*, *aqua fortis*, etc.

125. (2) If a foreign form will bear English inflections, or submit to English modes of syntax, the presumption is yet stronger in its favor. Thus, *adieus* would indicate that *adieu* had been thoroughly naturalized; *adieux*,

---

[1] *Standard English*, p. 338. [2] § 195 (2), *below*. [3] Oliphant, pp. 338, 339.

that it was still a French word, only resident in English. The old double plurals *cherubims* and *seraphims* show not only that *cherubim* and *seraphim* were fully naturalized in England three hundred years ago, but that their plural quality had been either utterly forgotten or never understood. The adverb *naïvely* speaks volumes for the truly English character of *naïve*, but *naïveté* indicates that *naïve* has not yet given birth to an English noun.

126. (3) Foreign forms intelligible to the average reader of English have presumably been anglicized; those that are known only "by sight" are probably still in waiting. Thus, *physique, protégé, chaperon*, are presumably adopted words; *au revoir, tête-à-tête, double entendre*, are perhaps still outside the pale.

127. These principles determine also the *pronunciation* of foreign words. (*a*) Naturalized forms have the English sounds of their letters; (*b*) words that have left their foreign moorings, but have not yet found full harbor in English, have either their native or their English sounds; (*c*) unquestioned aliens retain their foreign pronunciation as far as this is possible for English organs of speech.

Thus, (*a*) *Paris* (not *Pä-ree*), *Versailles* (not *Vare-sigh*), *Vienna* (not *Vee-ane*), *Ber-lin* (not *Bare-leen*), *Munich* (not *München*), *Columbus* (not *Colombo*). Some such words have been *translated* as well as *imported*,—for example, the family-names *Smith* (for the German *Schmidt*) and *Carpenter* (for *Zimmermann*); while not a few have been translated in Bottom the weaver's sense,—*sapsago* for the German *schabzieger*, *sicklygully* for the Indian *sakri-gali* (sacred pass), *Sir Roger Dowler* for *Siradzhu-d-daula*, *Peter Gower* for *Pythagoras* (via the French *Pytagore*).[1] (*b*) *Müller* (quite as often *Mül-ler* or *Miller* as with the German *ü*), *Hofmann* (not often distinguished from *Hoffman*), *Hi-mal-ya* or *Him-ä-lā-ya*. (*c*) *Göttingen*, *Molière*, *Goethe*,[2] *Corneille*.

[1] Haldeman, *Etymology*, p. 30.
[2] However well known a word may be, an impossible or difficult sound will long prevent its naturalization. Had *Goethe* admitted of translation, it would doubtless have been adapted long ago.

127*a*. Foreign languages are now so common an acquisition (and affectation so common a fault), that special care is often needed not to sacrifice unnecessarily the English sounds where these are preferable. Dr. Joseph Thomas's rules, (*Lippincott's Gazetteer of the World*, Introduction, and, more briefly, *Webster's Dictionary with Supplement*, Appendix), furnish an excellent guide through the many intricacies of this subject.

128. Many *provincialisms* are *archaisms* that have survived in a non-literary dialect ; as traditions or customs die out but slowly in families that mingle but little with the world. Such are *poke*, *while*, *guess*, *right* (as an adverb), and many more. They are often of purer stock than the words that have replaced them.

129. Technical terms are sometimes not only not objectionable, but actually preferable to other words. In professional language, in didactic works of all kinds, even in other prose, they can often be replaced only by absurd circumlocutions ; while, in poetry, the peculiarly poetic words lend no small part of the special charm of that kind of writing. Thus, a doctor of medicine, addressing a County Medical Society, may properly write, "The conditions under which *regular astigmatism* may develop are: *progressive myopia*, with and without *spasm of accommodation—spasm of accommodation* in an *emmetropic*, *myopic*, and *hyperopic* eye." Should he substitute non-professional language for the italicized words in this short passage, he would simply waste his own and his hearers' time. Even a *technical* definition of *regular astigmatism* requires many words,—"that form of *asymmetry* of the *cornea*, in which the *curvature* of the latter is different in the different *meridinal planes;*" and this, if expanded for lay readers by the writing of its technical terms in non-technical language, would grow much longer. In treatises intended to give instruction, the only restriction upon technicalities is that they shall not be used without full explanation ; and, even in ordinary

language, the law of intelligibility once satisfied, much that is technical may pass without challenge. In truth, as Whately pointed out long ago, "technical terms are a part of language," and the argument against the technicality may easily be made to prove too much,—"the uselessness of language altogether."[1] Indeed, in one sense all language is technical, since it depends for its usefulness upon the common understanding of its many sounds, words and phrases, constructions, *etc.* These are but *signs* of the things intended to be understood; and they have value as language only when and so far as they are correctly interpreted by the hearer or reader. Professional diction, then, is simply a body of signs, the meaning of which is known to but a limited portion of the people that use the language; and in this, of course, it differs vitally from non-technical speech; but in the one respect named it is certainly not unlike everything else in language.

130. The same argument (with a slightly different application) is put into the mouth of a young Englishman by a writer whose style, quite as much as the subject-matter of her works, has placed her in the front rank of English novelists;—[2]

"Are you beginning to dislike slang, then?" said Rosamond, with mild gravity.[3]

"Only the wrong sort. All choice of words is slang. It makes a class."[4]

"There is correct English: that is not slang."

"I beg your pardon: correct English is the slang of prigs who write history and essays. And the strongest slang of all is the slang of poets."

"You will say anything, Fred, to gain your point."

"Well, tell me whether it is slang or poetry to call an ox a *leg-plaiter*."

---

[1] *Elements,* § 4. [2] George Eliot, *Middlemarch,* ch. xl.
[3] Rosamond addresses her brother Fred, just home from Oxford.
[4] § 109, above.

OFFENCES AGAINST PURITY.

"Of course you can call it poetry if you like."

"Aha, Miss Rosy, you don't know Homer from slang. I shall invent a new game : I shall write bits of slang and poetry on slips, and give them to you to separate."

3. VIOLATIONS OF PRESENT USE.

131. Violations of Present Use are (1) *Archaisms*, forms that have entirely *passed out* of Good Use; (2) *Neologisms*,[1] forms that have not yet *come into* Good Use. For example ;—

(1) ARCHAISMS : *holden, proven, gotten*, and other participles in *-en* that have more modern forms, *receivēd, praisēd*, etc. (for *receiv'd, prais'd*, etc.), *a-men, can't, basket* (with the Italian *a*),[2] *maker* (for *poet*)[3], the *more* part,[4] *bow-pot* (for *bouquet*)[5], *dixonary*,[5] *yoops*,[5] the "Roman" pronunciation of words derived from the Latin, the fourteenth century pronunciation of Chaucer, and the Elizabethan sounds of the letters for Shakspere.[6]

(2) NEOLOGISMS : *viewiness*,[7] *exposition* (for *exhibition*), *vitative, vitativeness, solidarity*,[8] *to interview, to fully understand* (for *fully to understand* or *to understand fully*), *to cable*,

[1] Or *Neoterisms*, as they are sometimes called. But this word is an example of the very vice it names : it can not be found in the *body* of either Webster's or Worcester's dictionary, and is given in the Supplement to each without citation.

[2] Instead of *ā-men*, (with *a* as in *fate*), *can't* and *basket* (with the "intermediate" sound of *a*, the sound that lies between *ā* in *căn* and the Italian *a*.)—The false pronunciations are also provincialisms.

[3] Oliphant, *passim.*   [4] Freeman, *General Sketch of History, passim.*

[5] Thackeray, *Vanity Fair, in initio.* (But see § 160, *below*.)

[6] The *practical* point involved here is simple enough. A Roman of the Augustan age or an Englishman of the 14th or the 16th century would to-day be in great part unintelligible to the best Latin or English scholars; and the case would be much worse for "the people." Yet a pure pronunciation is one that can be "understanded of the people." Do not these (so called) "revivals" of sounds now gone forever, serve only to divorce the classic literatures of our own and other lands more and more from their modern readers?

[7] A "made" word denoting the vice of having opinions without knowledge. (John Henry Newman, *The Idea of a University*, p. xviii.) Cf. Miss Phelps, *The Story of Avis*, p. 8: "This was in the days when young ladies had not begun to have 'opinions' upon the doctrine of evolution, and before feminine friendships and estrangements were founded on the distinctions between protoplasm and bioplasm."

[8] Imported by Kossuth.

cablegram, ring (a *clique*), *unwisdom,*[1] *unfriend,*[1] *unfaith* (for *doubt, scepticism*),[2] *streeted,*[3] *wordship,*[4] *speechpartship,*[5] Dr. *Wattsiness* (for the prosaic in verse),[6] *dynamiteur*.[7]

132. Many neologisms have not yet escaped from the quarantine of the Vulgarism, and many are revivals of words long since forgotten. *To cable* (verb active and neuter) may find a lodgment in the tongue, although *to telegraph* would, in the same context, have the same meaning; but *cablegram* is an unnecessary and coarse hybrid. Like *to wire,* it may properly be avoided until necessity forces it upon the language. So, *to gather, to catch on,* (modern slang for *to understand,*) are wholly inexcusable. "'Why so much *weep?*' asked Artemus Ward; he little knew that he was reviving the Old English [Anglo-Saxon] *wóp*."[8] *Forewords* (for *preface*), *maker* (for *poet*), *rime* (for *rhyme*), are other examples of this revival.

133. Not all archaisms are objectionable. When "a word or phrase has been supplanted by something less apt, but has not become unintelligible,"[9] it is certainly preferable to the newer word. Not only *may* it be used; it *should* be chosen rather than the usurper.

(II.) VIOLATIONS OF PURITY WITH REFERENCE TO THE DEPARTMENTS OF GRAMMAR.

134. Of the three departments of Grammar named above,[10] Etymology treats of *words or phrases as such,* Syntax of their *construction,* Lexicography of their *meaning*. Offences against Etymology are named *Barbarisms,*[11] against Syntax *Solecisms,*[12] against Lexicography

---

[1] A revival in new meanings of old words. *Unwisdom* meant *ignorance; unfriend, enemy:* now the words correspond, respectively, to the adjectives *unwise* and *unfriendly*. Shakspere uses *unfriended* in the sense of *friendless*.
[2] Poetic.   [3] Howells.   [4] Grant White.   [5] Earle, *Philology*.
[6] Lowell, *Among My Books,* II. 202.
[7] Recent newspapers.—A French word, coined, apparently, to name that class of Irish conspirators against England who use dynamite *in terrorem*. It is not only a neologism, therefore, but an alienism and a hybrid as well. (See § 141, *below*.) *Dynamite-fiend* is certainly more expressive.
[8] Oliphant, p. 32.   [9] Lowell, *Among My Books,* II. 195.   [10] § 104.
[11] The Greeks called every one whose language they could not understand a *barbarian*.
[12] The city of *Soli* in Asia Minor was notorious for its bad Greek.

Improprieties. Hence, Barbarisms are *unauthorized words or phrases,* Solecisms *unauthorized constructions,* Improprieties words or phrases used in *unauthorized meanings.*

135. For English, this has been well stated by Dr. Campbell:—"Pure English implies three things; *first,* that the words be English; *secondly,* that their construction be in the English idiom; *thirdly,* that they be used in the precise meaning which custom has affixed to them. Accordingly, Purity may be injured in three ways. The *words* may not be English,—the fault called *Barbarism;* their *construction* may not be in the English idiom,— *solecism;* the words or phrases may not be used in their English *meaning,—Impropriety.*"[1]

I. BARBARISMS.

136. Barbarisms have been sub-divided into (1) *Radical words and phrases,* (2) *Inflections,* (3) *Derivatives,* (4) *Compounds.*[2] For example;—

(1) RADICAL WORDS AND PHRASES: *Skedaddle, gopher-hole, bummer,*[3] *enthuse, donate, swosh,*[4] *wellness, to bant, casuality, collaborator,*[5] *to plaque,*[6] *audition,*[7] *audient,*[8] *archaist*[8] or *anti-*

---

[1] Bk II. ch. iii.—The quotation is modernized and much condensed. Often the thought alone remains.

[2] Day, § 289.—(See § 137, *below.*) Compounds are composed of two or more entire words,—*horse-car, railroad-station;* derivatives, of entire words and affixes,—as *hardly, untruthful, archbishoprick.* But affixes were originally independent words; and to the scientific etymologist compounds and derivatives seem hardly separable. (Haldeman, *Outlines of Etymology,* p. 26.)

[3] Perhaps from the verb *bum,* to make a loud noise; the bummer being often an empty braggart as well as a good-for-naught.

[4] Ayres, *s. v.* The word was made by Mr. Ayres apparently to scarify Emerson with. One might guess in vain for its etymology.

[5] An imitation of the French *collaborateur.* Why not *fellow-workman?*

[6] The noun is still *alien;* to make a verb of it seems scarcely decent.

[7] A term invented by the spiritualists.

[8] Mrs. Browning (as cited in Worcester's *Supplement*),

quitarian[1] (for *antiquary*), *aspirator*,[2] *antipharmic* (for *antidotal*), *anywhen*,[3] *telegrammic* (for *curt, brief*), *solfamization* (for *solfaing*).

(2) INFLECTIONS: *bet* (for the preterite *beat*), *het* (for *heated*), the King *his* crown, *done, come* (and other perfect participles for the corresponding preterites),[4] *went* (and other preterites for perfect participles),[4] *hisself, theirselves* (for *himself, themselves*),[4] *ennuyé* (for *ennuied*),[5] *to taken, to washen* (and other infinitives in *-en*),[4] *takened, washened* (for *took, washed*, as if *taken* were present indicative),[4] *acceptant, admirant* (and other participles in *-ant* instead of *-ing*), *cherubims*,[6] *omnibi*,[7] *Scipii*,[7] *rostrae*,[7] and many other equally absurd plurals, *son-in-laws, son's-in-law, affiesdavit*.[7]

(3) DERIVATIVES: *matriculant* (for *matriculate*), *illy* (for *ill* as adverb), *firstly, lastly* (for *first, last*),[8] *direful* (for *dire*), *presumptive* (for *presumptuous*), *preventative* (for *preventive*),[9] *presentive* (for *presentative*),[9] *rendition* (for *rendering*), *jeopardize* (for *jeopard*).

(4) COMPOUNDS: *Health-Board, life-work, stand-point, self-affairs* (for *one's own affairs*), *self-evidence* (*evidence* that carries conviction *with itself*), *self-practice* (*practice without a teacher*),[10] *words-no-words*,[11] *calves-feet jelly, white-teethed*,[12] *brakeman* (for *brakesman*).[13]

---

[1] Milton, *Of Reformation in England*, Bk. I.
[2] Probably so called from its frequent use in helping the breathing.
[3] De Quincey (as cited in Worcester's *Supplement*).
[4] Vulgarisms.
[5] A laughable consequence of the importation of foreign inflections is the common error of writing the French adjective *fade*, tasteless, insipid, *fadé*, as if it were a participle and equivalent to English *faded*.
[6] Sternhold, quoted by Lowell, *Among My Books*, II. 133. Addison, *Spectator*, No. 327.
[7] Quoted by Hodgson, *Errors in the Use of English*, p. 83. *Scipii* and *rostrae* are inventions of Ouida's.
[8] Almost as well write *nextly*.
[9] The suffix *-ive* is added to Latin supine-stems. Cf. *cursive, penetrative*, etc.
[10] Compounds in *self* have this word as the object either of the other word in the compound or of a preposition naturally construed with *self*.
[11] Grant White, *Words and their Uses*, p. 201.
[12] Howells, *Italian Journeys*, p. 236.
[13] Both Webster and Worcester omit the *s*; but who ever heard of *a* brake on a railroad car? *Brakes*, like *scissors, tongs*, and *trousers*, (not to mention another article of dress,) go in pairs. One wheel may have *a* brake—a ratchet is such a brake—but wheels in pairs have *brakes*. As well write *scissor-grinder, tong-smith*, or *trouser-cutter*. The singular of any such word is certainly rare, if it occurs at all in good use.

OFFENCES AGAINST PURITY. 89

137. The classification of Barbarisms here adopted seems more logical than Campbell's division into "obsolete words," "new words," and "good words new-modelled." The Barbarism is a violation of Etymology; and Prof. Day's subdivisions rest on etymological distinctions. Campbell's subdivisions, on the contrary, are unsystematic as well as illogical; for "good words new modelled" are only one kind of "new words."

138. Mispronunciations and misspellings are special forms of the Barbarism; for the sounds of a language and the characters used to express them both come under the consideration of the etymologist. For example, *ī-ther, nī-ther*,[1] *clark* (for *clerk*),[2] *ravange* (for *revenge*),[3] *the* (so-called) *Spelling Reform, ra-ownd* (for *round*),[4] *dooty* (for *duty*),[5] *laughin, etc.* (for *laughing, etc.*),[4] *uv* (for *of = ŏv*),[4] *would uv* or *ŏv* (for *would have*),[4] many *compressions* of words (as *worshpful* for *worshipful*), unnecessary *extensions* (as *de-mon-stra-tor* for *demunstratur*).

139. Compound words, though natural to all languages and most abundant in older English, have not been numerously added to the English of more recent times; and new compounds are now regarded with suspicion. The entire history of language (as is well known) exhibits word-making as a most important factor in the growth of human speech; Elizabethan English was absolutely prolific in compounds; but recent Eng-

[1] Wrong both by analogy and by the usage of an overwhelming majority in England as well as in America. *Ei* has the sound of *i* in but few English words, and in these usually by "induction"; as, *sleight* from *sly*, *height* from *high*. "*I-ther*, or *ni-ther*, with the *i* long, is an affectation," says Grant White, "and, in this country, a copy of a second-rate British affectation." Recently, a shibboleth of fashionable society.
[2] Indefensible in America, whatever may be true of it in England.
[3] Ascribed to Henry Irving, but probably only a stage mannerism, if his at all.
[4] Vulgarisms.
[5] The *oo* sound is correct after "the sound of *sh* or *zh*," and (according to most orthoëpists) "when *u* is preceded by *r* in the same syllable." [Webster (1864), ¶¶ 29 ff., p. xliii.] In other cases, a slight *i* or *y* sound is heard before the *u*.

lish, while it retains many old words of the class, seems anxious to renounce its privilege of making new compounds, except in poetry. For example, Shakspere combined not only nouns, but adverbs, prepositions, verbs, and even whole phrases. *Wind-changing, giant-rude, steep-up, back-return, after-supper, falling-from* (*defection*), *carry-tale, find-faults, always-wind-obeying, ten-times-barred-up, to winter-ground* (to *bury* in *winter?*) *odd-even* (that darkest time of night when one can not distinguish *odd* from *even?*) are a few of his list.[1] Even *bilingual* compounds were made,—words in which the components are drawn from different sources, but mean the same thing; as, Spenser's *readie prest* (French *prêt*), the common *butt-end, etc.*[2] Shakspere's *weird sisters* in *Macbeth* is really a compound (*fate-sisters*), though it is usually written as a phrase. But very recent English has little or nothing to match with these examples. Such older compounds as *halcyon-days, college-student, sea-shore, milk-house, etc.*, remain in good use; but they tend more and more strongly to drop the hyphen and become phrases, as *winter solstice, autumn storms*, and many other compounds have done. Tennyson may write *seeming-wanton* and *tender-pencill'd* in a single stanza of the *In Memoriam;*[3] but *Health-Board* belongs to the newspapers, and *life-work* can not, perhaps, be defended by a single author of the first rank. On the other hand, many words, formerly compounds, have completely coalesced, till now they are scarcely distinguishable from integral words; as, *railroad, doughnut, tramway, hillside,* and many others. A few, however, as *horse-car, school-boy*, are kept apart by the evident integrity of their components; though this reason might hold as well in many cases of complete combination.

[1] E. A. Abbott, *A Shakespearian Grammar*, §§ 429-435.
[2] Cf. the tautologies *aid and abet, act and deed, null and void, acknowledge and confess, etc.* (But see § 196 (1), *below*.)
[3] Canto xlix. 3.

140. "Greek," says Mr. Oliphant, "has done much in the last three centuries to keep before us the fact, that English will lend itself readily to high-sounding compounds. Old Chapman long ago set us on the right tack; Milton followed; and our boys at school talk glibly of *wide-swaying* Agamemnon and *swift-footed* Achilles." But all this is as archaic as the schoolboys *wont* and *forsooth* for the Latin *soleo* and *videlicet;* and, if Greek and Latin contribute to the store of good English, (as they undoubtedly do when properly taught), both are often made the basis of an English style at once slovenly, archaic, and foreign. The Germans have, no doubt, been wise in keeping the power their tongue has always had of combining simple words; and many an English voice will echo Mr. Oliphant's wish, "Would that we could fasten any one of our prepositions to our verbs at will!" but the whole truth is that neither Chapman, nor Milton, nor even Tennyson, can to-day direct a prose writer in regard to what compounds he shall form, and that even in poetry Tennyson falls far behind Milton in his use of this class of words.

141. Hybridism (or Hybridity), the mingling in one word of elements derived from more than one language, is by most nations accounted an impurity; but English, a composite language, has admitted many hybrids. *A priori*, mongrelism in language, as in race, offends not only a cultivated (fastidious?) taste, but also that sense of the fitness of things to which man owes many a practical rule. A mongrel is expected to be ugly, is adjudged unnatural, and often is both coarse and repulsive. But, in all departments of nature, this *a priori* conclusion is often contradicted. Many hybrid plants are especially beautiful; and mixed races not infrequently show both strength and good looks. There is a smack of arrogance, to say nothing of the untruth involved, in the boasting of races that have continually "married in." In language, certainly, while many mongrel words are intolerable and unjustifiable, many more are not in any sufficient sense open to criticism. They have at least stood the test of use, they have fully established them-

selves in the language, they may be justified by the natural affinities of the languages uniting to form them, and their "pure" equivalents would, in many cases, be grotesque. For example, *naïvely*, *ailment*, *talkative*, *martyrdom*, *matronize*, *materialist*, *interloper*, *Christmas*, *cupboard*, *ostrich*, *target*, and a multitude more,[1] are "good English." *Unfrequent* holds its own with *infrequent;* Longfellow writes *undistinguishable;*[2] *linguistic* and *philological* have never been replaced by an equivalent of the German *sprachliche;*[3] and its hybridism (whatever else may hold the word back) will never prevent *scientist* from becoming the *best* English. So, *matronal*, though it can be found for *matronly* or *matronlike*,[4] would generally be accounted a purism; and *suprabalance* for *outbalance* or *guard du corps* for *body-guard* would be positively silly. On the other hand, *proseeing*, *forevision*, *telescribe*, *transwrite*, *logose*, *shortography* would undoubtedly be monstrous in place of *providence*, *foresight*, *telegraph*, *transcribe*, *verbose*, *stenography;* and *telegram*, much fought over as derived from *gramma*, a written character, instead of *graphe*, a writing, would, doubtless, have had a fiercer battle to wage, had it been proposed as *telescript*.

142. Abbreviated forms are at first sight barbarisms; but many are in good use, and can be justified (1) by analogy, (2) on the score of economy.[5] For example, *cab* for *cabriolet*, *hack* for *hackney coach*, *miss* for *mistress*,[6] *van* for *avant*, *penult* for *penultimate syllable*, have long been used, and, doubtless, by multitudes who never suspected that they were contractions. Not only do they save time for both speaker and hearer;[5] they have

---

[1] A long list is given in Skeat's *Etymological Dictionary*, Appendix.
[2] Sonnet I. prefixed to his translation of Dante's *Inferno*.
[3] As suggested by G. P. Marsh, *Lectures on the English Language*, p. 53.
[4] Both Webster and Worcester give it, Worcester citing Bacon in support.
[5] But see § 189, *below*.
[6] As a title: its use as a noun is a vulgarism.

numberless parallels in those crushed or crippled words of all modern languages whose ancestors stood in the full glory of undiminished length,—in *am, is, which, such,* words that once boasted two syllables each; in *mole,* from *moldiwarp;*[1] and in *alms,* a lineal descendant of *eleëmosyne.*[2] In fact, when curt forms are objectionable, they are so rather as neologisms or vulgarisms than as abbreviations. It may be inelegant or over-new to say *postal* for *postal card;* but the expression is not objectionable merely on the score of its diminished length. The superiority of the English and Continental *post-card* is not in its dropping a syllable, but in its avoiding the purism that can not accept *post* as an adjective. So, *five-twenties, governments, City 6's,* may smack of the stock exchange, but they are simply technical terms and in so far not amenable to strict literary rule. *Compo* for *composition* is not unknown to the world of artists;[3] and both it and *typo* are technical terms among printers.[4] *Chaff* (meaning *banter*) is from *chaffer;*[5] many Christian names are shortened, not for shortening's sake, but to express affection,—*Will, Tom, Sam, Rob,* Dickens's soubriquet *Bōz,*[6] and many more.

143. At the same time, there attaches to most such shortened forms a degree of disrepute that banishes them from literary composition; they are new or vulgar, and therefore unfit for the best use. For example, *phiz,*

---

[1] Earle, § 371.

[2] Contraction by Phonetic Decay—the wearing away of words—is of course different from that by Abbreviation—the dropping of syllables from words or of whole words from phrases; but the difference is in detail rather than in character.

[3] See a passage quoted from Eastlake's *Hints on Household Taste* by Earle, *Philology,* § 370.

[4] Of course, such forms are objectionable in purely literary use. (See § 162, *below.*)

[5] Earle, § 374.

[6] Short for *Moses,* a pet name of Dickens's younger brother, and "facetiously pronounced through the nose, Boses." (See Pierce & Wheeler's *Dickens Dictionary,* p. 1.)

cute, spec, specs, exam, confab, hyp'd, o. k., n. g., hôl, 'varsity, bus, tick,[1] *glasses,*[2] are either so recent or so contaminated by their associations as never to have been tolerated. *Gents* and *pants,* says Grant White, should "go together, like the things they signify. The one always wears the other."

"The curt form of *gent* as a less ceremonious substitute for the full expression of 'gentleman,' had once made considerable way, but its career was blighted in a court of justice. It is about twenty years ago that two young men, being brought before a London magistrate, described themselves as 'gents.' The magistrate said that he considered that a designation little better than 'blackguard.' The abbreviate[3] form has never been able to recover that shock."[4]

144. Abbreviated forms, whether authorized or not, may be classified as (*a*) shortened *words,* (*b*) shortened *phrases,* (*c*) *first words* of phrases. For example, (*a*) *incog* (for *incognito*), a *peal* of bells (for *appeal*), *story* (for *history*), *stress* (for *distress*), *mob* (for *mobile vulgus*); (*b*) *seven-thirties* (for *seven and thirty hundredths per cent. bonds*), *post-mortem* (for *post-mortem examination*), *locals* (for *accounts of local events*), *consóls* (for *consolidated annuities*); (*c*) *casual* (for *casual lodger*), *arctics, gums, rubbers* (for *arctic, gum, rubber, shoes*). The last construction is of constant occurrence in Latin and Greek— *boni* for *boni homines, hē barbarōs* for *he barbaros gē*— and is not unknown to even poetic English—"*The good* is oft interrëd with their bones"; "*the young* may die, but *the old* must!"

2. SOLECISMS.

145. Solecisms are errors in (1) *Concord,* (*agreement* or *government*); (2) *Grammatical Arrangement,* the ordering of the sentence to express grammatically the

---

[1] For *ticket,* itself a contraction from *etiquette.* (Earle, § 334.)
[2] For *eye-glasses.*
[3] § 131 (1), *above.*   [4] Earle, § 370.

thought intended; (3) *Grammatical Propriety*, the use of the proper grammatical element; (4) *Grammatical Precision*, the use of the precise number of words required to express the thought.[1] For example;—

(1) ERRORS IN CONCORD: (*a*) **Nouns and Pronouns**;—[2] An *alumni*, a *dicta*, this *phenomena;* such of his *litera scripta* [*literæ scriptæ, manuscripts*] as have escaped.—If *ye* from *your* hearts forgive not *every one his* brother *their* trespasses.[3] —Let *us* study God's word more diligently, and devote *yourselves* to his service.—*Everybody* can ride as soon as *they* are born.—I hope the *members* of the University will, *each* as far as lies in *his* power, exert *their* influence.—*Each* of the teachers made *their* report.—In Europe *no one* marries unless *they* have the certain means of supporting *their* children.[4] —You will live to marry a better woman than *I*.[5]—They trav-

---

[1] Day, § 290.—*Rhetorical Arrangement, Propriety,* and *Precision* are quite distinct attributes of the sentence.

[2] The following specifications by no means exhaust the errors into which even good writers and speakers fall. Fuller lists may be found in Day's *Art of English Composition,* Bain's *English Grammar,* A. S. Hill's *Principles of Rhetoric,* W. B. Hodgson's *Errors in the Use of English,* and many other similar works. Some of the examples used here are borrowed from one or another of the books named—especially Hodgson. Doubtful cases may commonly be met by a reference to general principles.

[3] Matt. xviii. 35.—The confusion is in the Greek, notoriously careless about such things. The Revisers of 1881 write it, "If *ye* forgive not *everyone his* brother from *your* hearts."

[4] Most common, when the reference is to persons of both sexes. *His or her* is even worse—outside of a law-paper; and Bain (quoted by Hodgson) claims that *their* has excellent usage at its back, even when the sex-difficulty is not present. Fortunately, several forms of expression are possible, (*all* for *every* or *everybody, both* for *each, people do not marry* for *no one marries*); but *his* may safely be written, unless *only* women are meant. In "nobody ever put so much of *themselves* into *their* work," *nobody* meaning Charlotte Brontë, *herself* and *her* would be the correct forms: when *nobody* means *no man or woman,* the natural principle that the masculine takes precedence of the feminine, as both masculine and feminine take precedence of the neuter, justifies *his*. The sentence "no *man* or *woman* marries unless *he* has," would be harsh; "*men* and *women* do not marry unless *they* have" would be far preferable; but "No *man* or *woman* marries unless *they* have" is the worst form conceivable. A recent writer has proposed a new pronoun for this use, *thon* (contracted for *that one*).

[5] Isabel Archer, in *The Portrait of a Lady*, by Henry James, Jr.

elled as fast as *him.*—Beelzebub, than *who*,[1] Satan except, none higher sat.—Them that honor me I will honor ; and *them*[2] that despise me shall be lightly esteemed.—Consider *who* the king your father sends.—Even papa, *who* Penelope told me she had seen.—Arthur, *whom* they say is killed to-night.— Francis, who fidgets them both to death, and *whom* I was so thankful was not coming.—Saladin, than *whom* no greater name is recorded in Eastern history.—*He*, who had always inspired in her a respect . . . , she now saw the object of open pleasantry.—

> "Mont Blanc is the monarch of mountains—
> They crowned him long ago ;
> But *who* they got to put it on
> Nobody seems to know."[3]

God forbid that John Hawkins's wife should refuse her last penny to a distressed mariner, and *he* a gentleman born.—Every one present, except *he*, guessed why.—This did not prevent John being inaugurated Duke of Normandy.—He earnestly protested against *them* embarking in the enterprise.—*These* kind of books, *those* sort of men ; *this* two hours, *that* twenty miles ;[4] a hundred dollars *are* too much for this.

(*b*) **Verbs;**—A keen passion like vanity, a strong one like love, or a subtle one like that of immediate personal sway, *transfigure* the resolve of such a nature, only so long as *they* may focus upon it.—A keen passion like vanity, a strong one like love, and a subtle one like that of immediate personal sway, *transfigures* the resolve of such a nature, only so long as *it* may focus upon it.—The greatest warrior of the age, conqueror of Italy, humbler of Germany, terror of the North, *contemn.*—The crippled baby, with all his many other failures, *were* forgotten.—Policy, as well as fashion, *dictate.* —The amount of discussion, equally with the valuable

---

[1] For euphony's sake, this philosophically correct nominative is written *whom*. (See Milton, Paradise Lost, ii. 299.)

[2] Properly written *they* in 1 Samuel ii. 30; but easily misread on account of the correct *them* in the first clause.

[3] These lines, signed "Albert Smith," Thackeray found in an album. He instantly wrote beneath them,—

> "I know that Albert wrote in a hurry;
> To criticise I scarce presume ;
> But yet methinks that Lindley Murray,
> Instead of *who*, had written *whom*."—(Hodgson).

[4] Correct when the idea is *collective*,—this (space of) two hours, that (distance of) twenty miles.

analysis, *are*.—The door of one [cell] is open; and within *stands* two cloaked figures.[1]—The game was played out, and the end was come, as the end of such matters generally *come*.[2]—To Marat, and Danton, and Robespierre *are* due the honor.[3]—I learned from him that not a line of the lectures *were* written.[3]—I have no feeling connected with my general recollection of them, but *those* to which the combination of good sense, wit, and genius naturally *give* rise.—To be active in the affairs of one's native corporation, and in settling controversies among one's friends there, *are employments* of the most laudable kind.

The moody and savage state of mind of the sullen and ambitious man—*is* or *are?*—admirably drawn.—Clearly, *the moody and savage state of mind* ought to mean *one* state of mind, as *the sullen and ambitious man* means one man. Therefore, *is* drawn is correct. If two states of mind are intended, write *the moody and savage states* or *the moody and the savage state;* as, when two men are meant, *sullen and ambitious men* or *the sullen and the ambitious man*. But even this apparently simple rule often fails. Thus, in the sentence, Political and social science *have* brought about . . . , the sense is manifestly plural, but the expression singular. Compare, The report of the President and Cashier *are* herewith submitted.—Such cases may sometimes be relieved by repeating the noun—*political science and social science*—sometimes by placing the adjectives after the noun—*science, political and social, has*—sometimes by making the noun plural and repeating the article—*the reports of the President and the Cashier*—sometimes by repeating the article while the noun remains singular—*the report of the President and the Cashier*, that is, a report made by them jointly—sometimes by other expedients, and sometimes by rewriting the whole sentence.

On the table there *was* neatly and handily arranged two long pipes.—There *exists*, sometimes only in germ and potentially, sometimes more or less developed, the same tendencies and passions.—*There* and *it* lead to many such blunders. Of course, good writers use these expletives—for emphasis, as,

---

[1] Kingsley, *Westward Ho!* (ed. 1879), ch. xxii. p. 346. Hodgson thinks it due to the "bustle of composition"; but surely it is typographical.

[2] Id. ib. p. 498. (See the next note.)

[3] Dr. Abbott calls these faults "errors of proximity"; but the construction is really *ad intellectum*.

there can be no doubt that it is inhuman to torture living creatures, it can not be denied that x is y; but both words are oftener misused than used correctly.[1]

Neither he nor I—*am, is, are?*—your enemy.—*Are* is plainly impossible, the alternative construction requiring a singular predicate.[2] Between *is* and *am*, the principle that the first person takes precedence of the second, and the second of the third, seems applicable.

Congress—*has* or *have?*—adjourned.—No pains—*has* or *have?*—been spared.—*This* or *these?*—means.—What—*is* or *are?*—the news?—The tongs—*stand* or *stands?*—by the fire.— Here Good Use and Law are at one. If the *idea* (the thought expressed by the subject) is singular, the verb should be singular; if the idea is plural, the verb should be plural. Many such nouns, however, have lost, or never had, the doubleness of number that makes variation possible. Thus, *news, gallows, etc.*, are now always singular, *tongs, scissors, riches, etc.*, always plural. But *means, pains, etc.*, vary.

(*c*) **Non-agreements and Misagreements**;—We have described the helplessness of the workingman, whose lot being cast in a large city, *desires* to find.—The *property* which every man has in his own labor, as it is the original foundation of all other property, so it is the most sacred and inviolable.

> "A happy *lover* who has come
> To look on her that loves him well,
> Who 'lights and rings the gateway bell,
> And learns her gone and far from home;
> He saddens.[3]"

Sir Charles addressed the House for three hours; when, *being* fatigued by his exertions, their lordships adjourned to the following day. — *Being* early *killed*, I sent a party in search of his mangled body.—England must take every precaution to defend herself against such villains, and, when *found*, she

---

[1] In older English *there is* was used, like the French *il y a*, with either a singular or a plural subject; and the present misuse is clearly a survival. (See § 128, *above*.)

[2] *Enemy*, not *enemies*; therefore, *am* or *is*, not *are*. Yet "*quot homines tot sententiae*," says Hodgson: "indeed, opinions outnumber the grammarians, since" one writer first "finds" for *am*, and then, only four pages later, "elects in favor of" *are*. Day, (*English Composition*, § 368. 1), decides for "the person and number of the nearest" subject.

[3] By poetic license. *In Memoriam*, viii.

ought to make an example of them.[1]—As *one* of his most distinguished pupils, I am quite sure that you will have deeply participated in the sense of an irreparable loss.

(2) Errors in Grammatical Arrangement: (*a*) Of modifiers;—One combatant sustained a wound in the arm *of no importance.*—The Moor seizing a bolster, *full of rage and jealousy*, smothers her.—Paid to a woman whose husband was drowned *by order of the vestry* under London Bridge.—Erected to the memory of John Phillips accidently shot *as a mark of affection by his brother.*—The sale of Ford's Theatre, where Mr. Lincoln was assassinated, *for religious purposes.*—The editor of the Medical Times (England) says he dreamed that he was in Winchester Cathedral listening to an eloquent sermon on *Christ* cleansing the lepers *from the reverend the chairman, in aid of the funds of the County Hospital.*—Hence he considered marriage *with a modern political economist* as very dangerous.—They followed the advance of the courageous, step by step, *through telescopes.*—The noble use he made of valuable patronage must sufficiently exonerate him from the suspicion of acting from interested motives *in the eyes of any candid man.*—If the Westminster Reviewer will read over what we have written *twice or thrice with patience and attention.*[2]—This house can *only* be seen upon application.—It has been demonstrated that he could *only* claim any election at all, any superiority to the Gentile, in virtue of God's calling.—We can *only* be saved from our evil, so large a portion of which consists in our selfishness and isolation, when we confess.— The manufacture of chinaware has been practised in China from such an early period, that tradition is *even* silent.—I *never* remember to have heard.—I *scarcely ever* remember to have had a rougher walk.—Nearly or quite the most remarkable and earnest and powerful article we *ever* remember to have read.— His last journey to Cannes, whence he was *never* destined to return.—I am a man *also* under authority.[3]—What wilt thou, queen Esther? and what is thy request? it shall be *even* given thee to the half of the kingdom.

---

[1] Recent newspaper, editorially.

[2] The French say such constructions "*squint;*" Dr. Hodgson says, "In a homely English phrase, 'they have one eye on the pot and the other up the chimney.'"

[3] Meaning *I also am.* (Matt. viii. 9.) The Revisers have for once bettered the translation of 1611; but they immediately write Greek-English again,— "having under *myself* soldiers," instead of "having soldiers under *me.*"

(*b*) **Of Balanced Members**;—And yet with his simple human smile, he looked neither *like a young bullock* nor *a gladiator*.[1]—We shall take neither *the fear of things present* nor *future* as our standard in this discussion.—With neither *a word for the disloyal daughter* or *the gaping, gossiping neighbors*.—I am neither *an ascetic in theory* or *practice*.[2]—The great and noble were obliged not only *to learn Greek*, but *were ambitious everywhere to speak it*.—Every composition is fairly liable to criticism, both *in regard to its design* and *to its execution*.—Mr. Ris was not *happy because Nature had ordained it so beforehand*,[3] but *because* . . .

(*c*) **Of Connectives and Extraneous Elements**;[4]—It can not be impertinent or ridiculous, *therefore*, to remonstrate. —These instances may, *it is hoped*, be sufficient to satisfy every reasonable mind.—Still she preserved her humility, *however*, and shamefacedness, till her crescent had exceeded the first quarter.—It was a case of unpardonable breach of trust and gross disregard of official duty, *to say the least*.—A prudent general will avoid a general engagement, *generally speaking*, unless his forces are equal.—Five sets of sonnets may *then* be distinguished, as in the table.—The series of poems addressed to his friend *thus* closes gravely with thoughts of love and death.[5]

(*d*) **By dividing the Infinitive**;—To *accurately* define,[6] to have *ever* seen, to be *at once* expelled.

(*e*) **By a Cross-Construction**;—By day my limbs, by night my mind, For thee and for myself no quiet find.—Though I with death and with reward did threaten and encourage him.—A

---

[1] Henry James, Jr., *The Last of the Valerii*, p. 129.—The effect is that of "a pair of crookedly hung pictures"; but there is worse mischief in the construction than this. Such sentences *may* become ambiguous or obscure, or they may even convey a false meaning. (See ₴ 321 (*f*), *below*.) They certainly do not say what they mean, and, therefore, are at least in danger of saying what they do not mean.

[2] "Three errors in nine words." (Hodgson.)   [3] ₴ 321 (*e*), *below*.

[4] Most connectives begin their sentences or clauses; these, of course, are not referred to here. Extraneous elements are sentences or parts of sentences involved in the structure of other sentences; as, The greatest of English poets may—*at Wordsworth puts it*—have "unlocked his heart."

[5] Prof. Dowden properly begins this sentence with *Thus:* it is misprinted here. In the previous quotation, however, he is correctly reported. (*The Sonnets of William Shakspere*, Larger Edition, pp. 25 and 33.)

[6] The adverb in this construction limits the whole expression, *to define*, and, therefore, should not separate its parts. The history of the infinitive adds another reason why the modifier should not be so placed.

connection between virtue and vice on the one hand, and happiness and misery on the other.—A keen eye and a graphic pen see and set down for us the characteristic details.— The unfortunate foreigner was flogged on two following days for disobeying the imperial mandate—for not wearing, and for wearing, the obligatory, and the interdicted costumes.—Separated by mountains and by mutual fear.[1]

(3) ERRORS IN GRAMMATICAL PROPRIETY: (*a*) **The Possessive Case for the Objective with a Preposition**;—the *Church's* service, *Utica's* million-dollar blaze, *God's* love,[2] the *man's* description, *your* fear,[3] *its* imaginative terrors,[4] in *our* midst, true science *whose* flattery, a tale *whose* lightest word.

Mr. G. P. Marsh[5] objects to this construction, because the possessive case, whatever it may have denoted in older English, now denotes only possession. But the vice often lies deeper. Many such expressions are *ambiguous*, many *misleading*. See, for example, I Thess. i. 4, *your* election of God,—a passage almost always misunderstood. When the sense is perfectly clear, however, this use of the possessive is correct; as, the *King's* enemies, *one's* friends, a *month's* mind (not obsolete among one body of Christians, certainly), for *my* sake, *their* separation, a *day's* work, ten *year's* toil. Brevity, too, would recommend these expressions. The objection to *whose* with reference to things is especially weak, *viz.*, that "the use of one possessive form for both" persons and things is "inconsistent." No sufficient reason can be urged against the use, and Marsh concedes that the "distinction" is "by no means yet fully established," that until recently the best English writers used *whose* as a neuter, and that many good authorities still use it so "in certain combinations." Bain declares "the rule that *whose* applies only to persons" to be "altogether at variance with literary usage."

---

[1] Some writers declare unreservedly against this construction; but it has at least one merit, brevity. At the same time, there is no denying that it is poetic rather than prose-like, and may easily lead astray. The first and second examples are from Shakspere; the third and fifth certainly confuse, rather than communicate, thought; the fourth has something of epigrammatic surprise about it, and may be allowed occasionally as a deliberate evasion of strict rule; while the last (from Gibbon) carries contraction to its utmost,—in fact equals the Greek *zeugma*. A master in composition will probably have discernment enough to use such sentences judiciously; a beginner should ally himself with "discretion, the better part of valor," and seek intelligibility at any sacrifice.

[2] Meaning man's love *for God*.   [3] Fear *of you*.
[4] Imaginative terrors inspired *by it*.   [5] *Lectures*, I. 393 ff.

(b) **"Dodging" Pronouns in -self;**[1]—O, they take the part of a better wrestler than *myself*.[2]—Mr. —— and *myself*.[3]—*Yourself* and many other members.[4]—They are older than *myself* by twelve and ten years.[5]—Willing and anxious to receive *yourself* and Clifford.[6]

(c) **Who or which for that, and vice versa;**[7]—He is the true Propontic, which never ebbeth, the sea *which* taketh handsomely at each man's hand.—The first minister *who* waited behind him with a white staff now advanced.[8]—The cock, *that* is the trumpet to the morn, doth awake the god of day.[9]—Has not your sister here, *that* never disobliged me, as good a right as you?—Harry remained with his regiment *that*[10] was garrisoned at Brussels.—The political transactions *which* terminated with the death of Queen Anne.[11]

(d) **Wrong Moods;**—If Venice *were* blotted out from the sovereignties of Europe, it was, after all, because Venice with her own hands had taken off the crown.—If Keble was a scholar . . . , if he *were* exemplary . . . , so he was admir-

---

[1] That is, *myself, himself*, etc., the compound personal pronouns, for the simple personals *I* or *me, he* or *him*, etc., as the case may require. The object of the exchange is evident. By using the *uninflected* words, a lazy or indifferent or ignorant speaker evades the question of *case* raised when the *inflected* pronouns are used; and, though some of the examples cited, can not be explained on this ground, it seems clear that these examples, which are extremely rare even in the authors quoted, are mere slips due to the contagion of a bad habit. The best usage is overwhelmingly against the abuse; historically considered—see Morris's *Accidence, in loc.*—it is absurd; and the teachings of Grammar clearly condemn it.

[2] *As You Like It*, I. iii. 22.—Nearly every other case in Shakspere can be explained as the *intensive* use with the simple pronoun omitted, for example, Myself am Naples.

[3] Twice in a short—perhaps hastily written—but *published* note from the daughter of an eminent man of letters, herself a writer of fair fame. Once for Mr.—— and *I*, once for Mr.—— and *me*.

[4] Lord Beaconsfield. But, in the same letter, "they, and *you* among them." *Yourself* seems sometimes to be used for *courtesy*.

[5] Charles Lamb, Essays, II. 266 (Moxon ed.) But, in the next sentence, "May they persist in treating *me* as a stripling."

[6] Hawthorne, *The House of the Seven Gables*, p. 157; but in the mouth of Judge Pyncheon. (See § 160, *below*.)

[7] In other words, the *co-ordinating* for the *restrictive* or *defining* Relative, and *vice versa*. (See a full discussion of the distinction, §§ 146 ff, *below*.)

[8] What does this sentence mean?   [9] *Hamlet*, I. i. 150.

[10] Did Harry belong to several regiments at once?

[11] Thackeray, *English Humourists—Swift*.

able.—If our standard for man's and woman's education were on a level, if it *was* the natural thing for an intellectual woman to give as much time and energy to study as it is for an intellectual man.—Politics *would* become one network of complicated restrictions, so soon as women shall succeed.—

(*e*) **Wrong tenses**;—Surely it *would be* desirable that some person should be charged.—I *shall have* great pleasure in accepting your invitation.¹—I have often thought that when men *are* intent on cards, their countenances show far more of their real characters than when they *engaged* in conversation.—He *would have accomplished* a great deal more, if a different principle of action *were substituted*.—Both *might win* the contest and the palm *divide*, *had* not Cloanthus thus *invoked* the gods.²—As we remember to have heard a learned judge declare that he did not know what an articulator *was*, we may explain that it is, *etc.*—Two young gentlemen have discovered that there *was* no God.—I meant, when I first came, *to have bought* all Paris.³—It had been my intention *to have collected*. He was proved *to be born* in France.—We happened *to be* [or *to have been?*] present.—I *should like* very much *to have seen* him. It *was* his intention [before he was prevented] *to have introduced*.

(*f*) **Wrong Auxiliaries**;—I *will* drown, nobody *shall* help me.⁴—*Shall* you go, if your friend disappoints you?—Esther said she *should* go into the king contrary to the law, and if she perished, she perished.⁵—He *might*⁶ do as I ask him, if he would.—This *can* not be done : the law will not permit it.—*Can* I go? (meaning, Will you give me permission?)

¹ No one would think of writing, I *will accept* your kind invitation.—I *shall have* great pleasure in coming is, of course, correct.

² Virgil, v. 322.—The thoughtful translation of foreign languages has doubtless helped to make many a good English scholar, but it has also prevented the making of many a one. Much *bad* English is simply *Latin* or *Greek* or *French* or *German* English.

³ But "I meant *to have bought* all Paris before I left" is correct. The tense of the dependent verb is determined by that of the principal; and no little care is sometimes necessary in choosing. Help often comes from writing the dependent clause as a principal, and then yoking it to the other verb.

⁴ A good example, whether real or not.

⁵ See §§ 152 ff, *below*.

⁶ *May* commonly denotes permission, *can* ability. But *may* once meant *to be able*, while *can* meant to *know;* and the old significations occasionally "crop out,"—"Power cannot change them, but love *may;*" "*Can* you swim?" (French *savez*-vous.) The words are distinguishable, however, and (in good use) are *generally* distinguished.

(*g*) **Wrong Prepositions**;—Wounded *from* a blow; different *to* or *than; in* this point of view; the light *from* which they regard it; that church *into* whose maternal bosom she has found rest; that church *in*[1] whose bosom she has fled for rest; *between* the several universities of our nation; *over* the signature (meaning *under* the authority, protection, *etc.*, of the signature.)[2]

(*h*) **Change of Elements in Balanced Members**;—Those who *give* as well as those *receiving*.—The island *of which* he is a native, and has lived in *it* all his life.—Kossuth, the arrival of *whom* in England, and the eloquence of *his* speeches in English.—This prevents their attending enough to *what* is in the Bible, and makes them battle for *what* is not in the Bible, but they have put *it* there.[3]—To throw a light across the whole landscape bewilders *the young traveller*, to carry *whom* blindfold leaves him.—Neither *did I feel* nor *partook*.—China *being* not only the most populous country in the world, but its inhabitants *are* probably the most dress-loving people.—*Whether* this disaster was originated, or *that* the inventor had forgotten.—Fuseli made this observation not only *in reference to the physiognomic cast of David's countenance*, but *his face was also disfigured by a hare-lip*.[4]

(*i*) **Preposition for Adverb, Adverb for Adjective, etc.**;—This nation, *of* all others, has more to boast of.—The *then* Bishop of London.—Damages for smoke, noise, interference with comfortable living, and *otherwise*.—He *never* said anything to the Prince as to where he went *nor* how he busied himself.—A *more* settled and *happier* frame of mind.[5]

(*j*) **Comparatives for Superlatives, and vice versa**;—We would not impeach the scientific acumen of Drs. First, Second, Third and Fourth, although we have never before heard of either of the *latter* three.—Which structure is *best*, the loose or the periodic?

(4) Errors in Grammatical Precision: (*a*) **By Omission**;—This melancholy is as bad [*as*] or worse than the most giddy merriment.[6]—Giovanni dreamed of a rich flower and [*a*]

---

[1] *In* was once used for *into;* but the two words are now fairly distinguished, and with reason.

[2] A useful list of proper prepositions is given in Worcester's *Dictionary*, pp. xl. xli.   [3] Matthew Arnold, *Literature and Dogma*, p. 383.

[4] These pictures need re-painting as well as re-hanging.

[5] Only an *apparent* double comparative, of course; but *happier and more settled* avoids even this appearance of evil.

[6] See, also, § 233, *below*.

OFFENCES AGAINST PURITY.   105

beautiful girl.¹—The scowl and [*the*] smile.²—A middle position between the Jewish and [*the*] Gentile world.—Matthews, of whom Byron used to talk so much, and [*whom he*] regretted so deeply. —The husband to whom she had sold herself, and [*by whom she*] had been paid the strict price.—The ideas which we get or [*which*] are given to us.—A volume of more interest to me than any [*other*] book.—Mazzini did more for the unity of Italy than any [*other*] living man.—As serious in his sports as in any [*other*] act of his life.—You will bear it as you have [*borne*] so many things.—I never *have* [*allowed*], nor ever will allow literary work to interfere with pastoral.³—I never *have* [*attacked,*] and never will attack a man for speculative opinions.³—Their conduct placed them in a position [*in which*] it is to be regretted an English Government should appear.—She is a monument of what a human being is capable [*of*].—The audience massed itself directly in front [*of*] and around the platform.—To partake [*of*] an intellectual pleasure.

(*b*) **By Excess**;—Was a daily spectacle like this to be deemed a nuisance, or not rather a salutary and *a* touching object?⁴— No stronger and stranger *a* figure than his is described in the modern history of England.—Longfellow, the poet, *the* scholar, and *the* gracious old man, is dead.—The face he loved best of all *others*.—The steepest path I ever climbed *before*.—Mr. Gladstone, more than any *other* French prime minister.—The loveliest pair that ever since met.⁵—The laird's death, though it no doubt delayed, yet *it* was not.⁶—These I removed from the last edition, and embodied *them*.⁶—The Bishop of Natal having come to England on a mission of humanity, *he* was naturally asked.⁷—Some words of our Bible, which, though they may

¹ Unless, indeed, Hawthorne meant that flower and girl were one. "Flower and maiden were *different*," he says, "*and yet the same*, and fraught with some strange peril in either shape."—*Mosses*, I. 107.
² *The House of the Seven Gables*, ch. xv.—Cf. ch. iv., "Both the frown and *the* smile passed *successively* over his countenance."
³ § 233, *below*.   ⁴ Lamb, *Elia*, II. 344.   (Moxon Ed.)   Only *one* object is meant.
⁵ Milton, *Paradise Lost*, IV. 321.
⁶ The pronoun is a viceroy, says Hodgson, and, hence, is not needed when the King is present in person.
⁷ If the first clause is a nominative absolute, *he* ought to mean some one else than the Bishop; while, if *he* means the Bishop, it is unnecessary. Cf. (1) Clare had to wait an hour, till, Lady Harriet coming in suddenly, she [Clare] exclaimed. (2) Clare had to wait an hour, till Lady Harriet, coming in suddenly, exclaimed. But (1) is both awkward and ambiguous. Even such forms as *Herod being dead, the angel warned Joseph* seem rare in the *best recent* English.

not be . . ., yet, in themselves, *they* explain.[1]—We are in an age of weak beliefs, *and* in which such belief as men have is determined.—The young officer was a Corsican, Napoleon Bonaparte, *and* whom people remembered as prominent.[2]—Are not only offensive, but *are* repulsive.—More satisfactory to take *rather* than to use.

NOTE.

1. Who, Which, and That.[3]

146. The distinction indicated above between *who* and *which* on the one hand, and *that* on the other, may be briefly expressed in a rule:—

(*a*) Use *who* or *which* to join to its antecedent clause a statement *coördinate* with that clause; as, Yes, said Kenyon, *who* [*and he*] sat on the column, at her side.

(*b*) Use *that* to introduce a clause *restrictive* or *definitive* of the antecedent; as, The Pincian garden is one of the things *that* reconcile the stranger to the rule of an irresponsible dynasty.

147. Unfortunately, the distinction is not always observed by modern writers; but much can be said in favor of observing it. *First*, the failure to do so often leaves the sentence ambiguous. Thus, They set up a choral strain,—"Hail, Columbia!" we believe,—*which* those old Roman echoes must have found it exceeding difficult to repeat aright. [A choral strain *that* the echoes found it difficult to repeat, or a choral strain, *and this* the echoes found it difficult to repeat?] The old Roman literature creates for us an intimacy with the classic ages, *which* [*that* or *and this*?] we have no means of forming with the subsequent ones. *Secondly*, though something may

---

[1] "Two viceroys in the same territory." (Hodgson.)

[2] But the conjunction is necessary when a preceding relative clause is *expressed or understood;* as, "Guasconti returned to his lodgings somewhat heated with the wine [that] he had quaffed, *and* which caused his brain to swim with strange fantasies." (Hawthorne.) "She found a tall, good-looking young man standing [—who was standing] on the rug, *and* whom . . . ."

[3] § 115, (1) (*c*), *above*.

be lost in variety by not exchanging the relatives freely, more is gained in precision by differentiating them. The relative is a troublesome word, because it recurs so frequently; and anything that can be done by way of making it more tractable is well done.

148. Elizabethan English knew the distinction, and generally made it; but by the eighteenth century *that* had nearly usurped the relative functions. Accordingly, Steele, in his *Humble Petition of Who and Which*, prayed that these words might be restored to the language;[1] and his prayer was heard so fully, that to-day *which* is most constantly abused. If the rule only had no exceptions, it would, in all probability, be generally adopted; but the many necessary exceptions[2] furnish at least a partial explanation why it is not obeyed. The student may wisely give himself any trouble he finds necessary in order to understand the distinction and obey the rule.

149. Perhaps the true explanation of this distinctive use of *who* or *which* and *that* lies in the fact that *that* is a *lighter* relative than *who* or *which*, is more easily spoken and therefore more easily incorporated with the sentence in which it stands, and that for this reason it naturally introduces the adjective clause—a clause closely connected with the antecedent. *Who* and *which*, on the other hand, are more *formal*, less easily spoken, and therefore not closely connected with their antecedents. Hence, they introduce coördinate clauses. Several of the exceptions seem to confirm this supposition.

150. EXCEPTIONS.[3]—In many cases, *that*, although required by the rule, would be intolerable;—

(1) After the demonstrative pronoun *that;* as, What a queer consciousness *that* must be *which* accompanies such a man. —But *those* may take *that;* as, Those castles *that* one sees along the Rhine.[4]

(2) After a preposition; as, In those long days about *which* nobody will ever know anything now.—But, the preposition

---

[1] *Spectator*, No. 78.

[2] § 150, *below*.

[3] E. A. Abbott, *How to Write Clearly*, Rule 8.

[4] See, however, Exc. (8), *below*.

may follow its verb, adverb-like, and then the relative is *that;* as, All the vicious habits and practices *that* he had been used to.[1]

(3) When separated from the other words of its own clause; as, I keep a being *who,* as I know, has many weaknesses, out of harm's way.—There are many persons *who,* though unscrupulous, are commonly good-tempered.

(4) When remote from its antecedent; as,

> "And here's a prophet *that* I brought with me
> From forth the streets of Pomfret, *whom* I found."

A poor woman *that* was crying piteously for help, and *whom* he at last hauled safely to shore.

(5) For variety's sake; as, A being *that* was not worth the smallest regard of one *who* had so great a work under his care.

151. In the following cases, *that* is often unpleasant, but may sometimes be used with good effect;—

(6) After a defined antecedent; as, His English friends *who* [*that?*] had not seen him.

(7) With the conjunction *that* preceding or following; as, Remember *that* the same awful will of heaven *which* [*that?*] placed a crown on his head, made him dull of comprehension.—Others gravely tell the man *who* [*that?*] is miserable, *that* it is necessary, *etc.*

(8) After the indefinite pronouns *some, many, others, several, those, etc.;* as, There are many *who* [*that?*] can testify. Those *who* think must govern those *that* toil.

(9) Other cases probably occur in which a writer may hesitate between *who* or *which* and *that;* but, unless for sufficient reason, the rule should have sway.

2. Shall and Will.[2]

152. *Shall* and *Will* differ in meaning as well as in function; and their difference in the one respect springs from their difference in the other. *Shall* once meant *to owe,* and still has that sense latent in its ordinary use:

---

[1] Addison, *Spectator,* No. 130.—Blair and others object to this construction as harsh; but no English is more idiomatic. It is less formal, of course, than *to which;* but it occurs even with the longer prepositions; as, Such were the prejudices *that* he rose above. It has the especial advantage of allowing the omission of the relative; as, The errand he was going on was none of his. (George Eliot.)

[2] § 145, (3) (f), *above.*

OFFENCES AGAINST PURITY.

Will means *to wish*. Hence, since a man may properly use of himself a verb that "implies debt or compulsion," but may not in courtesy use this verb of others, the English future tense reads *I shall, thou will, he will, we shall, you will, they will*. But the same words are also used to express *resolve, promise, command, etc.;* and then they read *I* or *we will, thou shalt, he, you, they shall*. From this double function springs a nice distinction, which ought to be observed by all good speakers, but which is often neglected. The following Table, condensed from Sir E. W. Head's little book, *Shall and Will* (especially Appendix H), will help the student to understand the distinction and to make it in speaking or writing. *Will, would*, and *should*, (but not *shall*,) are also used as principal verbs; but the Table speaks of them only as auxiliaries. *Shall* was once the only future auxiliary, and even now *is always used unless courtesy requires Will*.

(*a*) IN STATEMENTS—

Of the *First* Person,	SHALL *foretells;* as, I *shall* perish, and never see thy face again. WILL expresses (*a*) *resolve;* as, I *will* walk here in the hall, till the king please: (*β*) *promise;* as, And for thy humour I *will* stay at home.
Of the *Second* and *Third* Persons,	WILL *foretells;*[1] as, Bloody *will* be thy end. SHALL expresses (*a*) *promise;* as, I overheard what you *shall* overhear: (*β*) *command;* as, Rosaline, this favour thou *shalt* wear. (*γ*) *threat;* as, These gallants *shall* be task'd.

[1] And, in the *third* person, when the subject is a *rational* being, adds the idea of *intention;* as, They *will* do this (= it is their intention to do this).

(b) IN QUESTIONS—

Of the *First* Person,	{ SHALL asks *permission* or *direction;* as, *Shall* we dance, if they desire us to 't? WILL is absurd; as, *Will* we [= is it our intention to] come to-morrow?		
Of the *Second* and *Third* Persons,	WILL or SHALL	is used according as, by (*a*), it may be expected in the answer; as,	*Will*'t be a match? It *will*. *Shall* they see us? They shall.[1]

(c) *Should* follows *Shall*, and *Would Will*.

153. EXCEPTIONS.—The following cases do not follow the general rule ;—

(1) A dependent clause whose subject is the same as that of the principal clause, takes the auxiliary it would have, were it principal; as, The princess says she *shall* stay to see the sport. (She said, "I *shall* stay.") He wants not spirit to say *he'll* turn your current in a ditch. (He said, "I *will* turn.") Compare, He says he *shall* die young, and, He says he *will* die young.—But if the subjects are different, the rule holds; as, I hear they *will* come. (They said, "We shall come.") Boyet says the King *will* invite the Princess to court. (The King had said, "I *shall* invite.") It is ordered that every knee *shall* bow. (The order was, "Every knee *shall* bow.")

(2) Contingent or hypothetical assertions take *shall* in the second and third persons, even when simple futurity is expressed; as, If ever (whenever) thou *shall* love.—Haply your eye *shall* light upon some toy.—I will thank you (will wait to thank you), when (until) your strong hand *shall* give him strength.—But if the assertion is not contingent, the rule holds; as, By that time, you *will* be married.—At the gate, you *will*

---

[1] The meaning is, Is it your *will, command, intention* that they *shall* see us.

light upon two beggars.—She will thank him after he recovers, when her gratitude *will* excite him less.—In contingent or hypothetical sentences, duty, command, *etc.*, can be expressed only by *must* or *ought*, or by the longer phrases *it is one's duty, etc.;* as, If you *must* or *ought*, if it *is your duty*, if you *feel under obligation*, to go, I shall (will) withdraw my protest.

(3) In official letters of direction, military orders, *etc.*, *will* is used by courtesy for *shall;* as, Captain : On receipt of this communication, you *will* proceed, *etc.*

(4) In questions of the second person, *shall* is perhaps unusual (though examples of it may be both heard and read). *Shall* you go to New York to-day, has, of course, no discourtesy in it; and the answer would undoubtedly be, I *shall* or I *shall* not. But between simple futurity and intention or wish there is, in such cases, so little difference, that usage has commonly adopted *Will* you. The present Do you is often substituted for the future; as, *Do* you have a chill to-day? (= Is this the day for your chill, and do you therefore expect it?) The following examples from Shakspere, and others like them, take *shall* by exception (2) ; as, What *shall* you ask of me that I'll deny?— When *shall* you see me write a thing in rhyme?—The asking and the writing in rhyme are looked upon as mere hypotheses, impossible in fact.

3. IMPROPRIETIES.

154. Improprieties are (1) *Single Words*, (2) *Phrases*. Of course, those words are most liable to misuse which resemble each other "in sound, or sense, or both ;"[1] but other words than these are misplaced.[2] For example ;—

(1) SINGLE WORDS: (*a*) **Alike in sound or appearance** ;[3] —*predicate* and *predict*, *officious* and *official*, *leave* and *let*, *observance* and *observation*, *felicity* and *facility*, *continuous* and *continual*, *decimate* and *devastate*.[4]

---

[1] Campbell, II. iii.

[2] See sub-divisions (*d*), (*e*) and (*f*), *below*.—" None but those who are grossly ignorant of our tongue," says Campbell, can misuse " words that have no affinity to those whose place they are made to occupy ;" but some of the examples given below are cited by Campbell himself.

[3] The words *or appearance* were added by Prof. A. S Hill.

[4] *Decimate* ought to mean *to destroy a tenth*, but Webster defines it as meaning *to devastate*, and Worcester gives an equivalent signification.

(*b*) **Alike in sense;**—*reduplication* and *repetition*, *all* and *only* (as, Her living-room and her bed-chamber were *all* the rooms she had.—Ouida, *In Maremma*, ch. ii.), *learn* and *teach*, *lengthened* and *long*, *eliminate* and *elicit*, *verbal* and *oral*.

(*c*) **Alike in both sound or appearance and sense;**—*converse, inverse, reverse* and *opposite; lay* and *lie; sit* and *set; raise* and *rise; replace, displace, take the place of, fill one's place, supersede, succeed*, etc.[1]

(*d*) **Resembling in meaning their foreign equivalents or etymological primitives;**—*apparent* and *evident* or *manifest*,[2] *to exploit* and *to achieve*,[3] *to ambition* and *to seek eagerly*,[3] *noted* and *known*,[4] *to disillusion* and *to undeceive*,[5] *has reason* and *is right*,[5] *articulate* and *frame* or *put together*.[6]

(*e*) **Misused for each other, though not alike in sound, appearance, or sense;**—*condone* (= *forgive*) and *compensate* or *atone for*, *constantly* and *frequently*, *precept* and *doctrine*, *veracity* and *reality*, *spare* and *grant*,[7] *want* and *be* or *do without*.[8]

(*f*) **Blunder-Words;**—*insiduous* (by analogy with *assiduous*) for *insidious*, *demean* for *debase* or *lower* (as if its last syllable were English *mean*), *reticence* (as if *retinence*) for *reserve*, *persuade* for *advise* (because Latin *suadere* = to exhort), *Chinee* and *Cyclop* (as if *Chinese* and *Cyclops* were plurals).

(2) PHRASES: (*a*) **Absurd, inconsistent, or contradictory in meaning;**—*Local items* (*items* of *local* news).—*Saloon-atic slaughter* (*murder* in a *bar-room*).[9]—The care such an august *Cause* [= God] may be supposed to *take about any action*. The *unprecedented* impudence of B—— *nearly equalled* that of his chief and master.—The last survivor of *his* honored predecessors.

---

[1] *Replace* has almost *displaced* all the other words of the group. An accurate writer, of course, distinguishes them carefully, but many good writers accept *replace* in a vast majority of instances. (See Hodgson, pp. 60–62.)

[2] Lat. *apparens*.—"Of my uncle's great estate .... not the half .... was *apparent* [could be found?] after his death." (*The House of the Seven Gables*, p. 270, Riverside Ed.)

[3] French *exploiter*, *ambitionner*. The English words are marked "Obs." in Webster.

[4] Latin *notus*.—Shakspere (Sonnet 76, 6) and colloquial.

[5] French. [6] Latin.

[7] "Mr. Macaulay might have *spared* a passing eulogy." But both Webster and Worcester give this sense, citing Roscommon.

[8] "I can not *want* it" = I *do* or shall *want* (*need*) it.   [9] § 115.

(b) **Apparent only;**—*God and his Son except, Created thing* naught valued he nor shunned.¹—Adam the goodliest man of men *since born his sons;* the fairest of *her daughters* Eve.¹

(c) **Rhetorical;** *i.e., used to heighten the effect;* — He [Cerberus] was a monster, with three separate heads, and *each of them fiercer than the two others*.²—This made several women look at one another slyly, *each knowing more than the others*.²

¹ Milton, *P. L.*, II. 678, IV. 323.—By poetic license: not to be imitated in prose.
² Quoted by A. S. Hill from Hawthorne and Blackmore respectively.

V

VARIETIES OF DICTION. EXCEPTIONS TO THE LAWS OF PURITY.

155. Diction varies for the several kinds of composition, and the laws of Purity vary accordingly. The diction of Prose is manifestly different from that of Romance or Poetry; and even within the limits of Prose, a wide variety is both possible and desirable. A letter to one's friend, for example, adopts a far different style from that of the journal of a traveller; the journal, a far different style from that of a history or a biography; history or biography, a different style from that of the scientific treatise—even the essay; and each of these, a different style from that of the oration. Hence, errors in Diction are neither so noticeable nor so blameworthy in a letter as in a journal, in a journal as in a history, a biography, a scientific treatise, or an oration. The more deliberate and exact the work, the more stringent the laws of Purity. Further, a prose work may have a special, well-defined purpose—satire, pathos, humor, wit; and it then enjoys almost a poetic license.

156. These statements are true, also, with regard to Style in its other phases,—to Phraseology and to Style Proper,—as well as to Diction; but since violations of Diction are more easily noted than offences in the other particulars, especial stress must be laid on the truth in this application.

157. 1. The characteristics of the Diction of Prose and of Poetry have been thus stated by Abbott and Seeley : [1]—

(1) *Speech is the Guide to Prose.*[2]—"A man speaks in a very different manner according as he is conversing at the dinner-table, or holding a literary discussion, or arguing in a law-court, or addressing a public meeting

---

[1] *English Lessons for English People,* Part II., chap's i. and ii.
[2] Certain exceptional forms of Prose (§ 158) are excluded from what is said here.

or a congregation ; and every different shade in speaking will be represented in writing." "The differences will consist almost entirely *in the rhythm of the sentences, in the use of question instead of statement, of short sentences instead of long ones; not in words, which will be very nearly the same throughout.*" But (*a*) *Writing is more exact than speech.*—One can not wait in speaking to get the exact word : in writing, one must always do this. The superlatives of conversation, which give it a flavor and arrest attention, the similes that will not bear critical analysis, the incessantly recurring *very's* and *quites*,—are intolerable in writing. "A clever fellow" must be distinguished as an *original*, a *thoughtful*, a *judicious*, a *sagacious* man ; a *most delightful* day must be described (perhaps) more cautiously as a *pleasant*, an *agreeable* day ; "he's as grave as a judge" becomes "he's remarkably sober in mien or speech ;" "it would be *very improper*" omits its adverb. The letter alone, of written communications, adopts the easy, inexact diction of conversation ; and even it is less inexact than talk. (*b*) *Writing is less brief than speech.*—Contractions (*don't*, *'s*, *I'll*) are not permissible in formal writing ; ellipses are not so common as in speech ; short, but expressive words—such as *mob, bore, pell-mell*—must be used, if at all, with caution. (*c*) *Writing is less varied in construction than speech.*—Speech naturally introduces "direct discourse," and shifts from this to the "indirect quotation and back again almost at will." Compare the two following accounts, one written by Sir Thomas North, a translator of Plutarch, the other *spoken* by Cassius in *Julius Cæsar;*—

"When they raised their camp, there came two eagles that, flying with a marvellous force, lighted upon two of the foremost ensigns, and followed the soldiers, which gave them meat and fed them until they came near to the city of Philippi, and there, one day before the battle, they both fled away."

"Coming from Sardis, on our former ensign
Two mighty eagles fell; and there they perch'd,
Gorging and feeding from our soldiers' hands;
Who to Philippi here consorted us.
This morning are they fled away and gone."

See, too, the well-known speech of Cassius, beginning

"Well, honour is the subject of my story;"[1]

and compare it with the next two speeches,[2] which are more in prose style.

(2) *Poetic Diction differs from that of Prose chiefly in the choice of words.* (a) *Poetic Diction is Archaic and Non-Colloquial.*—Such words as *hallowed, sojourn, wons*, for *holy, lodge, dwell*, as *thou* and *ye* for *you*, as *e'er* for *ever* and *ere* for *before*, as *woe, blissful, ken, dire, ire*, (words avoided in ordinary modern prose) are peculiarly poetic. (b) *Poetic Diction is Picturesque.*—"Poetry prefers picturesque images to the enumeration of dry facts. Compare the poetry of the following;—

'The blackbird whistles from the thorny brake:
The mellow bullfinch answers from the grove:
Nor are the linnets, o'er the flowering furze
Pour'd out profusely, silent . . . . . .
. . . . . . The jay, the rook, the daw,
And each harsh pipe, discordant heard alone,
Aid the full concert; while the rock-dove breathes
A melancholy murmur through the whole,'—[3]

with the prosaical or rather the comical effect of—

'Now, too, the feather'd warblers tune their notes
Around, and charm the listening grove. The lark,
The linnet, chaffinch, bullfinch, goldfinch, greenfinch.'"[4]

(c) *Poetic Diction substitutes an Epithet for the thing denoted;* as, the breezy *blue*, the dead *vast* of the night; *and ornaments itself with epithets that add nothing to the*

---

[1] *Julius Cæsar*, I. ii. 92-131.—The same liberty is used in narrative (history and the like), but more reservedly.

[2] Lines 135-175.   [3] Thomson's *Seasons*.   [4] Sheridan, *The Critic*.

sense; as, "His dog attends him ... and snatches up the drifted snow with *ivory* teeth." *Red* lightning and *white* wings of a swan are other examples. (*d*) *Poetry is averse to lengthiness, and* [*is*] *euphonious.*—(α) Conjunctions and Relatives are omitted;—"See that your *polished* arms be *primed* with care" (for polished *and* primed).—"So those two brothers with their *murdered* man [the man they intended to murder]. (β) Length without force, or even length for the *mere* purpose of clearness is avoided. *Scarce* is preferred to *scarcely*, *vale* to *valley*, *list* to *listen*, *whist* to *be silent*. (γ) Euphony is always considered; as, *Erin* for *Ireland*, the *Scorpion* sign for the *Scorpion's* sign, *Verona walls*. (δ) But, to give added *pleasure*, a longer expression, construction, figure of speech is common in poetry; as,

> "I to the world am like a drop of water
> That in the ocean seeks another drop,
> Who falling there to seek his fellow forth,
> Unseen, inquisitive, confounds itself;"

instead of "I am to the world like a drop of water that falls into the ocean and is lost there."

158. 2. Certain forms of Prose admit exceptions to the laws of Purity :—

(1) To lend to satire an added sting, or to render pathos more pathetic, diction may be slightly *archaic*, and by this means carry the reader back to the times portrayed. The picture is thus made *real;* something of almost poetic picturesqueness being added. Naturally, such archaism is not alone, or, perhaps, so much in the words and constructions used: it pervades the whole style, and gives the work a *flavor* of antiquity. For example ;—

"Here we are all on our knees. Here is the Archbishop of Canterbury prostrating himself to the head of his church, with Kielmansegge and Schulenberg with their ruddled cheeks grinning behind the defender of the faith. Here is my Lord Duke of Marlborough kneeling, too, the greatest warrior of all times; he who betrayed King William—betrayed King James II.—betrayed Queen Anne—betrayed England to the French, the Elector to the Pretender, the Pretender to the Elector; and here are my Lords Oxford and Bolingbroke, the latter of whom has just tripped up the heels of the former; and if a month's more time had been allowed him, would have had King James at Westminster. The great Whig gentlemen made their vows and congees with proper decorum and ceremony; but yonder keen old schemer knows the value of their loyalty. 'Loyalty,' he must think, 'as applied to me—it is absurd! There are fifty nearer heirs to the throne than I am. I am but an accident, and you fine Whig gentlemen take me for your own sake, not for mine. You Tories hate me; you archbishop, smirking on your knees, and prating about heaven, you know I don't care a fig for your Thirty-nine Articles, and can't understand a word of your stupid sermons. You, my Lords Bolingbroke and Oxford—you know you were conspiring against me a month ago; and you, my Lord Duke of Marlborough—you would sell me or any man else, if you found your advantage in it. Come, my good Melusina, come, my honest Sophia, let us go into my private room, and have some oysters and some Rhine wine, and some pipes afterwards: let us make the best of our situation; let us take what we can get, and leave these bawling, brawling, lying English to shout, and fight, and cheat in their own way.'"[1]

"What preacher need moralize on this story? What words save the simplest are requisite to tell it? It is too terrible for tears. The thought of such a misery smites me down in submission before the Ruler of kings and men, the Monarch Supreme over empires and republics, the inscrutable Dispenser of life, death, happiness, victory. 'O brothers!' I said to those who heard me first in America: 'O brothers! speaking the same dear mother-tongue; O comrades! enemies no more, let us take a mournful hand together as we stand by this royal corpse and call a truce to battle! Low he lies, to whom the proudest used to kneel once, and who was cast lower than the poorest; dead whom millions prayed for in vain. Driven off his throne; buffeted by rude hands; with his

---

[1] Thackeray, *The Four Georges, George the First*, p. 23 (London, 1869).

children in revolt; the darling of his old age killed before him untimely, our Lear hangs over her breathless lips, and cries, 'Cordelia, Cordelia, stay a little!'

> 'Vex not his ghost,—oh! let him pass,—he hates him
> That would upon the rack of this tough world
> Stretch him out longer.'

Hush! strife and quarrel, over the solemn grave. Sound, trumpets, a mournful march. Fall, dark curtain, upon his pageant, his pride, his grief, his awful tragedy."[1]

(2) Many writers for pathos, wit, humor, have chosen a form of Prose not inaptly called *Impassioned*.[2] It is thus described;—"A beautiful prose (dangerous to imitate) which resembles poetry[3] in having a perceptible rhythm, and [which] now and then borrows poetic *brevity* and forms poetic compounds,—e.g., *daisied*, *sun-filled*,—while yet it never trespasses on the poetic vocabulary."[2] For example;—

"Let us watch him with reverence as he sets side by side the burning gems, and smooths with soft sculpture the jasper pillars that are to reflect a ceaseless sunshine, and rise into a cloudless sky: but not with less reverence let us stand by him when, with rough strength and hurried stroke, he smites an uncouth animation out of the rocks which he has torn from among the moss of the moorland, and heaves into the darkened air the pile of iron buttress and rugged wall, instinct with work of an imagination as wild and wayward as the northern sea: creations of ungainly shape and rigid limb, but full of wolfish life: fierce as the winds that beat, and changeful as the clouds that shade them."[4]

"It is now sixteen or seventeen years since I saw the Queen of France, then the Dauphiness, at Versailles; and surely never lighted on this orb, which she hardly seemed to touch, a more delightful vision. I saw her just above the horizon, decorating and cheering the elevated sphere she just began to move in,—glittering like the morning star, full of life, and splendor, and joy. Oh! what a revolution! and what an heart must I have, to contemplate without emotion that elevation and

---

[1] *The Four Georges, George the Third*, p. 96.   [2] *English Lessons*, II. ii.
[3] Verse, rather. (See §§ 36, 68, *above*.)   [4] Ruskin.

that fall! Little did I dream when she added titles of veneration to those of enthusiastic, distant love, that she should ever be obliged to carry the sharp antidote against disgrace concealed in that bosom; little did I dream that I should have lived to see such disasters fallen upon her in a nation of gallant men, in a nation of men·of honor and of cavaliers. I thought ten thousand swords must have leaped from their scabbards to avenge even a look that threatened her with insult. But the age of chivalry is gone. That of sophisters, economists, and calculators, has succeeded, and the glory of Europe is extinguished for ever. Never, never more shall we behold that generous loyalty to rank and sex, that proud submission, that dignified obedience, and that subordination of the heart, which kept alive, even in servitude itself, the spirit of an exalted freedom."[1]

(3) With the same ends in view, but transgressing the utmost limits of proper Prose by using poetic *words* as well as poetic brevity and poetic compounds, certain authors,—Lamb, Coleridge, De Quincey, for example,—have written an exceptional prose, the more dangerous to imitate than the prose just exemplified, the more nearly it approaches Poetry.[2] For example;—

"I like to meet a sweep; understand me,—not a grown sweeper, (old chimney-sweepers are by no means attractive,) but one of those *tender* novices, blooming through their first nigritude, the maternal washings not quite effaced from the cheek; such as come forth with the dawn, or somewhat earlier, with their little professional notes sounding like the *peep, peep* of a young sparrow; or liker to the matin lark should I pronounce them, in their aërial ascents not seldom anticipating the sun-rise? I have a kindly yearning toward these dim specks—poor blots- innocent blacknesses. I reverence these young Africans of our own growth,—these almost clergy imps, who sport their cloth without assumption; and from their little pulpits, (the tops of chimneys,) in the nipping air of a December morning, preach a lesson of patience to mankind. When a

---

[1] Burke.

[2] Abbott and Seeley, *ut cit.*—How great the danger, and how complete the failure of the ambitious writer may be, the last example quoted in this paragraph will teach.

child, what a mysterious pleasure it was to witness their operation! to see a chit, no bigger than one's self, enter, one knew not by what process, into what seemed the *fauces Averni,*—to pursue him in imagination, as he went sounding on through so many dark stifling caverns, horrid shades!—to shudder with the idea that 'now, surely, he must be lost forever!'—to revive at hearing his feeble shout of discovered day-light—and then (O fulness of delight!) running out of doors, to come just in time to see the sable phenomenon emerge in safety, the brandished weapon of his art victorious like some flag waved over a conquered citadel! I seem to remember having been told that a bad sweep was once left in a stack with his brush, to indicate which way the wind blew. It was an awful spectacle certainly; not much unlike the old stage direction in Macbeth, where the 'Apparition of a child crowned, with a tree in his hand, rises.'"[1]

"This is *saloop*—the precocious herb-woman's darling—the delight of the early gardener, who transports his smoking cabbages by break of day from Hammersmith to Covent Garden's famed piazzas;—the delight, and oh! I fear, too often the envy, of the unpennied sweep. Him should'st thou haply encounter, with his dim visage pendent over the grateful steam, regale him with a sumptuous basin (it will cost thee but three-halfpennies) and a slice of delicate bread and butter (an added halfpenny); so may thy culinary fires, eased of the o'er-charged secretions from thy worse-placed hospitalities, curl up a lighter volume to the welkin; so may the descending soot never taint thy costly well-ingredienced soups nor the odious cry, quick-reaching from street to street, of the fired chimney, invite the rattling engines from ten adjacent parishes, to disturb for a casual scintillation thy peace and pocket!"[2]

"The whole school were in ecstacies to hear tales and stories from his genius; even like a flock of birds, chirping in their joy, all newly alighted on a vernal land. In spite of that difference in our age—or oh! say rather because that difference did touch the one heart with tenderness and the other with reverence,— how often did we two wander, like elder and younger brother, in the sunlight and the moonlight solitudes! Woods into whose

---

[1] Charles Lamb, *The Praise of Chimney Sweepers.*

[2] Id. ib.—Note, especially, the absence of verse-rhythm, with an exquisitely graceful rhythm of prose. If occasionally a group of words falls into regular rhythm, the next clause immediately breaks this rhythm up again.

inmost recesses we should have quaked alone to penetrate, in his company were glad as gardens, through their most awful umbrage; and there was beauty in the shadows of the old oaks. Cataracts, in whose lonesome thunder, as it pealed into those pitchy pools, we durst not by ourselves have faced the spray—in his presence, dinned with a merry music in the desert, and cheerful was the thin mist they cast sparkling up into the air. Too severe for our uncompanied spirit, then easily overcome with awe, was the solitude of those remote inland lochs. But as we walked with him along the winding shores, how passing sweet the calm of both blue depths—how magnificent the white crested waves, tumbling beneath the black thunder-cloud! More beautiful, because our eyes gazed on it along with his, at the beginning or ending of some sudden storm, the apparition of the rainbow."[1]

159. 3. Romance, which combines the characteristics of Prose and of Poetry,[2] takes at one time the strictest form of prose-diction, at other times one of the special forms described in § 158. In its non-dramatic parts,[3] it is often simple narrative or other plain discourse, and can claim no license as to diction; but again (and especially in the Romance Proper[4]) it rises into satire, humor, the pathetic, the sublime, the supernatural, and its kinship with Poetry gives it a warrant for greater or less elevation. George Eliot, Thackeray, Dickens, Blackmore, and many other novelists have availed themselves of this privilege,—some of them, perhaps, to an unwarrantable extent. Thus ;—

"The boat reappeared, but brother and sister had gone down in an embrace never to be parted; living through again, in one supreme moment, the days when they had clasped their little hands in love, and roamed the daisied fields together."[5]

[1] Wilson, cited in *English Lessons.*—Perhaps, this extract may be apologized for under § 159; but, wherever it belongs, it may well stand as a warning against a diction utterly run wild. Much unsuccessful newspaper and other periodical writing results from such attempts to imitate the all but inimitable style of Lamb and his school.

[2] § 74, *above.*
[4] § 63, *above.*
[3] For the law of the dramatic passages, see § 160.
[5] *The Mill on the Floss*, cited in *English Lessons.*

"She was dead. No sleep so beautiful and calm, so free from trace of pain, so fair to look upon. She seemed a creature fresh from the hand of God, and waiting for the breath of life; not one who had lived and suffered death. . . . And now the bell—the bell she had so often heard, by night and day, and listened to with solemn pleasure almost as [to] a living voice—rung its remorseless toll, for her so young, so beautiful, so good. Decrepit age, and rigorous life, and blooming youth, and helpless infancy, poured forth—on crutches, in the pride of strength and health, in the full blush of promise, in the mere dawn of life—to gather round her tomb. Old men were there, whose eyes were dim and senses failing—grandmothers, who might have died ten years ago, and still been old—the deaf, the blind, the lame, the palsied, the living dead in many shapes and forms, to see the closing of that early grave. What was the death it would shut in, to that which still could crawl and creep above it! Earth to earth, ashes to ashes, dust to dust! Many a young hand dropped in its little wreath, many a stifled sob was heard. Some—and they were not a few—knelt down. All were sincere and truthful in their sorrow. . . . Then when the dusk of evening had come on, and not a sound disturbed the sacred stillness of the place—when the bright moon poured in her light on tomb and monument, on pillar, wall, and arch, and most of all (it seemed to them) upon her quiet grave—in that calm time, when outward things and inward thoughts turn with assurances of immortality, and worldly hopes and fears are humbled in the dust before them—then, with tranquil and submissive hearts they turned away, and left the child with God." [1]

160. 4. Writings of the dramatic type, (those in which characters are introduced in their own person,) admit in the dialogue anything that is necessary duly to effect this characterization. Dogberry[2] must talk like "an ass," and Holofernes[3] like a pedant; nor does either give offence, so long as he talks as such a character should talk. So, diction grows coarse, provincial, impure in any or every particular, or, on the other hand, is refined,

---

[1] *The Old Curiosity Shop*, chap's lxxi., lxxii., *passim*.—Whole passages are almost unbrokenly in iambic measure.

[2] Shakspere, *Much Ado*.   [3] Id., *Love's Labours Lost*.

national,—purity itself, according to the character of the person speaking. The author, of course, is not chargeable with violations of purity put into his characters' mouths, unless they are inconsistent with his own portrayals of these characters. Indeed, peculiarities of speech may go far to individualize a character and at the same time to describe him the more fully. Thus, Fluellen, in *Henry V.*, would be much less the valiant Welsh gentleman, did he not use *f* for *v*, *p* for *b*, and otherwise show his contempt for the King's English; the pomposity of Mr. Trumbull[1] is chiefly pictured in his peculiar diction; and Mr. Swiveller and the Marchioness[2] have their characterizing modes of expression.

161. 5. *Literal* quotations are not chargeable against the quoting writer. The latter is responsible for introducing the quotation, but for nothing more. At the same time, excessive quotation in foreign languages has the effect of alienism; and, hence, many writers translate or paraphrase in their text, adding the original in footnotes. Especially, in technical works, in which the citation of authorities must be pushed very far, the footnote serves as a most useful storehouse for much that would embarrass or destroy the text.

162. 6. *Colloquialisms*, forms admissible only in conversation, are also excepted from the law of Purity that holds in writing or formal speech. One ought not to "talk like a book," if the talk is informal; for a certain *negligé* in conversation is a positive virtue. On the other hand, strictness will vary as speech becomes less and less colloquial; and even conversation must never sink into vulgarisms or other positive errors of speech.

---

[1] The auctioneer in *Middlemarch*, who "never used poor language without immediately correcting himself," and who therefore fell into numberless repetitions;—" A *very nice thing*, a *very superior publication*, entitled 'Ivanhoe.'"

[2] *The Old Curiosity Shop.*

VI.

DIVIDED USAGE.

163. Not infrequently, several "different, though resembling modes of expression for the same thing" are equally in good use. Competent authority can be urged for each, or the same good writer uses both forms. Usage is then said to be "divided;" and even the most assured believers in Good Use concede that the Standard of Purity must be found elsewhere. As a basis for the discussion of such cases, the following principles have been widely agreed upon.

164. *First*, the dissent (conscious or unconscious) of a single writer or coterie of writers does not set up a divided usage. The alternative form may not be a mere idiotism,—that is, it may have sufficient support to make it reputable; but it can not be said to *divide* usage, unless its supporting minority is respectable. The authorities on each side must be equal or nearly so. From an overwhelming weight of authority on one side may be inferred the support of underlying truth; and the feeble minority struggles in vain. Thus, the pronunciations *i-ther* and *ni-ther* are certainly heard in reputable use, but usage can not yet be said to be divided in this case, for the supporting minority is too small. "Custom, when wavering," says Dr. Campbell, "may be swayed, but, when reluctant, will not be forced. And in this department a person never effects so little, as when he attempts too much."[1] For this reason, it is to no purpose with Johnson to pronounce the word *news* a plural, whatever it might [may?] have been in the days of Sidney and Raleigh; nor is Johnson's rule well founded, that no noun singular should end with single *s*.[1]

[1] Campbell, II. ii. 1.

So, in spite of much opposition from conservative writers and speakers, *telegram* was quickly accepted as "good English;" *is being done* and other passive forms with *being* are widely used,[1] and the subjunctive mood is quite as widely disused.[2] On the other hand, though scholars of no mean rank have espoused the cause of *Phonetic Spelling*, it is still unadopted, and seems destined to share the fate of those other "reforms" that would write *Hērodotos* and *Keltic,* and pronounce Cæsar *Kaisar* and Virgil *Wergil* (with hard *g*.)

165. *Secondly*, in no case of Divided Usage can a man "be said to speak barbarously," whichever side he conforms to. Each of the contending forms has sufficient authority, and is, therefore, in good use. Thus, an important class of English words end indifferently in -*wise*, -*way*, or -*ways;* and the last ending (a genitive long since forgotten) is, perhaps, the most truly English form. Yet Dr. Johnson, in his *Dictionary*, condemns "all those who either write or pronounce" *noways* "ignorant barbarians." These, as Campbell points out, "are only Pope, and Swift, and Addison, and Locke, and several others of our most celebrated writers";[3] while the form is in no way a violation of Etymology.

166. At the same time, *thirdly*, one or another of such contending forms may be preferable, or the case can be settled by an appeal to underlying principles. The superiority of one of the disputing forms is so great as to give it a decided preference over the other, and thus virtually to settle the case between the two. Some of these principles—those most commonly appealed to— have been stated by Campbell in his famous "Canons,"

---

[1] At the same time, John Henry Newman and Grant White are not the only protestants against this latest coinage of the English mint. Many men of learning, judgment, and good taste, as well as of genuine sympathy with the true progress of the age, can not tolerate it.

[2] *Were* is perhaps the only exception.   [3] II. ii. 1.

a condensation of which, with examples, is given below. In using them, the student should always remember that other principles are equally valid, and that any principle *known* to be a law of thought or speech may be brought forward either in approval or in condemnation of a proposed use.

167. Canons for Divided Use;—

Of two (or more) forms equally in Good Use, that which is—

(1) Univocal,	is	(1) Equivocal,
(2) Analogous to other forms of its kind in the same language,	preferable	(2) Out of analogy,
(3) Euphonious,	to	(3) Harsh,
(4) Simple and brief, or	one that	(4) Complex and lengthy, or
(5) According to the older usage.	is	(5) Recent.

168. Examples of the application of these rules may be given as follows, the numbers referring, of course, to those of the canons.

(1) *Beside*, as preposition to mean "by the side of," "aside from," "out of," and *besides*, (*a*) as preposition to mean "in addition to," (*b*) as adverb or conjunction to mean "moreover," "beyond," are better than *beside* or *besides* used indifferently. Some of the confusion, at least, that has existed and still exists between the forms is cleared away by the distinction.[1] So *forward, upward, backward, etc.*, the adjectives, may be distinguished from *forwards, upwards, backwards, etc.*, the adverbs; unless, indeed, the fact that, in these cases, the part of speech is always made clear by the meaning as determined by the context, is to be considered a sufficient reason for writing both adjectives and adverbs without the *s*. (See the last foot-

---

[1] Skeat, *Etymological Dictionary*, says the oldest form was *beside*, that the *s* was added because many English adverbs ended in *s*, that *besides* as a preposition is really incorrect, but that the s-form in both uses is very old. The same is true of many other adverbs in *s*.

note; and add Grant White's chief objections that the s-forms increase the already constant sibilation of English, and that all these words were originally written without *s;* in other words, that the omission of *s* is right under Canons 3. and 5). *By consequence* is preferable to *of consequence,* where the meaning is *consequently,* because *of consequence* may also mean *of importance. Scarce,* as adjective, and *scarcely,* as adverb. *Recall* rather than *recal,* as more likely to suggest its meaning, *call back. Bi-cȳ-cle* rather than *bi-cȳ'-cle* or even *bi'-cȳ-cle,* if only because *cycle* has now a meaning so remote from *wheel,* that *bi'-cȳ-cle* is most certain to be understood. *Sideways, lengthways, crossways, etc.,* and *nowise, likewise, otherwise, etc.,* seem right, since the terminations *ways* and *wise* are of different derivation and meaning; the forms in *-ways* being preferable whenever the ending means *direction,* and those in *-wise* when the ending means *manner* or *mode.* But the distinction has been lost sight of; and, under the influence of Canon 2, *-wise* is gradually usurping the place of *-ways.* Hence, *noways,* often used for *nowise,* would seem to have a province of its own; but the confusion of *way=direction* with *way=mode, manner,* easily promotes an exchange of the two forms.

(2) *Ever so wise,* rather than *never so wise; whether or not,* rather than *whether or no; needs* and *dares,* when the verbs are principal, as "he *needs* no influence," "he *dares* as much as man may dare;" but *need* and *dare,* (by analogy with *can, will, shall, may, etc.,*) when they are auxiliaries; as, "he *need* (*dare*) not act in that way;"[1] *sang* as past tense, rather than *sung.*[2]

(3) For *conscience'* sake, not *conscience's; boys',* not *boys's;*[3] *godly,* not *godlily; scarcity,* rather than *scarceness; most proper,* rather than *properest; more delightful,* rather than

---

[1] *Need* and *dare* are often *conditional;* as, he *need* (*dare*) not try, whatever should occur, meaning, he would be under no necessity (he would not have the courage) to try, whatever should occur.

[2] *In Memoriam,* xxx.;—

"Then echo-like our voices rang;
We *sung,* tho' every eye was dim,
A merry song we *sang* with him
Last year: impetuously we *sang.*"

"Once more we *sang.*"

[3] But the *'s* should be written, for clearness' sake, whenever Euphony allows. *Chambers'* is not so clear either to the eye or to the ear as *Chambers's;* and, in not a few such cases, the double *s* is not intolerably harsh.

delightfuller;[1] *on* the floor, rather than *upon* the floor;[2] *to*, rather than *unto;*[2] *round*, rather than *around.*[2]

(4) *Admit, approve, meet, attain*, rather than *admit* or *approve of, meet with, attain to*. So, *gather together, come in*, (as a reply to a knock), *trace out, examine into*, and many other compound verbs may properly lose their adverbs, unless the sense plainly requires them. *Endeavour oneself* long ago gave way to *endeavour*.

(5) *To let, for sale* are older (and shorter) than *to be let, to be sold; to do* (as "what is there to do") than *to be done; begin*, than *commence;* and the house *is building* than the house *is being built.*[3] *Point of view, man of science, the work of his life*, and many other such phrases are preferable by Canon 5; but Canon 4 may yet fasten upon the language *stand-point, scientist,*[4] *life-work, etc*. Both Johnson and Webster sought to "restore the ancient usage," the former by writing *u* in the ending *-our*, as in *honour, parlour, etc.*, the latter by dropping it: simplicity and brevity have decided the question (for America, at least); and this, although the sound *heard* is *ŭ* and not *o*. On the contrary, Canon 5 has kept *Saviour*, as it has *traveller,*[5] *recall,*[5] *programme,*[5] *coquette*, and many others.

Under Canon 1 many dissyllabic verbs are distinguished from nouns or adjectives of the same spelling,[6] and a few nouns from their adjective-doubles,[7] by a difference of accent. But the older usage (Canon 5) still controls not a few such cases. *Pérfect* is still the verb as well as the adjective; *cemént* and *detáil* are all but universal as nouns. Between *cóntents, pró-*

---

[1] Many such comparatives and superlatives are hard to pronounce, as well as of harsh sound.

[2] Defensible, also, by Canon 4; but the rhythm of verse often, as the rhythm of prose sometimes, demands the longer form.

[3] Clearness, however, may require the form with *being*. Thus, "just as the rogue *was flogging*" would not say clearly that the rogue was *being flogged*. Occasionally, too, the active form would be intolerable for other reasons. Thus, "when the stone *was raising* into its place" would forcibly suggest the vulgarism of *raise* for *rise;* and this, although stones do not *rise*, but *are raised*.

[4] Especially, this word, so much shorter and simpler than *man of science*, and objected to for reasons comparatively so weak.

[5] Most words of the *trável* class, however, do not double their final letter: *rebel* ((from *bellum*) drops one *l;* and *anagram, diagram, etc*. (taken *directly* from the Greek) never had final *-me* in English.

[6] For example, recórd and récord.   [7] For example, aúgust and áugust.

ceeds, álly, etc., and *conténts, procéeds, ally', etc.*, Canon 1 is fast securing a verdict; as, in the case of the nouns *pérmit, prótest, pérfume, íncrease, rétail, súrvey*, it perhaps has been successful. In *contról* no difference of accent seems ever to have been suggested; while *cómbat*, the only form known to the dictionaries, is often spoken *combát* when it is a verb. *Gállant*, adjective and noun, becomes *gallánt* in the special meanings of "attentive to ladies" and "suitor," and is always *gallánt* as a verb. Under Canon 5, *it is me, it is him, etc.*, are undoubtedly preferable to *it is I, it is he;* but Canon 2, is fast striking the balance in favor of the nominative construction. The modern use seems to be due to the Bible of 1611, Matt. xiv. 27, where the translators wrote *it is I*, for the Greek ἐγώ εἰμι (Latin *ego sum*).[1] Shakspere had, indeed, used the nominative;[2] and a curious failure to distinguish the English cases had characterized other writers before as well as in his time; but Mr. Ellis's words are doubtless true,—"I consider that the phrase *it is I* is a modernism, or rather a grammaticism—that is, it was never in popular use. The Anglo-Saxon form was *I am it*,[3] the form still used in German; while the other Teutonic languages had and have either *I am it* or *it is me*. The translators of 1611 of course knew nothing of all this, and so selected the form that doubtless recommended itself to their minds as most accordant with classical usage in regard to predicates. On the same principle, the pronoun *either*, restricted by its derivation to mean *one or the other of two*, may mean *one of any number;* for, as a conjunction, it is not so restricted, and, by analogy, often takes the broader meaning.[4] Canon 5, however, has so far proved stronger than Canon 2; and the best literary use to-day is overwhelmingly in favor of limiting the meaning of the word.

169. Of the five canons, 1 is generally decisive; but, even it may sometimes be set aside. Next in weight come 4, 5, 3, 2 (in the order named); but 5 necessarily admits many exceptions, the borderland between the archaic and the present being narrow, indefinable, and easily passed unconsciously. Canon 2 has compara-

---

[1] Cf. v. 28, *if it be thou for* εἰ σὺ εἶ (*si tu es*).
[2] *V. and A.*, 993; *As*, III. ii. 267; and elsewhere.
[3] March, *Grammar*, § 366, 5. [4] So, too, of course, *neither*.

tively little influence, unless it has the field to itself.
The rule laid down above[1] that the surest road to Purity
is the cultivation of a refined literary feeling, applies with
peculiar force in cases of Divided Use. In no case will
this literary sense be more valuable than in deciding the
many delicate questions raised when both Use and Law
are divided against themselves.

[1] § III.

(B) THE ELEMENTS OF STYLE.

SUB-DIVISIONS.

170. Mechanically considered, language consists of *words* (including *phrases* and *clauses*), *sentences* (or collections of words that express statements, commands, or questions),[1] *paragraphs* (groups of sentences—sometimes a single sentence—relating to one particular point in a discourse), and *whole compositions*. The larger divisions of entire works, *sections, chapters, parts, books, volumes, etc.*, are really whole compositions upon the limited themes discussed within their bounds. Hence, the following sub-divisions of the Elements of Style; —*I. Vocabulary, II. The Sentence, III. The Paragraph, IV. The Whole Composition.* To these may be added, for convenience' sake, *V. Figures of Speech;* for, though figures are generally treated as special devices to promote force,[2] they tend quite as often to clearness,[3] to ornament,[4] or to some other end, and, hence, belong rather with the Elements of Style as preparatory to the consideration of the Qualities of Style.

171. These sub-divisions (except the last) are determined by the principle of *Unity*, the law that *each division of a whole work shall contain within its own limits only one part of that work.* This law controls all rational procedures, but is of especial importance in Composition; for, since it is impossible that the same mental faculties shall be engaged at identically the same moment in two or more different ways, the *communication* of thought is in even a stronger sense impossible *without confusion*, unless the law of Unity be strictly observed. Hence, the value of the distinctions between words, phrases, sentences, etc., not only as truths of Grammar, but also as laws of Rhetoric,—not only to the student of language, but to the writer as well.

---

[1] When a single word seems to constitute a sentence, there is always an ellipsis; as, *Yes.—No.—Never!—Read* (imperative).—*Pshaw!* The shortest non-elliptical sentence contains at least two words, a subject and a predicate. [2] § 325, *below*. [3] § 318, *below*. [4] § 339, *below*.

I.

VOCABULARY.

1. THE CHOICE OF WORDS.

172. "There is reason to think," says George P. Marsh,[1] "that the vocabulary of English is among the most extensive now employed by man. The number of words not yet obsolete, but found in good authors, or in approved usage by correct speakers, including the nomenclature of science and the arts, does not probably fall short of one hundred thousand." How this total was reached, Mr. Marsh does not say; but, if it was a fair estimate in 1861, an additional ten or twenty thousand words may safely be assumed for the language to-day, and the English-speaking nations may justly pride themselves on their noble inheritance. Even by comparison with German, a language of most copious vocabulary, English does not suffer; Jacob Grimm himself, in a well-known passage, ascribing to it "a veritable power of expression, such as perhaps never stood at the command of any other language of men," and saying that even German "must first rid itself of many defects, before it can enter boldly into the lists as a competitor with the English."[2]

173. The latest editions of Webster and Worcester[3] contain about one hundred and nineteen and one hundred and sixteen thousand words respectively. Of these many are obsolete, and a few (beyond question) mere "dictionary" words; so that one hundred and fifteen thousand is, perhaps, a safe estimate of the total number of present English words as shown by these works.

[1] Lectures, I. 181. (Fourth Ed. 1861.)

[2] *On the Origin of Language* (quoted and translated by Trench, *English Past and Present*, Lect. I.)

[3] Unabridged, with Supplement.—The numbers are given by the courtesy and with the authority of the editors and publishers.

Grieb's *German Dictionary* (Am. Ed. 1857), as comprehensive for its day as Webster or Worcester of the same date, contains apparently about ninety-five thousand words; and, hence, on the supposition of an increase since 1857 of from ten to twenty thousand words, German to-day may have between one hundred and five and one hundred and fifteen thousand words.[1]

174. Few writers or speakers of English, however, use more than a fractional part of this abundant wealth of their mother-tongue. "There are persons who know the vocabulary in nearly its whole extent, but they understand a large proportion of it much as they are acquainted with Greek or Latin, that is, as the dialect of books, or of special arts or professions, and not as a living speech, the common language of daily and hourly thought. Or if, like some celebrated English and American orators, living and dead, they are able, upon occasion, to bring into the field in the war of words even the half of this vast array of light and heavy troops, yet they habitually content themselves with a much less imposing display of verbal force, and use for ordinary purposes but a very small proportion of the words they have at their command."[2] "Few writers or speakers use as many as ten thousand words, ordinary persons of fair intelligence not above three or four thousand."[2] The "all-embracing Shakspere wrote his plays with about "fifteen thousand words;" the "all-knowing Milton" his poems with about "eight thousand."[2] The Bible of 1611 (without the Apocrypha) contains rather less than six thousand words,[3] and Edwin Abbott's *Concordance to Pope* perhaps eleven thousand.[4] The Egyptian hieroglyphic symbols and the words used in Italian opera count each about

---

[1] The method of counting *Grieb* had, unfortunately, to be rough. The number of words on a dozen or twenty pages was averaged, and this average multiplied by the number of pages in the volume. The results, uncertain as they no doubt are, can not be seriously astray.

[2] Marsh, pp. 181, 182.   [3] Marsh, p. 263.

[4] Estimated by the plan described in foot-note [1], *above*.

eight hundred;[1] the vocabularies of business and of travel are very small;[2] and a wholly uneducated man "gets on" with probably not above three or four hundred words.[3]

175. The explanation of these at first astonishing facts is correctly given by Mr. Marsh.[4] *First*, any one running over the pages of a dictionary finds that a large proportion of its words are such as he himself never uses. *Secondly*, although few words are "absolutely synonymous, yet every important thought, image, and feeling, has numerous allied, if not equivalent forms of expression, and out of these every man appropriates and almost exclusively employs those which most closely accord with his own" habits, tastes, opinions, reading, *etc.* "One man will say a *thankful heart*, another a *grateful spirit;* one *fancy*, another *imagination;* one's friend is of a *sanguine temperament*, another's of a *hopeful spirit;* one *regards* a winter passage around Cape Horn as a *very hazardous voyage*, another *considers* it a *peculiarly dangerous trip.* Men of moderate passions employ few epithets, with verbs and substantives of mild signification; excitable men use numerous intensives, and words of strong and stirring meanings. Loose thinkers content themselves with a single expression for a large class of related ideas; logical men scrupulously select the precise word which corresponds to the thought they utter." *Thirdly*, many words are the *technica* of science or art, and are but little known or used outside of their own domains.

176. At the same time, "command of language is the author's first requisite. A good memory for words is no less indispensable to the author than a good memory for forms is to the painter. Words are the material that the author works in, and it is necessary above everything [else] that he should have a large store at his command."[5]

[1] Marsh, pp. 181, 182.   [2] A. S. Hill.
[3] A mere guess, and perhaps too low. It is based upon a close observation for several years of eight or ten men, who could all read a little, but (with one or two exceptions) could not write. The most noticeable fact in their talk was its *lack of synonyms:* a few words did duty for whole classes of terms.
[4] *Ut cit.*—Even within the quotation-marks, liberties have been taken by way of condensation. The whole lecture from which the extracts are made is important in this connection.
[5] Minto, *Manual*, p. 2.

Or, to change the figure, an author fights with his vocabulary as a general with his army; and he shows his skill, not only in marshalling and disposing his forces, but also in keeping a sufficient number ready for battle, and in making his details. No expenditure of time or labor, therefore, can be too great, which proves necessary to the acquisition of an extensive and well-chosen vocabulary. Indeed, on the principle of *noblesse oblige*, the student of English, who has at his disposal an almost unlimited store of words,[1] should feel bound in honor to use his vocabulary most fully and discreetly.

177. What, then, does command of language imply, and how shall it be obtained? (1) Command of language implies (*a*) Copiousness and Variety in Words, (*b*) Skill in Selection. (2) It may be obtained (*a*) by the Extended Reading of Standard Authors, (*b*) by using works of Reference, (*c*) by Practice in Composition. Each of these statements deserves detailed consideration.

178. (1) (*a*) Poverty or monotony of language is the sure road to grammatical impurity, to violations of Brevity,[2] to irretrievable dullness. The constant use of slang and other forbidden but more familiar substitutes for correct expressions, the slovenly and the exaggerated use of words, the exchange of words that resemble each other or are in some other way falsely suggested to the mind, the absurd (and, surely, "vain") repetitions, circumlocutions, and prolixities that characterize the language of "poor" speakers, the sameness of word and phrase from sentence to sentence that paints the whole picture (as it were) in one color,—all these vices are bred in a meagre and unvaried vocabulary. Even the ear is offended; for the constant recurrence of the same sounds, whether harsh or pleasant, is monotonous, and an active mind either sinks under the load or else escapes from it by refusing to read or listen.

[1] § 172 ff., above.   [2] § 191, below.

179. (*b*) Unskilful selection of words leads to obscurity and weakness;—to language that *befogs* the reader by leaving its meaning ambiguous or unintelligible; language that fails of its purpose because it lacks the vigor derivable only from "the fitness of things." "A word fitly spoken," wrote the wisest man of antiquity, "is like apples of gold in pictures of silver."

180. (2) (*a*) If reading is to promote command of language, it must be extended, varied, interesting to the reader, and critical. As noted above, also, it should be chiefly of *standard* authors. At the same time, an occasional hour spent on inferior writers is not wholly wasted. There are valuable exercises in false Rhetoric, as well as in false Syntax. The danger in reading only a few authors is that their mannerisms and other peculiarities in language shall be acquired, while what is best in their style is lost sight of. Style, even in respect of vocabulary, is undoubtedly the man himself;[1] but, beneath what is peculiar and individual, there lies a broad foundation, which is common to all writers. To build upon this foundation, one must know, not a few authors, but many. For the same reason, reading must be varied. The writers of each class of books use to a great extent the same words: they certainly use words of the same class. The diction of Poetry (as has been said above) is not that of Prose, and even the several kinds of Prose differ in this respect. To have a specialist's knowledge of words in many different subjects is not often possible; but a man of the higher culture may justly be expected to know many words outside of the topics of his own profession or his own special reading. Further, reading must interest the reader, and be critical. Perfunctory work—so many hours, so many pages a day, done listlessly or in a fit of absence of mind—is simply idle.

[1] § 312, *below*.

The rule to read at least so much a day is beyond all question good; but, if the reading is done mechanically or inattentively, the rule is as little fulfilled as the injunction to pray always is obeyed by carrying about a prayer on one's hat-band or by sewing it in the hem of one's coat. At the same time, no truce should be made with the temptation to indulge morbid appetites. It is a part of the duty of an educated man to cultivate his taste for what is good in itself; and, if he finds a deficiency in any direction within the limits proper for him, he is bound assiduously to develop himself in that direction. Sir Joshua Reynolds, returning heart-broken from the continent because he had been unable to admire the works of the great masters in Art, and setting himself to study more closely and to train more rigorously his own powers, is an example worth volumes of homily. On his next trip abroad he was abundantly rewarded: pictures that before had repelled him, now attracted him most powerfully. Of course, critical observation of standard authors will not be possible, until after the student has acquired some knowledge of the rules of Rhetoric, and has had some practice in Composition. Ignorant criticism is simply barbarous.[1] At the same time, if an *uncritical* habit of reading is once acquired, it is most difficult to correct; and, on this account, the habit of reading thoughtfully—critically so far as one does know—should be cultivated early in life. To read with one's eyes open, one need not wait till the sight has begun to fail.

181. (*b*) Works of Reference, though of only secondary value, are not to be lightly esteemed. They do not, indeed, make usage; still less, the laws of Rhetoric: they simply record these things. But, when prepared by authors of learning and skill, especially when they have passed the editorship of several generations, their record is of great value. *Liddell and Scott's Greek*

---

[1] Appendix, p. 333.

Dictionary, Webster's and Worcester's English Dictionaries, The Encyclopædia Britannica, doubtless have their weak places; but are they therefore to be discarded? So, books of synonyms—Smith's *Synonyms Discriminated* is of the first rank—have their place among a writer's "tools." At the same time, knowledge derived from works of reference has not the life, and, therefore, not the power, of that obtained by personal contact with actual literary products; and a man who knows only the dictionaries, *etc.*, knows his language very much as a physician knows medicine who has never been at the bedside.

182. (*c*) Practice in Composition, too, tends to enlargement of vocabulary. At the moment of composing, indeed, words are chosen unconsciously; but revision brings forward many questions that must be answered, shows when and why the right word or its opposite has been taken, and so defines and extends critical knowledge. More than this, words are but counters till they are used in composition: then they are real in a sense true never before.

183. The principles on which a wise choice of words is made are many and various. Some of them have already been stated; some will be met hereafter. Three seem especially to belong here. These are—

(1) Other things being equal, native words—in English, words of Anglo-Saxon origin—are preferable to those derived from other sources.

(2) Short words—monosyllables and dissyllables— have some advantages over longer ones.

(3) "Proper words in proper places."[1]

184. (1) The reason for preferring native words to those that have come into the language from other sources, is evident. A writer naturally uses best the words of his own linguistic stock. These are to his manner born:

---

[1] "Swift's definition of a good style."—A. S. Hill.

other words have had to accommodate themselves to that manner, and have not always succeeded. An Englishman,[1] therefore, since his language is Teutonic in grammar, and (so far as the words he uses most constantly are concerned) overwhelmingly Teutonic in vocabulary,[2] an Englishman naturally concedes to "Anglo-Saxon English" an eldest son's prerogative. Besides, in English, the words of native stock name, as a rule, things in every-day use, and are, hence, both simple and brief. Archbishop Trench's comments on this fact have long been familiar;[3] and the experience of every one in the main confirms that writer's views.[4]

185. Further, an etymological analysis of the English vocabulary points the same way. (*a*) Taken in bulk, about *sixty* per cent. of English words are from the Anglo-Saxon, *thirty* from the Latin (including Latin through the French), *five* from the Greek, and *five* from all other sources.[5] (*b*) A careful examination of the total vocabularies of the English Bible, Shakspere, Milton's poetry, and of selected passages from several other authors,[6] justifies the inferences that the best English authors use very large proportions of Anglo-Saxon words, and that a writer who to-day habitually falls below *seventy* per cent. of Anglo-Saxon is un-English. Some results may be given here;—

---

[1] That is, any one who speaks English as his mother-tongue.

[2] Cf. § 185, *below*.

[3] *On the Study of Words*, Lect. III. Trench instances the great features of nature, *sun, moon,* and *stars, earth, water* and *fire;* all the prime social relations, *father, mother, husband, wife, son, daughter;* the words *house, roof, home, hearth, board; boor, hind, churl; flail, plough, sickle, spade; wheat, rye, oats, bere* (=barley); *ox, deer, cow, calf, sheep, swine, deer, fowl;* and then notes that the list might be much extended.

[4] But see §§ 186 ff, *below*.

[5] Trench, *ut cit.*—Skeat, *Ety. Dict.*, App., gives lists from which (counting roughly, to be sure) the proportion of Anglo-Saxon to Latin may be stated at about 18: 8 or 9,—a result not materially different from Trench's.

[6] G. P. Marsh, *Lectures*, I. 119 ff.

Chaucer,	88–93	per cent. of Anglo-Saxon.
Spenser,	86	" "
New Testament,	90–96	" "
Shakspere,	88–91	" "
Milton,	80–90	" "
Addison,	82	" "
Swift,	68–85	" "
Johnson,	72	" "
Hume,	73	" "
Gibbon,	70	" "
Irving,	77–85	" "
Macaulay,	75	" "
Bryant,	84–92	" "
Mrs. Browning,	70–92	" "
Tennyson,	87–89	" "
Longfellow,	87	" "
Ruskin,	73–84	" "

186. But the preference thus established for Anglo-Saxon must not be either misstated or misunderstood.

(*a*) It implies no law against other English, only a conclusion in favor of large percentages of Anglo-Saxon. Well-meaning but over-zealous advocates often forget this, and leave the impression that a man who uses more than a mere sprinkling of Latin or other non-Teutonic words is a sinner "above all the Galileans." For example, Mr. Oliphant's dictum for "the best of English" is "old Teutonic words, with a *dash* of French terms mostly naturalized in the Thirteenth Century,'"—a dictum that would bind the tongue in this age with mediæval fetters.[2] On the other hand, Marsh justly says that not only must the relative proportions of Anglo-Saxon and Latin in the vocabulary at any time be considered, but also that the subject of the work must be borne in mind. "Had words of Latin and French etymology been proportionally as numerous in the time of Johnson and of Gibbon as they now are, those authors, instead of employing twenty-

[1] *Standard English.*

[2] Its effect on Mr. Oliphant's own style is exemplified below (¿ 188).

eight or thirty per cent. of such words, would scarcely have contented themselves with less than fifty. And had either of them attempted the æsthetical theories so eloquently discussed by Ruskin, with the knowledge and the stock of words possessed by that masterly writer, their Saxon would have been confined to particles, pronouns, and auxiliaries, the mere wheel-work of syntactical movement."[1] So, in one of two passages from Washington Irving, Mr. Marsh finds *eleven* per cent. of foreign words, in the other, nearly *thirty-eight* per cent.[2]

(*b*) The several reasons assigned in favor of Anglo-Saxon English have force, if at all, only in cases that admit a choice; and such cases are much more rare than is commonly believed. (*a*) No two English words, perhaps, have *precisely* the same meaning. Synonyms are words of *like*, not of *the same* signification, and, even when they come closest in sense, are still separable. Thus, two words nearer in meaning than *begin* and *commence* could not be found; and yet the alphabet *begins*—it could not be said to *commence*—with the letter *a*. After five hours' walking I *began* to feel tired; but, I *commenced* walking at five o'clock.[3] So, in a multitude of other examples differences of sense will be found that can not be set aside in pursuit of any etymological theory. (*β*) Words that come close in meaning are not always of different derivation. Thus, neither *fancy* nor *imagination*, however they compare in sense, is Teutonic; and the same is true of both words in the following pairs, —*regard* and *consider*, *very* and *peculiarly*, *hazardous* and *dangerous*.[4] (*γ*) Many notions are not expressed in English by words of Anglo-Saxon origin. Thus, Trench[5] says that "of the seventy words whereof the

---

[1] *Lectures*, I. 127.
[2] *Bracebridge Hall* and *The Sketch Book*. (Marsh, pp. 129-131.)
[3] Smith, *Synonyms Discriminated*. [4] § 175, *above*.
[5] *English Past and Present*, Lect. I.

Lord's Prayer consists[1] only the following six claim the rights of Latin citizenship: *trespasses, trespass, temptation, deliver, power, glory.*" For these, he thinks, might be substituted (respectively) *sins,* [*sin*], *trials, free, might,* and *brightness.* But, surely, *sins* and *trespasses* are not co-extensive in meaning; nor are *brightness* and *glory.* In Luke xi. 4, to be sure, *sins* is substituted for *trespasses;* but it is explained by *indebted* in the following clause.[2] So, *glory* may mean *brightness,* as in 1 Cor. xv. 41, "one glory of the sun, and another glory of the moon, and another glory of the stars;" but, when the devil shows Jesus "the kingdoms of the world, and the *glory* of them" (Matt. iv. 8), and especially when Jesus prays, "O Father, *glorify* thou me with thine own self with the *glory* which I had with thee before the world was" (John xvii. 5), the word has surely a far different sense. This sense, moreover, is that intended in the prayer, and one that no other English word exactly expresses. As to *trials* and *temptation,* Trench himself concedes a difference—how great a difference he hardly seems to feel. *Deliver,* too, though it may mean to *set free,* also means to *protect from,* as *free* does not. *Might* perhaps denotes *lawful* power, what one *may* do: *power* does not thus limit itself.

187. The truth is that, while the recommendation to be Anglo-Saxon in diction is most strenuously to be insisted upon—a recommendation first made, apparently, by Trench, but echoed by numbers of able writers, Marsh, Oliphant, Herbert Spencer, Bain, Austin Phelps, —yet it must not be allowed to hamper, still less to fetter, the writer. Unfortunately, it has sometimes been ridden as "a hobby," only to its rider's discomfiture. Language that is simple, clear, precise, good in any way,

---

[1] According to the English Prayer Book. The American Book shows *seventy-one* words; a shorter form in both books, *fifty-six;* Matt. vi., *sixty-six;* Luke xi., *fifty-eight.* [2] Cf. *debts* and *debtors.* Matt. vi. 12.

is always, no matter what its derivation, superior to that which is raised to a preference by an arbitrary standard. When nothing else is lost by excess of the Anglo-Saxon element in composition, rhythm and other musical qualities may be sacrificed. Few things try one's style so severely as an unbroken succession of very short words;[1] and yet (as has been said) Anglo-Saxon words are apt to keep within two syllables. As to other musical qualities, Byron's contrast between Italian and English,—

> "I love the language, that soft bastard Latin,
>   Which melts like kisses from a female mouth,
> And sounds as if it should be writ on satin,
>   With syllables that breathe of the sweet South,
> And gentle liquids gliding all so pat in
>   That not a single accent seems uncouth,
> Like our harsh Northern, whistling, grunting guttural,
>   Which we are obliged to hiss, and spit, and sputter all,"—

may well warn the writer at least to flavor his sentences with the more Southern tones.

188. A few amusing instances of the riding of this hobby may be cited. Mr. Oliphant's whole book is an attempt to exemplify a truly English diction.[2] Yet he garnishes his pages with alienisms,[3] and is often driven to desperate shifts not to use a non-Teutonic word. He writes *maker* for *poet*, calls the Latin brought into England by the Benedictines in the seventh century, "our first *batch* of Latin *ware*," says that "the lecture and the reading desk speak to the *folk*," and abundantly praises such Christian names as *Edith*, *Ethel*, and *Frideswide*. As a consequence, his style is manneristic to a degree,—scarcely English, in fact, although it overflows with Anglo-Saxon words. Herbert Spencer, too, praises Anglo-Saxon English as economizing the reader's attention; yet his own vocabulary is highly Latinized. Thus, in the third paragraph of his *Essay on Style*, which contains 233 words, only 152, or less than 66 per cent., are of Anglo-Saxon derivation; while of the 123 *different* words the paragraph contains, only 60, or less than 49 per cent., are

---

[1] § 189, *below*.   [2] As defined by himself. (See § 186, *above*.)

[3] § 117, *above*.

Anglo-Saxon. Further, if the form-words (the prepositions, conjunctions, articles, *etc.*, "the joints or hinges of the sentence,") be omitted, of 159 principal words, only 78, or about 49 per cent., are Anglo-Saxon; or, not counting repetitions, only 48 in 111, or less than 44 per cent. In his philosophical writings the case is commonly worse, as the notions to be expressed are more generally those for which Anglo-Saxon English has no equivalents. Thus;—

"The *assumption* of an *objective source* for the *subjective relation* of *Difference*, is *implied* in the last two *assumptions*. If, as shown above, all *special cognitions* of *spaces* and times *involve cognitions* of *differences;* and if, as shown above, *Space* in *general*, which is *resolvable* into *relations* of *Co-existence*, and Time in *general*, which is *resolvable* into *relations* of *Sequence*, are *separable* from one another as being *respectively constituted*, the last by *difference* of *order*, and the first by no-*difference* of *order;* it is *clear* that the *postulation* of *objective sources* of these *subjective forms*, *implies postulation* of an *objective source* of *Difference*. And this *postulation* of an *objective source* of *Difference*, *equally implied* in all the *arguments* which *prove* the *relativity* of the *conception* of *Difference*, has for its *ultimate* warrant the deepest *assignable* warrant—the *Persistence* of *Force*. Though the *relation* of *Difference*, *constituted*, as we have seen, by a *change* in *consciousness*, cannot be *identified* with anything beyond *consciousness;* yet that there is something beyond *consciousness* to which it is *due*, is an *inevitable conclusion;* since to think otherwise is to think of *change* taking *place* without an *antecedent*."[1]

The italicized words are non-Teutonic. If every word is counted (195 in all), less than 64 *per cent.* are Teutonic; while, of the 86 different words, only 47 words, 54½ *per cent.*, are Teutonic. Form-words omitted, the percentage is lower still. Nor is this example unfairly technical. The result is very little better in a less technical passage. For example, in the following unusually Saxon extract from Spencer,—

"On the *approach* of any *large* body, the shrimps left in a tide *pool* make *convulsive darts* which may end in *removing* each of them to a greater *distance* from the *approaching* body, or in bringing it nearer, or in leaving it almost where it was. The random leaps which a flea makes in *attempting* to

[1] *Psychology*, Part II. ch. iv.

escape are of like *nature;* showing, as they do, no *perception* of the whereabouts of the *pursuer*. On the other hand, the *movements* of a crab or a fish when *alarmed*, are, like those of all higher *creatures*, away from the *object* to be *escaped*. The *particular direction* of something in the *environment* is *responded* to by *appropriately-adjusted motions* of the *organism*— the *correspondence* is *comparatively special*,"[1]—
though 95 of the 124 words, nearly 77 *per cent.*, are Teutonic, yet of the 71 different words, only 46 or less than 65 *per cent.* are Teutonic.[2] Once more, a laughable story is told of a certain Englishman, so strong in his love of Church and State, that he could brook nothing Roman, lest it should prove Popish. Declaiming against innovations in the Prayer Book, he cried out, "Give me the good old Anglo-Saxon 'Table of Proper Lessons.'"

189. (2) English has, no doubt, a large proportion of short words; and the advantages they possess over longer ones are clear,—(*a*) economy of space in printing and of time in speaking, (*b*) compactness of structure, (*c*) simplicity and clearness of meaning. But here again *other things must be equal.* (*a*) When addressed to the ear, (perhaps, even when written,) an unbroken series of short words leaves the mind but little chance to catch the thought expressed. One word follows another so rapidly, that the listener's attention is distracted, and he has no little difficulty in grasping the meaning intended. Long words on the other hand, are often recognized in their context by their first or their first two syllables; and the mind is thus allowed the time occupied in uttering (or reading) the remaining syllables in which to catch the idea. Thus the truest economy is served, as it often is, by the largest expenditure.[3] (*b*) For the same reason, the closest compactness of structure is not always desirable. True terseness implies grace and elegance,

---

[1] *Psychology*, III. vi.

[2] *Pool*, a Celtic word, is counted against Spencer, but *random*, French from the Teutonic, in his favor.

[3] Proverbs, xiii. 7.

qualities impossible, perhaps, unless variety of tone, accent, and movement is obtained. Even in verse, with all its advantages of regular rhythm, a succession of monosyllables is often bald to an extreme. Thus,—

" Think not that strength lies in the big round word,
 Or that the brief and plain must needs be weak.
To whom can this be true, who once has heard
 The cry for help, the tongue that all men speak
When want, or woe, or fear, is in the throat,
 So that each word gasped out is like a shriek
Pressed from the sore heart, or a strange wild note
 Sung by some fay or fiend ! There is a strength
Which dies if stretched too far or spun too fine,
 Which has more height than breadth, more depth than length,
Let but this force of thought and speech be mine,
 And he that will may take the sleek, fat phrase,
Which glows but burns not, though it beam and shine—
 Light, but no heat—a flash, but not a blaze ! "[1]

Or, compare with each other—

(1)   "That is a step
On which I must fall down, or else o'erleap,
For in my way it lies. Stars, hide your fires ;
Let not light see my black and deep desires :
The eye wink at the hand ; yet let that be,
Which the eye fears, when it is done, to see."[2]

(2) " Me thought I heard a voice cry 'Sleep no more !
Macbeth does murder sleep,' the innocent sleep,
Sleep that knits up the ravell'd sleeve of care,
The death of each day's life, sore labour's bath,
Balm of hurt minds, great nature's second course,
Chief nourisher in life's feast."[2]

In prose, the monotony of accent due to an unbroken succession of short words may even set up a regular rhythm out of all keeping with the subject and the character of the work.[3] (c) Short words are not always simple

---
[1] Addison Alexander, in Marsh, II. 98.—One of two sonnets written to illustrate the capabilities of the monosyllable. They are not, says Marsh, " models to be followed in the selection of words."

[2] *Macbeth*, I. iv. 48 and II. ii. 35.   [3] ¿¿ 158 ff, above.

or even clear; nor are long words necessarily abstruse or obscure. *Faith, sin, scorn, doubt, wit, humor,* are no easier to define than *confidence, trespass, derision, hesitation, ingenuity, pleasantry;* and *affection, cataract, imagined, never-lighted* are as easy to understand as *love, falls, fancied, unlit.* The child knows *gingerbread* quite as well as *cake;* and the baby calls a *dog boo-boo* or *bow-wow.* In fact, the length of a word is a mere accident,—an accident that would hardly have attracted attention, had not so many abstruse or technical terms been polysyllabic, and had not pedants and pretenders fallen into the error of supposing that longer words are necessarily dignified and graceful. The evil in many long words is their unfamiliarity or their absurd pretentiousness;[1] but these faults are not invariably cured by the use of monosyllables. The only valid rule in regard to length of words, is, as in regard to their derivation, to choose the words that best express the thought intended. Especially, in speaking to the young or the ignorant, a wilful selection of short words, like a wilful simplicity of style, often exposes the speaker to a charge of undervaluing the capacity of his listeners. Besides, the advantage that a natural diction gives the speaker by way of stimulus to the hearer, is literally thrown away, and success in speaking correspondingly endangered. Dr. E. A. Freeman's *General Sketch of History* loses much of its value by this mannerism.[2] For example;—

England *had a good deal to do* with the Western Empire during the time of the Saxon Emperors.—Olaf was persuaded to become a Christian and to make peace with England; *so* he *went home* to Norway and began to *bring in* Christianity there. —He [Sforza] *was one of* a class of men of whom *there were then many* in Italy, mercenary generals who *went about with bands* of soldiers *hiring themselves out* to *fight for* any prince or commonwealth *that would pay them.*

[1] § 113, *above.* [2] Dr. Freeman is also excessively Anglo-Saxon.

190. (3) Vocabulary varies with the thought to be expressed, the subject of the composition, the purpose of the work, the mental capacity of the reader, the feelings natural to the writer or to the characters speaking, and, doubtless, with other circumstances. Hence, Swift's statement that monotony is a sign not only of verbal and mental poverty, but also of insensibility. It is "out of the heart" that "the mouth speaketh," and in no sense more truly than in that intended here. To stimulate a reader, one must be deeply stirred oneself.

2. The Number of Words.

191. The number of words required to express a given thought varies, perhaps, more than any other feature of discourse. At one time, every added word spoils the effect; at another, the writer must grow all but garrulous. "Brevity is," indeed, "the soul of wit"; but what constitutes Brevity in a given case? Had Dr. Campbell reflected further, he would surely have been less "certain that of whatever kind the sentiment be, witty, humorous, grave, animated, or sublime, the more briefly it is expressed the energy is the greater, or the sentiment is the more enlivened, and the particular quality for which it is eminent the more displayed." The burning glass does, indeed, (as Campbell goes on to say,) collect more rays of the sun into one focus, the smaller that focus is; the liquor distilled is the stronger, the further the distillation is carried; but sometimes one wants diffused light and whiskey well-watered. The usual belief that Brevity implies the smallest number of words possible, is much mistaken, and has led many a good man into ambiguity and other violations of clearness, actually defeating his purpose in writing. No doubt, faults in the direction of excess are far more common than those in the direction of deficiency; but, here again, the truest economy is often

in the largest expenditure—sometimes in apparent waste. The true doctrine undoubtedly is that a composition should contain every *necessary* word, but not one word more—every word necessary, not only to express the thought intended, but to express it in the way, to the end, under the characterization, *etc.*, intended. Judicious BREVITY does not reside at a fixed point midway between DEFICIENCY, on the one hand, and DIFFUSENESS, on the other: it rather occupies the entire space between these two extremes, sliding now toward that, now toward this, as occasion or sufficient reason may warrant. The opposing considerations in any case are like opposing forces in nature, and Brevity is their *resultant*. Among these considerations are Grammatical and Rhetorical Precision, Clearness and Force,[1] the Kind of Composition; the Purpose in Writing, the Capacity of the Minds addressed, Euphony, Rhythm, *etc.*; but no one of them weighs always on the same side of the scale. The student can not be given an absolute rule: he must be guided by his best judgment in each special case, remembering that, his chief end being always to communicate thought—whatever his special purpose—Clearness, the prime quality of Style, must ever be aimed at first.

192. For example, the historian Gibbon, writing for scholars —certainly for students—naturally carries Brevity much farther than Thackeray, the novelist and essayist, whose aim is to instruct by pleasing. Compare;—

"The soil is fruitful, and the climate mild and temperate: the *happy* region was ignorant of earthquake and pestilence: the emperor's throne was turned towards the East, and a golden wolf on the top of a spear seemed to guard the entrance of his tent. . . . 'The Turks,' he said, 'are not equal in number to one hundredth part of the inhabitants of China. If we balance their power, and elude their armies, it is because we *wander without any fixed habitations in the exercise of war and hunting. Are we strong? we advance and conquer: are we feeble? we re-*

---
[1] §§ 251 and 262, *below*.

lire and are concealed. . . . No chastisement could be inflicted too severe for *the rare and inexpiable guilt of cowardice.*"[1]

"'I hear,' said he, '*that* there has actually been no war between us of France and you *men* of England for *well* nigh fifty year. Ours has ever been a nation of warriors. And besides her regular men-at-arms, 't is said the English *of the present time* have more than a hundred thousand *of* archers with weapons that *will* carry *for* half a mile. And a multitude have come amongst us of late from a great Western country, never *so much as* heard of in my time—valiant men and great drawers of the long bow, *and they say they* have ships in armour that no shot can penetrate. Is it so? Wonderful; wonderful! The best armour, gossips, is a stout heart. * * * Of late, there came amongst us a good knight, Messire de Cambronne, who fought against you *English* in *the country of* Flanders, being captain of the guard *of my Lord the King of France*, in a famous battle where you English would have been utterly routed but for the succour of the Prussian heathen. This Messire de Cambronne, when bidden to yield *by you of England,* answered *this,* "The guard dies but never surrenders;" and fought *a* long *time afterwards,* as became a good knight.'"[2]

The difference, it will be noted, is not merely in the words italicized; it pervades the entire structure of the two passages.

193. So, in a single work, different passages will vary as to brevity. Compare,—

>   (1) "Then echo-like our voices rang;
>   We sung, though every eye was dim,
>   A merry song we sang with him
>   Last year: impetuously we sang:
>
>   "We ceased: a gentler feeling crept
>   Upon us: surely rest is meet:
>   'They rest,' we said, 'their sleep is sweet,'
>   And silence follow'd, and we wept."
>
>   (2) "My own dim life should teach me this,
>   That life shall live forevermore,
>   Else earth is darkness at the core,
>   And dust and ashes all that is;
>
>   "This round of green, this orb of flame,
>   Fantastic beauty; such as lurks
>   In some wild Poet, when he works
>   Without a conscience or an aim."[3]

---

[1] Gibbon, ch. xlii.   [2] Thackeray, *Roundabout Papers, Dessein's.*
[3] Tennyson, *In Memoriam,* xxx., xxxiv.

In the first stanza of the first passage, the narrative moves naturally forward, and no ellipsis would be tolerable; but, with silence, and while the gentler feeling crept upon the singers, came reflections, that, no doubt, presented themselves as brokenly as Tennyson details them. In the second quotation, the nature of the thought explains the condensation.

194. Hence, Violations of Brevity result from Deficiency as well as from Excess. On either side they occasion *obscurity, ambiguity, imprecision,*[1] *feebleness, flatness, tediousness;* the vice of the construction lying really in these effects, not in the number of words used. For example, Robert Browning, it is often said, is "*caviare to the general.*" And why? Surely, not alone because the subject-matter of his poetry is abstruse: the riddles that he sets his readers are quite as often due to the excessive condensation of his style.[2] Even in his best work, his translations from Euripides, the sense is not always clear; while in his own dramas, especially *Aristophanes' Apology*, he is often unpardonably difficult.[3] Longfellow, too, usually as limpid as a mountain brook, confuses his reader now and then in *The Divine Comedy* —a translation, to be sure, of a work none too easy of comprehension in the original.[2]

195. On the side of Excess, Violations of Brevity are (1) TAUTOLOGY, unnecessary *repetition;* (2) PLEONASM, or REDUNDANCY, unnecessary *addition;* (3) VERBOSITY, unnecessary *fullness.* Verbosity includes (*a*) *Circumlocution*, or *Periphrasis*, "the long way round" for "the short way home;" (*b*) *Paraphrase*, intentional amplification; (*c*) *Prolixity*, the accumulation of unimportant details or of things that may be assumed to be known.

---

[1] A rare word, but one that expresses most accurately the opposite of *precision*.

[2] See § 197, *below*.

[3] Yet Browning can be as clear as sunlight when he gives his thought room. Such poems as *Incident of the French Camp* and *The Boy and The Angel* confuse no one.

Tautology and Pleonasm can generally be corrected by *omitting* the unnecessary words; Verbosity can be cured only by *recasting* the whole work. For example;—

(1) TAUTOLOGY: A *universal* panacea for *all* the ills that flesh is heir to.—It was almost intolerable *to be borne.*—The messenger brought tidings of good *news.*[1]—Perspicuous and *transparent.*—If he lives to become their *future* emperor.—A neutral is bound to use *due* diligence.

(2) PLEONASM: The reason why witchcraft was ridiculed was *because, etc.*—Until we *both* meet face to face in heaven.—Her position was by no means *of an* agreeable *character.*—I wrote you a *letter.*—*Wet* waves, *white* milk, the *glorious* sun, *ivory* teeth.[2]

(3) VERBOSITY: (*a*) **Circumlocution**;—Pope professed *to have learned his poetry from* Dryden, whom, *whenever* an opportunity *was presented,* he praised *through the whole period of his*[3] *existence* with unvaried liberality. (=Pope professed himself the pupil of Dryden, whom he lost no opportunity of praising with unvaried liberality).[4]

(*b*) **Paraphrase**;—Wherefore he that shall not only hear and receive these my instructions, but also remember, and consider, and practise, and live according to them, such a man may be compared to one that builds his house upon a rock; for as a house founded upon a rock stands unshaken and firm against all the assaults of rains and floods and storms, so the man who, in his life and conversation, actually practises and obeys my instructions, will firmly resist all the temptations of the devil, the allurements of pleasure, and the terrors of persecution, and shall be able to stand in the day of judgment, and be rewarded of God.[5]

[1] "*Good* tidings of great joy" (Luke ii. 10) is correct under § 196, (1), *below*.

[2] But see § 157. (2) (*c*), *above*. Prose, however, usually avoids such epithets.

[3] Whose?

[4] Quoted and corrected by Bain, I. ii. Bain omits "with . . . liberality;" but the sense of the original is not completely reproduced without this phrase.

[5] Cf. Matt. vii. 24, 25.—Campbell says the author of this rendering of the text "is far from deserving to be accounted either the most verbose, or the least judicious of the tribe" of paraphrasts. Franklin ridicules this "tribe" in his *Proposed New Version of the Bible.* The Bible needs modernizing, he says ironically. How much better it would read, if Satan, in Job i. 9, should not say, "Doth Job fear God for nought?" but "Does Your Majesty imagine that Job's good conduct is the effect of mere personal attachment and affection?" (Works, Ed. Sparks, Boston, 1836, ii. 166.)

(c) **Prolixity**;—I have always longed to know what that story was (or what collection of histories), which a lady had in her mind to whom a servant of mine applied for a place, when I was breaking up my establishment once and going abroad.[1] (=What story or collection of histories could a lady have had in mind to whom a servant of mine once applied for a place!)[2]

> "But, O my Muse, what numbers wilt thou find
> To sing the furious troops in battle join'd?
> Methinks I hear the drum's tumultuous sound
> The victor's shouts and dying groans confound;
> The dreadful burst of cannon rend the skies,
> And all the thunder of the battle rise.
> 'Twas then great Marlborough's mighty soul was prov'd,
> That, in the shock of charging hosts unmov'd,
> Amidst confusion, honor, and despair,
> Examin'd all the dreadful scenes of war;
> In peaceful thought the field of death survey'd,
> To fainting squadrons sent the timely aid,
> Inspir'd repuls'd battalions to engage,
> And taught the doubtful battle where to rage."[3]

196. The following exceptions, however, must be noted. They are, in fact, only apparent; for they are fully justified by the importance of the ends they achieve:—

(1) **Synonyms**, especially when derived from different languages, are often combined to express a thought not otherwise expressed so fully or so emphatically; as, *act*[4] and *deed*,[5] *ways*[5] and *means*,[4] *acknowledge*[5] and *confess*,[4] *assemble*[4] and *meet together*,[5] *head*[5] and *front*,[4] *end*[5] and *aim*,[4] *aid*[4] and *comfort*,[4] the *vision*[4] and the *faculty*[4] *divine*,[4] *aid*[4] and *abet*.[6]

(2) **Clearness or other rhetorical ends** may be promoted by violations of Brevity; as, The poet is *born, not made.*—Your sensibility *is your livelihood*, my worthy friend. You feel a pang of pleasure or pain? It is noted in your memory, and some day or other *makes its appearance in your manuscript.*—You tell me that the Venus de Medici is beautiful, or Jacob Omnium is tall. Que diable! *Can't I judge for myself? Haven't I eyes and a foot-rule?*—How *hospitable* they were, those Southern men! In the North itself *the welcome was not kinder*, as I, who *have eaten Northern and Southern salt*, can testify.—Lest at any time they should see *with their eyes*, and hear *with their ears*, and should understand *with their heart*, and should be converted,

---

[1] Thackeray, *Roundabout Papers, On a Hundred Years Hence.*
[2] But see § 196. (2), below.   [3] Addison, *The Campaign.*
[4] Latin.   [5] Anglo-Saxon.   [6] Scandinavian.

and I should heal them.—Addison describes a fan as "this *little modish machine*"; Swift called Defoe "the *fellow that was pilloried,* I have forgot his name"; Milton suggests, not only by a periphrasis, but by a clear tautology, the height from which Vulcan fell,—

> "*from morn*
> *To noon he fell, from noon to dewy eve,*
> *A summer's day; and with the setting sun*
> *Dropt from the zenith like a falling star*
> *On Lemnos, the Ægean isle;*"

and, instead of *chancel*, Tennyson writes—

> "*where the kneeling hamlet drains*
> *The chalice of the grapes of God.*"

Euphemisms are often long ;—*to fall asleep; the shadow fear'd of man; the reeling Faun; are borne to their long home; the undiscover'd country, from whose bourn no traveller returns;*

> " She likes herself, yet others hates
> For that which in herself she prizes ;[1]
> And, while she laughs at them, forgets
> She is *the thing that she despises.*"

For emphasis, such expressions are common as, '*Twill be a long day in which* that happens (=I doubt that's ever happening); set himself up above *all that was ever called sovereign in England.*

(3) **Strong feeling** often disposes the mind to dwell upon the object of the feeling; as, I am *astonished*, I am *shocked*, to hear such principles *confessed;* to hear them *avowed* in this house and this country.—All is *little*, and *low*, and *mean* among us.—And, so speaking, I say that to countenance the Brahminical idolatry, and to discountenance that religion which has done so much to promote justice, *and* mercy, *and* freedom, *and* arts, *and* sciences, *and* good government, *and* domestic happiness, *which* has struck off the chains of the slave, *which* has mitigated the horrors of war, *which* has raised women from servants and playthings into companions and friends, [*I say that to countenance that religion and discountenance this*] is to commit high treason against humanity and civilization.—Cicero uses four nearly equivalent verbs to describe Catiline's flight from Rome, *abiit, excessit, evasit, erupit.*

(4) **Epithets** may be used sparingly for rhetorical effect ; as, I can't pretend to quote scenes from the *splendid* Congreve's

---
[1] Note, too, the circumlocution in this line.

plays.[1]—The moon's *soft* light stands in striking contrast with the *glaring* light of the sun or the *lurid* flames of a conflagration.—*Bloody* revolution, *practical* man, *battle-torn* greenback, may point a moral or even a sophism.—The phrase, the dollar of our *fathers*, aimed to give respectability to silver as a legal tender; the nickname, the dollar of our *daddies*, may yet consign the coin to the melting pot.

197. On the side of Deficiency, Violations of Brevity have never been classified; but the following specifications may, perhaps, lead to such a classification;—

(1) **One part** of a compound or joint expression, the whole of which is usual in expressing the sense intended may be omitted; as, Treason against the United States consists only in levying war against them, or in giving *aid*[2] to the enemy.—So, *butt-end* of a gun or a club, rather than *butt* or *end*.

(2) **Necessary words,**—yet such as the context or the evident meaning of the sentence might supply, were the sense only clear,—may be omitted; as, A little *dinner, not more than the Muses*, with all the guests clever, and some pretty, offers human life and human nature under very favorable circumstances.[3]

(3) **The structure of the sentence** as a whole may be too compact; as, Above the esplanade, on points of rock forming shelves, the women looked down on the dance, in holiday costume; a great scarlet hood, a body embroidered in silver, or in silk with violet flowers; a yellow, long-fringed shawl; a black petticoat hanging in folds, close to the figure, and white woolen gaiters.[4]—I have seen people who laughed at the music; "the air is monotonous," they say, "contrary to all rule, it has no ending; those notes are false." At Paris that may be; but here, no. Have you remarked that wild and original expression? How it suits the landscape!—Even Poetry, which courts brevity, may carry this contraction too far;—

---

[1] Thackeray, *English Humorists.*—A world of sarcasm is in that word *splendid.* Congreve was a sad example of the brilliant man of the world in that most dissolute age which he himself portrays.

[2] The mind expects *and comfort.* (See § 196, (1), *above.*)

[3] Benjamin Disraeli (quoted by A. S. Hill).—The clew to the puzzle was brought to the author by Mr. R. W. Davids, (Sopho., U. of Pa., 1880-81; B.S., 1883,) from Isaac Disraeli's *Curiosities of Literature,* Am. Ed. 1872, II. p.434:— "The elegant Romans declared that a repast should not consist of less in number than the Graces, nor of more than the Muses."

[4] Taine, *A Tour through the Pyrenees,* translated by Fiske.—The meaning is clear, but condensation is carried very far.

"Shall I sonnet-sing you about myself?
  Do I live in a house you would like to see?
  Is it scant of gear, has it store of pelf?
  'Unlock my heart with a sonnet-key?'

"Invite the world as my betters have done?
  'Take notice: this building remains on view,
  Its suites of reception every one,
  Its private apartment and bedroom too;

"'For a ticket, apply to the Publisher?'
  No: thanking the public, I must decline—
  A peep through my window, if folks prefer;
  But, please you, no foot over threshold of mine!

"'Hoity, toity! a street to explore,
  Your house the exception! "*With this same key
  Shakespeare unlocked his heart*," once more!'
  Did Shakespeare? If so, the less Shakespeare he!"[1]

"' As he willed, he worked:
  And, as he worked, he wanted not, be sure,
  Triumph his whole life through, submitting work
  To work's right judges, never to the wrong,
  To competency, not ineptitude.
  When he had run life's proper race and worked
  Quite to the stade's end, there remained, to try
  Its turning, should strength dare the double course.
  Half the diaulos reached, the hundred plays
  Accomplished, force in its rebound sufficed
  To lift along the athlete and insure
  A second wreath, proposed by fools for first,
  The statist's olive as the poet's bay.
  Wiselier, he suffered not confuse his sight,
  Retard his pace a twofold aim, at once
  Poet and statist; though the multitude
  Girded him ever.'"[2]

"''Twas at the time when Juno was enraged,
  For Semele, against the Theban blood,
  As she already more than once had shown,
  So reft of reason Athamas became,
    That, seeing his own wife with children twain
    Walking encumbered upon either hand,
  He cried: 'Spread out the nets, that I may take
    The lioness and her whelps upon the passage';
  And then extended his unpitying claws,
  Seizing the first, who had the name Learchus,
  And whirled him round, and dashed him on a rock;
  And she, with the other burthen drowned herself."[3]

---

[1] Robert Browning, *House*, stt. 1-3 and 10.—Note especially the last stanza.
[2] Id., *Aristophanes' Apology*, ll. 212 ff.
[3] Dante, *Inferno*, xxx., (translated by Longfellow.)

Very concise prose accounts of Bacchus and Athamas (needed to understand these verses) fill twenty-eight lines, two hundred and fifty words, in Anthon's *Classical Dictionary*, as opposed to the twelve short lines, ninety-one words, of this passage.

198. The Means to Brevity are too numerous to be mentioned in detail. Some have already been described; others will be spoken of below. The following seem to require special notice here ;—

(1) **Aptly-Chosen words**[1]; as, One of the gentlemen *noted down the proceedings of the journey, for which* Hogarth *and a brother artist made drawings*. (That is, One of the gentlemen *took notes, and* Hogarth, *etc*.)

(2) **Compact grammatical structure**; as, *It would appear that they slept most of them* in one room, *and the chronicler of the party describes them all as waking* at seven o'clock, *and telling* each other their dreams. (That is, *Most of them seem to have slept* in one room; and, *according to the chronicler of the party, all woke* at seven o'clock and *told* each other their dreams.)—*I have thus gone through the circumstances of a life* which till lately passed pretty much to my own satisfaction, and I hope in no respect *injurious* to any other man.—(That is, *Such, then, was my life*, which till lately . . . satisfaction and (I hope) in no respect injuriously to . . . .)

(3) **Suggestion or Implication**; as, We Indian children were consigned to a school of which our deluded parents had heard a favourable report, but which was governed by a horrible little tyrant, who made our young lives so miserable *that I remember kneeling by my little bed of a night, and saying*, "*Pray God, I may dream of my mother!*"—Most of us tell old stories *in our families*. The *wife* and *children* laugh for the hundredth time. The *old servants* nod and smile a recognition at the well-known anecdote.[2]

(4) **Figures of speech**, especially *Antithesis, Metaphor, Interrogation, etc*.[3]

(5) **Apt Quotation**, especially of *familiar* (but not *trite*) passages; as, The bells [of Antwerp cathedral] go on ringing.

---

[1] § 179, *above.*
[2] Even in Thackeray's time, the implication in "*old* servants" was so doubtful that the text reads, "old servants (though old servants are fewer every day.)"
[3] §§ 235 ff, *below.*

Quot vivos vocant, mortuos plangunt, fulgura frangunt;[1] so on to the past and future tenses, and for how many nights, days, and years! Whilst the French were pitching their *fulgura* into Chassé's citadel, the bells went on ringing quite cheerfully. Whilst the scaffolds were up and guarded by Alva's soldiery, and regiments of penitents, blue, black, and gray, poured out of churches and convents, droning their dirges, and marching to the place of the Hôtel de Ville, where heretics and rebels were to meet their doom, the bells up yonder were chanting at their appointed half-hours and quarters, and rang the *mauvais quart d'heure* for many a poor soul. This bell can see as far away as the towers and dykes of Rotterdam. That one can call a greeting to St. Ursula's at Brussels, and toss a recognition to that one at the town hall of Oudenarde, and remember how after a great struggle there a hundred and fifty years ago the whole plain was covered with the flying French cavalry—Burgundy, and Berri, and the Chevalier of St. George flying like the rest. "What is your clamour about Oudenarde?" says another bell (Bob Major *this* one must be). "Be still, thou querulous old clapper! *I* can see over to Hougoumont and St. John. And about forty-five years since, I rang all through one Sunday in June, when there was such a battle going on in the corn-fields there, as none of you others ever heard tolled of. Yes, from morning service until after vespers, the French and English were at it, ding-dong." And then, calls of business intervening, the bells have to give up their private jangle, resume their professional duty, and sing their hourly chorus out of *Dinorah.*

By this principle, also, may be explained the value of some proverbs and the offensiveness of others. There is, indeed, a flavor of vulgarity in the continual quotation of trite, over-worked sayings of this sort; but there is great effectiveness, and sometimes a high degree of elegance, (as Trench has shown,) in the apt quotation of sayings which, while they are on the people's tongues, are yet not hackneyed by use.

---

[1] A common inscription on bells in the old cities is *Vivos voco, mortuos plango, fulgura frango.* Without the quotation the paragraph would lack connection and significance.

II.

THE SENTENCE.[1]

199. The importance of a correct structure for the sentence can hardly be overestimated. Success in this particular naturally leads to success in other respects; since correctness of form in every sentence implies a high degree of perfection for the whole composition. At the same time, sentence-building is not the whole of Style. "Take care of the Sentence," say some teachers, "and the Composition will take care of itself;" but the maxim is only half true. There is more in the construction of discourse than the construction of its several divisions; and it is only when the work as a whole—not as made up of parts—is completed, that composition (in its fullest signification) can be said to have taken place. This will appear the more clearly, the further the student advances in either the theory or the practice of his art.

1. THE ORDER OF WORDS AND CLAUSES IN THE SENTENCE.

200. In every language, Grammar teaches certain principles of Syntax—the *marshalling* of words and clauses. These principles Rhetoric accepts, and then proceeds to base on them laws of its own for the greater efficiency of discourse. For English, these laws are four in number;—

201. (1) *Words must stand as near as possible to the words they modify.* For example;—

The estates of the province and the magistracy of the city appealed *to his Majesty* from the decision of the Duke. The case did not *directly* concern the interests of religion, for although

---

[1] § 170, *above*.

the heretical troubles of 1566 furnished the nominal motives of the condemnation, the resistance to the tenth and twentieth penny was the real crime for which they were suffering. The King, *therefore*, although far from clement, was not extremely rigorous. He refused the object of the appeal, but he did not put the envoys to death[1] by whom it was brought to Madrid. This would have certainly[2] been the case *in matters strictly religious*, or *even had the commissioners arrived two years before*, but *even* Philip believed, *perhaps*, that *for the moment almost enough* innocent blood had been shed.

The words italicized are better placed than they could be anywhere else in their sentences; but, in the following examples, the italicized words are misplaced;—

The clergy, *too*,[3] of the Province, having invoked the bull "*in Coena Domini*," by which, *etc.*—The hundredth penny *would amount*,[4] as he calculated, to at least five millions.— Occasion will presently arise to show how this has happened, *with some detail*.[5]

202. The want of inflections in English gives to the position of words in that language special importance. Were English words "ticketed," as Latin words are, much less would be sacrificed by bad arrangement; but in a language whose syntax is almost wholly "flat" or "phrasal," (determined by the position of its words or phrases,) misinterpretation is only too likely to follow disorder. Confusion, ambiguity—all the offences against that prime quality of Style, Clearness—wait upon misarrangement, and betray the author to his worst enemies, the readers who, because his language is not unmistakably clear, force upon it a meaning he never

---

[1] Or, *put to death the envoys?*   [2] *Certainly have been?*

[3] *Too* really limits the phrase *the clergy of the province*, and ought, therefore, to stand after *province*. If it would then seem to limit only that word, and the emphasis on *clergy* would be lost, the words *of the province* must be omitted or, perhaps, be expressed by the adjective *provincial*.

[4] Correctly arranged by Motley.

[5] Lanier, *The Science of English Verse*, p. 23.—The more singular an oversight, because the author generally shows a remarkable command of language.

intended it to bear. Strike out the commas after *calculated* and *happened*, in the two last examples in § 201, and the sentences have a meaning quite different from that which the eye, helped by the commas, sees that they have. But how shall these commas help the ear of a hearer? Besides, punctuation is a lame support for the meaning of a sentence,—a communication of thought from mind to mind.

203. (2) *Modifiers commonly precede the words they modify;* as,—

"When *rosy* plumelets tuft the larch,
    And *rarely* pipes the *mounted* thrush;
    Or *underneath the barren brush*
Flits by the *sea-blue* bird of March."

"Oh that *this too too solid* flesh would melt!"

But inversions are common, and not only for emphasis;—

(*a*) In poetry, for the sake of the peculiar effect desired or of metre; as, the Table *Round*,

"An holy-water-sprinckle, dipt in deowe,
With which she sprinckled favours *manifold*."
"By some soft touch *invisible*."

(*b*) Even in prose;—(α) When the modifier is phrasal; as, a thing *to be well attended to*, formulas *so widely divergent*,[1] not *of itself* a strong fortress, will lop out *year by year* the weakest, was heard *on all sides;* (β), though very rarely, when the modifier is flat; as, devastation *universal*, seed *royal*.

204. (3) *The Principle of Emphasis.* (*a*) In all languages, inflected or not, any unusual order of words or clauses attracts attention, and so declares[2] the meaning

---

[1] Really a predicate (formulas *that are* so widely divergent). Cf.—

"A forester of Dean,
Wet from the woods, with notice of a hart
*Taller than all his fellows, milky-white,
First seen that day;*"

Participles are often so construed. The omission results, however, in a postpositive modifier.

[2] The Greek word for *declares* in this sense is ἐμφαίνει (*emphainei*), and from it is derived the noun *emphasis*.

more strongly. (*b*) It is a law of thought that the beginning and the end of a sentence are its most emphatic places, and, hence, that special care must be taken both *to put emphatic words or clauses into these emphatic places* and *to keep out of the emphatic places matter that is not of particular importance*. "As in an army on the march, the fighting columns are placed front and rear, and the baggage in the centre, so the emphatic parts of a sentence should be found either in the beginning or the end, subordinate and matter-of-course expressions in the middle."[1] Thus ;—

(*a*) **Unusual Arrangements** ; (α) By *inversion ;* as, *Within*, the house is full of pictures, engravings, etc.—*Silver and gold* have I none.

"And ever met him on his way
With wishes, thinking, *here to-day*,
Or *here to-morrow will* he come."

The Rev. T. T. L. was, *if ever man was*, a religious genius.— Among these [my friends], *though I did not personally know him*, I can not but reckon him. (β) By *prefixing* a conjunction, an interjection, the case of address, or something else *unemphatic*, in order to throw special stress on what immediately follows ;[2] as, I am very sorry that I was not at home when you were so kind as to call. When *next* you come to town, *etc*.— Alas! that *any one* should ever feel either teaching or learning to be a drudgery !

"O friend, who camest to thy goal
So early, leaving me behind,
I would the great world grew like thee,
Who grewest not alone in power
And knowledge, but by year and hour
In reverence and in charity."

Of *sarcasm*, as morally distinguished from satire, he was everywhere and always incapable.—Nay, *more*, there is scarcely a handicraft, *etc*.—In like manner, *the imagination* foretells things. (γ) By *intentional repetition, pleonasm, or ellipsis ;* as,

"Alone, *alone*, all *all alone*,
Alone on a wide *wide* sea !

---

[1] Bain (Am. Ed.), p. 135.
[2] This construction has been aptly compared to the poise or halt of the blacksmith's hammer, when he would change the rhythm of his blows.

The lad can not leave his father: for if he should leave *his father, his father* would die.[1]—Haste ye, *and go* up to my father.—Your fathers, where are they?

> "Unwatch'd, the garden bough shall sway,
> Unloved, the sun-flower, shining fair,
>   *Ray round* with flames her disk of seed,
>   And many a rose-carnation[2] *feed*
> With summer spice the humming air;
> Unloved, by many a sandy bar,
>   The brook shall babble down the plain,
>   At noon, or when the lesser wain
> Is twisting round the polar star;
> Uncared for,[3] *gird* the windy grove."

(*b*) **Emphatic Places**;—"*What a pretty snuff-box!*" he remarked, as I handed him mine, which *I am still old-fashioned enough to carry.*—And *this* I declare *upon my honour.*—I appeal to Mr. Hart, *the landlord*—I appeal to James, the *respectful and intelligent waiter, if this statement is not true.*—Boy! it was happy for thy grandam that she loved me *not.*—Nay (for I am making a clean breast, and liberating my soul), perhaps of all the novel-spinners now extant, the present speaker is the *most addicted to preaching.* I cry "peccavi" *loudly and heartily.*—*Sir*, said I, knowing him to be an old friend whom I had met.—*Far, far away into the past I look*, and see the little town with its friendly glimmer.—The good old ladies would have pronounced her to be *a little idle thing, occupied with her silly books and neglecting her housekeeping.*

205. "There is nothing more urgently required for the improvement of our sentences," says Mr. Minto,[4] "than a constant study to observe this principle. It is difficult to conceive when there would be an impropriety in placing important words where the reader naturally expects to find them. The reader's attention falls easily and naturally upon what stands at the beginning and what stands at the end, unless [this is] obviously introductory in the one case, or obviously rounding off in the other. The beginning and the end are the natural places for important words. This arrangement is conducive both to clearness and to elegance: it prevents confusion, and is an aid to justness of emphasis. As

---

[1] Gen. xliv. 22.   [2] Sc. *shall.*   [3] Sc. *the brook shall.*   [4] *Manual*, p. 10.

important words need not occupy absolutely the first place nor absolutely the last, but at the beginning may be preceded by qualifying clauses, and at the end may be followed by unemphatic appendages that are not of a nature to distract attention, we are not required to make unnatural inversions or to take unidiomatic liberties of any kind. If a writer finds a construction stiff and unnatural, he may be sure that he has not succeeded in throwing the emphasis where it should be thrown; if he has not buried the important words in the depth of the sentence, he has probably done worse: he has probably drawn off the reader's attention from the words altogether, and fixed it where it should seldom or never be fixed—upon the form."

206. Yet Mr. Minto thinks "the following out of this principle" far from easy. One may "hang as long over his sentences as Mr. Tennyson is said to hang over his lines, and yet commit blunders after all." Thus;—

We spake anon of the inflated style of some writers. What also if there is an *afflated* style,—when a writer is like a Pythoness on her oracle tripod, and *mighty words, words which he can not help, come blowing, and bellowing, and whistling, and moaning* through the speaking pipes of his bodily organ?[1]

> " Thus he came at length
> To find a stronger faith his own;
> And Power was with him in the night,
> Which makes the darkness and the light,
> And dwells not in the light alone,
> But in the darkness and the cloud,
> As over Sinai's peaks of old,
> While Israel made their gods of gold,
> Altho' the trumpet blew so loud."[2]

[1] Thackeray, *Roundabout Papers.*—The thought is that the writer is *taken possession of*—like the Pythoness. Arrange, therefore, "oracle tripod, and through the speaking pipes of his bodily organ come *blowing, and bellowing, and whistling, and moaning, mighty words, words which he can not help.*" Thus arranged, the passage has the effect of a climax. (§ 278, *below.*)

[2] Tennyson, *In Memoriam,* xcvi.—Verse has, of course, its liberties; but the order of this sentence weakens it more and more from "night" on,—certainly from the word "cloud." In l. 4, *darkness* is the emphatic word; the sense evidently being, not only the light but the darkness as well. (Compare the next two lines; but remember that this criticism refers only to the thought expressed, not to the words as constituting a verse of poetry.)

207. The secret of success in applying this principle of Emphasis lies in long-continued drill,—in practice controlled by the resolve never to leave a sentence unfinished in this respect. The evil results are least, of course, when sentences thus misconstructed are spoken; for the speaker's voice or manner generally interprets them. But no such help is at hand for the reader: he must trust wholly to the position of the words or clauses; and, if unemphatic words get into emphatic places, or emphatic words into unemphatic places, the meaning can often be detected only by a sort of divination. With the help of the context, to be sure, one can sometimes make out what the writer must have meant; but the setting of such puzzles always threatens the author's success, and may prove fatal to it. Thus ;—

If they had *only* imputed to that friend *in after times* certain celestial attributes, how would that have hindered such utterances.[1]—I *merely* allude to it *for the purpose.*—You did not know, poor Anne, when you framed those lofty purposes, that suffering is just as hard to bear whether one is noble or ignoble, good or bad. In the face of danger the heart is roused, and in the exaltation of determination forgets its pain; it is the long monotony of dangerless days that tries the spirit hardest.[2]

208. (4) *Modifying clauses either precede or follow their principals.* The *natural*, or *indirect*, order,—the order most common, perhaps, in free, unguarded, informal composition—*postpones* the modifier; the *inverted*, or *direct*, order *anticipates* it. Thus ;—I had a capital half-hour with Jacob Faithful last night, *when the last sheet*

---

[1] Dr. Maurice meant, If it was *only in after times* that they imputed, or, If they had imputed to that friend certain celestial attributes *only in after times.* Such a misstep is rare in the usually firm tread of Dr. Maurice's style.

[2] The emphatic words are, *in the face of danger, in the exaltation of determination,* and *the long monotony of dangerless days.* The last of these three phrases is correctly placed; but few readers, perhaps, are quick enough not, on *first* reading, to emphasize *the heart is roused* and *forgets its pain.*

was corrected, when "Finis" had been written, and [when] the printer's boy, with the copy, was safe in Green Arbour Court; but, *As some bells in a church hard by are making a great holiday clanging in the summer afternoon,* I am reminded.

209. But too much must not be inferred from the words *natural* and *inverted*. Perhaps, as Herbert Spencer suggests,[1] *indirect* and *direct* would be better terms, since these words express the fact of the construction without embarrassing inferences. Certainly it would be most unfortunate to interpret *natural* as implying that the inverted (direct) order is *unnatural*. Style does, indeed, grow more and more direct, as it grows more and more formal,—that is, as it casts aside more and more the *negligé* of conversation or letter-writing, the free, unguarded, informal mode of discourse already mentioned; but neither order is ever unnatural, neither is always better in any style of composition. Monotony and feebleness necessarily result from the excessive use of either; and, hence, however informal a composition may be, it may use both constructions; while no style ought ever to become so formal, so grave or dignified, as wholly to reject the indirect order. Thus, in a humorous letter to the lady he was soon to marry, Dr. Hodgson writes, A host of dresses, *etc.*, are prepared, *which* [= *although they*] *become old-fashioned long before they can be worn out, and the moths fall heirs to half the properties;* but, only a few lines below, By the way, I am not sure whether I told you that, *before you can be married in valid form*, you must pass an examination in Economics. So, in a more formal letter,—I have delayed reply . . . . , *until I should be able*, and, *If the difficulty be insuperable* . . . . , how much greater is *etc.?* Even a philosophical writer like Herbert Spencer uses the indirect order, although (as will appear) the

[1] *Essay on Style.*

direct order is more common in such compositions;[1]— Of the engineers, contractors, and various others concerned, it may be admitted that, though daily custom has induced laxity of principle, yet they would be harshly judged, *were the transactions that may be recorded against them, used as tests.*

210. The reason for prefixing a modifier to its modified word, and a qualifying to a principal clause, has been clearly stated by Herbert Spencer to be *economy of the reader's or hearer's attention.* In this order, he affirms, the whole thought is grasped by the time the last word expressing it has been uttered; as, *a black horse; if A is B, C is D;* whereas, in the other order, a different idea may be conceived by the mind addressed, before the whole thought is uttered; as, *a horse* [bay? grey? brown? no,] *black; C is D,* [always? if X is Y? no,] *if A is B.*[2] The chief reasons for inverting the direct order are *variety* (either *absolute* or *as occasioned by the kind of writing*), *emphasis, etc.* For example, Verse may require the inversion for the sake of either the metre or the rhyme; the Drama and the Novel naturally introduce the indirect order in dialogue; in the first of the following sentences, emphasis requires the words *do much the same* at the end, and, therefore, places the italicized modifiers after the words they modify; in the fourth sentence, the modifier *while . . . . enemy* is last placed apparently for variety's sake; while in the same sentence, the adverb *at . . . . employer* must stand either where it is or (and ludicrously, of course) after *disbelieve :—*

"Men *taken at random from higher and lower ranks,* would, most likely, *if similarly circumstanced,* do much the same. Indeed, the mercantile world might readily recriminate. . . . . Does the condemnation come through the press? The con-

---

[1] And also although the particular writer named is an enthusiastic advocate of anticipation on the principle of economy. (See § 210, *below*.)

[2] But see § 211, *below*.

demned may remind those who write,[1] of the fact that it is not quite honest to utter a positive verdict on a book merely glanced through, or to pen glowing eulogies on the mediocre work of a friend *while slighting the good one of an enemy;* and may further ask whether those who, *at the dictation of an employer*, write what they disbelieve, are not guilty of the serious offence of adulterating public opinion."[2]

211. But all these reasons may tend to directly the opposite conclusions: economy may demand the indirect order; emphasis, *etc.*, the direct order. "Carrying forward each qualifying clause costs some mental effort;" and, hence, when there are several such clauses, or when the time occupied by them is considerable, more is lost by the direct order than is gained, and economy itself requires the indirect order. On the other hand, statements made in principal clauses are generally more emphatic than those found in dependent members; variety may, of course, overrule other considerations on either side; and so on.[3] Nothing will more severely try the student's judgment and taste than to balance the opposing considerations that affect this question.

212. Sometimes the same principal clause is qualified by two or more dependents and it may then be a good plan to distribute the dependent clauses on either side of their principal clause. For example;—

At last, after much fatigue, through deep roads and bad weather, we came, with no small difficulty, to our journey's end;[4] or better, At last, with no small difficulty, and after much fatigue, we came, through deep roads and bad weather, to our journey's end.[5]

[1] Better, *the writers*, in order to avoid the collocation *write of.*

[2] Herbert Spencer, *Essays* (N. Y. 1874), p. 260.

[3] See the examples already given.—The student should be required to give in each case the apparent reason for the order chosen.

[4] Whateley's arrangement of "We came to our journey's end, at last, with no small difficulty, after much fatigue, through deep roads, and bad weather."

[5] Spencer, *Essay on Style*, p. 26.—Spencer points out that to anticipate all the modifiers "would not produce a satisfactory effect": he might have said, would produce an effect as unsatisfactory as that of the original order.

2. THE PERIOD AND THE LOOSE SENTENCE.

213. The principles thus set forth lead directly to the distinction between the *Periodic* and the *Loose* Sentence. When a sentence follows the indirect order, whether of clauses or of words, it is said to be *loose*, or, if the effect of this order is bad, to be *viciously loose*. On the contrary, when predicates precede what they are predicated of, and qualifications come before the words they qualify,— that is, when the order is direct,—the structure is called *periodic*, or, if the effect is bad, *excessively periodic*. The sentence so produced is called *a Period*. Moreover, the predominance of one or the other of these modes of arrangement gives its special character to style, rendering it predominantly loose or predominantly periodic, viciously loose or viciously periodic.

214. Hence, the proper term by which to express the essential character of the Period is *Anticipation*, and not, as is commonly said, *Suspense*. Campbell's definition of the Period, a *complex* sentence in which the meaning is *suspended* until the close, has long since been abandoned in its first part; while, in its second, it has been boldly challenged by one writer, and ingeniously explained away by another. (1) A single example will suffice to show that the periodic effect, even though defined as *suspense*, can be produced in a sentence not complex ;—

In contemplation of her goodness his hard heart melts into pathos, his cold rhyme kindles and glows into poetry, and he falls down on his knees (so to speak) before the angel whose life he had embittered, confesses his own wretchedness and unworthiness, and adores her with cries of remorse and love.[1]

(2) Prof. H. N. Day, defining the periodic structure as "one in which the leading thought of the sentence is presented in the closing member," and the loose order

---

[1] The words *in contemplation of her goodness* are not only emphatic, but modify *all* the following clauses.

as "one in which the sentence terminates with one or more dependent members," cites the following loose sentence, which, however, satisfies Campbell's criterion of suspending the sense till the close;—

"One party had given their whole attention, during several years, to the project not only of enriching themselves and of impoverishing the rest of the nation ; but, also, by these and other means, establishing their dominion under the government and with the favor of a family who were foreigners that they might easily believe they were established on the throne by the good-will and strength of this party alone."

In like manner, Mr. Minto, though he thinks "it is probably difficult to go farther [than Campbell's definition] without committing one's self to general statements that will not apply to every period," yet reaches by his analysis a conclusion virtually the same as Prof. Day's.

215. The word *suspense*, it is true, is no less useful than *anticipation* in expressing the whole doctrine of the Period; for, as *anticipation* suggests the bringing forward of predicates and qualifications, so *suspense* suggests the postponement of the principal (leading) element or member. But the term is not commonly used in this sense. As defined by Campbell, it is the postponement, not of the leading member of the sentence, but of the complete meaning of the sentence for the purpose of better securing the reader's attention. Are readers, then, so hard to engage? Must a reader be enticed with postponements of the *dénouement* in any case, as a balking horse with a wisp of hay? Must a writer resort to unworthy tricks, in order to secure attention? Surely, he should rather trust to the weight, the attractiveness in itself, of the thought he has to communicate. Besides, as already said, *suspense*, if put forward as the *differentia* of the Period, fails to define the peculiar structure intended. If the word is to be used at all, it should be

limited to denote the correlative of *anticipation*—the postponement of the principal elements or members of sentences for economy's sake or for other sufficient reasons.

216. "The effect of the periodic structure is to keep the mind in a state of uniform or increasing tension until the *dénouement*. This is the effect stated in its ultimate and most general form. The effect that a reader is conscious of receiving varies greatly with the nature of the subject matter. When the subject is easy and familiar, the reader, finding the sentence or clause come to an end as soon as his expectations are satisfied, receives an agreeable impression of neatness and finish. When the subject-matter is unfamiliar, or when the suspense is unduly prolonged, the periodic structure is intolerably tedious, or intolerably exasperating, according to the temper of the reader. In impassioned writing the period has a moderating effect, the tension of the mind till the key-word is reached preventing a dissipation of excitement. Gravity, dignity, and such effects are not necessary attributes of the period," [1] but only of long periodic sentences. "A lively interest may be sustained as well as a grave interest." [1] For example;—

(1) My companions were utterly bored, and called down curses on France. Their minds, *strained by the rude passions of politics, by the national arrogance,* [2] *and the stiffness of scriptural morality,* needed repose. They wanted a smiling and flowery country, . . . The sunburnt peasants, *dull of countenance, sitting near a pool of mud,* were disagreeable to them. For repose, they dreamed of pretty cottages set in fresh turf, fringed with rosy honeysuckle." [3]

(2) "*Much as a story which, passing from mouth to mouth, and securing a slight exaggeration at each repetition, comes round to the original narrator in a form scarcely to be recognized;* so, *by a little improper influence on the part of landowners,* a

---
[1] Minto, *Manual*, pp. 6, 7 (condensed).
[2] They were Englishmen.   [3] Taine, *Among the Pyrenees*.

little favouritism on the part of members of Parliament, a little intriguing of lawyers, a little manœuvring by contractors and engineers, a little self-seeking on the part of directors, a little understatement of estimates and overstatement of traffic, a little magnifying of the evils to be avoided and the benefits to be gained—it happens that shareholders are betrayed into ruinous undertakings by grossly untrue representations, without any one being guilty of more than a small portion of the fraud."[1]

This example shows the effect of the periodic structure in "unfamiliar subject-matter." The following absurdity is an example of "suspense unduly prolonged."

(2) "*Through great, low-lying fields of golden grain, over which the evening breezes swept with impetuous, light feet, blending the radiant yellow of the corn and the bright, blood-red of the poppies in a glorious arabesque of gold and green and scarlet: past dark green woods and gently rising knolls of grassy green: away round moss-lichened boulders, topped by dark green firs, through which gleamed the red berry of the rowan: circling round towering crags, from whose frowning peaks ivy-mantled ruins of hoary castles stood out bodily against the glorious autumn sky,* the river stole; and, *as the dreamer lazily guided the easy tiller and gently bellying sail,* a great happiness filled his soul, and he felt that this in very deed was Paradise."

(3) "And from that cup of sorrow, *which upon all lips is pressed in some proportion,* they must submit, *by the very tenure on which they hold their gifts,* to drink, if not more profoundly than others, yet more perilously as regards the fulfilment of their intellectual mission."[2]

The "tension," which grows greater and greater as far as the word *drink,* is *gradually* relaxed by the two modifiers that follow and *loosen* the sentence. The effect of stopping at *drink* would have been almost that of a shock. Compare the sudden halt of the next example.

"The faces of infants, *though they are divine as flowers on a savanna of Texas, or as the carolling of birds in a forest,* are, *like flowers on a savanna of Texas, or the carolling of birds in a forest,* soon overtaken by the pursuing darkness that swallows up all things human."[2]

[1] Herbert Spencer, *Essays*, p. 262. [2] De Quincey (cited by Minto.)

217. The student has now before him the grounds for a decision which structure is better, the periodic or the loose. Clearly, neither order is *always* better. *First*, though the direct order is, perhaps, more formal than the indirect, yet both are used in all kinds of writing. *Secondly*, "in light subjects neatness or finish is generally regarded as an acquisition;" but, even here, "a caution is needed; rounded neatness, if it recurs too frequently, may become tiresome. .... Be not *too periodic* neither, but let your own discretion be your tutor."[1] "In unfamiliar subjects, care must be taken that the considerations kept in suspense [placed last, that is, because of the anticipations] be not too numerous or too abstruse." In this case, (as De Quincey has remarked,) exhaustion both mental and physical follows the effort to carry along to the conclusion the endless *protases* on which this conclusion, the suspended *apodosis*, depends.[2] *Finally*, on all these points, the court of last resort is the judgment of the particular writer upon the particular case, guided, of course, by broad knowledge and refined taste. The writer alone has before him all the conditions necessary to a judicious choice; and he must make this choice anew in each case as it arises.

3. Explicit Reference.

218. The reference of every word, phrase, or clause in a sentence must be clearly indicated. Otherwise, the sense grows doubtful or obscure, and the reader is left either to guess at the writer's meaning or to despair of divining it. To a great extent, Explicit Reference depends on arrangement;[3] to some extent, it is effected

---

[1] Minto, *ut cit*.

[2] See the examples in § 216 (2), *above*.—De Quincey himself, however, sets a bad example on this head; and yet the sentences quoted from him in § 216 (3), are by no means the worst examples that could be found in his works.

[3] § 145 (2), above.

by the close connection of the thought expressed; but, in another part, it is promoted by certain special devices, the rhetorical bearings of which need to be considered here. These devices are (1) the use of *connectives*, (2) *intentional repetitions*.

219. (1) Connectives are (*a*) *conjunctions*, including *adverbs* and *adverbial phrases used conjunctively*, (*b*) *pronouns* and *pronominal phrases*. The following examples show the value now of inserting, now of omitting, connectives of the several classes.

(*a*) "Boabdil, however,[1] had again retired to Velez el Blanco, on the confines of Murcia, where he could avail himself, in case of emergency, of any assistance *or* protection afforded him by the policy of Ferdinand. His defeat had blighted his reviving fortunes, *for* the people considered him as inevitably doomed to misfortune. Still, *while* he lived, El Zagal knew he would be a rallying point for faction, *and* liable at any moment to be elevated into power by the capricious multitude. He had recourse, therefore,[1] to the most perfidious means to compass his destruction. He sent embassadors to him, representing the necessity of concord for the salvation of the kingdom, *and* even offering to resign the title of king, *and* to become subject to his sway, on receiving some estate on which he could live in tranquil retirement. But,[1] *while* the embassadors bore these words of peace, they were furnished with poisoned herbs, which they were to administer secretly to Boabdil; *and if* they failed in this attempt, they had pledged themselves to dispatch him openly, *while* engaged in conversation.[2]

(*a*) "The rain came *and* covered all objects with its blinding veil. An hour later, the drained clouds were creeping along half way up the height; the dripping rocks shone through a dark varnish, like blocks of polished mahogany. Turbid water went boiling down the swollen cascades; the depths of the gorge were still darkened by the storm; *but* a tender light played over the wet summits, like a smile bathed in tears. The gorge opened up; the arches of the marble bridges sprang lightly into the limpid air, *and*, sheeted in light, Luz was seen

---
[1] ¶¶ 250 ff, *below*.
[2] Irving, *The Conquest of Granada*, vol. i., ch. xlv.—The passage exemplifies, perhaps, the *maximum* number of conjunctions in ordinary cases.

seated among sparkling meadows *and* fields of millet in full bloom."[1]

(*a*) He attaches to himself all the placeholders, with their numerous connexions, *and also* [= *as well as*] all the expecters *and* hopers of places, which will form a strong party in promoting his views.[2]—The style, being obsolete, *and thence* less agreeable, is perhaps one reason why the reading of that excellent book is of late so much neglected.[2]—This is, *in some measure*, to be attributed to their situation, . . . , *but* is *also* to be attributed, *etc.*—*As* fully *as* brevity permits, I will state some of my views on general questions, *as well as* on this special subject.

(*b*) All *that* he said made his students feel that Economics only played, *etc.*—He used to tell of a student of natural history, *who*, when addressed as an entomologist, exclaimed, *etc.*—Those *who* knew Dr. Hodgson's career must have recognized that he was a man of the widest intellectual sympathies; and it was *this* width of sympathy *that* made his teaching on Economics so interesting and so true.—Such a requisition *as* will shield.—Dr. Hodgson's class was small, and it was *on this account* easier for him to know each man.[3]

220. The excessive use of connectives is a violation of Brevity, and necessarily enfeebles the style.[4] When the arrangement of the sentence or the close connection of the thought expressed suffices for explicit reference,[5] the use of any special device is, of course, a waste of force, and should be carefully avoided. But the persistent and unreasoning omission of connectives is equally a violation of judicious Brevity,[4] and is equally to be shunned. Between these two extremes, lies a field within which, not Brevity alone, but the further consideration of Explicit Reference, controls the insertion or the omission of connectives. The following examples illustrate the question as thus generally stated ;—

---

[1] Taine, *Pyrenees*, p. 171.—A good example of perhaps the *minimum* use of conjunctions in an ordinary case.
[2] Franklin, Works ed. Sparks (Boston, 1836), vol. ii. p. 166.
[3] Other examples may be found in the quotations above and in those of the next paragraph.
[4] §§ 191 ff, above.   [5] § 218, *above*.

(1) "I knew two, *that* were Competitors for the Secretaries Place, in Queen Elizabeths time, *and yet* kept good Quarter between themselves; *And* would conferre, one with another, upon the Businesse; *And* the one of them said, *That* to be a Secretary, in the Declination of a Monarchy, was a Ticklish Thing, *and that* he did not affect it."[1]

(2) "This Orthon, the familiar spirits, Queen Mab, are the poor little popular gods, children of the pool and the oak, engendered by the melancholy *and* awe-struck reveries of the spinning maiden and the peasant. A great state-religion then overshadowed all thoughts; doctrine ready-made was imposed upon them; men could no longer, as in Greece or Scandinavia, build the great poem which suited their manners and mind."[2]

(3) "*If* ever there was a proselyte of *whom* a proselyting sect would have been proud, *it* was Lord George [Gordon]; *not only because* he was a man of high birth and rank; *not only because* he had been a member of the legislature; *but also because* he had been distinguished by the intolerance, nay, the ferocity, of his zeal for his own form of Christianity."[3]

(4) Lord George [Gordon] was a proselyte of *whom* a proselytising sect might well have been proud. He was a man of high birth and rank; he had been a member of the legislature; he had been distinguished by the intolerance, the ferocity, of his zeal for his own form of Christianity.

(4) "It was therefore absolutely necessary *to ascertain* what resources each party possessed, *to bring* the long and intricate account between them to a close, and *to assign* to each a fair portion of assets and liabilities."—Insert *in order* before either *to ascertain* or *to bring*, and the sense is materially changed.

221. The excessive use of the Relative Pronoun and other relative words as connectives is a special indication of weakness. Such constructions as, the rock *on which* his fortress was built; Christian captives, *who* had been carried off by these war-hawks of the mountains; Hamet el Zegri had scarcely returned to Ronda, *when* he received intelligence; *etc.*, are, of course, quite unobjec-

---

[1] Bacon's *Essays*, Ed. W. Aldis Wright, pp. 93, 94.

[2] Taine, *Among the Pyrenees*, translated by Fiske, p. 166.—But one connective (the italicized *and*) is used that could possibly have been left out.

[3] Macaulay, *Speeches*, Tauchnitz Ed., I. 141.

tionable, and are incessantly occurring; but even these and other legitimate uses of the relative must not occur too often. Nothing, perhaps, is more puerile; nothing, perhaps, is less to be defended. Older English, it is true, imitating Greek and Latin, used the relative, not only between clauses, but even between sentences;[1] but more recent English has sought to correct the abuse. As will be seen,[2] Unity is often destroyed by "tagging" a relative construction to a complete thought; and, even when this is not the case, the relative has such a propensity to occur again and again, that variety often demands the substitution of other constructions. The following hints on this subject are given by Dr. Abbott;[3]—

Equivalents for the Relative;—(*a*) *Participle* or *Adjective;* as, Men *thirsting* for Men *that thirst.*—Cæsar, *dead* and *turned* to clay, for Cæsar, *when dead.*—But this construction is sometimes ambiguous,—as, Fluellen, *touch'd* with choler,—and, if the subject is modified—as, *Those* men *thirsting*—is very harsh.

(*b*) *Infinitive;* as, He was the first *to enter* (*that entered*) the room.

(*c*) *Clause with if, when, because, etc.;* as, *If* a man *has* no music in his soul ('The man *that has*).

(*d*) *What;* as, *That which* you know (*What* you know.)

(*e*) *Omission of the Relative;* as, The errand (*that*) he was going on.[4]

(*f*) The demonstrative or personal pronoun with a conjunction; as, He did his best, *and this* (*which*) was all that could be expected of him.

222. (2) Repetitions for the sake of Explicit Reference need not be classified: almost any repetition would be tolerable by which clearness, force, or emphasis was secured, and other important considerations not lost sight of. Still, since such repetitions can not (like certain other devices

---

[1] § 255, *below*.   [2] § 213 ff, *below*   [3] *How to Write Clearly*, R. 10.
[4] Dr. Abbott mentions, also, (*f*) the old relative words *whereby, wherein, etc.*, as, The means *whereby;* but the construction is archaic.

of style) be *concealed*, they should be used sparingly. The following examples must be studied carefully ;—

This is the advice of one *who* has been their servant, *who* has served them loyally, and *who* is still sincerely anxious *for* their credit and *for* the welfare of the empire of which they are the guardians,—a country which enjoys the blessings *of* a pure religion, *of* freedom, *of* order.—So much for the first charge, *the charge* of disobedience.—*On the* most important *questions, on the question* whether a war shall be declared, *on the question whether* a treaty shall be concluded, *on the question whether* the whole system of land revenue established in a great province shall be changed, his single vote, *etc.*—Suppose *that* George the Third had not recovered, *that* [1] the rest of his long life had been passed in seclusion, Great Britain and Ireland would then have been, *etc.*[2]—He ordered *that* none should sally forth to skirmish, without permission from their commanders ; *that* none should set fire to the woods on the neighboring mountains ; and *that* all word of security given to Moorish places or individuals, should be inviolably observed.[3]

4. LONG AND SHORT SENTENCES.

223. Another important question is the *Length* of the Sentence. Not that any sentence is objectionable *simply* because it is very short or *simply* because it is very long; for the length of every sentence is determined chiefly by the thought it has to convey. But a sentence is certainly *too* short if it restricts the proper expansion of the thought, and *too* long if it expands the thought too far, or grows involved and therefore obscure. "Jesus wept" is as complete a sentence as "For I am persuaded, that neither death, nor life, nor angels, nor principalities, nor powers, nor things present, nor things to come, nor height, nor depth, nor any other creature, shall be able

---

[1] Were this word left out, the following clause would naturally be taken for the conclusion, at least until the word *then* was reached.

[2] Macaulay's *Speeches*.

[3] Irving, *Conquest of Granada*, ii. 2.—The sense might be clear without the *that's*, but it is certainly clearer with them.

to separate us from the love of God, which is in Christ Jesus our Lord;" but "The sixteenth century was comparatively a time of light," is too short, because it leaves the reader perplexed, till, as he continues the paragraph, he learns,—

"Yet even in the sixteenth century a considerable number of those who quitted the old religion followed the first confident and plausible guide who offered himself, and were soon led into errors far more serious than those they had renounced. Thus Matthias and Kniperdoling, apostles of lust, robbery, and murder, were able for a time to rule great cities. In a darker age such false prophets might have founded empires; and Christianity might have been distorted into a cruel and licentious superstition, more noxious not only than Popery, but even than Islamism."[1]

So, "John Eliot, the 'Apostle to the Indians,' was born in England and educated at the University of Cambridge, coming to Boston in 1631, and accepting as his life-mission, the next year, the conversion of the Indians, who were evidently, in his opinion, the descendants of the lost tribes of Israel," is too long, because it confuses the birth and education of Eliot with his coming to Boston, his accepting a certain mission, and his being of such and such an opinion.[2]

224. At the same time, a writer can not be too strictly on his guard to keep his sentences from running to an extreme on either side,—into disjointedness, on the one hand—into intricacy, on the other. Early English prose is much disfigured by excessive length of sentence. The writers "did not know when to stop. They seem to have been afraid to let a sentence out of their hands till they had tacked on all the more important qualifications of the main statement." On the other hand, some writers have affected brevity of sentence, and have

---

[1] Throw the first two sentences together.

[2] Write, "John Eliot . . . Cambridge. Coming . . . 1631, the next year he accepted as his life-mission, the conversion . . ."

thereby produced a style that Coleridge calls *asthmatic,*—a style "purposely invented for persons troubled with the asthma to read, and for those to comprehend who labour under the more pitiable asthma of a short-witted intellect." Nor is either fault only ancient. In most recent times, excesses have been committed in both directions. Ruskin, for instance, often lets his Pegasus get away with him, and is unable to pull up until after a long run. One paragraph in *The Poetry of Architecture*[1] contains *four hundred and eight* words, and only *seven sentences.* Of these two are reasonable in length, four quite long, and one contains *one hundred and five words*, comprising *nine clauses.* On the other hand, a recent writer of historico-religious novels has *ten sentences* in a single paragraph of *one hundred and twenty words*, the longest sentence containing only *twenty-six* words and *four clauses.*

225. The effects produced by the short sentence are lightness, vivacity and disjointedness; by the long sentence, dignified seriousness and continuousness. Each has its advantages. The former is easier to apprehend; the latter "affords more room to expand the sense." To this may be given a stateliness of march; that is the vehicle of impetuous or interrupted speech. The intellect dictates long sentences; shorter ones flow from the feelings, or express decisions of the will. Variety, if nothing more, would demand an alternation; so that, "here, too, discretion is the tutor." Excess in the one way produces brokenness, a want of sequence in the thought, and a sense of *unsatisfiedness;* in the other direction, prolixity, ambiguity, and a general sense of *becloudedness.* In the former case, the mind has not time enough to dwell upon each thought as it is presented; in the latter, the sentence weighs on the mind like a fog that will not lift. For example;—

[1] Published anonymously, but evidently Ruskin's. Cf. *The Stones of Venice,* ch. xvi. 10, 2d paragraph. One sentence has *eighty-six words* and *six clauses.*

(1) "Corruption, you all know, is the subject of penal laws. If it is brought home to the parties, they are liable to severe punishment. Although it is not often that it can be brought home, yet there are instances. I remember several men of large property confined in Newgate for corruption. Penalties have been awarded against offenders to the amount of five hundred pounds. Many members of Parliament have been unseated on account of the malpractices of their agents. But you can not, I am afraid, repress intimidation by penal laws. Such laws would infringe the most sacred rights of property. How can I require a man to deal with tradesmen who have voted against him, or to renew the leases of tenants who have voted against him? What is it that the Jew says in the play?

> 'I'll not answer that,
> But say it is my humour.'

Or, as a Christian of our own time has expressed himself, 'I have a right to do what I will with my own.' There is a great deal of weight in the reasoning of Shylock and the Duke of Newcastle."[1]

In these sentences, disjointedness is carried almost (perhaps, quite) to abruptness; but other sentences immediately following, redeem in some measure their predecessors. Besides, as Minto remarks, "the use of a startling series of short sentences may almost be said to be a feature of English oratory." It certainly is a feature (and a marked feature) of Macaulay's oratory.

(2) "From an early age I have felt a strong interest in Edinburgh, although attached to Edinburgh by no other ties than those which are common to me with multitudes; that tie which attaches every man of Scottish blood to the ancient and renowned capital of our race; that tie which attaches every student of history to the spot ennobled by so many great and memorable events; that tie which attaches every traveller of taste to the most beautiful of British cities; and that tie which attaches every lover of literature to a place which, since it has ceased to be the seat of empire, has derived from poetry, philosophy, and eloquence a far higher distinction than empire can bestow. I do not mean to say that thought, discussion, and the new phenomena produced by the operation of a new representative system, have not led me to modify some of my views on questions

---

[1] Macaulay, *Speech on the Edinburgh Election*, May 1839.

of detail; but, with respect to the fundamental principles of government, my opinions are still what they were when, in 1831 and 1832, I took part, according to the measure of my abilities, in that great pacific victory which purified the representative system of England, and which first gave a real representative system to Scotland. Even at that time, gentlemen, the leaning of my mind was in favour of one measure to which the illustrious leader of the Whig party, whose name ought never to be mentioned without gratitude and reverence in any assembly of British electors, I mean Earl Grey, was understood to entertain strong objections, and to which his Cabinet, as a Cabinet, was invariably opposed."[1]

Aided, though it is, by a special artifice,[2] the first sentence grows tedious, though not ambiguous or confused; the thought expressed by the second sentence is certainly not easily carried along to the close; and the last sentence has two parentheses. Still, no one of these sentences reaches the dense fogginess of the next example.

(2) Certainly, if we examine that love of power, which enters so largely into most practical calculations—nay, which our Utilitarian friends have recognized as the sole end and origin, both motive and reward, of all earthly enterprises, animating alike the philanthropist, the conqueror, the money-changer, and the missionary—we shall find that all other arenas of ambition, compared with this rich and boundless one of Literature, meaning thereby whatever respects the promulgation of Thought, are poor, limited, and ineffectual.

226. But even quite long sentences may not be on that account objectionable. Thus;—

"As for me, I was, as I have already said, very quick and lively, easily moved by novelty, fond of intellectual pleasures, interested in observing so many persons all unknown to me; and I found favor with my new sovereign, because, as I have said elsewhere, I took pleasure in listening to him."

"Although Bonaparte would have been angry if any one had seemed to doubt the sincerity of his utterances, which were at this period entirely republican, he introduced some novelties into his manner of life every day, which tended to give the place of his abode more and more resemblance to the palace of a sovereign."

[1] Macaulay, *Speech on the Edinburgh Election*, May 1839.   [2] § 222, *above*.

227. Length of sentence often results from excessive periodicity; but there is no necessary connection between the Period and the Long Sentence. When the periodic form is used to promote neatness or finish, the sentence is often very short, never unreasonably long; while loose sentences, simply because they are loose, seem longer than they really are. At the same time, periodicity and length of sentence are so common together, that the phrase *Periodic Style*[1] would never, perhaps, be used of work in which short sentences predominated, or *Abrupt Style* (*Style coupé*)[2] of work in which long sentences were in the majority. The examples already given sufficiently illustrate this point.

228. When a sentence must, in the judgment of the writer, grow unusually long, its several members should be most carefully connected in accordance with the rules for Explicit Reference. Any device, not otherwise objectionable, may be resorted to, provided it serves the purpose of guiding the reader more surely through the maze. For example ;—

"Bad as a despotism is, *yet, where* anarchy is the only alternative, *we must say, that, as* anarchy would bring greater suffering than despotism brings, despotism is justified by the circumstances. *And similarly,* however inequitable in the abstract were the beheadings, [*the*] hangings, and [*the*] burnings of ruder ages, *yet, if* it be shown *that without penalties thus extreme,* the safety of society could not have been insured —*if, in their absence,* the increase of crime would have inflicted a larger total of evil, *and that, too,* on peaceable members of the community; *then* it follows *that* morality warranted this severity."

5. THE BALANCED SENTENCE.

229. Sentences that have their *different* parts *alike in form*, are said to be *balanced:* the parts are equal or nearly equal both in the amount of thought expressed and in the number of words used to express it, and, hence, they may properly be said to be *weighed against* each other. Thus ;—

---

[1] § 213, *above.*
[2] A style marked by disjointedness due to shortness of sentence. (§ 225, *above.*)

THE BALANCED SENTENCE.   185

We might *have held out hopes of public employment to converts*, and *have imposed civil disabilities on Mahometans and Pagans.*—Our *plain clothing commands far more reverence* than all the *jewels* which the most *tawdry Zemindar* wears; and our *plain language carries with it far more weight* than the *florid diction* of the most *ingenious Persian scribe.*[1]

230. The Balanced Sentence is commonly defined as a *compound* sentence whose *clauses* are similar.[2] But the balanced parts are not always clauses, nor need the sentence be compound; as, *Emblems of vice* are *objects of public worship*. Acts of *vice* are acts of *public worship*. Crimes against *life*, crimes against *property*, are not only *permitted* but *enjoined* by this odious theology. Such members are sometimes said to be *assimilated;* but, when weighed against each other in this way, they are also balanced. So, three or even more parts of a single sentence may be balanced, or the balance may be between whole sentences, with or without balance between their different members. For example, As this superstition is of all superstitions *the most irrational*, and of all superstitions *the most inelegant*, so is it of all superstitions *the most immoral.*—*We might have acted* as the Spaniards acted in the New World. *We might have attempted* to introduce our own religion by force. *We might have sent missionaries* among the natives at the public charge. *We might have held out, etc.*

231. The parts of a balanced sentence are different in *meaning*, alike in *grammatical structure*, in *sound*, or in *other particulars*. The effects produced are enhanced by the peculiar structure, rather than caused by it; for mere balance is nearly always weak, while strong thought is made the stronger by the special form. Compare the following example with the examples in § 229;—

---

[1] The last sentence is really *doubly* balanced; each clause within itself, and the two clauses against each other.
[2] For example, Bain, Part I., § 137. In §§ 141 ff, however, are cited as balanced,—Words are the *counters* of *wise* men, and the *money* of *fools;* *High* life *below* stairs; As if a number of *worldlings* made a *world; etc.*

"I wrote once a little book of shooting: King HENRY gave me a living for it; when *he* lost his *life*, *I* lost my *living;* but noble King Edward again did first *revive* it by his *goodness*, then did *increase* it by his *liberality;* thirdly, did *confirm* it by his *authority* under the great seal of England," etc.

232. The advantages of this structure are many, but it has also some disadvantages. On the one hand, it aids the memory, it causes pleasure—especially, if a difference of meaning can be reached by juggling (as it were) with the same words[1]—and it leads to the correct placing of emphatic words. On the other hand, the weapon is a dangerous one. Let a writer's ear once be enchanted by the balanced structure, and he forgets how painful are the impressions he is making upon his reader. Like verse-rhythm in prose,[2] the balanced structure cannot be disguised: to disguise it is to destroy it. Periodic sentences may be so varied as to leave the reader unaware from whence their stimulating effect is derived; but series of balanced sentences are necessarily monotonous.[3] Pleasing at first, their sweetness at length cloys the taste. Besides, excess of balance leads to tautology, (for the sentence must be filled out, and with a repetition, if with nothing else,) to the insertion of unnecessary allusions and other details, (by way of securing the "see-saw,") and to similar vices brought on by "the irresistible craving for the familiar measure." Like drunkenness, this craving becomes a disease. Macaulay is one of its notorious victims; while of a certain American writer, still living, it has been wittily said, "His pages make one sea-sick." The following instances of repetition and unnecessary additions should be especially noted;—

[1] For example, What is *Hecuba* to *him*, or *he* to *Hecuba?*—A *juggler* is a *wit* in *things*, and a *wit* is a *juggler* in *words*. The examples already given sufficiently illustrate the other points.

[2] 158 (2), *above*.—Minto notes that "in impassioned prose, balance has something of the effect of metre."

[3] Minto, pp. 9-10.

"He has opposed many bills introduced by the present Government; but *he has opposed them* on such grounds," *etc.* [Strike out the words in italics, and change the semicolon to a comma.]

"What I do anticipate is this, that he will attempt to keep his party together by means which will excite grave discontents, and yet that he will not succeed *in keeping his party together;* that he will lose the support of the Tories without obtaining the support of the nation; and that his government will fall from causes purely internal." [The words in italics are pleonastic, and each of the last two clauses repeats what the first had already said. "He" was a Tory.]

233. A not unusual, but most objectionable form of Balanced Sentence is that produced by the so-called "splitting" of two allied constructions; for example, As bad *as*, or worse *than*, his predecessor; interest in, and responsibility for, the world's condition; I never *have allowed*, and never *will allow*, literary labor to infringe on pastoral.—Whatever may sometimes be gained in brevity by this arrangement, much more is lost in elegance; so that the construction should commonly be avoided. Indeed, sometimes even brevity is sacrificed. The first sentence cited above is shorter when properly arranged,—As bad as his predecessor or worse. So, I never have allowed literary labor to infringe on pastoral, and never will.

234. The Balanced Structure is often joined with *antithesis, epigram*,[1] or *climax*.[2] The Proverbs of Solomon and many other familiar sayings—such as, Waste not, want not—To hesitate is to be lost—Not that I loved Cæsar less, but that I loved Rome more—are examples of balance combined with antithesis and epigram; Tennyson's "dowered with the hate of hate, the scorn of scorn, the love of love," of balance and climax. In the following sentence, antithesis is neglected, and balance suffers accordingly;—Take the human being at the right period of life, and prevention is as easy as [at a later period] cure is difficult.

[1] ¶ 301, *below*.   [2] ¶ 278, *below*.

A style in which balance predominates, especially if antithesis, *etc.*, are joined with it, is called *Pointed.*

6. THE CONDENSED SENTENCE.

235. In imitation of the classical construction called *zeugma*, a few English writers occasionally join under one government or agreement two or more terms that do not strictly admit of being so construed ; as, Of nineteen tyrants, not one *enjoyed* a life of peace or a natural death.—The Russian grandees came to court dropping pearls and vermin. "In the present day," says Minto,[1] "when used at all," the condensed sentence chiefly serves "comic purposes. Readers of Dickens and his imitators are familiar with such" expressions "as 'drew tears from his eyes and a handkerchief from his pocket.'" But Tennyson[2] has shown that the construction is still powerful for higher uses ;—

"The circuits of thine orbit *round*
A higher height,[3] a deeper deep."

7. UNITY.

236. Unity requires that "every part of the sentence shall be subservient to one *principal* affirmation." Thus ;—

This is indeed worth your attention.—Of course all mankind are, as Mr. Gladstone says, of our own flesh and blood.—But you know how often it happens in England that a cultivated person, a person of the sort that Mr. Charles Sumner describes, talking to one of the lower class, or even of the middle class, feels, and cannot but feel, that there is somehow a wall of partition between himself and the other, that they seem to belong to two different worlds.—Thoughts, feelings, perceptions, susceptibilities, language, manners,—everything is different.—France brings the Alsatians into a social system so full of the goodness and agreeableness of life ; we offer to the Irish no such attraction.—A nation pursues social equality, supposed to

[1] *Manual*, p. 10.   [2] *In Memoriam*, lxiii. 3.   [3] Sc. *fathom*.

be an utterly false and baneful idea; it arrives, as might have been expected, at fearful misery and deterioration by doing so; and yet, at the same time, it is high, if not the first, in the scale of civilized nations.

Each of these sentences sets forth only one *principal* idea. This idea may be unmodified, as in the first sentence; slightly modified, as in the second; involved in a net-work of modifiers, as in the third; or even consist of a longer or shorter series of specific statements that together make up the one, generic idea intended, as in the last three sentences. In each case the thought conveyed is single, the impression received by the mind also single.[1]

237. For precisely the opposite reason, *viz.*, that they set forth more than one principal idea each, the following sentences violate Unity;—

In this uneasy state, Cicero was oppressed by a new and cruel affliction, the death of his daughter Tullia; which happened soon after her divorce from Dolabella; whose manners and humours were entirely disagreeable to her.[2]—My dear friend, if you look at the last essaykin (though you may leave it alone, and I shall not be in the least surprised or offended), if you look at the last paper, where the writer imagines Athos and Porthos, Dalgetty and Ivanhoe, Amelia and Sir Charles Grandison, Don Quixote and Sir Roger, walking in at the garden-window, you will at once perceive that NOVELS and their heroes and heroines are our present subject of discourse, into which we will presently plunge.[3]—It seemed to me that from his long fingers two quivering flames issued, sputtering, as it were, which penetrated me, and forced me back into one of the chairs—the broken one—out of which I had much difficulty in scrambling, when the strange glamour was ended.[3]

How completely these sentences violate the rule; can be seen by writing them correctly;—

In this uneasy state, a new and cruel affliction befell Cicero. His daughter Tullia had been married to Dolabella, but had

---

[1] The first four sentences stand consecutively in a single paragraph in Matthew Arnold's *Mixed Essays, Equality.*
[2] Quoted by Blair. [3] Thackeray, *Roundabout Papers.*

been divorced because her husband's manners and humours were entirely disagreeable to her. Shortly after the divorce, she died.—My dear friend, . . . essaykin, where the writer . . . subject of discourse. Into this . . . plunge.—It seemed to me . . . as it were, penetrating me, and forcing me back . . . broken one. Out of this, when . . . ended, I had . . . scrambling.[1]

238. As commonly stated, however, the rule becomes "dogmatic and cramping." No sentence, it is said, should contain more than "one entire thought or mental proposition;" "things which are separated in reality" should not be "connected in language;" "in every sentence there ought to be one main assertion." But every page of every good English writer, as well as the philosophy of the sentence, contradicts these statements, and confirms the more moderate rule laid down above. It must be remembered, too, that "a statement merely explanatory or qualifying, put into a sentence apart, *acquires a dangerous* (!) *prominence.*" In a word, "the only universal caution that can be given, is to beware of distracting from the effect of the main statement by particulars not immediately relevant," to "leave something for the next sentence," to "distinguish between the Unity of a Sentence . . . and the Unity of a Paragraph." Even Blair's rules command too much. As condensed by Bain, they are,—

(1) In the course of the same sentence not to shift the scene;
(2) To avoid crowding into one sentence heterogeneous ideas;
(3) To avoid excess of parenthetical clauses; (4) Not to add members after a full and perfect close.

A careful examination of them will show how far they exceed the valid rule.

239. (1) What Blair intended by *shifting the scene* appears from his own explanation.

[1] Or, perhaps, It seemed to me . . . were. These penetrated . . . chairs—the broken one; and I had much difficulty, when . . . ended, in scrambling out of it.

THE SENTENCE—UNITY.   191

"We should not be hurried," he says, "by sudden transitions from person to person, nor [*sic*] from subject to subject. There is commonly, in every sentence, some person or thing, which is the governing word. This should be continued so, if possible, from the beginning to the end." For example, "'After we came to anchor, they put me on shore, where I was welcomed by all my friends, who received me with the greatest kindness.' In this sentence, though the objects contained in it *have a sufficient connexion with each other*, yet, by this manner of representing them, by *shifting* so often both *the place* and *the person*, *we* and *they*, and *I*, and *who*, they appear in such a disunited view, that the sense of connexion is almost lost."

Plainly, Blair's idea of shifting the scene is changing the subject or the construction of the sentence;[1] and so he has commonly been quoted as teaching. But, surely, if the objects contained in a sentence have "a sufficient connexion" with each other, there is no want of unity. The sentence may lack *force* and *clearness*, as Blair's example does; it may be *loose*, as Blair's example is; it may have other faults, perhaps; but unity is left, though obscured. Shifting the scene (in Blair's sense) may lead a writer into confusing in one sentence two ideas that ought each to have a sentence of its own;[2] but it is not the change of subject or construction that destroys unity: it is the herding together of disparate thoughts. The form of the sentence is certainly objectionable; but, if this form necessarily destroys unity, the only legitimate form of sentence is that of Example 1st, § 235, and every other sentence quoted in that paragraph as obeying the rule really breaks it. But no one, perhaps, will say this; certainly, no one familiar with the English tongue and its sentence-forms and constructions.

240. (2) Blair's second rule is undoubtedly a rule of Unity, and is exemplified by all the examples quoted or to

---

[1] Blair's correction proves this:—"Having come to anchor, I was put on shore, where I was welcomed by all my friends, and received with the greatest kindness."

[2] See Ex. 1st, § 236.

be quoted under this head.   The student must remember, however, to define "heterogeneous" with distinguished liberality.   All over-statements of the true principle of Unity have been due to narrowing the meaning of this word.

241. (3) Parentheses, like a change of subject or construction, may destroy unity, but only when they introduce foreign thought.   The parenthesis—even an excess of parentheses—is not objectionable in itself, but only because of its effects.   These effects are vicious looseness of structure, monotony, mannerism, confusion as opposed to clearness; but neither they nor any other evil results of the parenthesis are results of the form only; the evils complained of are in the thought.   On the contrary, parentheses are sometimes actually advantageous.[1]   The following examples, if studied carefully, will illustrate these remarks;—

> Every man who has been coached through the famous "Faust" of Goethe (thou wert my instructor, good old Weissenborn, and these eyes beheld the great master himself in dear little Weimar town!) has read those charming verses which are prefixed to the drama.—Years ago I had a quarrel with a certain well-known person (I believed a statement regarding him which his friends imparted to me, and which turned out to be quite incorrect).—I wonder if the rascal is alive—an elderly scoundrel he must be by this time; and a hoary old hypocrite, to whom an old schoolfellow presents his kindest regards—parenthetically remarking what a dreadful place that private school was; cold, chilblains, bad dinners, not enough victuals, and caning awful!—Are you alive still, I say, you nameless villain, who escaped discovery on that day of crime?—And if I remember right (protesting I have not read the book for forty-two or three years), Robert Bruce made a speech to his soldiers.—If I were a mother (which is absurd), I

---

[1] The attempt to get rid of the vicious results of the parenthesis by substituting commas or dashes for the parenthesis-marks shows this. The consequences are not unlike those of the ostrich's hiding its head in the sand, in order to escape pursuit, or the child's closing his own eyes, that nobody may see him.

should like to be, *etc.*—For myself, being also *du métier*, I confess, *etc.*—He ranks with your Uncle Toby, Sir Roger de Coverley, Falstaff—heroic figures, all—American or British.

242. So, too, (4) the adding of members after a full and perfect close may result in only loosening the sentence, not in destroying its unity. For example, His legatee inherits these modest possessions by virtue of a codicil to his lordship's will, written, "strange to say upon a sheet of paper bearing the 'Athenæum Club' mark," is a loose sentence, but not out of unity.[1] On the other hand, the final clause of the second example in § 237, states a fact not subservient to the main statement, and, hence, is in violation of unity. So, also, are the final clauses of the two following sentences;—

The gentleman who received it, having looked at the draft with terror in his countenance, then looked at me, then called to himself two of his fellow clerks, and queer it was to see all their aquiline beaks over the paper.—The invention created some little conversation amongst scientific men at the time, though I remember a machine in Edinburgh of a very similar construction, two hundred—well, many, many years ago—and at a breakfast which Guillotin gave he showed us the instrument, and much talk arose amongst us as to whether people suffered under it.

243. The relative clause is especially apt to be thus "tagged" to a completed sentence; and unity suffers accordingly. Thus;—

We passed from Shepherd's Inn into Holborn, and looked for a while at Woodgate's bric-à-brac shop, which I can never pass without *etc.*—I saw a headless man seated, with his head in his lap, which wore an expression of piteous surprise.—A postboy was shot by an Irish gentleman on the road near Stone, in Staffordshire, who died in two days, for which the gentleman was imprisoned.—The eighteenth century had now become rich in the names of great Americans, one of the most

---

[1] Re-arranged—By virtue of ... will (written, ... mark) his legatee inherits these modest possessions—the sentence is certainly not out of unity: why is Thackeray's form, which throws the emphatic clause to the last, any worse?

remarkable of whom was Benjamin Franklin, who had all the versatility of Roger Williams and Increase Mather, and was a master in whatever branch of learning he touched.[1]

244. Added clauses and other violations of unity are sometimes used purposely, for humor's sake or for some other sufficient reason; but the construction must be considered a license, and be used sparingly. For example;—

Can you be fond of these? Of Pope I might: at least I might love his genius, his wit, his greatness, his sensibility—with a certain conviction that at some fancied slight, some sneer which he imagined, he would turn upon me and stab me. —Yes, Eve never took the apple—it was a cowardly fabrication of the serpent's.—There is poor Sophia Dorothea, with her furious jealousy regarding her husband (though she loathed and cheated him).—Really, if their complexions were a *little* better, don't you think they would be nice-looking girls—by candle-light?—" Ha! ha!" replied Jingle; "I say—she's very well—desires her compliments—begs you won't trouble yourself—love to *Tuppy*—won't you get up behind?—drive on, boys."—I kept my eyes carefully from him at first, for I knew what he little thought—and I gloried in the knowledge—that the light of madness gleamed from them like fire.

8. Due Proportion.

245. The several parts of a sentence "should have bulk and prominence according to their importance." Modifiers, whether words, phrases, or clauses, should not outweigh the principal statement, lest what is subordinate should appear to be of chief importance, and what is really important be lost sight of. Thus;—

It is extraordinary how cool any party but the principal can be in such cases.[2]—"Snodgrass," he said, in a voice tremulous with emotion, "if I fall, you will find in a packet which I shall place in your hands a note for my—for my father."[2]—The officer

---

[1] Sentences like the two last, which "tag" not one but several relative clauses to a complete construction or to each other, have been aptly said to be in "the House that Jack built" style. (See, also, § 221, *above*.)

[2] In due proportion.

THE SENTENCE—DUE PROPORTION. 195

evinced his consciousness of their presence by slightly beckoning with his hand ; and the two friends followed him, at a little distance, as he walked away.[1]—The doctor took snuff with everybody, chatted with everybody, laughed, danced, made jokes, played whist, did everything, and was everywhere.[1]— Mr. Snodgrass dropped the hand which he had, in the spirit of poesy, raised towards the clouds, as he made the above appeal, and assumed an attitude of attention.[2]—Three or four buxom girls speedily dispersed in search of the different articles in requisition, while a couple of large-headed, circular-visaged males rose from their seats in the chimney-corner, (for although it was a May evening, their attachment to the wood fire appeared as cordial as if it were Christmas,) and dived into some obscure recesses, from which they speedily produced a bottle of blacking and some half-dozen brushes.[3]—At one end of that old, cold, glassy, glittering, ghostly, marble hall there stands a throne, on which a white marble king ought to sit with his white legs gleaming down into the white marble below, and his white eyes looking at a great white marble Atlas, who bears on his icy shoulders a blue globe as big as the full moon.[2]

[1] In due proportion.   [2] Out of proportion.
[3] Full of defects: the sentence needs " heroic " surgery.

III.

THE PARAGRAPH.[1]

246. A Paragraph is in fact a whole composition in miniature, and sometimes constitutes a whole composition.[2] The laws that it obeys are of the highest importance; Prof. Bain's injunction in regard to it being more nearly true than the similar rule for the sentence (not Prof. Bain's) criticized above.[3] "Look to the Paragraphs," he says,[4] "and the Discourse will look to itself; for, although a discourse as a whole has a method or plan suited to its nature, yet he that fully comprehends the method of a paragraph, will also comprehend the method of an entire work."[5] The several sentences of a paragraph bear to each other precisely the same relations that the several paragraphs or other larger divisions of a composition bear to themselves; and, hence, no one who can construct a satisfactory paragraph, can readily fail in constructing a whole work.

247. And yet, strange as it may sound, paragraph-arrangement has been much neglected by even the best English writers. Mr. Minto, after examining "at considerable length the paragraph arrangements of" a number of different authors, concludes that "very few writers in our language seem to have paid much attention to the" subject, and that "none of them can be recommended as a model." Prof. Bain seems to have been the first to state formally any rules for the paragraph; Campbell, Blair, and even Whately stopped with the sentence;

---

[1] § 170.　　　　　　　　　　[2] As in the newspaper or other periodical.
[3] § 199.　　　　　　　　　　[4] Part I., § 178.
[5] Thus guarded, the injunction corresponds exactly with what was said about the whole composition and its divisions in § 170, *above*.

and one may still hear the doctrine laid down, as if not contradictable, that the whole of Style lies in sentence-building.

248. The principal rules for the paragraph[1] are as follows.

1. Initial Theme, or Topic, Sentences.

249. Unless obviously preparatory, the opening sentence is expected to indicate the subject of the paragraph. An initial sentence is, of course, unusually prominent, and, hence, is ill fitted to set out merely introductory matter. When it must do this, its character should be distinctly marked. Thus ;—

"*Peace was made; but would peace endure?* [Topic-sentence.] There was little chance of it, and this for several reasons. First, the native fickleness of the Iroquois, who, astute and politic to a surprising degree, were in certain respects, like all savages, mere grown-up children. Next, their total want of control over their fierce and capricious young warriors, any one of whom could break the peace with impunity whenever he saw fit ; and, above all, the strong probability that the Iroquois had made peace in order, under cover of it, to butcher or kidnap the unhappy remnant of the Hurons who were living, under French protection, on the island of Orleans, immediately below Quebec."[2] [The paragraph continues amplifying this last statement.]

"*In the summer of 1653, all Canada turned to fasting and penance, processions, vows, and supplications. The saints and the Virgin were beset with unceasing prayer.* [Manifestly introductory.] The wretched little colony was like some puny garrison, starving and sick, compassed with inveterate foes, supplies cut off, and succor helpless."[3] [Subject of several following paragraphs.]

"I went away sick at heart, despite that victory [as an actor in a French provincial theatre] on which my old companions so generously felicitated me. A victory over these poor boors who knew not one letter from another ! What was it worth ?

[1] Bain, Part 1. §§ 158 ff, (re-arranged and often altered.)
[2] Parkman, *The Old Régime in Canada*, ch. i.   [3] Id. ib.

"*In the great cities, no doubt, they would have hissed down my acting. For the first time, my career seemed miserable, and any successes in it seemed ridiculous either to seek or to prize.* [No hint of what is to follow, and the first sentence misleading as to the purpose of the second.] For, in imagination, I followed the bright creature [a young girl who had laughed at him as ugly and stupid] to her home, and heard her laugh in her solitude as she thought of me, an ugly wretch who fancied if ploughmen laughed at him, or kitchen wenches wept, that he had fame!" [The error is due to the presence of the first sentence in this paragraph: it belongs to the preceding paragraph.]

2. EXPLICIT REFERENCE.

250. "The bearing of each sentence upon what precedes must be explicit and unmistakable." Otherwise, the sense grows doubtful or obscure, and the reader is left to guess at the writer's meaning or to despair of divining it. A break in the connection between sentences is far more damaging than a disjointing of the thought within the sentence; and it is far more likely to occur. For, although a paragraph deals with a distinct topic, there is, of course, a greater break between independent sentences than between the parts of a single sentence, and the writer is, therefore, the more easily thrown off his track. Thus, were all the means neglected that are taken to preserve the connection of thought in the following paragraph, the labor of the reader would be much increased;—

"The adventurous spirits of the cavaliers were inflamed by *this suggestion;*[1] in their *sanguine confidence*,[2] they already beheld Malaga in their power, and they were eager for the enterprise. The marques of Cadiz, [*however?*] endeavored to interpose a little cool caution.[2] He *likewise* had apostate adalides, the most intelligent and experienced on the borders; among *these*, he placed especial reliance on one named Louis Amar, who knew all the mountains and valleys of the country. He had received from *him* a particular account of these moun-

[1] Refers to a preceding paragraph. [2] Is this phrase tautological?

tains of the Axarquia. *Their* savage and broken nature was a sufficient defence for the fierce people who inhabited them, *who*,[1] manning their rocks and their tremendous passes, which were often nothing more than the deep dry beds of torrents, might set whole armies at defiance. Even if vanquished, *they*[2] afforded no spoil to the victor. Their houses were little better than bare walls, and they would drive off their scanty flocks and herds to the fastnesses of the mountains."[3]

251. When the sentences are short, and the thought at best somewhat broken, the effect is far worse. Thus, should the words italicised in the following extract be omitted, the thought would be much more difficult to follow ;—

"It is a miserable State of Minde to have few Things to desire and many Things to feare. *And yet* that commonly is the Case of Kings; Who being at the highest, want Matter of desire, which makes their Mindes more Languishing ; And have many Representations of Perills and Shadowes, which makes their Mindes the lesse clear. *And* this is one Reason *also* of that Effect which the Scripture speaketh of; That the King's Heart is inscrutable. *For* Multitude of Jealousies and Lack of some predominant desire, that should marshall and put in order all the rest, maketh any Man's Heart hard to finde or sound. Hence it comes *likewise* that Princes," etc.[4]

252. Explicit Reference in the paragraph, like that within the sentence,[5] is often secured by special devices; but a close relation of thought or a close syntactical relation may alone be sufficient to bind sentences together, and many sentences are so remotely connected as to defy linking by any formal tie. In all these cases, the sentences simply follow each other ;[6] but care must always be taken that the sequence of thought is clear. If, in any case, this is not so, the presumption is either

---

[1] *And who?*   [2] *These mountaineers?*
[3] Irving, *The Conquest of Granada*, i. ch. xii.
[4] *Bacon's Essays*, Ed. W. Aldis Wright, p. 75.—The old punctuation only obscures the sense, and is therefore changed.
[5] § 218, *above*.   [6] For examples, see § 254, *below*.

that a connecting device of some kind is needed, or that there is a gap in the thought which requires bridging by one or more intermediate sentences.

253. The special devices for explicit Reference are (1) *Connective particles,* "the joints or hinges on which sentences turn,"—(*a*) *conjunctions,* (*b*) *adverbs* or *adverbial phrases used conjunctively,* (*c*) *pronouns,* including *demonstrative clauses, similarly used;* (2) *Repetitions,* (*a*) *literal,* (*b*) *in substance;* (3) *Inversions* and *other unusual arrangements of the sentence.* The following extracts exemplify all these devices;—

(1) "There would really seem an almost Arcadian simplicity in *such* demands, coming from so practised a statesman as the Lord Treasurer, and from a woman of such brilliant intellect as Elizabeth unquestionably possessed. *But* we read the history of 1587, not only by the light of subsequent events, but by the almost microscopic revelations of sentiments and motives, which a full perusal of the secret documents in those ancient cabinets afford.[1] *At that moment* it was not ignorance nor [*sic*] dulness which was leading England towards the pitfall so artfully dug by Spain. There was trust in the plighted word of a chivalrous soldier like Alexander Farnese, of a most religious and anointed monarch like Philip II. English frankness, playing cards upon the table, was no match for Italian and Spanish legerdemain,—a system according to which, to defraud the antagonist by every kind of falsehood and trickery was the legitimate end of diplomacy and statesmanship."[2]

"When Burghley read *these* fine phrases, he was much impressed; and they were pronounced at the English court to be 'very princely and Christianly.' An elaborate comment, *too*, was drawn up by the comptroller on every line of the letter. 'These be very good words,' *said the comptroller.*"[2]

(2) "It was pleasant, *no doubt,* to be applauded by high churchmen and low churchmen, by the Sheldonian Theatre and by Exeter Hall. *It was pleasant* to be described as the champions of the Protestant faith. *It was pleasant* to hear your opponents called by every nickname that is to be found in the foul vocabulary. . . . *It was pleasant* to hear that they were

---

[1] *Affords?*   [2] Motley, *United Netherlands,* ch. xvii.

the allies of Antichrist. . . . *But* when all this slander and scurrility had raised you to power, *etc.*"[1]

"*At the very beginning of the year* the King of Denmark had made an offer to Philip of mediation. *The letter*,[2] entrusted to a young Count de Rantzau, had been intercepted.

(3) He never scrupled, on repeated occasions, to insinuate that Barneveld [and others][3] had organized a plot to sell their country to Spain. Of *this*[4] there was not the faintest evidence; but it was, *etc.*—*As for powers*, say that you, as my governor-general, will entrust them to your deputies, in regard to the Netherlands. *For all other matters*, say that you have had full powers for many months, but that you cannot exhibit them till conditions worthy of my acceptance have been offered."[5]

254. Three classes of sentences are so closely related in thought as not commonly to need formal binding together:—(1) Iterative and explanatory sentences; (2) Cumulative statements; (3) Sentences added by way of consequence. Examples of each class will be found in the following paragraphs. Sentences closely related by syntax do not need classification; and those whose connection is remote do not admit of it. Thus;—

And there sat the patient letter-writer in his cabinet, busy with his schemes. His grey head was whitening fast. He was sixty years of age. His frame was slight, his figure stooping, his digestion very weak.—And there he sat at his table, scrawling his apostilles. The fine innumerable threads which stretched across the surface of Christendom, and covered it as with a net, all converged in that silent cheerless cell. France was kept in a state of perpetual civil war; the Netherlands had been converted into a shambles; Ireland was maintained in a state of chronic rebellion; *etc.*[6]—There were many who thought as I did, but we were not asked, were not counted. We had but to hold our tongues, and stand quiet and see the Germans enter Paris.—"This winter," she said slowly, "my children have all died for want of food—one by one, the youngest first. Ever since then I want [have wanted?] to hurt something—always."[7]

---

[1] Macaulay, *Speeches, The State of Ireland.*
[2] Sc. *of mediation.* (Case (2) (*b*).)   [3] Motley names them all.   [4] Sc. *plot.*
[5] Motley, *ut cit.*   [6] Motley, *ut cit.*   [7] Ouida, *A Leaf in the Storm.*

—I was cooped up in the city: it [?] was much worse than the first siege. I went out in many sorties. I made no doubt he was at Versailles. Then you know this other war came—the civil war. I was in the capital still. It [?] seemed to me that the people were in the right. I can not argue, but I think so still."[1]

255. The relative pronouns and other relative words were once used in English (as in Latin and Greek) to unite both independent sentences and remotely connected members of compound sentences; but their use as connectives would now seem to be restricted to the joining of clauses closely related in thought.[2] Thus, the following examples are undoubtedly archaic;—

The Inconveniences that have been noted in calling and using Counsell, are three. For *which* Inconveniences the Doctrine of Italy hath introduced Cabinet Counsels.[3]—I wish also, in the very Middle, a Faire Mount, with three Ascents and Alleys enough for foure to walke abreast; *Which* I would have to be Perfect Circles.[3]—They cast them into prison, charging the jailor to keep them safely: *who* thrust them into the inner prison.[4]

" My name is Thomas Mowbray, duke of Norfolk,
 Who hither come, engaged by my oath."[5]

But the following are correct;—

In the east, *where* [*i.e.*, although there] they knew the sun was rising, they could only[6] see the livid light of the still towering flames.[7]—The threads are twisted into a strong cord, *which* [=and it] is dragging us to an evil doom.[8]—We have a destiny *which* [*that*] we must needs fulfil together.[8]—In all these hundred paces, *while* we have been watching him, he has not made one of those caprioles in the air, *which* are a characteristic of his natural gait.[8]

256. The sufficient reasons against the older construction are, (1) that the demonstrative or the personal pronoun, with or without a connective as the case may require, is more definite,

---

[1] Ouida, *A Bunch of Lilacs*.   [2] § 221, *above*.   [3] Bacon, *Essays*.
[4] Acts xvi. 23, 24.   [5] Shakspere, *Rich II.*, 1. iii. 16.
[6] Place this word properly.   [7] Ouida, *A Leaf in the Storm*.
[8] Hawthorne, *The Marble Faun*, *passim*.

and therefore clearer, than the relative; and (2) that the law of Unity[1] is violated by the union of two sentences so far independent in thought.

257. With this single exception, all English connectives may unite independent sentences as well as the members of a compound sentence or the still more closely related elements of the simple sentence. For example;—

"*But*[2] I perceive, my dear auditors, that you are impatient for the remainder of my discourse. Impute it, I beseech you, to no defect of modesty, if I insist a little longer on so fruitful a topic as my own multifarious merits. It is altogether for your good. The better you think of me, the better men and women will you find yourselves. I shall say nothing of my all important aid on washing days; though on that account alone, I might call myself the household god of a hundred families. Far be it from me also to hint, my respectable friends, at the show of dirty faces which you would present without my pains to keep you clean. *Nor* will I remind you how often, when the midnight bells make you tremble for your combustible town, you have fled to the Town Pump, and found me always at my post, firm amid the confusion, and ready to drain my vital current in your behalf. *Neither* is it worth while to lay much stress on my claims to a medical diploma. Let us take, *etc.*— Summer or winter, nobody seeks me in vain; *for*, all day long, I am seen at the busiest corner, just above the market, stretching my arms to rich *and* poor alike; *and* at night, I hold a lantern over my head, *both* to show where I am, *and* [to] keep people out of the gutters."[3]

258. Objections have been brought, however, to four other connectives as initial words in the sentence,—to *and, but, for,* and *however.* As early as Campbell's time,[4] "some critics," had remarked that *and* is correct only within the sentence; Mr. G. P. Quackenbos[5] finds in the period that separates independent sentences a bar to beginning these sentences with *and* or *for* or *however;*

---

[1] § 236, *above.* [2] Begins a paragraph.
[3] Hawthorne, *A Rill from the Town Pump* (in *Twice-Told Tales*, vol. i.)— Three sentences in nine begin with conjunctions.
[4] *Rhetoric*, III. ii. [5] *A Course in Composition and Rhetoric.*

an anonymous newspaper book-reviewer thinks that "a professor of rhetoric should *know* that a sentence usually should not begin with the conjunction *but, and*, or *for;*" while Prof. A. S. Hill[1] writes as follows;—

"The judicious use of connective particles—'the joints or hinges on which sentences turn'—is a merit of style; but their misuse is a serious blemish. ... A connective which serves no purpose is worse than useless, and one used for an unsuitable purpose leads astray.

"*And* and *but* are frequent offenders in both ways. They should always connect words or clauses closely related in meaning and similar in construction,—*and*, by way of addition (as in 'poor *and* honest'); *but*, by way of subtraction or opposition (as in 'poor *but* honest').

"A composition should never begin with *and* or *but;* for, if nothing comes before the conjunction, there is nothing for it to connect with what comes after; and a paragraph should rarely so begin, for a new paragraph indicates that there is a break in the sense too important to be bridged by a conjunction. A similar objection might be taken to the employment of these words at the beginning of a sentence; but for this there is much good usage."

259. But all this is plainly without sufficient ground in either reason or authority. Campbell dissented from the remark he quotes; Quackenbos's reason is simply laughable; and though Prof. Hill has so adroitly mixed sound sense and empty argument in a circle, that he has doubtless deceived himself, yet he not only is contradicted by every good author and by the philosophy of the construction, but is inconsistent with himself. These statements, however, must be made in detail and supported by argument.

259 *a*. Campbell's "critics" and the newspaper Minos do not condescend to give reasons for their ostracism. Perhaps, like the Attic clown who voted to banish Aristides, they "hate" the inoffensive monosyllables because these have made themselves so useful in the commonwealth of Language. Perhaps, like

---

[1] *Principles*, p. 116.

one who must be nameless here, but who withdrew his objection the moment he found how full his best-loved English books were of the initial connectives, they think these words *inelegant*. Quackenbos's reason can have weight with such writers only as dare not unite by a link-word what a law of punctuation has put asunder; who believe, forsooth, that punctuation governs expression, not that it is a mere mechanical device to assist the eye in reading. Prof. Hill's argument will be reviewed after the following general considerations in the case have been set out.

260. *First*, whatever can be truthfully alleged against any of the four proscribed connectives *as connectives*, holds, of course, with equal force against all connectives; for, in their office of connective, all words that unite sentences or parts of sentences, whatever their technical names among the parts of speech are simply conjunctions; and whatever one conjunction can do, as a conjunction, all conjunctions can, of course, do equally well. Hence, if *and* or *but* or *for* or any other connective can not or should not unite independent sentences, no connective can or should do so; and both sentences and paragraphs, to an extent little dreamed of till their structure is closely examined, must fall apart like uncoupled railroad cars. This alternative can hardly recommend itself to any thoughtful student of English: indeed, it would seem far preferable, not only that four particular connectives should be abused, but that the pages of English books should be riddled with misused connectives. Of course, if some special disability can be alleged against these particles that does not hold against other connectives, this argument fails. But no such special disability is alleged. *And, but, etc.* are not more inelegant than other words of their class; that they are inelegant at all is disproved by the fact (established below[1]) that the purest English writers use them freely. Even Prof. Hill's contention, that *and* and *but* are peculiarly liable to be abused, argues only for their judicious use—not for their disuse; and caution is necessary against the abuse of every means of expression by language.[2]

[1] §§ 264, 267.

[2] And, by the way, in no respect more than in the use of conjunctions *within* the sentence—the special province, according to Prof. Hill, of *and* and *but*. Where one offence is committed with *and* or *but*, as initial words, scores of offences are committed with these words internally, (§ 220, *above*); and as a teacher of composition, Prof. Hill knows this. Indeed, his first words quoted above show that he does; but, with his further statement, "They should always connect," *etc.*, he commits himself hopelessly.

261. *Secondly*, most English connectives (especially *and, but, etc.*) are so insignificant in size, and so unapt to attract attention in any way, that they may be used the oftener without injury to style; while the substitutes for them,—such words as *also, however,*[1] *because*—being longer, are the more unmanageable, whether placed first in the sentence or not.

262. *Thirdly*, if even a single alternative means of expression or form of construction is cut off from the language by unnecessary proscription, Style loses in variety, or even in clearness or force, and the writer is proportionately crippled.[2] What folly, then, to lay down a rule that, in its logical consequences, banishes all connectives from the first place in the sentence—to diminish one's resources, reduce one's armory, and then expect to fight the better the battle of efficient communication of thought!

263. In the light of these truths, Prof. Hill's argument must appear weakness itself. It plainly rests on two grounds, one for the whole composition, another (or two others much alike) for the paragraph and the sentence;—(1) "If nothing comes before the conjunction [*and* or *but*] there is nothing for it to connect with what comes after;" (2) "A new paragraph (sentence) indicates that there is a break in the sense too important to be bridged by a [that is, *any*] conjunction." Further, though Prof. Hill distinctly limits his first statement to "*and* or *but*," the reason he gives why these words can not begin a whole composition is, of course, an equally good reason why no connective can be so employed. Hence, the second statement is unconsciously broadened, till the general assertion is made, that the gap between paragraphs or sentences is too great for any conjunction (and therefore any connective) to bridge.

<small>In a personal letter, quoted here by permission, Prof. Hill claims that all that can fairly be inferred from his text is that initial connectives must not be abused. "The sum and substance of what I say about *and* and *but* is that they should never be used without a good reason." But surely, this statement is utterly incompatible with his printed words, "*And* and *but* . . . should *always* connect *words* or *clauses*"—not sentences, be it observed—and with the fact that not a single initial *and* or *but* can be found between the covers of his *Principles*, except in quotation. (See, also, § 263, *below*.)

[1] *However* is not always a full substitute for *but*. (See the next foot-note and *Webster's Dictionary*, s. v.)

[2] Thus, "I, however, can not approve of it" and "I can not, however, approve of it" certainly differ in meaning; while, "However, I cannot approve of it" is not only a variation in form, but, doubtless, a more emphatic summing up of what has gone before,—that in opposition to which the new sentence is set.</small>

264. But (1) there may be, and in actual literary products there sometimes is, not a little before the whole composition with which an initial *and* or *but* may properly connect what comes after. Thus, the prophet Jonah, in the English version, begins, "*Now* the word of the Lord came unto Jonah, the son of Amittai, saying," *etc.* In Hebrew, the initial word is literally *And;* the thought in Jonah's mind seeming to be, "The word of the Lord has been sent to many prophets, who have thus revealed His will to man. And now to me, too, Jonah the son of Amittai, has this mighty revelation come: Jonah, too, is a prophet of the Lord." So, Dickens opens his *A Message from the Sea* with these words, "'And a mighty sing'lar and pretty place it is' . . . said Captain Jorgan, looking up at it." The conjunction connects much that is told later in the story, but which is really antecedent to Captain Jorgan's remark, with the rest that follows in the course of the tale. Compare, "And so it was announced in all the newspapers of Paris, that Prince Moleskine, . . . , was about to return to his own country."[1] Of course, such openings are abrupt and brusque; but often an abrupt or even a brusque opening is exactly the beginning desired or even necessary.[2] It must be confessed, however, and it ought to be noted by the student, that such cases are extremely rare. Prof. Hill errs simply in forgetting the few examples that make his "never" too strong, and in limiting his remark to *and* and *but.*

265. (2) Prof. Hill's other allegation, that a new paragraph or a new sentence indicates a break in the sense too important to be bridged by a conjunction, is (to characterize it mildly) a bald assumption. Not one scrap of evidence is adduced by him to support his statement; while the fact that the best English writers habitually begin both paragraphs and sentences with conjunctions abundantly proves that a conjunction *can* bridge the gap indicated by these breaks.[3]

[1] E. C. Grenville-Murray, (a powerful rather than a finished writer.)

[2] Three other examples are not English; but they may be given with a view to noting how writers of two most cultivated peoples thought fit to begin their works. Aristophanes, *Lysistrate*, l. 1, sets a character to exclaiming, by way of prologue, 'ΑΛΛ' εἰ τις εἰς Βακχεῖον αὐτὰς ἐκάλεσεν; and Euripides, *Medea*, opens with a phrase that, though called interjection, really *connects* the whole play with the legend of the Golden Fleece, Εἴθ' ὤφελ' Ἀργοῦς μὴ διαπτάσθαι σκάφος. So, Virgil, *Æneid*, iv. 1, "*At* regina gravi jamdudum saucia cura Vulnus alit venis."

[3] § 267, *below.*

266. Hence, Prof. Hill's whole argument falls. The question raised is, *Ought* a conjunction to do so and so? The point at issue is, *Can* a conjunction do this work? No, says Prof. Hill, it can not, and therefore it ought not. But, surely, this is not reasoning. It is a bold, ill-concealed, begging of the whole question; and this directly in the face of Prof. Hill's own concession that "much good usage" can be found for the construction. Initial *and* and *but* DO bridge the gap between sentences: yet they CAN not![1]

267. Finally, the authority of both rhetoricians and standard writers is uncompromisingly against any such proscription of connectives. Campbell (as has been said) assails the position taken by some of his contemporaries;[2] Blair seems never to have heard of the objections that Campbell notes;[3] Lord Kames was engrossed by the higher questions of his art; Whately, Bain, nearly the whole catalogue of professed rhetoricians, either ignore the rule or laugh it to scorn. Against these names, the *ad captandum* decisions recorded above weigh literally as the dust in the balance. Usage, too, is undeniably on the same side. Initial *and's*—and especially *but's* and *for's*—can be found on the pages, not only of average writers,

[1] § 397, *below*.—There are really two questions raised in this discussion, (1) Ought a conjunction to begin a whole composition? (2) Ought it to begin a sentence or a paragraph? but the rare case of a whole composition beginning with a conjunction is neglected here as practically of no importance.

[2] His chief argument is usage; but he urges also the inconsiderable size of *and*, *now*, etc., and the greater length and unwieldiness of the longer connectives, as well as the loss in variety entailed by the cutting off of even a single form that is in good use, and to which no valid objection has been brought.

[3] *Lectures*, XII.—Blair speaks of the misuse of *and* internally, but does not say one word about initial *and*. Yet it is not impossible—it seems, perhaps, probable—that Campbell meant Blair by his "some critics." In 1760, when Campbell was writing at Aberdeen, Blair was lecturing at Edinburgh, and this with such success that his lectures were actually "*pirated*" and published surreptitiously. Now, a hundred miles in Scotland, *anno* 1760, was a long distance, and Campbell might easily have been imposed upon by an illegitimate copy of Blair's book. Prof. Meiklejohn (*Life and Letters of W. B. Hodgson, LL. D.*, p. 9,) notes the fact that prayers were said at Edinburgh for George IV. six months after that monarch was dead; and, if this was possible in the second quarter of the 19th century, what need be doubted of the third quarter of the eighteenth? Assuming, then, that Blair was misunderstood and misrepresented—as, of course, he could easily have been on such a point—nothing would have been more natural than for Campbell to expose *in a parliamentary way* the reported blunder of his great contemporary and rival.

but of the best—indeed, of all—writers. Even Addison, who (compared with most other writers) uses a singularly small number of initial connectives of any sort, nevertheless begins many a paragraph and sentence with one or another of the four words in question.[1] In Shakspere, in Spenser, Milton, (both verse and prose), in Southey, Carlyle, De Quincey, Macaulay, Motley, Bancroft, Prescott, Washington Irving, Hawthorne, George Eliot, in the most imaginative, as well as in the most matter-of-fact writers, the construction can be found and abundantly.[2] Indeed, such arbitrary and unfounded statements as those of Mr. Quackenbos and Prof. Hill would have been scouted at once by all habitual readers of good English, had not the connectives complained of been so common and (except *however*) so inconsiderable in size as scarcely to attract the ordinary reader's attention. Nor could *and* or *but* or any other initial conjunction have impressed itself so painfully on any sensible man's literary feelings, had he not been suffering from that rhetorical hysteria which, while it exalts the sensibilities, depraves the taste and debauches the judgment.

3. Parallel Construction.

268. "When several consecutive sentences iterate or illustrate the same idea, they should, as far as possible, be formed alike."[3] The parallelism of form is a natural

---

[1] In *The Spectator*, No. 329, there are fifteen paragraphs and thirty independent sentences. Only four paragraphs and one sentence are introduced by connectives,—*indeed, further, in the next place, then* (twice), and none of them standing first. Yet in No. 335, one sentence begins with *however*, another with *but*, and a third with *and;* while, in No. 414, one paragraph and two sentences begin with *but*.

[2] How abundantly the following statements may prove. They could be multiplied almost indefinitely. Motley, *The United Netherlands*, ch. xv., begins *thirty-four* sentences with one or another of the four condemned copulatives;—Edition of 1868 (Harper and Brothers, N. Y.), vol. II, p. 216, 2; 219, *220*, 221, *222*, each 1; 223, *225*, each 3; 230, *232*, 236, *237*, *238*, each 1; 239, *241*, each 2; 244, 245, *246*, 247, 248, *249*, 250, *251*, *252*, each 1; *254*, 2; 255, 259, each 1. (Page-numbers in italics refer to examples of these words beginning paragraphs. Quoted matter is not counted.) Hawthorne, *The Marble Faun*, vol. ii. chap's viii. to x., shows *seventeen* examples:—Edition of 1860 (Ticknor and Fields, Boston), pp. 93, 94, 95, *96d*, *97d*, 103, 106, *108*, 111, 112*d*, *113*, 115*d*, each 1; 116*d*, 117*d*, each 2; 118, 1. (Examples in dialogue are marked *d*.)

[3] Bain, *ut cit.*

mode of expressing the parallelism of thought; just as a change of form is the natural mode of suggesting a change of thought. Thus ;—

(1) "Now, Sir, the first charge which I bring against Lord Ellenborough is, that he has been guilty of an act of gross disobedience, that he has done that which was forbidden in the strongest terms by those from whom his power is derived. The Home Government says, Do not interfere in the concerns of heathen temples. Is it denied that Lord Ellenborough has interfered in the concerns of a heathen temple? The Home Government says, Make no presents to heathen temples. Is it denied that Lord Ellenborough has proclaimed to all the world his intention to make a present to a heathen temple? The Home Government says, Do not decorate heathen temples. Is it denied that Lord Ellenborough has proclaimed to all the world his intention to decorate a heathen temple? The Home Government says, Do not send troops to do honour to heathen temples. Is it denied that Lord Ellenborough sent a body of troops to escort these gates to a heathen temple!"[1]

(2) "No sooner had they arrived than Laval and Mézy, the new governor, proceeded to construct the new council. Mézy knew nobody in the colony, and was, at this time, completely under Laval's influence. The nominations, therefore, were virtually made by the bishop alone, in whose hands, and not in those of the governor, the blank commission had been placed."[2]

269. When joined with Balance, this assimilation, produces an even stronger effect; as, "Agitation and rebellion, you say, are in kind the same thing: they differ only in degree. Sir, they are the same thing in the sense in which to breathe a vein and to cut a throat are the same thing. There are many points of resemblance between the act of the surgeon and the act of the assassin. In both there is the steel, the incision, the smart, the bloodshed. But the acts differ as widely as possible both in moral character and in physical effect."[3] Had the last three sentences read,—They are the same thing in the sense in which the act of the surgeon and the act of the assassin are the same thing: in both . . . bloodshed. But the acts are far from being

---

[1] Macaulay, *Speeches, The Gates of Somnauth.*
[2] Parkman, *The Old Régime in Canada,* ch. vii.
[3] Macaulay, *Speeches, The Ministry of Lord Melbourne.*

the same thing in . . . effect,—the parallelism would have been yet more complete. (But see § 271, *below*. Macaulay wisely decided in favor of Variety.)

270. Two means to Parallel Construction have been noted;—(1) "The principal subject and the principal predicate should retain their positions throughout;" (2) Corresponding expressions should have corresponding places. For example;—

(1) "He [Mézy] seems to have been one of those natures that run with engrossing vehemence along any channel into which they may have been turned. At the Hermitage he was all devotee; but climate and conditions had changed, and he or his symptoms changed with them.[1] He found himself raised suddenly to a post of command, or one which was meant to be such. The town major of Caen[2] was set to rule over a region far larger than France."[3]

(2) "The summer of 1661 was marked by a series of calamities scarcely paralleled even in the annals of this disastrous epoch. Early in February, thirteen colonists were surprised and captured, next came a fight between a large band of laborers and two hundred and sixty Iroquois;[4] in the following month, ten more Frenchmen were killed or taken; and henceforth, till winter closed, the settlements had scarcely a breathing space."[5]

271. But the laws of Variety[6] and Emphasis[7] often set this rule aside. When parallel constructions become monotonous, especially when they lead to the misplacing of emphatic or unemphatic words, they cannot be preferable to varied forms, ever fresh and correctly emphatic. Thus;—

(1) "Fortune had been strangely bountiful to him.[8] The nations of Europe, exhausted by wars and dissensions, looked

---

[1] Better,—but with a change of climate and conditions, he or his symptoms had changed.

[2] That is, Mézy himself.   [3] Parkman, *ut cit.*, ch. viii.

[4] Better,—a large band of laborers met and fought two hundred and sixty Iroquois.

[5] Id. ib. ch. ii.   [6] § 338, *below*.   [7] § 204, *above*.   [8] Louis XIV.

upon him with respect and fear. Among weak and weary neighbors, he alone was strong. The death of Mazarin had released him from tutelage ; feudalism in the person of Condé was abject before him ; he had reduced his parliaments to submission ; and, in the arrest of the ambitious prodigal Fouquet, he was preparing a crushing blow to the financial corruption which had devoured France. Nature had formed him to act the part of King. Even his critics and enemies praise the grace and majesty of his presence, and he impressed his courtiers with an admiration which seems to have been to an astonishing degree genuine. He was a devout observer of the forms of religion ; and, as the buoyancy of youth passed away, his zeal was stimulated by a profound fear of the devil. Mazarin had reared him in ignorance ; but his faculties were excellent in their way, and, in a private station, would have made him an efficient man of business. The vivacity of his passions, and his inordinate love of pleasure, were joined to a persistent will and a rare power of labor. The vigorous mediocrity of his understanding delighted in grappling with details. His astonished courtiers saw him take on himself the burden of administration, and work at it without relenting for more than half a century. Great as was his energy, his pride was far greater. As king by divine right, he felt himself raised immeasurably above the highest of his subjects ; but, while vindicating with unparalleled haughtiness his claims to supreme authority, he was, at the outset, filled with a sense of the duties of his high place, and fired by an ambition to make his reign beneficent to France as well as glorious to himself."[1]

The construction is carried into the two next paragraphs, and always with the same variety and correctness of emphasis. A finer example of intentional non-parallelism, where parallel construction would have been unendurably monotonous, can not easily be found. The student should rewrite the passage with *he* as the subject throughout, and then note the inferiority of the latter form. On the other hand, the parallel construction of so many sentences in the following extract grows extremely wearisome, and would be utterly unbearable, were it not for the interrupting passage, "But we did none of these things . . . to be perpetrated in open day."

---

[1] Parkman, *ut cit*, ch. x.

(2) "Now, Sir, it is a difficult matter to determine in what way Christian rulers ought to deal with such superstitions as these. We might have acted as the Spaniards acted in the New World. We might have attempted to introduce our own religion by force. We might have sent missionaries among the natives at the public charge. We might have held out hopes of public employment to converts, and have imposed civil disabilities on Mahometans and Pagans. But we did none of these things; and herein we judged wisely. Our duty, as rulers, was to preserve strict neutrality on all questions merely religious; and I am not aware that we have ever swerved from strict neutrality for the purpose of making proselytes to our own faith. But we have, I am sorry to say, sometimes deviated from the right path in the opposite direction. Some Englishmen, who have held high office in India, seem to have thought that the only religion which was not entitled to toleration and to respect was Christianity. They regarded every Christian missionary with extreme jealousy and disdain; and they suffered the most atrocious crimes, if enjoined by the Hindoo superstition, to be perpetrated in open day. It is lamentable to think how long after our power was firmly established in Bengal, we, grossly neglecting the first and plainest duty of the civil magistrate, suffered the practices of infanticide and suttee to continue unchecked. We decorated the temples of the false gods. We provided the dancing girls. We gilded and painted the images to which our ignorant subjects bowed down. We repaired and embellished the car under the wheels of which crazy devotees flung themselves at every festival to be crushed to death. We sent guards of honor to escort pilgrims to the places of worship. We actually made oblations at the shrines of idols. All this was considered, and is still considered, by some prejudiced Anglo-Indians of the old school, as profound policy. I believe that there never was so shallow, so senseless a policy. We gained nothing by it. We lowered ourselves in the eyes of those whom we meant to flatter. We led them to believe that we attached no importance to the difference between Christianity and heathenism. Yet how vast that difference is! I altogether abstain from alluding to topics which belong to divines. I speak merely as a politician anxious for the morality and the temporal well being of society, and, so speaking, I say that to countenance the Brahmanical idolatry, and to discountenance that religion which has done so much to promote justice, and mercy, and

freedom, and arts, and sciences, and good government, and domestic happiness, which has struck off the chains of the slave, which has mitigated the horrors of war, which has raised women from servants and playthings into companions and friends, is to commit high treason against humanity and civilization."[1]

A careful study of the passage will show beyond all doubt that Macaulay intended no emphasis on his constantly recurring subject *we*—still less on *I* in the last three sentences; and yet unless such emphasis were intended, and even if it were intended, the many repetitions of the same construction are terribly damaging.[2]

272. Where emphasis is intended, however, the parallel construction is a most certain means by which to secure it. Thus;—

"An army, a navy, a preventive service, a police force, may do their work whether the public feeling be with them or against them. Whether we dislike the corn laws or not, your custom houses and your coast guard keep out foreign corn. The multitude at Manchester was not the less effectually dispersed by the yeomanry, because the interference of the yeomanry excited the bitterest indignation. There the object was to produce a material effect; the material means were sufficient; and nothing more was required. But *a Church* exists for moral ends. *A Church* exists to be loved, to be reverenced, to be heard with docility, to reign in the understandings and hearts of men.[3]

4. METHOD.

273. "A paragraph should be consecutive, or free from dislocation"; that is, the several thoughts expressed in it should follow each other in their natural order, and the whole paragraph move forward step by

---

[1] Macaulay, *The Gates of Somnauth.*

[2] See § 272, *below.*—Of course, allowance must be made for the fact that the extract is from a speech. Macaulay perhaps never wrote so ill in his *History* or his *Essays.*

[3] Id., *The Church of Ireland.*—The parallelism of the concluding sentences is all the more marked because of the intentional variety of form of the other sentences.

step from the topic-sentence to the close. "Each paragraph," says Prof. Bain, "has a plan dictated by the nature of the composition. According to such plan, every pertinent statement has a suitable place; in that place, it contributes to the general effect; and, out of that place, it makes confusion." Orderly arrangement of course assists the reader by concentrating his attention: a want of method embarrasses him by unnecessarily taxing his attention. Of the two examples that follow, the first is correct, the second contains serious dislocations;—

(1) "When the news that he[1] had been stopped, insulted, roughly handled, and plundered, and that he was still a prisoner in the hands of rude churls, reached the capital, many passions were roused. [Topic-sentence.] Rigid Churchmen, who had, a few hours before, begun to think that they were freed from their allegiance to him, now felt misgivings. He had not quitted his kingdom. He had not consummated his abdication. If he should resume his regal office, could they, on their principles, refuse to pay him obedience? [First Specification.] Enlightened statesmen foresaw with concern that all the disputes which his flight had for a moment set at rest would be revived and exasperated by his return. [Second specification.] Some of the common people, though still smarting from recent wrongs, were touched with compassion for a great prince outraged by ruffians, and were willing to entertain a hope, more honourable to their good nature than to their discernment, that he might even now repent of the errors which had brought on him so terrible a punishment." [Third specification.][2]

(2) "Norwich was the capital of a large and fruitful province. [Topic-sentence.] It was the residence of a bishop and of a chapter. It was the chief seat of the chief manufacture of the realm. Some men distinguished by learning and science had recently dwelt there; and no place in the kingdom, except the capital and the universities, had more attractions for the curious. [The second of these three specifications properly belongs first; so that the first and the third, closely related, may stand

[1] James II.   [2] Macaulay, *History of England*, ch. x.

together.] The library, the museum, the aviary, and the botanical garden of Sir Thomas Browne, were thought by the Fellows of the Royal Society well worthy of a long pilgrimage. [Correctly placed.] Norwich had also a court in miniature. [This 'court in miniature' is then most amply described, but the paragraph closes abruptly.] In the year 1693, the population of Norwich was found, by actual enumeration, to be between twenty-eight and twenty-nine thousand souls." [A statement utterly misplaced after the "court in miniature," and properly belonging either with or even before the earlier specifications. Its fittest place would seem to be immediately after the topic-sentence.][1]

5. UNITY.

274. Unity requires that every statement in the paragraph shall be subservient to one *principal* affirmation. This principal affirmation is, of course, the topic-sentence, which sets forth the subject of the paragraph. To this everything that has any right to a place in the paragraph must be related, either as explanation, specification, illustration, or in some other definite way. Anything not so related forms a digression, and, according to its length and its subject-matter, more or less diverts the reader's attention. Such a digression should be put into an independent paragraph. Thus ;—

(1) "On returning to our own frontiers, I had an opportunity of displaying my exemplary greenness. [Topic-sentence.] That message to my brother with all its *virus* of insolence I repeated as faithfully for the spirit, and as literally for the expressions, as my memory allowed me to do; and in that troublesome effort, simpleton that I was, fancied myself exhibiting a soldier's loyalty to his commanding officer. [Specification.] My brother thought otherwise: he was more angry with me than with the enemy.—I ought, he said, to have refused all participation in such *sans culottes*[2] insolence ; to carry it was to acknowledge it as fit to be carried. [Contrasting Sentence.] One grows wiser every day; and on this particular

---

[1] Macaulay, *History of England*, ch. iii.
[2] The spelling in the *Author's Library Edition* (Boston, 1873.)

day I made a resolution that, if again made prisoner, I would bring no more 'jaw' (so my brother called it) from the Philistines. If these people *would* send 'jaw,' I settled that, henceforwards, it must go through the post-office.'' [Reflection.][1]

(2) "My father was a merchant; not in the sense of Scotland, where it means a retail dealer, one, for instance, who sells groceries in a cellar, but in the English sense, a sense rigorously exclusive; that is, he was a man engaged in *foreign* commerce, and no other; therefore, in *wholesale* commerce, and no other —which last limitation of the idea is important, because it brings him within the benefit of Cicero's condescending distinction as one who ought to be despised certainly, but not too intensely to be despised even by a Roman senator. [Though punctuated as a sentence, this medley contains three independent statements, each of which should be in a sentence by itself. The third mars the unity of the paragraph even worse than the further digression described below.] He—this imperfectly despicable man—died at an early age, and very soon after the incidents recorded in this chapter, leaving to his family, then consisting of a wife and six children, an unburdened estate producing exactly sixteen hundred pounds a year. Naturally, therefore, at the date of my narrative—whilst he was still living —he had an income very much larger, from the addition of current commercial profits."[2]

The paragraph then broadens into a detailed discussion of the scale of living common in an English merchant's family. It cites facts, proves England "the paradise of household servants," makes a contrast in this respect between merchants' and the poorer noblemen's families, comments on the consequent "disturbance upon the usual scale for measuring the relations of rank," and warns the reader not to think De Quincey's family of higher rank than it really was. In a word, after this trying digression, it ends exactly where it began, "My father was a merchant." If the digression was in any sense necessary, it should have been put into a paragraph by itself. (Compare the next example.) But De Quincey painfully often neglected Unity, and crowded his paragraphs (as he did his sentences) with digressions, till the reader's patience is (and should be) quite exhausted.

[1] De Quincey, *Autobiographic Sketches*, ch. ii.
[2] *Autobiographic Sketches*, ch. i.

(3) "The circumstances which attended the sudden dissolution of this most tender connection I will here rehearse. And, that I may do so more intelligibly, I will first describe that serene and sequestered position which we occupied in life.

"Any expression of personal vanity, intruding upon impassioned records, is fatal to their effect—as being incompatible with that absorption of spirit and that self-oblivion in which only[1] deep passion originates or can find a genial home. It would, therefore, to myself be exceedingly painful that even a shadow, or so much as a *seeming* expression of that tendency, should creep into these reminiscences. And yet, on the other hand, it is so impossible, without laying an injurious restraint upon the natural movement of such a narrative, to prevent oblique gleams reaching the reader from such circumstances of luxury or aristocratic elegance as surrounded my childhood, that on all accounts I think it better to tell him, from the first, with the simplicity of truth, in what order of society my family moved at the time from which this preliminary narrative is dated. Otherwise it might happen that merely by reporting faithfully the facts of this early experience, I could hardly prevent the reader from receiving an impression as of some higher rank than did really belong to my family. And this impression might seem to have been designedly insinuated by myself.

"My father was a merchant;" *etc.* (as in Ex. (2), *above*.)[2]

275. The rule, however, admits many exceptions; and dogmatic or cramping statements of it are to be as carefully avoided as are similar statements of the rule for Unity in the sentence. Poetry, especially, may violate the law; and naturally, for its object is to please rather than to instruct. But even in Prose, sentences that are "merely explanatory or qualifying" may acquire a "dangerous prominence," if placed in a paragraph alone. Thus ;—

"Meanwhile the old man looked through the sketches and studies with which the room was strewed.

"'You do not finish your things?' he said abruptly.

"René flushed darkly.

[1] *Alone.*
[2] Id. ib.

"'Oil pictures cost money,' he said briefly, 'and—I am very poor.'

"Though a peasant's son, he was very proud: the utterance must have hurt him much.

"*The stranger took snuff.*

"'You are a man of singular genius,' he said simply. 'You only want to be known to get the prices of Meissonier.'"[1]

276. At the same time, the rule may be made more stringent for the paragraph than for the sentence. Paragraph-digressions occupy more room, and, hence, create the greater confusion. Sometimes a connective may be introduced to mark the change of track, and, of course, should be, if possible, even at the beginning of independent paragraphs.[2]

6. Due Proportion.

277. The several sentences or parts of sentences in a paragraph must be in due proportion: the principal statements must not be outweighed by the subordinates, but, as in the sentence, everything must "have bulk and prominence according to its importance." Thus;—

(1) "I have mentioned already that we had four male guardians, (a fifth being my mother.) These four were B., E., G., and H. The two consonants, B. and G., gave us little trouble. G., the wisest of the whole band, lived at a distance of more than one hundred miles; him, therefore, we rarely saw; but B., living within four miles of Greenhay, washed his hands of us by inviting us, every now and then, to spend a few days at his house."[3] [In proportion.]

(2) See Example (2), § 274, *above*.—In it the modifying statements far outweigh the principals, and require condensa-

---

[1] Ouida, *A Provence Rose*, III.—Some allowance must be made for the fact that the stranger is on the point of proposing to the starving artist to do a dishonorable act.

[2] For example, De Quincey begins a paragraph digression, *Now*, to any man who is acquainted with commercial life as it exists in England.

[3] De Quincey, *ut cit.*, ch. ii.

tion. The bare facts that it relates, are, (*a*) My father was an English merchant, (*b*) He died at an early age soon after the incidents recorded in this chapter, leaving his wife and six children an unburdened estate of sixteen hundred pounds a year, (*c*) Naturally, therefore, his own income had been much larger. Now, these facts may, of course, be appreciably expanded by modifying statements, and yet the proportion of the paragraph be undisturbed; but much of what De Quincey has crowded in must be thrown into a separate paragraph or be omitted. Thus, the following re-writing probably carries the insertion of modifying matter to its extreme ;—

My father was an English merchant; that is, one engaged in foreign, and therefore wholesale, commerce. As a wholesale dealer, he came within the benefit of Cicero's condescending distinction as one who certainly ought to be despised, but not too intensely even by a Roman Senator. He died, *etc.*, as in (*b*), *above*. Naturally, therefore, *etc.*, as in (*c*) *above*.

In Scotland, the word *merchant* means a retail dealer, one, for instance, who sells groceries in a cellar; but the English sense of the term is rigorously exclusive. The limitation of the term is important; for it leaves my father only an imperfectly despicable man—a man whose current commercial profits made him undeniably rich.

But the additional paragraph is an unnecessary digression and therefore weak.

7. CLIMAX. BATHOS.

278. A paragraph or even a single (compound) sentence may be so arranged that its "first part prepares the way for the middle, and the middle for the end, in a kind of ascent."[1] This ascent is called Climax; its opposite descent, Bathos. Either may be intentional or accidental; but Climax is always an excellence, unintentional Bathos a glaring defect. Intentional Bathos may be humorous or pathetic or witty,—may create a good-natured laugh or start a tear or point a stinging sarcasm. Thus ;—

---

[1] Abbott, *How to Write Clearly*, R. 39.

(1) "An open (*a*), tolerant (*a'*), and kindly (*a''*) temper, that welcomes confidence (*b*), that overlooks faults (*b'*), that makes much of any good in other men (*b''*), that easily forgives wrong (*b'''*)."[1]

"As the railroad track sweeps through the towns which string themselves along it (*a*), climbs mountains and plunges into valleys (*a'*), hides itself in forests and flashes out again into broad plains and along the sides of happy lakes (*a''*), and evidently cares nothing for them all except as they just give it ground on which to roll out its length towards its end by the shore of the Pacific (*a'''*),—so this man's life pierces right on through all the tempting and perplexing complications of our human living (*b*), and will not rest until it has attained the mastery of legal power (*b'*)."[2]

"The same is true about the sympathy of the rich (*a*) with the poor (*b*), of the believer (*a'*) with the doubter (*b'*), of the hopeful (*a''*) with the despondent (*b''*), of the liberal (*a'''*) with the bigoted (*b'''*); aye, even of the saint (*a''''*) with the sinner (*b''''*)."[3]

"And herein lies the great miracle of speech, the strongest proof of its living (*a*), organic (*a'*)—I had almost said divine (*a''*)—power, that even as the processes of vegetable life build up (*b*), assimilate (*b'*), vivify (*b''*), and transform into self-sustaining (*c*), growing (*c'*), and fruitful (*c''*) forms (*b'''*) the dead material of mechanical nature, so language" *etc.*[4]

(2) "Sir, they[5] are grand, they are splendid; there are not twelve men, sir, in Boston who could have written those plays."[6]

"Such a derangement must have reduced society to its first elements, and led to a direct collision of conflicting interests."[4]

"Language can inform them[7] with the spiritual philosophy (*a'*) of the Pauline epistles (*b'*) the living thunder (*a''*) of a Demosthenes (*b''*), or the material picturesqueness (*a*) of a Russell (*b*)."[8]

---

[1] Phillips Brooks, Sermons, vol. ii. p. 226.   [2] Id. ib. p. 114.

[3] Id. ib. p. 120.   [4] G. P. Marsh, *Lectures*, i. 288.

[5] The plays of Shakspere.   [6] Quoted by Hodgson, *Errors in English.*

[7] Inexpressive articulate sounds.

[8] Geo. P. Marsh, *Lectures*, i. p. 289. (Cited by A. S. Hill, p. 135.) Singularly enough, the same sentence contains the three exceptionally fine climaxes last quoted under (1), *above*.

(3) "Then fill a fair and honest cup, and bear it straight to me;
　　The goblet hallows all it holds, what'er the liquid be;
　　And may the cherubs on its face protect me from the sin,
　　That dooms one to those dreadful words,—'My dear, where *have* you
　　　　been?'"[1]

"May the blossom of your heart—
　　Eleanore—
Be a rose whose petals part
　　But to pour
Sweets of love;—and if there be
Tears as well as smiles for thee,
May they be the dew that He
　　Doth restore.

"So, a kiss before you go,
　　Eleanore,
(Reaching up to me tiptoe
　　From the floor;—
With the gold around your head,
And your dimpled cheeks so red,)
There—be off with you to bed,
　　Eleanore!"[2]

"But changing hands, it[3] reached at length a Puritan divine,
Who used to follow Timothy, and take a little wine,
But hated punch and prelacy; and so it was, perhaps,
He went to Leyden, where he found conventicles and schnaps.

[From Leyden the bowl comes over in the *Mayflower*, and Miles Standish and his soldiers drink "a long and solemn draught" from it on the eve of a battle with the Indians.]

"That night, affrighted from his rest, the screaming eagle flew,
He heard the Pequot's ringing whoop, the soldier's wild halloo;
And there the sachem learned the rule he taught to kith and kin;
'Run from the white man when you find he smells of Hollands gin.'"[4]

"When George the Fourth was still reigning over the privacies of Windsor, when the Duke of Wellington was Prime Minister, and Mr. Vincy was mayor of the old corporation in Middlemarch, Mrs. Casaubon, born Dorothea Brooke, had taken her wedding journey to Rome."[5]

---

[1] O. W. Holmes, *On Lending a Punch-Bowl*, st. 13.

[2] C. H. L. (in the Philadelphia *Evening Bulletin*), st. 5, 6.

[3] Dr. Holmes's punch bowl.

[4] Holmes, *ut cit.*, st. 4, 8.　　[5] George Eliot. (Cited by Prof. Hill, p. 135.)

IV.

THE WHOLE COMPOSITION.[1]

279. The laws that control the composition as a whole are derived in great part from the nature of the thought expressed, and belong, therefore, to Invention;[2] but there are certain other rules that apply to all compositions, and are in part, at least, laws of form. These belong here.

1. The Parts of a Composition.

280. Considered as a whole, the Composition has four parts, two *essential* and two *non-essential*;—two that should be found in every composition; two that may be present, but need not be. The essential parts are;—

(1) The PROPOSITION, which sets forth *the limits within which* or *the end for which* the subject of the composition is to be discussed, or else states *the precise form in some other particular* that the work proposed is to take;

(2) The DISCUSSION, which is *the body* of the composition, and contains *what is said* of the theme as limited in the Proposition.

The non-essential parts are;—

(1) The INTRODUCTION, which contains necessary *preliminary* matter;

(2) The CONCLUSION, which contains necessary matter by way of *summary*, of *general enforcement* of the truths taught, *etc.*

281. Thus, Matthew Arnold's essay *On Translating Homer*[3] opens as follows;—

---

[1] § 170, *above*.   [2] Part Second, *below*.
[3] *Essays in Criticism* (New York, 1877), pp. 284 ff.

"It has more than once been suggested to me that I should translate Homer. That is a task for which I have neither the time nor the courage; but the suggestion led me to regard yet more closely a poet whom I had already long studied, and for one or two years the works of Homer were seldom out of my hands. The study of classical literature is probably on the decline; but, whatever may be the fate of this study in general, it is certain that, as instruction spreads and the number of readers increases, attention will be more and more directed to the poetry of Homer, not indeed as part of a classical course, but as the most important poetical monument existing. Even within the last ten years two fresh translations of the Iliad have appeared in England: one by a man of great ability and genuine learning, Professor Newman; the other by Mr. Wright, the conscientious and painstaking translator of Dante. It may safely be asserted that neither of these works will take rank as the standard translation of Homer; that the task of rendering him will still be attempted by other translators. [Introduction.] It may perhaps be possible to render to these some service, to save them some loss of labor, by pointing out rocks on which their predecessors have split, and the right objects on which a translator of Homer should fix his attention." [Proposition.]

Then follows an elaborate discussion,[1] comprising, of course, the bulk of the essay; and then another single paragraph,[2] concluding the whole matter;—

"Here I stop. I have said so much, because I think that the task of translating Homer into English verse both will be re-attempted, and may be re-attempted successfully. There are great works composed of parts so disparate, that one translator is not likely to have the requisite gifts for poetically rendering all of them. Such are the works of Shakspere, and Goethe's Faust: and these it is best to attempt to render in prose only. People praise Tieck and Schlegel's version of Shakspere: I, for my part, would sooner read Shakspere in the French prose translation, and that is saying a great deal; but in the German poets' hands Shakspere so often gets, especially where he is humorous, an air of what the French call *niaiserie!* and can anything be more un-Shaksperian than that? Again; Mr. Hayward's prose translation of the first part of Faust—so good that it makes one regret Mr. Hayward should have abandoned the line of translation for a kind of literature which

[1] Pp. 285-367.   [2] Pp. 367-8.

is, to say the least, somewhat slight—is not likely to be surpassed by any translation in verse. But poems like the Iliad, which, in the main, are in one manner, may hope to find a poetical translator so gifted and so trained as to be able to learn that one manner, and to reproduce it. Only, the poet who would reproduce this must cultivate in himself a Greek virtue by no means common among the moderns in general, and the English in particular—*moderation*. For Homer has not only the English vigor, he has the Greek grace; and when one observes the boistering, rollicking way in which his English admirers—even men of genius, like the late Professor Wilson—love to talk of Homer and his poetry, one cannot help feeling that there is no very deep community of nature between them and the object of their enthusiasm. 'It is very well my good friends,' I always imagine Homer saying to them, if he could hear them : 'you do me a great deal of honor, but somehow or other you praise me too like barbarians.' For Homer's grandeur is not the mixed and turbid grandeur of the great poets of the north, of the authors of Othello and Faust; it is a perfect, a lovely grandeur. Certainly his poetry has all the energy and power of the poetry of our ruder climates; but it has, besides, the pure lines of an Ionian horizon, the liquid clearness of an Ionian sky."[1]

282. Unless something *must* be said by way of introduction or conclusion, the work consists of Proposition and Discussion alone. Especially if a work grows too long, or if there is danger of wearing out the reader's attention by unduly postponing "the gist of the matter," or by allowing the interest to flag after the discussion is fairly ended, an excellent rule is, Cut down the composition by lopping off both introduction and conclusion. For example ;—

Mr. Arnold's essay *The Literary Influence of Academics*[2] opens abruptly thus ;—

"It is impossible to put down a book like the history of the French Academy, by Pellison and D'Olivet, which M. Charles

---

[1] Pp. 368–424, *Last Words*, really constitute a separate essay, with its own introduction (pp. 368–370), double proposition (p. 370), double discussion (371–389 and 389–423), and conclusion (423–424).

[2] Id., pp. 39 ff.

Livet has lately re-edited, without being led to reflect upon the absence, in our own country, of any institution like the French Academy, upon the probable causes of this absence, and upon its results. [Proposition.] A thousand voices will be ready to tell us that this absence is a signal mark of our national superiority; that it is in great part owing to this absence that the exhilarating words of Lord Macaulay lately given to the world by his very clever nephew, Mr. Trevelyan, are so profoundly true; 'It may safely be said that the literature now extant in the English language is of far greater value than all the literature which three hundred years ago was extant in all the languages of the world together.' I dare say this is so; only, remembering Spinoza's maxim that the two great banes of humanity are self-conceit and the laziness coming from self-conceit, I think it may do us good, instead of resting in our pre-eminence with perfect security, to look a little more closely why this is so, and whether it is so without any limitations." [The same thought expanded.]

To be sure, the paragraphs that immediately follow this proposition contain, by way of preparation, "a very few words on the outward history of the French Academy;" but these belong to the discussion, not to the essay as a whole, and are aimed at making this discussion the more intelligible: they are introductory, of course, but only to the discussion, not to the whole work. So, the concluding paragraph of the essay—Mr. Arnold's opinion as to the kind of academy England will some day found—is rather a last paragraph of the discussion than a conclusion to the essay as a whole.

Obedience to this rule would have saved a certain preacher the mistake of correcting the excessive length of his sermons by making them (in his deacon's words) "all introduction."

283. But the rule must be construed liberally. Although, as Bacon says, "to use too many Circumstances, ere one come to the matter, is Wearisome," it is also true, as he says, that "to use none at all is Blunt;" and while a reasonably abrupt opening is by no means objectionable, excessive abruptness is commonly to be avoided. A brief introduction or conclusion may, therefore, be admitted, even when one is not in the strictest sense *necessary*. Thus ;—

The essay *On Translating Homer* might have ended without the conclusion quoted above, and might have begun as follows; —"It may safely be asserted that the task of rendering Homer into English will be attempted by yet other translators; and it may perhaps be possible" *etc.;* but the opening would then have been less graceful, the mention of Newman's and Wright's translations (which are, in fact, reviewed in the essay) must have been made elsewhere, and perhaps awkwardly; while the reader would have missed the last two sentences of the essay, two as beautiful sentences as were ever penned by English writer.

At the same time, the relative proportions of the non-essential parts of this essay—and the particular example is most instructive—may serve to emphasize the rule. Of nearly eighty-five closely-printed post-octavo pages they fill but two; and even these two might have been omitted. The rule is a good working *dictum*,—arbitrary, perhaps, and quite as often to be violated as to be obeyed; but it expresses a great truth, *viz.*, that it is always better to begin at once, even at the sacrifice of important matter, even at the risk of a moderately abrupt opening or close, than to allow a delay in coming to the point or an undue prolonging of the subject to exhaust or even severely tax a reader's—much worse, a hearer's—patience. The strain on the attention, to say nothing of the confusion of thought caused by an irrelevant introduction or conclusion, is so great as to make the omission of even admissible matter safer than the insertion of matter that is of doubtful importance.

284. It is not pretended that, in every work by a competent writer, these parts of the composition are thus clearly defined. Even the Proposition and the Discussion may not be marked off by as much as a paragraph-break. The whole matter may be left to the good sense and discrimination of the reader. But, of course, in any work in really good form, both the limitation of the subject that it is the office of the Proposition to set clearly before the reader, and the several statements about this Proposition that it is the office of the Discussion to make, will be so presented that the reader can easily and at once discover them. Thus, to take yet another example from the same writer;—

Mr. Arnold's essay *Marcus Aurelius*[1] opens by quoting John Stuart Mill's assertion that Christian morality is inferior to the best morality of the ancients ; criticizes this remark by showing the true ground and the inspiring motive of any system of morals, and that Christian morality both rests on this ground and has this motive; cites Epictetus and Jesus side by side ; claims that Jesus' statements of certain great truths are far superior to those of Epictetus ; has a sly "rap on the knuckles " for Mr. Mill ; and then (in the first sentence of a new paragraph) *suggests* the subject of his essay, as follows ;—"That which gives to the moral writings of the Emperor Marcus Aurelius their peculiar character and charm, is their being suffused and softened by something of this very sentiment whence Christian morality draws its best power."[2] The balance of the essay cares as little for orderly arrangement, and leaves the reader as unassisted as before. It mentions a "recently published" translation of Aurelius, praises this translation and then brings "one or two little complaints against" it, speaks critically of Aurelius's Greek, gives a brief biography of the Emperor, and finally quotes from his *Meditations* by way of illustrating his ethical opinions. The close is quite as abrupt and disjointed. In one paragraph, it remarks the catholicity of Aurelius's moral code ; in a second, it speaks of the natural affinity of the Roman persecutor of the Christians for Christian morality, and raises the at once vain, yet alluring, question, What effect would this morality have had upon this persecutor of Christians, could he only have known it in its reality?

285. But this plan is attended with no little danger. Unless the Proposition (not formally expressed) is (1) perfectly clear in the writer's own mind, and (2) made equally clear to the reader or hearer, the whole work not only may become inartistic in form and unmethodical in its development of the subject, but also may violate the law of Unity ;[3] the writer becoming confused by the details of his work, and failing of his mission because the reader receives nothing intelligibly. The man who himself does not know where he is going will hardly guide others aright : he who is led blindfolded conceives

---

[1] *Id.*, pp. 253 ff. [2] P. 257. [3] ¶ 289 *below.*

many a false idea of his destination, may have many a stumble or even fall.

285 *a*. A fair test of this doctrine is to read side by side two compositions such as the essays last quoted from. That on the Academies is clear, because its plan is distinctly laid down from page to page, and every step taken in pursuance of this plan is distinctly announced. The writer knows where he is going, and the reader where the writer is taking him. After the opening quoted above (one page), three pages and a half tell the history of the French Academy; two pages more comment on the hostility any plan to set up a high standard in matters of intellect and taste is sure to encounter; five pages discuss certain peculiar characteristics of the English nation; and the rest of the essay (except one paragraph) is filled with examples of what an English Academy might do for English literature. But the essay on Aurelius is a continual surprise. Mr. Arnold doubtless knew what he meant to say in his paper; yet his work looks very much as if he had started writing with only a vaguely defined purpose,—perhaps to review Mr. Long's translation. The consequence is a disjointed essay which, bold as the criticism may seem, makes most unwarrantable demands upon one's attention and ingenuity. The reader sets out with the broad subject *Marcus Aurelius;* learns, after four pages of tossing about, that Mr. Arnold intends to speak of Aurelius's code of morality; is then rudely carried off into five pages on Mr. Long's translation and the Emperor's Greek; meets then nine pages on the life of Aurelius and cognate questions; and is at last allowed (in eleven pages out of twenty-nine that he has read thus far) to hear what moral principles this remarkable man jotted down in his *Meditations.* The close (in two pages more) makes at least three separate remarks cognate with the general discussion of the subject rather than with the matter that has *immediately* preceded. Such a contrast as that between these essays could not exist, perhaps, in the work of a single writer, except as a result of difference of method; and no candid reader can hesitate for a moment, one would think, to say which method is preferable. Even Mr. Arnold's Homer paper, eighty-five pages long, is easily followed through its every winding; and this, quite as much because the clew to the maze has been securely placed in the reader's hand in that last sentence of the first paragraph, as for any other reason.

285 *b*. Important exceptions—or, rather, apparent exceptions —to this principle will be met under the heads of Excitation and Persuasion.[1]

286. Of course, anything *mechanical* in this use of method will impair a writer's success; but the artist must everywhere "conceal his art;" and an extreme of formality were better, one would think, than confusion or failure. The chief end of discourse is to communicate thought; and failure in this particular is, therefore, total failure. Yet how many worthy books are not read, how many excellent addresses are not listened to, simply because their method is so outrageously bad, that readers and hearers alike refuse the labor necessary to be instructed by them! The assertion often made that a strict arrangement develops only formality, stiffness and awkwardness, and hampers or even dwarfs or enfeebles the mind of the writer, tying him down to mechanical processes when he most needs to be free,—this assertion can not possibly be true in all cases—is not true (as many teachers will testify) even in the elementary work of students. An orderly arrangement may guide a writer without affecting his liberty; while (as has been said), without such orderly arrangement, clear in his own mind, and clearly impressed upon the mind of his reader, he may fall into confusion, or spend his well-meant labor in vain.

287. To facilitate this methodical planning and construction of discourse, a synopsis of the whole work, ("skeleton" it is often called), may be clearly thought out or even written down, before the actual labor of composition begins. Even a systematic notation of the several divisions of the work by figures or letters may be employed; though this notation does not commonly appear in the finished work, except in compositions intended only to instruct or to set out statistics or similar details. Text-books use such a notation, and

[1] Part Second, *below*.

properly; but literary products (distinctively so called) commonly do not. Of course, such an outline must never be allowed to fetter the writer: it must be used, some one has aptly said, only as the mason uses his scaffolding, as a means to an end. Points may be omitted from it; new points be added; in fact, any liberty may be taken with it that tends to improve the composition. Sometimes, a writer works better without a synopsis. The subject, in its broad, general outline, is clear to him, and he can readily follow it through its every part. In such cases, let him by all means decline a "scaffolding": only let him be sure that his work, when finished, is as clear to his reader as to himself. Of course, too, if, at any point, when working without such help, he becomes embarrassed, he can jot down his outline, and so recover his "bearings." Freedom in one's methods of work is too precious to be lightly bartered away.

288. The forms that the several parts of the composition take are determined mainly by the subject-matter: the Proposition, however, needs a few words of special remark. Many writers state it definitely, as Matthew Arnold, in the first two of his essays quoted above; or Lord Macaulay, who begins his *History*, "I purpose to write the history of England from the accession of King James the Second down to a time which is within the memory of men still living." But other writers (or the same writers at other times) merely imply it in a sentence the chief purpose of which is different; as Mr. Arnold in his third essay named above. Sometimes it is found in an opening sentence or in the last sentence of the introduction; and it may even be fully expressed in the title of the work. To insist upon any one form,—indeed, not to insist upon variety in this as in other respects,—is a foolish as well as a useless dogmatism. A writer can ill afford to allow his openings to become so habitually alike that they constitute a mannerism. The solitary

horseman climbing a long hill, so much affected by a certain writer, has provoked for him the *soubriquet* of "the one-horse man." The danger in trusting to the title to announce one's proposition lies in the carelessness with which a title is often read. Indeed, the common (but most mistaken) practice of many persons is to "skip" title, preface, and all kindred matter.

288 *a*. The Proposition is not necessarily a judgment the truth or falsity of which is to be enforced on the reader. In Argument,[1] of course, such a judgment stands as proposition; but in Narration, in Description,[2] in other kinds of composition, the Proposition sets forth only the purpose of the writer, the circumstances of his writing, *etc.*

2. Canons.

289. The Composition as a whole, no matter what its subject, obeys four general rules. They are;—

(1) Unity. Each part of the composition must be subservient to one theme, and one proposition under that theme.

Everything else must be rigidly excluded; or, if anything out of strict unity is admitted, its insertion must be justifiable on sufficient grounds. Even in extended works, much interesting matter has always to be left out, lest the attention be unduly diverted from the main line of thought. A reasonable quantity of such material, however, is sometimes inserted in foot-notes or appendices; but even here the limits of advisability are soon reached. Speaking of De Quincey, confessedly a great sinner in this respect, Mr. Minto sums up the case most cleverly;— "Should these digressions, obviously breaches of strict method, be imitated or avoided? The experienced writer will please himself, and consult the effect that he intends to produce. But if he digresses after the model of De Quincey, he may rest assured that he will be accused of affectation, and will offend all that read for direct information concerning the subject in hand."

---

[1] § 395, *below*.   [2] §§ 372 ff, *below*.

(2) METHOD. The development of the subject must follow a natural (that is, the logical) order.

This canon has already been applied in the section on the parts of a composition, but it is equally applicable to every other detail. As no little force is gained by properly distributing the greater divisions of the whole work, so a like force is imparted by assigning to every sub-division, every paragraph, every sentence, just its own place,—the place determined for it by the nature of the thought expressed, by the special work which that particular part of the discourse has to do, and by other considerations, to be mentioned under several heads of Part Second, *below*.

(3) SELECTION. From the matter found to be relevant by Canon (1), the writer must choose what is most important in accordance with his proposition and his purpose in writing.

This rule is most binding, of course, when the composition is limited in extent; but it has force in all cases. The wider the scope of the author, the greater is the mass of material he collects, and the greater the necessity for a judicious selection from this mass of just those things which *he* especially needs to set down. Hence, no rule of Composition—not even the law of Unity—can be of greater importance than this law of Selection. A wise choice of material ensures the success of a book; the failure to make this choice may so heavily "handicap" the work as to leave it no chance in the race. Such unassorted work is sometimes said to be "padded." De Quincey's failures in this particular are often commented on, and would doubtless have ruined the chances of works less remarkable in other respects. And here again can the value of a commanding use of method be seen. In most cases, the writer will choose his material wisely, only after he has grasped securely and held before his mind (like a visible object between his finger and his thumb) the whole outline of his composition.[1] *Vice versa*, the

---

[1] De Quincey is a conspicuous exception. The law of Method he practises most successfully, using artistically the several means of indicating the plan of his work, apologizing for his digressions, giving notice of his return from them, and in every way carrying his reader along with him. Yet he had not learned the law of Unity—much less its more exacting sister-rule of Selection.

secret of many a failure in Method has been a failure in Selection; the want of power to choose wisely serving, as a rule, to debar the writer from making a judicious arrangement of material.

(4) COMPLETENESS. The proposition must be discussed fully.

Everything *essential*, everything that is necessary to set the subject as defined in the proposition completely before the reader, must be included. The sin of incompleteness is, of course, far less common than its opposite of overcrowding and irrelevancy; but its effects are none the less injurious to the work, and the vice itself, therefore, none the less carefully to be guarded against.[1] A judicious Brevity may leave one's readers or hearers wishing that the book, the sermon, the lecture had been longer: Incompleteness leaves the mind unsatisfied, as a piece of music leaves the ear, when it closes upon any chord but that of the tonic. One cannot help feeling that the writer has pledged himself to more than he has fulfilled, or, perhaps, has attempted more than he was able to accomplish.

[1] Appendix, p. 335.

V.

FIGURES OF SPEECH.[1]

290. "A Figure of Speech is a deviation from the plain and ordinary mode of speaking, with a view to greater effect;"[2] as, That *lamp lighted in Paradise*, instead of *Love;* Saturn, *quiet as a stone*, for Saturn *motionless*. So;—

The *vanward clouds* of evil days.—To sit *upon an Alp as on a throne.—Tragedy!* O, sir, *nothing of the kind!*—For *thou, dear, noble Elizabeth*,[3] around whose ample brow I fancy a tiara of light or a gleaming aureola.

"A casement . . . .
. . . *diamonded* with panes of quaint device
Innumerable, of *stains* and splendid *dyes*,
As are the tiger-moth's deep *damasked* wings."

291. It is a question, perhaps, whether the many "artifices of style gradually accumulated" by rhetoricians under the head of Figures of Speech admit of strict classification. "Such an accumulation," says Mr. Minto,[4] "could hardly be other than heterogeneous;" and even Prof. Bain,[5] who attempts only "the most common figures," and whose division is based on the "three simple modes of working" to which "all our intellectual powers are reducible," leaves one group of figures unclassified. Some points, however, have been made towards a classification; and by combining these points, all the most important figures can be grouped under certain well-defined heads.

292. (1) "A limited number of figures" are deviations from the ordinary modes of speech in the "use of *single words*."[6] Thus, *lamp, clouds, diamonded, stains* and *damasked*, in the examples cited above,[7] all contain figures of this sort. They are easily distinguishable both from the formal similitudes there cited, *quiet as a stone, upon an Alp as on a throne*, and from such peculiar sentence-structures as are observable in the fifth and sixth examples of that paragraph. Now, for these single-word figures Mr. Minto has proposed to reserve the name

---

[1] § 170, *above*.   [2] Bain, Part I.   [3] De Quincey's sister, long dead.
[4] *Manual*, p. 14.   [5] Part I., §§ 2, 40 ff.   [6] Minto.   [7] § 290.

trope—"at present, a kind of general synonym for a figure of speech," but defined by the ancients in a narrower sense,[1] and undoubtedly a useful word when properly restricted in meaning. Prof. Day, twenty years before Minto published his *Manual*, used the term in the same meaning; and Aristotle's word *metaphor*, as opposed to *simile*, included just about the same group of figures.[2] The advantage of the plan lies in its giving a convenient common designation to a small class of figures much used by certain writers who do not affect the longer similitudes; —by De Quincey, for instance, who (on this understanding) is rich in *tropes*, as opposed to Macaulay, who is rich in *similes*,[3] and to Carlyle, who abounds in *exclamations, etc.* The figures a writer uses often give valuable suggestions as to the character of his mind and the sources of his information ; and, hence, a convenient nomenclature must be of great service in rhetorical criticism.

293. (2) Another ancient term was re-proposed for modern use by John Quincy Adams,[4]—namely the Greek word *schemata*, or (as Mr. Adams boldly wrote it) *schemes*. Cicero says the word denoted figures that affect the sentence or the whole discourse,—in other words, figures that have to be *stated at length*. Such are the *Simile*, the *Allegory, etc.*,—another group that it is convenient to be able to name in a single word. Mr. Adams's word *schemes* is, unfortunately, too closely associated with its modern meaning to permit its being used here ; but the Greek plural answers every practical purpose.

294. (3) All figures of speech may be divided into two classes ;[5]—(*a*) *Figures of Diction*, in which the deviation from the ordinary mode of speech is in the *language ;* (*b*) *Figures of Thought*, in which it is in the *form of the sentence.* In figures of class (*a*), the language cannot be altered without destroying or at least changing the figure ; in class (*b*), so long as the form of expression is retained, the figure remains. Thus, the sentence " *Out, out, hyæna !* "[6] contains two figures,—a *meta-*

---

[1] Appendix, p. 336.

[2] *Poetic*, xxi. (See, also, Ritter's note, Buckley's translation of Aristotle in Bohn's Classical Library.)—Hence, plainly, the modern and erroneous use of *metaphorical* to characterize a style noticeable for its habitual use of such figures. (Minto, p. 15.)

[3] Minto, *ut cit*.   [4] *Lectures*, II. xxx.

[5] Also an ancient distinction, and recognized by Mr. Adams, *ut cit*.

[6] Milton, *Samson Agonistes*, 748.

phor in *hyæna* (that is, *Dalila*), and the *exclamation*. But, had Milton written, *Be gone, wild beast!* there would still have been a metaphor in *wild beast*,[1] though it would have been a different metaphor; whereas the sentence-form, the *exclamation*, would have remained untouched. The phrase *figures of thought* is valuable also as a term of reference; for, like *tropes* and *schemata*, it names a well-defined group of figures for which it is a convenient designation. In characterizing Carlyle above,[2] it was said, *he abounds in exclamations, etc.*: it may now be said, *he abounds in figures of thought.*

295. There results, then, the following classification;—

Figures of Speech.

(1) Of Diction.   (2) Of Thought.

(*a*) Tropes.   (*b*) Schemata.

(1) (*a*) The chief Tropes are,—

(α) **Metaphor,** *implied comparison;* as, The barky *fingers* of the elm;

(β) **Metonymy,** *the substitution of an accompaniment for the thing it accompanies;* as, The shepherd, with his *home-spun* lass;

(γ) **Synecdoche,** *a similar substitution of a part for the whole, or vice versa;* as, Truth forever *on the scaffold;* wrong forever *on the throne;*

(δ) **Personification,** *the attributing of life or even human feelings and purposes to an inanimate object;* as, The *sleepless* Ocean.

(1) (*b*) The chief Schemata are,—

(α) **Simile,** *comparison in terms,* i. e., *stated at length;* as, *Such* stuff *as* dreams are made of;

(β) **Allegory,** *detailed comparison of objects that but remotely resemble each other;* as, the comparing of lower animals with men in Æsop's *Fables;*

(γ) **Antithesis,** *the explicit contrasting of things already opposed in meaning;* as, The petition originated, *not* with the King, *not* with the parliament, *not* with the people, *but* with a section of the clergy themselves;[3]

---

[1] Such word-phrases are, in effect, single words, and, therefore, tropes. From the present point of view, they are essentially different from such phrases as *quiet as a stone,* or *gently, like dew upon the grass.*

[2] 292.   [3] Froude. (Cited by Bain.)

(δ) **Epigram**, "*conflict or contradiction between the form of the language and the meaning really conveyed;*"[1] as *Bread is bread*, (meaning, it is unusually high-priced);

(ε) **Irony**, *the unmistakable saying of what is not meant, in order the more clearly or forcibly to say what is intended;* as, A *pretty* plight;

(ζ) **Hyperbole**, *exaggeration designed only to make a deeper impression;* as, The *infinite* magnificence of heaven;

(η) **Euphemism**, *the softening of a harsh or indelicate expression, or the substitution for it of one that is euphonious or delicate;* as, When Stephen had said this, he *fell asleep*.

(2) The most important Figures of Thought are,—

(α) **Interrogation**, *affirmation or denial strengthened by being thrown into the form of a question;* as, Is thy servant a dog, that he should do this thing?

(β) **Exclamation**, *a mode of expression dictated by "sudden and intense emotion;"* as, How wonderful is Death,—Death and his brother Sleep!

(γ) **Apostrophe**, *an address to an absent or imaginary auditor, as if he were present;* as, Come, pensive nun, devout and pure![2]

296. A much longer list might easily be made; but, as Prof. A. S. Hill has well said, "The figures of speech are the very *stuff* of human language"; and many so called figures are not in any strong sense deviations from the ordinary mode of speech, but only devices of the sentence or the paragraph, or even downright violations of Syntax. Asyndeton, for example, is simply an omission of connectives; Ellipsis, the omission of other easily supplied words—perhaps, merely for Brevity's sake. Anacolouthon, the failure of a sentence to follow the lead of its beginning, is absolutely a vice—certainly a vicious mannerism—in some speakers, however rare it may be in writing. To include everything called a figure by the ancient or other writers who have emphasized this topic, would be only to collect an interminable catalogue of mere names. The ambition to make such lists was the fatal disease of mediæval rhetoricians, as well as of some more recent writers.[3]

---

[1] Bain. [2] Milton's invocation to Melancholy.

[3] For instance, John Sterling, D.D., whose *System of Rhetoric*, (London, 1795, pp. 25) is simply a double list of *ninety-four* figures of speech, first in English heroic couplets, with English examples and a translation of the technical terms; secondly, in Latin hexameters, with Latin examples and the derivation of the technical terms from the Greek.

The division here proposed has at least one merit. It avoids minute sub-division—that over-classification which rarely or never classifies, but only bewilders.

297. In illustrating more fully the several figures by examples of each, the order of the classification will not be adhered to: the student will better understand the necessary distinctions, and at the same time find the classification itself more clear, if the figures that can be effectively compared or contrasted are brought together.

298. (1) Two figures consist in the comparison of objects that closely resemble each other;—(*a*) METAPHOR, an *implied* comparison; (*b*) SIMILE, a comparison *stated at length*. Thus, De Quincey writing of his *sister*, uses a metaphor,—*Pillar of fire* that didst go before me to guide and to quicken. Had he written, Thou who didst go before me, *like a pillar of fire*, to guide and to quicken, he would have used a simile. So ;—

(*a*) *Pillar of darkness*, when thy countenance was turned away to God.—Anger so constantly discharging its *thunders*.—Reason, the twinkling *lamp* of wandering life.

"With head uplift above the wave, and eyes
That sparkling *blazed*."

"To you, my purse, and to none other wight,
Complain I, for ye be my *lady* dear."

(*b*) They had glimmering eyes, red, *like the eyes of ferrets*.—I rose, *as if on billows*.—Hastily, therefore, I kissed the lips that I should kiss no more, and slunk, *like a guilty thing*, with stealthy steps from the room.

"He, above the rest
In shape and gesture proudly eminent,
Stood *like a tower*."

"Fat *as a whale*, and walkëd *as a swan*."

299. (2) Two figures consist in the comparison of objects that but remotely resemble each other,—objects that are *brought* into comparison by the figure ;—(*a*) ALLEGORY, a *sustained* comparison ; (*b*) PERSONIFICATION, the comparison of *inanimate* with *animate* objects. Thus ;—

(*a*) *The Pilgrim's Progress*, a detailed comparison between the Christian life and a pilgrimage to a distant country.[1] Other

[1] Cf. Hebrews, xiii. 14.

familiar examples are Swift's *Gulliver's Travels*, Chaucer's *House of Fame*, and Spenser's *Faëry Queene*.

> (b) "Such an act
> That *blurs* the *grace* and *blush* of modesty,
> Calls virtue hypocrite, takes off the rose
> From *the fair forehead* of an innocent love,
> And *sets* a blister there, makes marriage-vows
> As false as dicers' oaths: O, such a deed
> As from the *body* of contraction *plucks*
> The very *soul*, and sweet religion *makes*
> A rhapsody of words; heaven's *face* doth glow:
> Yea, this solidity and compound mass,
> *With tristful visage*, as against the doom,
> *Is thought-sick* at the act."

300. (3) Two figures consist in the *substitution* of one thing for another;—(a) METONYMY, of an *accompaniment* for the thing it accompanies; (b) SYNECDOCHE, of a *part* for the whole or *vice versa*. Thus;—

(a) The *scarlet hat* of the Cardinal, the *silver cross* of the Legate, were no more, (meaning *cardinals* and *legates* were no more).—Philip heard him read *the prophet Esaias*.—One day nigh weary of her irksome *way*, (*i. e.*, her *journey*).—In secret *shadow* far from all men's sight, (*i. e.*, in a shaded, and therefore secret place).—*Blood* for *life;* a *sunshine* instead of a *bright light; roses* (in a cheek) as a sign of *health*, or *blushes* as a sign of *modesty*.

> (b) "The boy had fewer *summers*, but his heart
> Had far outgrown his years."
>
> "I can not see what flowers are at my feet,
> Nor what soft *incense* hangs upon the boughs."
> "And with rich *metal* [i. e., gold] loaded every rift."
>
> "And kiss thy fair large ears, my gentle *joy*."
>
> "O that this too too solid flesh would melt,
> Thaw, and resolve itself into a *dew*."

To *spur* or *goad* for to *drive; steel* for *sword;* a *Daniel* come to judgment; *slothful* shade; his *lazy* bed; "the holy priest that to her speaks and blesseth her with *happy* hands."

301. (4) Five figures coincide in presenting *the unexpected;*—(a) ANTITHESIS, by way of *contrast;* (b) EPIGRAM, in *conflicting or contradictory forms of expression;*

FIGURES OF SPEECH.

(c) IRONY, in *oppositeness of meaning;* (d) HYPERBOLE, in *self-evident exaggeration;* (e) EUPHEMISM in the *avoidance of anything unpleasant.* Thus ;—

(a) Amidst *luxuries* in all things *else*, we were trained to a *Spartan simplicity* of diet.

> "There's a divinity that *shapes* our ends,
> *Rough hew* them how we will."
> "Our remedies oft in *ourselves* do lie,
> Which we ascribe to *heaven*."

(b) At creation three kinds of people were made,—*men, women,* and *Harveys*.[1]—A man resolved *to do good that evil might come*.—He went to his *imagination* for his *facts*, and to his *memory* for his *tropes*.—*Verbosity* is cured by a *wide vocabulary*.[2]

(c) However, for this once, my cynic must submit to be told he is wrong. *Doubtless*, it is *presumption* in me to suggest that his sneers can ever go awry, *any more than the shafts of Apollo*. But still, *however impossible* such a thing is, in this one case it *happens* that they *have*.[3]

> (d) "A man so various that he seemed to be
> Not one, but *all mankind's Epitome :*
> Stiff in opinions, *always* in the wrong,
> Was *everything* by starts and nothing long;
> But, *in the course of one revolving moon,*
> Was chemist, fiddler, statesman, and buffoon."
>
> "Can any mortal mixture of earth's mould
> Breathe such *divine enchanting ravishment?*"

Milton, to give an idea of Satan's physical prowess, says,

> "With *head uplift above the wave,* and *eyes*
> That *sparkling blazed, his other parts besides,*
> Prone on the flood, extended long and large,
> Lay floating *many a rood*."

(e) The *departed* or the *deceased* for the *dead* is a familiar euphemism. Other examples are ;—

---

[1] The Harveys meant were those of Lord Bristol's family "at the beginning of the last century."—De Quincey, *Autobiographic Sketches*, chap. ii., says the epigram was ascribed (he knew not how truly) to Lady Mary Wortley Montague.

[2] Cited by Bain, who restricts the meaning of epigram as is done here. The word once meant a short, pointed poem : Bain selects the play upon words as "the most frequent device for brevity and point employed in such compositions."

[3] De Quincey, *A Sequel to the Confessions*, Part 1.—The words italicized are especially pointed.

> "My necessaries are embark'd: farewell:
> And, sister, as the winds give benefit
> And convoy is assistant, do not *sleep*,
> But let me hear from you."
>
> "Beware
> Of entrance to a quarrel, but being in,
> Bear 't *that the opposed may beware of thee.*"

302. (5) The three FIGURES OF THOUGHT;[1]—

(*a*) Doth Job fear God for nought?—Can a man weigh off and value the glories of dawn against the darkness of hurricane?—Shall he expire, and unavenged?

> "When fades at length our lingering day,
> Who cares what pompous tombstones say?"

(*b*) O burden of solitude, that cleavest to man through every stage of his being!—The Parliament of living men, Lords and Commons united, what a miserable array against the Upper and [the] Lower House composing the Parliament of Ghosts! —Methought I heard a voice cry, Sleep no more!

(*c*) " Earth, ocean, air, beloved brotherhood!
If our great Mother have imbued my soul
With aught of natural piety to feel
Your love, and recompense the boon with mine;
. . . . . . then forgive
This boast, beloved brethren, and withdraw
No portion of your wonted favor now!"

" Life of Life! thy lips enkindle
With their love the breath between them!"

" My daughter! with thy name this song began,—
My daughter! with thy name thus much shall end,—
I see thee not, I hear thee not,—but none
Can be so wrapt in thee; thou art the friend
To whom the shadows of far years extend."

Mighty and essential solitude!—that wast, and art, and art to be!—Hadst thou been an idiot, my sister, not the less I must have loved thee, having [2] that capacious heart overflowing, even as mine overflowed, with tenderness, and stung, even as mine was stung, by the necessity of being loved.—Cloud, that hast revealed to us this young creature and her blighted hopes, close up again.—O thou fervent reformer,—whose fatal tread he that puts his ear to the ground may hear at a distance coming onwards upon every road,—if too surely thou wilt work for me and others irreparable wrong and suffering, work also for us a little good!

[1] §§ 294 ff, *above*.   [2] § 145 (1) (*c*), *above*.

303. The following special forms of Metonymy (1) and Synecdoche (2) are noted by Prof. Bain ;—(1) (*a*) the Sign, or Symbol, for the Thing Signified, (*b*) the Instrument for the Agent, (*c*) the Container for the Thing Contained, (*d*) an Effect for a Cause, (*e*) an Author for his Works ; (2) (*a*) the Species for the Genus, and *vice versa*, (*b*) the Individual for the Species (*Antonomasia*), (*c*) the Concrete for the Abstract, (*d*) the Material for the Thing Made, (*e*) the Passion for the Object that inspires it, (*f*) the Transferred Epithet. Examples of each form have already been given.[1]

304 Comparison is figurative, only when the objects compared are different in kind. Otherwise, it is literal. Thus,

"How the red *roses* flush up in her cheeks,
And the pure snow with goodly *vermeil stain*,
Like *crimson dyed in grain*,"—

contains both a figurative and a literal comparison. *Roses* for *blushes* is figurative ; but *vermeil stain like crimson dyed in grain* simply notes the particular shade of red the bride blushed —namely, as pure a vermillion as results from dyeing with kermes.[2]

305. Rhetoricians lay down a number of rules for the use of Figures ; but the following general principles seem to cover the ground ;—

(1) All Figures should be in keeping with both the occasion and the feelings natural to a speaker on that occasion. They must *seem* to be spontaneous, even if they are not. Any appearance of their having been *hunted*—having been gone after through the lanes and hedges of thought—of their having been compelled to come in—is fatal to their efficiency. Thus, an orator, fired with his topic, may properly write,—

"Have I any unkind feeling towards these poor people? No more than I have to a sick friend who implores me to give him a glass of iced water which the physician has forbidden. No more than a humane collector in India has to those poor peasants who in a season of scarcity crowd round the granaries and beg with tears and piteous gestures that the doors may be opened and the rice distributed. I would not give the draught

---

[1] § 300, *above*.   [2] See G. P. Marsh, *Lectures*, i. 66.

of water, because I know that it would be poison. I would not give up the keys of the granary, because I know that, by doing so, I should turn a scarcity into a famine. And in the same way I would not yield to the importunity of multitudes who, exasperated by suffering and blinded by ignorance, demand with wild vehemence the liberty to destroy themselves."

A cooler, more dispassionate reasoner would probably have said,—

It is not, Mr. Speaker, that I have any unkind feeling towards these poor people: I simply can not yield to their importunity, suffering and ignorant as they are, and give them the means to their own destruction.

So, compare the stilted lines (*a*) with the following "strains like the breath of the morning which has swept over flowery meads" (*b*);[1]—

(*a*) "Was this the face that launch'd a thousand ships,
And burnt the topless tow'rs of Ilium?
Sweet Helen, make me immortal with a kiss.
Her lips suck forth my soul! See, where it flies.
Come, Helen, come, give me my soul again.
Here will I dwell, for Heav'n is in these lips,
And all is dross that is not Helena.
I will be Paris, and, for love of thee,
Instead of Troy shall Wittenberg be sack'd;
And I will combat with weak Menelaus,
And wear thy colours on my plumed crest;
Yea I will wound Achilles in the heel,
And then return to Helen for a kiss.
Oh! thou art fairer than the evening air,
Clad in the beauty of a thousand stars:"[2]—

(*b*) "Come live with me and be my love,
And we will all the pleasures prove,
That hill and valley, grove and field,
And all the craggy mountains yield.
There will we sit upon the rocks,
And see the shepherds feed their flocks
By shallow rivers, to whose falls
Melodious birds sing madrigals."[3]

[1] Alfred H. Welsh, *Development of English Literature and Language*.
[2] Marlowe, *Faustus*.   [3] Marlowe, *The Passionate Shepherd to his Love*.

(2) Figures should not be too numerous in any composition, nor should the same figure be too often repeated. In the passage just cited from Marlowe's *Faustus*, the figurative applications of Helen's share in causing the Trojan war are numerous and unvaried *ad nauseam*.

(3) All figures should both be clear in themselves and promote clearness in their context. To this latter end, they should be clearer than literal statement. Thus, the literal statement, The heat of the oven was 1400° Fahrenheit, would have been far less clear to the average reader than the hyperbole, The furnace was heated "one seven times more than it was wont to be heated," indefinite as this statement is. So, it may be questioned what is meant by

> "The noble sister of Poplicola,
> *The moon of Rome:*"

certainly one may doubt whether the figure is as clear as a literal statement would have been.[1] But no one need ask what Homer meant by

> "Soft as *the fleeces of descending snow*,"

or Tennyson by

> "Him, like *the working bee in blossom dust*,
> Blanched with his mill, they found."

(4) The accumulation in the same context of incongruous figures, the combining of literal and figurative language, and the "mixing" of figures—that is, the drawing of the parts of a single figure from different sources—are alike forbidden.[2] All these errors may be noted in the following short passage;—

"*Pillar of fire* that didst go before me to guide and to quicken,—*pillar of darkness*, when *thy countenance was turned*

---

[1] Bain says it is *admissible* on the ground that "the absence of intellectual similarity is consistent with emotional keeping"; but he does not *translate* it.

[2] The mixed Metaphor is especially condemned by rhetoricians,—probably, because the Metaphor is so striking a figure.

away to God, that didst too truly *shed* the shadow of death over my young heart,—in what scales should I *weigh* thee? Was the blessing greater from thy *heavenly* presence, or the *blight* which followed thy *departure?* Can a man *weigh off* and value the glories of dawn against the darkness of hurricane?"[1]

Here are at least fourteen figures—the words in italics, the Apostrophe (sustained from "Pillar of fire" to "departure"), the Euphemism in "turned away to God," and the three Interrogations;—surely a goodly number, even were they more congruous in thought. But they come from so many and so different sources, that the mind can scarcely follow the rapid changes of imagery. In the second place, the allusion to the miraculous leading and lighting of the children of Israel on their way from Egypt[2] is suddenly changed into a reference to the shining of the planets by reflected light, and this immediately made to do duty as a euphemism for his sister's death.[3] Finally, "the blessing from thy heavenly presence," a literal statement except for the adjective, is badly contrasted with "the blight which followed thy departure"—a strong figure.

"So, then, one chapter in my life had been finished. Already, before the completion of my sixth year, this first chapter had *run its circle*, had *rendered up its music* to the final chord—might seem even, *like ripe fruit from a tree*, to have *detached itself forever* from all the rest of the *arras* that *was shaping itself* within *my loom of life.*"[4]

[1] De Quincey, *Sequel to the Confessions*, Part I.

[2] Exodus xiii. 21, 22; xiv. 19, 20.—De Quincey's figure varies the account, but not so seriously as to impair its fidelity or to obscure the reference.

[3] A euphemism, be it noted, singularly beautiful in itself, and one that would have been a rare ornament, had it been properly employed.

[4] De Quincey.

(C) THE QUALITIES OF STYLE.

DEFINITION AND SUB-DIVISIONS.

306. The properties of language denoted by the phrase Qualities of Style[1] are easily distinguished from both the grammatical and the mechanical properties, and yet they are not easily defined. The meaning of the qualifying adjective *subtler*, used above,[1] will be best reached, perhaps, by remembering the distinction between the outward and bodily and the inward and spiritual form of a composition.[2] The grammatical and the mechanical properties of language belong to the one, the subtler properties to the other. The former lie on the surface of discourse, and are sensible to the eye or the touch; the latter lie deeper, and must be appreciated by the sensibilities, rather than detected by the senses. The former can be localized; the latter belong to the composition as a whole. In a word, the qualities of style appeal to and stimulate the higher intellectual life in man, excite in him intenser and more exalted feelings, and most powerfully influence his will. The student will have no greater difficulty, however, in coming to know these qualities than he has had in learning to recognize the more superficial and, therefore, the more patent properties of language exhibited under the heads of Grammatical Purity and the Elements of Style.

307. The Qualities of Style admit of distribution under two heads;—I. *The Subjective Qualities*, II. *The Objective Qualities*. Language, considered as the medium of communication, may be viewed in its relation either to the speaker or to the person addressed; that is, either subjectively or objectively. Hence, the two classes of Qualities of Style.[3]

[1] § 77, *above*.   [2] § 17, *above*.   [3] Day, *Art of Discourse*, § 244.

I.

THE SUBJECTIVE QUALITIES.

308. The Subjective Qualities of Style are (1) *Significance*, (2) *Continuousness*, (3) *Naturalness*.

(1) SIGNIFICANCE.

309. Significance implies two things;—(*a*) "that the speaker have some thought to communicate"; (*b*) "that the words employed actually express some meaning." "Discourse in which the speaker does not design to communicate any thought" is *Spurious Oratory;* that in which he uses "the forms of speech," indeed, but "with no thought or sentiment expressed in them," is *The Nonsensical.* Thus;—

Launcelot Gobbo's talk with his blind father is at first intentionally meaningless: "I will try confusions with him," says Launcelot.[1]

"*Gob.* Master young gentleman, I pray you, which is the way to master Jew's?

"*Laun.* Turn up on your right hand at the next turning, but, at the next turning of all, on your left; marry at the very next turning, turn of no hand, but turn down indirectly to the Jew's house.

"*Gob.* By God's sonties, 'twill be a hard way to hit. Can you tell me whether one Launcelot, that dwells with him, dwell with him or no.

"*Laun.* Ergo, Master Launcelot. Talk not of Master Launcelot, father; for the young gentleman, according to Fates and Destinies and such odd sayings, the Sisters Three and such branches of learning, is indeed deceased, or, as you would say in plain terms, gone to heaven."[2]

The Nonsensical, too, is exemplified by Shakspere;—[3]

[1] *The Merchant of Venice*, II. ii. 38.
[2] Such "talk for talk's sake" does not always have even Launcelot's excuse, an idle wish to tease: it has been used to retard legislation, or to wear out opponents in debate.
[3] *Love's Labours Lost*, iv. ii. 51.

"*Hol.* Sir Nathaniel, will you hear an extemporal epitaph on the death of the deer? And, to humour the ignorant, call I the deer the princess killed a pricket.

"*Nath.* Perge, good Master Holofernes, perge; so it shall please you to abrogate scurrility.

"*Hol.* I will something affect the letter, for it argues facility.

> "The preyful princess pierced and prick'd a pretty pleasing pricket;
> Some say a sore; but not a sore, till now made sore with shooting.
> The dogs did yell: put L to sore, then sorel jumps from thicket;
> Or pricket sore, or else sorel; the people fall a hooting.
> If sore be sore, then L to sore makes fifty sores one sorel.
> Of one sore I an hundred make by adding but one more L."

310. The Humorous[1] sometimes approaches the nonsensical, but never reaches it. Thus;—

"*Launce.* Nay, 'twill be this hour ere I have done weeping; all the kind of the Launces have this very fault. I have received my proportion, like the prodigious son, and am going with Sir Proteus to the Imperial's court. I think Crab my dog be the sourest-natured dog that lives: my mother weeping, my father wailing, my sister crying, our maid howling, our cat wringing her hands, and all our house in a great perplexity, yet did not this cruel-hearted cur shed one tear: he is a stone, a very pebble stone, and has no more pity in him than a dog: a Jew would have wept to have seen our parting; why, my grandam, having no eyes, look you, wept herself blind at my parting. Nay, I'll show you the manner of it. This shoe is my father: no, this left shoe is my father: no, no, this left shoe is my mother; nay that cannot be so neither: yes, it is so, it is so, it hath the worser sole. Now, sir, this staff is my sister, for, look you, she is as white as a lily and as small as a wand: this hat is Nan, our maid: I am the dog: no, the dog is himself, and I am the dog—Oh! the dog is me, and I am myself: ay, so, so. Now come I to my father; Father, your blessing: now should not the shoe speak a word for weeping: now should I kiss my father; well, he weeps on. Now come I to my mother: O that she could speak now like a wood woman! Well I kiss her; why there 'tis; here's my mother's breath up and down. Now come I to my sister; mark the moan she makes. Now the dog

---

[1] § 331, *below.*

all this while sheds not a tear nor speaks a word; but see how I lay the dust with my tears."[1]

(2) CONTINUOUSNESS.

311. Continuousness of style is its quality of being connected. It implies (*a*) that the thought expressed be set in its proper relations; (*b*) that it move regularly forward from the beginning, step by step, to the end. Much has necessarily been said on this subject above,—under the Sentence, the Paragraph, the Whole Composition. An additional remark or two will answer here. (*a*) Brokenness of style—Sententiousness, it is often called—ought to denote intensity of feeling—feeling too deep for utterance or too abrupt and broken for a flow of words. Affected sententiousness is not only weak, but generally betrays its artificial character. (*b*) As an example of "talking in a circle," may be mentioned a funeral prayer twenty minutes long, yet revolving about the single petition that God would bless the afflicted family.

(3) NATURALNESS.

312. Naturalness of style is its representing the peculiar mode of thought and manner of expression of the particular writer. Every man is in some respects *sui generis* —incapable of classification; and, hence, though a writer should avoid all mannerisms and affectations, though he should never *aim* at being individual, he should allow himself only his own style. "The speaker's own manner best becomes him,"[2] "*Le style c'est l'homme*,"[3] "A simple and natural style, the eloquence of nature, enchants us for the reason that while we are looking for

---

[1] *The Two Gentlemen of Verona*, II. iii. 1.—The grains of "salt" that keep such buffoonery "sweet" are the scattered thoughts suggested by the passage. Absurdly as these are turned from their true and usual associations, they are still there, and start the mind in several directions.

[2] Day, § 301.   [3] Buffon,

an author we find a man."[1] "The speaker must ever be himself,"[2]—are but varying expressions of this truth. On the other hand, imitation of another, whether in mode of thought or in manner of expression, commonly ends in the copying of all his faults, without attaining any of his excellences. A writer's *mannerisms* are easily mimicked, may even be burlesqued—that is, be grossly exaggerated: his *individuality* is inimitable. The many unprofessed imitators of Longfellow or Tennyson or Browning, as well as the confessed imitations of *Excelsior*, or *Break, break, break*, or *How They Brought the Good News from Ghent to Aix*, exemplify this truth.

313. Naturalness of style is affected by "*the subject* and *the occasion* of the discourse." These influence the mind of the writer, and "leave their impressions on his style, in rendering it more earnest and elevated, more stately and dignified, or more light and familiar."[3] Thus, compare the following descriptions of a sun rise;—

"The saffron morn, with early blushes spread,
Now rose refulgent from Tithonus' bed,
With new-born day to gladden mortal sight,
And gild the course of heaven with sacred light."[4]

"The sun had long since in the lap
Of Thetis taken out his nap;
And, like a lobster boiled, the morn
From black to red began to turn."[5]

Burke, a friend of America, describes the rapid growth of the colonies by saying that, while England talks of "the mode of governing two millions" of Americans, "millions more" spring up to be managed: Dr. Johnson, an enemy to all "whigs," says the Americans "multiply with the fecundity of their own rattlesnakes."

---
[1] Pascal, translated by Shedd, *Literary Essays*, p. 81.
[2] Gabriel Harvey, an English rhetorician in the reign of Elizabeth—the college-mate of Spenser, and the friend of Sir Philip Sidney. His book is extremely rare, and is quoted here from Morley's *First Sketch of English Literature*.
[3] Day, ¿ 305.—The examples, too, are cited by Day.
[4] Homer.   [5] Butler's *Hudibras*.

II.

THE OBJECTIVE QUALITIES.

314. Considered in their relation to the person addressed, the qualities of style are, 1. *The Intellectual Qualities*, 2. *The Emotional Qualities*, 3. *The Æsthetic Qualities*. Class 1 includes (1) *Simplicity*, as opposed to *Abstruseness;* (2) *Clearness*, as opposed to *Confusion*.[1] Clearness admits of sub-division into (*a*) *General Clearness*, or *Perspicuity;* (*b*) *Minute Clearness*, or *Precision*.[2] Class 2 contains (1) *Force*, (2) *Pathos*, (3) *The Ludicrous;* Class 3, (1) *Melody*, (2) *Harmony*, (3) *Variety*, (4) *Elegance*.

1. The Intellectual Qualities.

(1) Simplicity.

315. Simplicity is the quality of being *readily comprehended*, of being easily grasped by the mind and understood completely. The term denotes more than Clearness, the quality of being readily *apprehended;* for comprehension implies that the thing understood is grasped in its entirety, whereas apprehension implies intelligibility only in part. Thus ;—

The meaning of the word *electricity* can be easily apprehended; but no one, perhaps, would claim that he comprehends the term. Even such "everyday" words as *earth, air, fire, water, man, woman, child, father, mother, uncle, aunt*, mean a vast deal more to some minds than to others; while certain scientific terms, readily intelligible in a general way, are completely understood only by special students of the sciences to which they belong. For example, such words as *conscious, aware, perceive, conceive, think, remember, imagine*, are separated by well-ascertained boundaries, of which a speaker untaught in

[1] Bain. [2] Minto.

Mental Science knows nothing. So, of the following lines, the first four are, perhaps, universally intelligible; the last four speak to far fewer minds;—

> "I saw from the beach, when the morning was shining,
> A bark o'er the water move gloriously on;
> I came when the sun o'er that beach was declining—
> The bark was still there, but the waters were gone.
> And such is the fate of our life's early promise,
> So passing the spring-tide of joy we have known;
> Each wave that we danced on at morning ebbs from us,
> And leaves us at eve on the bleak shore alone."

316. Hence, "Simplicity and Abstruseness (its opposite) are relative terms," and "want of simplicity is a fault only in relation to the persons addressed." To be sure, "whatever is hard to understand is not simple, is abstruse, recondite;" but "what is hard for one man may be easy for another,"[1] and, for this reason, the degree of simplicity required in any writing depends entirely upon the readers that may reasonably be expected for it. "A writer addressing himself purposely to a learned audience only wastes his strength by beating about the bush for language universally familiar."[2] On the other hand, the difficulty in speaking to children lies in the essential abstruseness (to them) of many subjects about which one may wish to inform them or they may wish to learn.

317. In some part, however, the attainment of Simplicity depends on the kind of words employed or the construction of the sentence, the paragraph, or even the whole composition. Hence, many principles of Style already laid down apply here; and the following may be added;—

(1) Familiar terms—such as "represent common and familiar objects and actions"—are simpler than "rare or remote" terms.[3] Thus, so far as words are concerned, the last example cited in § 315 is simplicity itself: its last four lines are less simple than the first four only because the total thought presented is less easily grasped.

[1] Minto, p. 19.   [2] Minto, p. 20. (See, also, § 129, *above*.)   [3] Bain.

(2) Particular terms are simpler than generals; especially, the names of persons, than the names of classes. Thus, Chaucer's account of the Prioress, Madame Eglantyne, a fine lady of his day, says, not that she avoided profanity, but that

> "Her greatest oath was but by Saint Loy;"[1]

not that she had all the good breeding of her time, but that

> "At metë[2] well ytaught was she withal,
> She let no morsel from her lippës fall,
> Nor wet her fingers in her saucë deep.
> Well could she carry a morsel, and well keep
> That no dropë ne fell upon her breast;"

not that she had a tender conscience, but that

> "She was so charitable, and so pitous,[3]
> She woldë[4] weep if that she saw a mouse
> Caught in a trap, if it were dead or bleddë;"[5]

not that she was foolishly fond of her pets, but that

> "Of smallë houndës had she, that she fed
> With roasted flesh and milk and wastel bread.[6]
> But sorë weptë she if one of them were dead,
> Or if men smote it with a yerdë smartë."[7]

So Thackeray, by way of assigning Irving and Macaulay their places in modern literature, calls them "the Goldsmith and the Gibbon of our time." Once more, in Chaucer's *Nonne Prestes Tale*, when Pertelote makes game of Chaunteclere for doing "force of dremës"—setting store on his dreams—Chaunteclere gives her *instances* in which dreams have come true, and opposes these most confidently to Cato's *opinion* that dreams mean nothing.

(2) CLEARNESS.

318. Clearness, the quality of being readily *apprehended*, is either general or minute. General Clearness has aptly been called Perspicuity; Minute Clearness, Precision.[8] The opposite of Clearness is Confusion, Ambiguity, or Uncertain Reference; and hence, Clear-

---

[1] *Prologue to the Canterbury Tales*, 120. [2] Meat—her meals.
[3] Pitiful. [4] Would. [5] Bleeding.
[6] Cake-bread, made of the whitest flour. [7] Struck it sharply with a stick.
[8] The terms are not always so distinguished. Most writers use only a single term, Perspicuity, to express all that is here intended by Simplicity, Perspicuity and Precision. Blair defined Precision as "the highest part" of Perspicuity; but Bain and Minto, whose views are here set forth, seem more logical.

ness is not a relative term. "Ambiguous language may mislead learned and unlearned alike. Confused expression is not justifiable under any circumstances, unless, indeed, it[1] is the writer's deliberate purpose to mislead. The educated reader will guess the meaning sooner than the uneducated; but neither should be burdened with the effort of guessing."[2] For this reason, Clearness is a quality "*of obligation.*" Unlike Simplicity, it is always attainable, and, for this reason, may always be insisted upon. Discourse *must* be intelligible, and intelligible in only one sense; not only so clear that it *may* be understood, but so clear that it *must* be understood by every one of sound mind,—so clear that it cannot be misunderstood by any rational interpreter.

319. In all cases, Clearness in expression is impossible, unless the writer is capable of *thinking* clearly. Whatever the character of the subject, simple or abstruse, a writer who can not think clearly easily grows confused, and his style ambiguous: in a difficult subject he is sure to be defeated. At the same time, it is not true, as is sometimes asserted, that clear thinking necessarily leads to clear writing. A man who knows perfectly well what he wants to say may yet blunder in his expression of it. He may choose a wrong word, an inapt word, a form of expression of any kind that does not really say what he intends; and so he may set down either something the meaning of which is ambiguous, or a thought quite different from that in his own mind. Between the author and his reader lies the whole domain of Style—the *Form* of thought expressed in language. Certain considerations, therefore,—some already presented, others to be presented now as more specifically promoting Clearness, —must be carefully borne in mind.

320. Before detailing these considerations, however, one preparatory remark must be made. All the laws of Form as

---

[1] § 321 (*d*), *below.*   [2] Minto.

thus far set out,—the laws of Grammatical Purity, of Vocabulary, the Sentence, the Paragraph, the whole Composition,—may contribute to Clearness. Constant reference to this fact has been made throughout the preceding pages; and even more constant reference might have been made to it. Indeed, unless these laws do contribute to the more successful, and, therefore, the clearer expression of what one has to say, they are scarcely worth the time and attention they justly receive in books of Rhetoric. The truth is that all deparments and sub-departments of Rhetoric in some sense overlap. Mr. Minto adverts to this fact (in part, at least) when he says that were an examination of an author's style to be "ideally thorough" under any one of the three divisions, Elements and Qualities of Style, and Kinds of Composition, such an examination would exhaust everything that could be said. The convenience of treating, not Style only, but Rhetoric, from several different points of view justifies even some repetition.[1] The student will remember, therefore, that any means of expression, any rhetorical device of any kind, may assist him in determining a point of Clearness; and that, since Clearness is a quality of obligation, the quality most essential to the effective communication of thought, he may gratefully accept to this end any help, from whatever source it comes. At the risk, therefore, of repeating what has been already said, the following specifications of Means to Clearness are set down.

321. (*a*) Many English words have several meanings, and should therefore be so used as to indicate in each case the particular meaning intended.[2] Thus ;—

A man who has lost his eye-sight has in one *sense* less consciousness than he had before.—The phrase, the art of *painting* proved in a certain sentence, to mean the art of *rouging*.—An American clergyman once printed the statement that American preaching was less *from* the Bible than was preaching in England. He meant it was less *on* the Bible, less *explanatory* of the Bible; but he was understood to mean *more on secular topics*. He appeased his brethren by a manly public confession that he had not expressed himself clearly.—The English auxiliary verb *will* expresses not only futurity, but willingness or desire. Hence, the common misunderstanding of "Ye *will*

---

[1] *Manual*, p. 3.   [2] Specifications (*a*), (*b*), (*c*) are given by Bain.

CLEARNESS. 257

not [=are not willing, do not wish to] come unto me that ye may have eternal life."—The preposition *for* may mean either *because* or *seeing that:* hence, a common mis-interpretation of Luke vii. 47.

(*b*) Two meanings of the same word should not occur in the same context. Thus ;—

Truth is, error and *truth* are blended in their minds.—This is my *duty* so long as I keep within the bounds of *duty*.—He *left* this world, *leaving* handsome fortunes to his children.—The *letters* of many men of *letters* are not distinguished above those of ordinary *letter*-writers.

(*c*) Clearness is promoted by using every word in its exact sense and by always expressing that sense with that word.

Examples of words easily confused in meaning have been given above.[1]—A serious error of the English translators of the Bible (1611) was their expressing the same Greek word by different English words and different Greek words by the same English word. For example, in Rom. vii. 7, 8, *lust, covet* and *concupiscence* all express the same idea, *coveting;* in John xiii. 10, *wash* stands for two different Greek words, *to take a bath* and *to wash*.[2]

On the other hand, Variety or Euphony may demand a change of word, even when the sense changes but little or not at all. "Our occidental taste in matters of rhetoric—or rather our *English* taste, for it is doubtless traceable mainly to the influence of the blended Norman and Saxon elements in our language—makes us like a euphonious change in the phraseology,[3] even when there is no change in the sense."[4] For example, *blameless* and *guiltless* in Matt. xii. 5, 7, *separate* and *divideth* in Matt. xxv. 32, *diversities* and *differences* in 1 Cor. xii. 4, 5, "most readers, looking merely at the *English*,

---

[1] § 154.

[2] Prof. Thayer, in *Bible-Revision*, pp. 133 ff.—The paper also lays down the necessary limits within which the principle can be applied in translation. The Revision of 1881 has mended both places.

[3] Diction, as the terms are used in this work. [4] Prof. Thayer, *ut cit.*

would prefer to let stand as they are, rather than substitute in each [case] some single identical term."[1] But neither Variety nor Euphony should be allowed to outweigh Clearness. When the easy or the full understanding of a passage depends on the repetition of the same word even many times, the repetition is vastly preferable to any exchange of the repeated word for other terms however euphonious or varied. For example, in Gen. xliv. 22, "The lad can not leave his *father;* for if he should leave his *father*, his *father* will die," not a word can be changed without destroying the intelligibility of the sentence. Hence, the rule against repeating an important word in the same context,—a rule often taught in so severe a form as, "Never repeat an important word on the same page,"—is actually *vicious*, unless it is understood to be simply a principle of taste,—merely a law of form, to be set aside whenever Clearness requires,—a law true only in the light of its converse,—Always repeat a word in any context, provided no other word expresses precisely the thought intended.

(*d*) The reference of many Pronouns is ambiguous. For example ;—

"*He* told the coachman that *he* would be the death of *him* if *he* did not take care what *he* was about and mind what *he* said."[2]

"A bull-dog attacked a man in an area. *It* is thought that by careful nursing *he* will pull through."

"The steamer Danish Monarch, from Barrow, experienced a succession of heavy gales during the entire passage, *which* stove in a boat and the rail, swept the decks of everything movable, and filled the cabin with water."

"As the matter stands now, while the belief exists that L. will be elected, he will be hotly pressed by R., championed, as *he* is, . . ."

"*He* [a friend of John Inglesant's] was very particular in inquiring after Father St. Clare, and whether Inglesant knew of

---

[1] Prof. Thayer, *ut cit.*   [2] Quoted by Abbott and Seeley, *English Lessons,* p. 118.

anything *he* was engaged in ; but John could give *him* no information, not knowing anything of the Jesuit's plans. They were hard times, *he* said."[1]

"When the gentleman had related this incident, *he* invited Johnny—for *he* was very courteous—to come on to *his* house and stop with *him.*"

It is especially a sinner; for it has two faces, or, rather, may now turn its face towards an antecedent, and now towards a following noun. Thus ;—

"English literature is postponed to almost everything else : *it* can hardly gain admission at all. The most that can be got for *it* is merely such fag-ends of time as . . . We think *it* a fine thing to have our children studying Demosthenes or Cicero, but do not mind their being ignorant of Burke and Webster."[2]

Dr. Abbott lays down the rule, "Pronouns should follow the nouns to which they refer without the intervention of another noun ;" and, although there are many clear exceptions to this rule,[3]—cases in which "one of two preceding nouns is decidedly superior to the other in emphasis,"—yet the student had better obey the rule, unless the case is so clearly exceptional that no ambiguity of reference is possible. For example, the following lines are clear enough and unobjectionable in Poetry ;—

" So sorrow's heaviness doth heavier grow
For debt that bankrupt sleep doth sorrow owe ;
Which now in some slight measure *it* will pay,
If for *his* tender here I make some stay ;"[4]

but a prose writer who demanded so much of his reader's intelligence would certainly be to blame. Still, even in Prose, the pronoun need not always refer to the last noun. For example ;—

---

[1] *John Inglesant*, ch. iii.—The context makes it plain that the last *he* means Inglesant's friend.

[2] The sentence is condensed from its original form; and the jarring of the *it's* is not only the more noticeable, but actually worse than in the original.

[3] As Dr. Abbott himself admits,—*How to Write*, R. 25.

[4] Shakspere, *A Midsummer-Night's Dream*, III. ii. 84.—*His* is for *its* (*sleep's*).

"Kenyon made haste along the Via Sistina, in the hope of overtaking the model, whose haunts and character *he* was anxious to investigate for Miriam's sake. *He* fancied that *he* saw *him* a long way in advance; but before *he* reached the Fountain of the Triton, the dusky figure had vanished."[1]

(*e*) *If not* and other negative words construed with conjunctions often become ambiguous; as;—

The writings of a great number, *if not* the majority, of celebrated authors.[2]—He was *not* sad *because* some intruder had cast a shadow on their mirth.—The remedy for drunkenness is *not* to be ascetic.[3]—A house of business employing *not* less than a hundred clerks at *any* time.[3]

(*f*) Often the obscurity is in the entire structure of the sentence; as;—

"He was twice married, and left six children. One grandchild, the daughter of his daughter Mary, *wife* of———, is now his only surviving descendant."

"The widow called the boy Andrew again, whenever she felt careless about her spiritual condition, and the youth behaved himself, but used the name of Sapphira's husband," *etc.*

"A Rising Sun man was so intent on making his wife sorry *that* he spent the money for an organ *that* he had been saving to pay the taxes with *that* he resolved to make death more than doubly sure."

322. Simplicity, Perspicuity, and Precision, then, are degrees of Intelligibility. Precision reaches minuteness of detail; Perspicuity is contented with general outline; Simplicity, in subjects that admit of it, is produced by the use of certain classes of words and a certain structure of sentence. Hence, Simplicity is essentially incompatible with Precision; for exactness often can not be secured except by the use of terms that are technical and unfamiliar,—terms the very opposite of those that promote simplicity. Perspicuity and Precision are more or less

---

[1] Hawthorne, *The Marble Faun*, i. 144.—The secret here is the maintaining of a single pronoun in reference to the subject, and the changing of this pronoun to a noun again only when the subject changes.

[2] ¿ 98, *above*.   [3] Cited in *English Lessons*, p. 120.

incompatible; since "to dwell with minute precision on the details tends rather to confuse our impressions as to the general outlines."[1] Simplicity and Perspicuity are not necessarily incompatible; for "the general outlines of things can be conveyed in familiar language."[1] Thus, to describe the earth as "round" is to speak with the utmost simplicity, but to convey only a general outline of its form; to say that it is "a sphere flattened at the poles" is to be perspicuous, but to "remove ourselves from the easy comprehension of many of our countrymen;"[1] to call it "an oblate spheroid" is to be precise, but to address the understanding of but a handful of English speakers.

323. Hence, Blair's rule, that "whatever a man conceives clearly, it is in his power, if he will be at the trouble, to put into distinct propositions, that is, to express clearly to others," is truly (as Mr. Minto terms it) absurd. For Blair uses but one term Perspicuity to denote the three degrees of intelligibility; and his rule must therefore mean that not only precision, not only general clearness, but even simplicity, is attainable in every case. But, surely, the inherent difficulty of a subject *may* be pleaded as an excuse for want of simplicity or even of perspicuity; since some subjects require for their intelligible presentation a microscopic minuteness of detail, and this (as has been shown) is always incompatible with simplicity, often with perspicuity. How shall the anatomy of the nerves be made simple, or the principles on which the construction of the steam engine rests? Certain mathematical propositions, clear as the light of day, precise as a Newton or a La Place can state them, are yet abstruse to a vast majority of the human race. Many minds fail even to formulate certain problems of Astronomy; yet to other minds these problems are as familiar as the face of one's intimate friend.

[1] Minto.

2. The Emotional Qualities.

324. Rhetoricians usually recognize only one Emotional Quality, *Vivacity*, or, as they indifferently call it, *Strength, Energy, Force*. Bain is right, however, in naming, also, (2) *Pathos* and (3) *the Ludicrous;* for, although the last two are often so characteristic of whole compositions as to constitute distinct modes of discourse, they may also, beyond doubt, be qualities of style in any kind of discourse. *Force*, the more generic word of the first group of names, and, perhaps, a better translation of the Greek ἐνέργεια than even *energy* itself, is preferred here as the name of the quality intended.

(1) Force.

325. Force is the quality of Style that produces *active* pleasurable excitement,—that pleasurable excitement which stimulates the mind to action. Mr. Minto's list of synonyms gives a clearer idea of the meaning of the term;—"Animation, vivacity, liveliness, rapidity, brilliancy; nerve, vigour, strength, energy, fervour; dignity, stateliness, splendour, grandeur, magnificence, loftiness, sublimity;" and his sub-groups (as indicated by the semi-colons) distinguish the three most marked degrees of the quality. Exactly to define these terms, however, would be impossible; their intention being necessarily general so long as different men feel differently or are different in character. Indeed, it is, perhaps, not even desirable that such terms should be weighed with accuracy; for substantial agreement in applying them will the sooner be reached, if they are not too narrowly marked off from each other. At their extremes, they are easily distinguished : it is only at their points of contact that they trench upon one other,— the points where animation (for example) in its liveliest form, brilliancy, passes into nerve, or where fervour and dignity overlap. A style that is only animated is rarely adjudged sublime; nor is one that is grand easily mistaken for one that is only vivacious.

326. Force in composition depends chiefly on the capacity of the writer to *feel* strongly. The language used, the structure of the sentence, other kindred devices, may *promote* force in expression; but they are not the *sources* of the quality.[1] True force springs either from the Possession or the Exercise of Power by oneself, or from Sympathy with Displays of Power in others or in Nature.[2] Thus, Satan in Hell is at first "vanquished, rolling in the fiery gulf, confounded"; but

> "the thought
> Both of lost happiness and lasting pain
> Torments him: round he throws his baleful eyes,
> Mixed with obdurate pride and steadfast hate;"

and then, lashed to madness, he boldly defies God;—

> "What though the field be lost?
> All is not lost—the unconquerable will,
> And study of revenge, immortal hate,
> And courage never to submit or yield."

Even after he has raised himself from the burning lake and surveyed its horrors, he is not dismayed, but exclaims,—

> "The mind is its own place, and in itself
> Can make a Heaven of Hell, a Hell of Heaven;
> To reign is worth ambition, though in Hell:
> Better to reign in Hell than serve in Heaven."

Step by step, as he recovers from his dejection, and recognizes the power that even the Omnipotent, in accordance with eternal decrees, can not take from him, his language rises in power, till it breaks into that sublime address,—

[1] See § 328, *below*. [2] Bain.

> "Powers and Dominions, Deities of Heaven!—
> For, since no deep within her gulf can hold
> Immortal vigour, though oppressed and fallen,
> I give not Heaven for lost."

In like manner, Satan's rising spirits carry with them all the lesser fiends. The assembly that has been sneeringly addressed,—

> "Have ye chosen this place
> After the toil of battle to repose
> Your wearied virtue? . . .
> Or in this abject posture have ye sworn
> To adore the conqueror?"—

is now a body in which "out-fly"

> "Millions of flaming swords, drawn from the thighs
> Of mighty Cherubim; the sudden blaze
> Far round illumines Hell. Highly they rage
> Against the Highest, and fierce with graspéd arms
> Clash on their sounding shields the din of war,
> Hurling defiance toward the vault of Heaven."

So, the animated, the vigorous, the grand in Nature have stirred men's minds, and charged their pens with a diction more than usually powerful.

> "The upper air burst into life!
> And a hundred fire-flags sheen;
> To and fro they were hurried about!
> And to and fro, and in and out,
> The wan stars danced between.

> "And the coming wind did roar more loud,
> And the sails did sigh like sedge;
> And the rain poured down from one black cloud;
> The moon was at its edge.

> "The thick black cloud was cleft, and still
> The moon was at its side;
> Like waters shot from some high crag,
> The lightning fell with never a jag,
> A river steep and wide."

327. As the deepest feelings often lack expression, so true force in writing often chooses language the most self-restrained. That divinest of all prayers, the prayer on the cross, is an example. The Saviour's rebuke to the renegade Peter was conveyed by a look. Mere display of force, language without a corresponding elevation of thought is *Bombast;*[1] it

> "frets its hour upon the stage
> And then is heard no more : it is a tale
> Told by an idiot, full of sound and fury,
> Signifying nothing."

Even so clever a writer as Mr. Blackmore has given the rein to this false sort of Pegasus. Describing a famous storm that swept over England, he writes ;[2]—

"Suddenly, ere a man might say Good God! or Where are my children? every tree was taken aback, every peat-stack reeled and staggered, every cot was stripped of its thatch, on the opposite side to that on which the blow was expected.

"The first squall of that great tempest broke from the dark south-east. It burst through the sleet, and dashed it upwards like an army of archers shooting ; ere a man could stay himself one way, it had caught him up from another. The leaves from the ground flew up again through the branches which had dropped them ; and then a cloud of all manner of foliage, whirling, flustering, capering, flitting, soared high over the highest tree-tops, and drove through the sky, like dead shooting-stars.

"All the afternoon the squalls flew faster, screaming onward to one another, furious maniacs dashing headlong, smiting themselves and everything. Then there came a lull. So sudden that the silence was more stunning than the turmoil. A pause for sunset ; for brave men countless to see their last of sunlight.

"All that night it blew and blew, harder and harder yet ; the fishermen's boats on the beach were caught up, and flung against the gravel-cliff; the stout men, if they ventured out, were snatched up as a mother snatches a child from the wheels of a carriage ; the oaks of the wood, after wailing and howling,

---

[1] Originally, cotton used to stuff out doublets. Hence, "to bombast out a line," to stuff it " full of sound and fury signifying nothing."

[2] *Cradock Nowell*, ch. xxxi, xxxii.

as they had done to a thousand tempests, found that outcry go for nothing, and with it went themselves. Seven hundred towers of nature's building showed their roots to the morning. The old moon expired at 0.32; and many a gap the new moon found, where its mother threw playful shadows. The sons of Ytene are not swift-witted, nor deeply read in the calendar; yet they are apt to mark and heed the great convulsions of nature. The old men used to date their weddings from the terrible winter of 1787: the landmark of the young men's annals is the storm of 1859."

Many much-vaunted descriptions in the modern novel are scarcely better than this; many are far worse. The older English dramatists, too,—even Shakspere in his earliest authorship—erred in this way. Thus;—

Marlowe's Tamburlaine, drawn in his chariot by two captive Kings, fairly raves;—

> "Holla, ye pampered jades of Asia!
> What, can ye draw but twenty miles a day,
> And have so proud a chariot at your heels,
> And such a coachman as great Tamburlaine,
> But from Asphaltis, where I conquer'd you,
> To Byron here, where thus I honour you?
> The horse[1] that guide the golden eye of heaven,
> And blow the morning from their nostrils,
> Making their fiery gait above the clouds,
> Are not so honour'd in their governor
> As you, ye slaves, in mighty Tamburlaine.
> The head-strong jades of Thrace Alcides tam'd,
> That King Ægeus fed with human flesh,
> And made so wanton that they knew their strengths,
> Were not subdu'd with valor more divine
> Than you by this unconquered arm of mine.
> To make you fierce, and fit my appetite,
> You shall be fed with flesh as raw as blood,
> And drink in pails the strongest muscadel:
> If you can live with it, then live, and draw
> My chariot swifter than the racking clouds;
> If not, then die like beasts, and fit for naught
> But perches for the black and fatal ravens.
> Thus am I right the scourge of highest Jove;
> And see the figure of my dignity,
> By which I hold my name and majesty!"

So, Shakspere's *Love's Labours Lost* begins with more sound than sense;—

[1] Old plural.

> "Let fame, that all hunt after in their lives,
> Live registered upon our brazen tombs
> And then grace us in the disgrace of death;
> When, spite of cormorant devouring Time,
> The endeavour of this present breath may buy
> That honour which shall bate his scythe's keen edge
> And make us heirs of all eternity.
> Therefore brave conquerors,—for so you are,
> That war against your own affections
> And the huge army of the world's desires,—
> Our late edict shall strongly stand in force:
> Navarre shall be the wonder of the world;
> Our court shall be a little academe,
> Still and contemplative in living art."

328. Further conditions to Force in Composition are *Originality*—freshness of matter or newness of form—*Variety*, and *Economy*. Were the *rifacimenti*[1] of Shakspere his only dramas, his works would be as little read to-day as are the miracle-plays or the interludes. His later works, many of which are grounded on histories or novels well-known in his day, so transform the baser metals of their originals, that they are virtually his own invention.[2] Many a talented novelist has made shipwreck by employing too repeatedly the same plot, scenery, or aim in writing. For example, George Macdonald, whose *Alec Forbes of How Glen*, and Mrs. Muloch-Craik, whose *John Halifax, Gentleman*, rightly earned them high rank among novelists, later dissipated their strength in stories the sole purpose of which seems to have been to preach. Even Sir Walter Scott's archæology grows wearisome; Thackeray's *Virginians* is less interesting than *Henry Esmond*—especially, after *Henry Esmond;* excessive length, as much as his many defects in style, has consigned Richardson to the limbo of books forgotten; and both the *Paradise Lost* and the *Faëry*

---

[1] Old plays *touched up*—Shakspere's apprentice-work.

[2] *As You Like It*, for instance, tells a story already told in *The Cook's Tale of Gamelyn;* *Julius Cæsar* and *Macbeth* were largely drawn from North's *Plutarch* and Hollinshead's *Chronicle;* but the most minute comparison leaves Shakspere's credit for originality unhurt.

Queene would be oftener read and better known, were their riches less embarrassing.

(2) Pathos.

329. Pathos is the Quality of Style that produces *passive* pleasurable excitement,—pleasurable excitement that quiets rather than arouses the mind,—excitement of the more tender feelings, such as love, pity, benevolence, humanity. The term is not always so restricted, however; the most agitating "representations of pain and misery" being often included under it. But such representations are not always of one character. They may be used by way of suggesting motives to action, and then they are forcible rather than pathetic; but they may also be used for the so-called poetic end of giving melancholy pleasure, and then they are pathetic rather than forcible. This distinction may not be found in the words *pathos* and *force* as commonly used: distinctions between the several modes of mental action rarely are observed in the popular use of even the technical terms that name them. But such distinctions are none the less useful, none the less to be observed in technical use. An example or two will make the matter clearer.

A lawyer pleading for his client's life, a preacher aiming to move his audience to deeds of charity, will avoid no detail of horror, of pain, of mental suffering, however harrowing; but the novelist, the dramatist, the poet, will ordinarily reject details that would carry his reader beyond the limits of passive, into the domain of active excitement. At the most, he will admit such details, only that he may the more fully please his reader by allaying the mental excitement they have produced, by righting wrong, by vindicating suspected virtue, by exhibiting what has rightly been termed poetic justice. Or, if his purpose is to "hold the mirror up to nature," to portray real life with all its actual grief and pain and wrong, its sickening, saddening load of genuine misery, he will commonly have the further purpose of showing the alleviations, the consolations that man so burdened may find in philosophy, in virtue, in religion. Examples of novels, plays, poems, to which these remarks apply are scarcely necessary; a few examples of the apparent exceptions may be given. The novels of Charles Dickens, for instance, have been criticized as overstepping the bounds of reason in this respect. They carry us, it is said, into scenes of actual, not ideal, horror: they make too urgent demands upon our sympathy; they portray real and present suffering, suffering that stands at our doors and waits for alleviation from us. And so they undoubtedly do. Dickens does transcend the limits of passive excitement; for he had a higher mission than merely to please his countrymen: he wrote also to correct abuses. True, he allures men to listen; but chiefly, that he may spur them on to action. He might, indeed, have written essays, tirades against existing wrongs, satires clever and fresh; but, in that case, no master of Dotheboy's Hall would ever have come to London to bring suit against Dickens for libel in revealing the secret crimes of his school, nor would generation after generation have pored over the many pages that teach such deep-sinking lessons of sympathy, of pure humanity, of neighborly kindness and love. George Macdonald's *Alec Forbes*, too, heart-rending as its details are, probably went far to banish the brutal *tawse* from Scotch schools, and presents a sufficient alleviation in the death together, at a moment of perfect mutual understanding and reconciliation, of the repentant schoolmaster and his long-suffering pupil, the victim of his unrestrained passion. The dismal picture of Denmark drawn in *Hamlet* is not all shadow: a "light" breaks upon it "at eventide" from the hope one may entertain that the state, purified by the many storms it has passed through will enter on a new and loftier career. *King Lear*, except the death of Cordelia, *Othello*, except the sacrifice of Desdemona, may be explained on the same principle. If Cordelia and Desdemona *could* not be spared because of "the logic of events," then it must be freely conceded that in these cases Shakspere has passed beyond the limits of poetry into the confines of history, has portrayed the horrible, not the pathetic.

330. Pathos, like Force, can not be achieved merely by the use of supposedly pathetic language. Beneath the language used must be genuine pathetic thought, tender emotion either felt or sympathized with by the writer, and giving character to his style. Mere pathos

of language is *Sentimentality*, the corresponding vice to Bombast. Even poets of high rank,—Wordsworth and Tennyson, for instance,—have fallen into this error ;—

> "'T is said, that some have died for love :
> And there is one whom I five years have known :
> He loved,—the pretty Barbara died ;
> And thus he makes his moan :
> 'O move, thou Cottage, from behind that oak !
> Or let the aged tree uprooted lie,
> That in some other way yon smoke
> May mount into the sky!
> The clouds pass on ; they from the heavens depart :
> I look,—the sky is empty space ;
> I know not what I trace ;
> But when I cease to look, my hand is on my heart.'"[1]

> "Full knee-deep lies the winter snow,
>   And the winter winds are wearily sighing :
> Toll ye the church bell sad and slow,
> And tread softly and speak low,
>   For the old year lies a-dying.
>   Old year, you must not die ;
>   You came to us so readily,
>   You lived with us so steadily,
>   Old year, you shall not die."[2]

[1] *Poems Founded on the Affections*, xlii.
[2] *The Death of the Old Year*, st. 1.—The very personification seems absurd, and the two lines next to the last are absolutely nonsensical. Contrast with this whole poem Tennyson's truly strong and pathetic verses, *In Memoriam*, cvi. ;—

> "Ring out wild bells to the wild sky,
>   The flying cloud, the frosty light :
>   The year is dying in the night ;
> Ring out, wild bells, and let him die.
>
> "Ring out the old, ring in the new,
>   Ring, happy bells, across the snow
>   The year is going, let him go ;
> Ring out the false, ring in the true.
>
> "Ring out old shapes of foul disease ;
>   Ring out the narrowing lust of gold ;
>   Ring out the thousand wars of old,
> Ring in the thousand years of peace.
>
> "Ring in the valiant man and free,
>   The larger heart, the kindlier hand ;
>   Ring out the darkness of the land,
> Ring in the Christ that is to be."

Carried to an extreme, Sentimentality becomes mawkish, produces a mental nausea.

(3) The Ludicrous.

331. The Ludicrous, or the Laughable, is a generic term for whatever promotes laughter. This may be (*a*) the degradation of an object (person or thing) ordinarily dignified; (*b*) the unexpected and ingenious association of objects not usually connected. Further, the degradation constituting form (*a*) may be (*a'*) malicious, intended to sting, or (*a''*) good-natured. (*a'*) is *Satire;* (*a''*), *Humor.* (*b*) is *Wit.*[1] Thus;—

(*a'*) "Close to those walls where Folly holds her throne
 And laughs to think Monroe would take her down,
 Where o'er the gates, by his fam'd father's hand,
 Great Cibber's brazen, brainless brothers stand;[2]
 One cell there is concealed from vulgar eye,
 The Cave of Poverty and Poetry.
 Keen, hollow winds howl thro' the bleak recess,
 Emblem of Music caus'd by Emptiness.
 Hence Bards, like Proteus long in vain tied down,
 Escape in Monsters, and amaze the town. [38]
 Hence Miscellanies spring, the weekly boast
 Of Curl's chaste press, and Lintot's rubric post:[3]
 Hence hymning Tyburn's elegiac lines[4]
 Hence Journals, Medleys, Merc'ries, Magazines;
 Sepulchral Lies,[5] our holy walls to grace,
 And New-Year Odes,[6] and all the Grub-street race.

[1] Bain and Minto.

[2] Monroe was physician to Bedlam Hospital; Cibber was Poet Laureate; his father had made two statues of lunatics, which were placed over the Bedlam Hospital gates.

[3] Curl and Lintot were booksellers: the latter advertised his books in *red* letters.

[4] Criminals executed at Tyburn sang psalms (sometimes published elegies on their own deaths).

[5] Alluding to fulsome epitaphs on church walls, *etc.*

[6] Written annually by the Poet Laureate to be sung at Court on New Year's Day. Cibber's were especially famous.

"In clouded Majesty here Dulness shone;
Four guardian Virtues, round support her throne:
Fierce champion Fortitude, that knows no fears
Of hisses, blows, or want, or loss of ears:
Calm Temperance, whose blessings those partake
Who hunger and who thirst for scribbling sake:
Prudence, whose glass presents th' approaching jail:
Poetic Justice, with her lifted scale,
Where, in nice balance, truth with gold she weighs
And solid pudding against empty praise."[1] [54]

(a'') "At one of these ['two groceries' in Cambridge] the unwearied students used to ply a joke handed down from class to class.

"*Enter A*, and asks gravely, 'Have you any sour apples, Deacon?'

"'Well, no, I haven't any just now that are exactly sour; but there's the bell-flower apple, and folks that like a sour apple generally like that.' (*Exit A.*)

"*Enter B*. 'Have you any sweet apples, Deacon?'

"'Well, no, I haven't any just now that are exactly sweet; but there's the bell-flower apple, and folks that like a sweet apple generally like that.' (*Exit B.*)

"There is not even a tradition of any one's ever having turned the wary Deacon's flank, and his Laodicean apples persisted to the end, neither one thing nor another."[2]

(*b*) "Here lies, or lie,—decide the question, you,
If they were two in one or one in two,—
P. and S. Snow, whose memory shall not fade,
Castor and Pollux of the oyster trade:
Hatched from one egg, at once the shell they burst,
(The last, perhaps, a P. S. to the first,)
So homoousian both in look and soul,
So undiscernibly a single whole,
That whether P. was S., or S. was P.,
Surpassed all skill in etymology;
One kept the shop at once, and all we know
Is that together they were *the* great Snow,
A snow not deep, yet with a crust so thick
It never melted to the son of Tick;
Perpetual? nay, our region was too low,
Too warm, too Southern, for perpetual Snow.

---

[1] Pope, *The Dunciad*, I. 29-54.

[2] James Russell Lowell, *Cambridge Thirty Years Ago* (in *Fireside Travels*, p. 33.)

> But Snow is gone, and, let us hope, sleeps well,
> Buried (his last breath asked it) in a shell;
> Fate with an oyster-knife sawed off his thread,
> And planted him upon his latest bed.
> Him on the Stygian shore my fancy sees
> Noting choice shoals for oyster colonies,
> Or at a board stuck full of ghostly forks,
> Opening for practice visionary Yorks.
> And whither he has gone, may we too go,—
> Since no hot place were fit for keeping Snow!
> *Jam satis nivis.*"[1]

332. The opposition here affirmed between Satire and Humor is generally alleged between Humor and Wit; but "the proper antithesis to Humour is Satire: Wit is common to both."[2] And, surely, if Wit has been correctly defined, this judgment holds. The "unexpected and ingenious association of objects" may certainly be used either for the malicious or the good-natured promotion of the Ludicrous; that is, Wit may be combined with either Satire or Humor; but it may also exist alone and for its own sake, uncomplicated by any intention whatever, simply for the sake of being witty. There certainly is such a thing as pure Wit; as there are, also, pure Satire and pure Humor. For example, Dr. Holmes's verses *My Aunt* are in the main pure satire, but each stanza closes (as is often Dr. Holmes's method) with a flash of wit;—

> "My aunt, my poor deluded aunt!
> Her hair is almost gray;
> Why will she train that winter curl
> In such a spring-like way?
> How can she lay her glasses down,
> And say she reads as well,
> When, *through a double convex lens*
> *She just makes out to spell?*
>
> "Her father . . . .
> . . . . sent her to a stylish school;
> 'Twas in her thirteenth June;
> *And with her, as the rules required,*
> *Two towels and a spoon.*"

On the other hand, his *Evening—By a Tailor* seems to have no other intention than to contrast the pensive, almost poetic mood of the soliloquist with the grotesque figures he uses in description: it is pure Wit. Thus;—

---

[1] James Russell Lowell, *Cambridge Thirty Years Ago* (in *Fireside Travels*, p. 38.)
[2] Minto.

"Day hath put on his jacket, and around
His burning bosom buttoned it with stars.
Here will I lay me on the velvet grass,
That is like padding to earth's meagre ribs,
And hold communion with the things about me—
Ah me! how lovely is the golden braid
That binds the skirt of night's descending robe!
The thin leaves, quivering on their silken threads,
Do make a music like to rustling satin,
As the light breezes smooth their downy nap.

"Is that a swan that rides upon the water?
O, no, it is that other gentle bird,
Which is the patron of our noble calling.
I well remember in my early years,
When these young hands first closed upon a goose;
I have a scar upon my thimble finger,
Which chronicles the hour of young ambition.
My father was a tailor, and his father,
And my sire's grandsire, all of them were tailors;
They had an ancient goose,—it was an heirloom
From some remoter tailor of our race.
It happened I did see it on a time
When none was near, and I did deal with it,
And it did burn me,—oh, most fearfully!"

So Pope's satire, quoted above, is absolutely free from wit, (unless in lines 37, 38 and 53, 54), and is certainly guiltless of humor; while Mr. Lowell's story of the grocer is simply humorous, lacking the witty as completely as it lacks the satirical.

333. The Humorous and the Pathetic are apt to be joined in the same composition—sometimes in the closest union. Thus, Mr. Swiveller and the Marchioness[1] stand in marked contrast to Little Nell and her grandfather. The truly pathetic death-scene of the child follows hard upon some of the most amusing chapters of the book. Launcelot Gobbo is not out of place in *The Merchant of Venice.* Dr. Holmes joins in the same short poem[2] the two following stanzas;—

"The mossy marbles rest
    On the lips that he has prest
        In their bloom,
And the names he loved to hear
    Have been carved for many a year
        On the tomb.

[1] Dickens, *The Old Curiosity Shop.*   [2] *The Last Leaf.*

"I know it is a sin
    For me to sit and grin
        At him here;
    But the old three-cornered hat,
    And the breeches, and all that,
        Are so queer!"

334. The distinction just made between the Ludicrous produced by degradation and that produced by unexpected association will lead the student intelligently through the mazes of such terms as Sarcasm, Travesty, Burlesque, Mock-Heroic, *etc.* He need only distinguish elements of the kind (*a*) from those of class (*b*), and his way is clear.

3. THE ÆSTHETIC QUALITIES.

335. The Æsthetic Qualities are those that serve to refine the style. This refinement may be in the language used, in the relations of the thought expressed to the language, or in the total effect produced by both thought and diction. Hence, the Æsthetic Qualities are (1) *Melody*, (2) *Harmony*, (3) *Variety*, (4) *Elegance*. A more elaborate division could easily be made; but a minute classification, interesting as it might be, hardly seems necessary.

(1) MELODY.—(2) HARMONY.

336. Melody and Harmony are technical terms of Music, but are easily transferred to Style;—*Melody*, the effect produced by the *succession* of pleasing sounds; *Harmony*, the effect of several such sounds heard *together*. In Rhetoric, the definition of Melody remains unchanged; but Harmony is the agreement, not of several sounds with each other, but of Sound with Sense. The limiting word "pleasing" points to *Euphony* as a quality implied in Melody; while the truth that sounds in language (as in music) are either accented or unaccented, suggests *Rhythm*[1] as a further implication in

---
[1] § 36, *above.*

the term. Harmony may be *Imitative* or *Symbolical;*— *Imitative*, when the words used mimic in sound the thought intended; *Symbolical*, when they "designate sensible objects or scenes" that "symbolize or image forth the sense."[1]

The following examples illustrate these qualities;—

"Methinks I see in my mind a noble and puissant nation rousing herself like a strong man after sleep, and shaking her invincible locks; methinks I see her as an eagle mewing her mighty youth, and kindling her undazzled eyes at the full mid-day beam; purging and unscaling her long-abused sight at the fountain itself of the heavenly radiance; while the whole noise of timorous and flocking birds, with those also that love the twilight, flutter about, amazed at what she means, and in their envious gabble would prognosticate a year of sects and schisms."[2]

Pleasing in themselves, the sounds follow one another without jar or break; while the accents are so admirably distributed, that, although the ear receives an agreeable sense of rhythmic movement, there is no offensive regularity of rhythm.[3] So,—

"At summer eve, when Heaven's ethereal bow
Spans with bright arch the glittering hill below,
Why to yon mountain turns the musing eye,
Whose sun-bright summit mingles with the sky?
Why do those cliffs of shadowy tint appear
More sweet than all the landscape smiling near?
'Tis distance lends enchantment to the view,
And robes the mountain in its azure hue.
Thus, with delight, we linger to survey
The promised joys of life's unmeasured way,
Thus, from afar, each dim-discovered scene
More pleasing seems than all the past hath been,
And every form, that Fancy can repair
From dark oblivion glows divinely there."[4]

Euphony and Melody at every point, and a regular Rhythm, as becomes verse.

"But Ida with a voice, that like a *bell*
Toll'd by an earthquake in a *trembling tower*,
Rang ruin, answer'd full of grief and scorn."

"But had you stood by us,
The *roar* that *breaks* the *Pharos* from his base
Had left us *rock*."[5]

---

[1] H. N. Day, by whose classification this whole paragraph has been suggested.
[2] Milton, *Areopagitica*.   [3] § 40, *above*.
[4] Campbell, *The Pleasures of Hope*.   [5] Tennyson, *The Princess*, vi.

The italicized words are especially imitative; but there is a further agreement of Sound and Sense in each passage as a whole. Of passages that *symbolize* the sense expressed the following are good examples;—

> "How calm, how beautiful, comes on
> The stilly hour when storms are gone;
> When warring winds have died away,
> And clouds, beneath the glancing ray,
> Melt off, and leave the land and sea
> Sleeping in bright tranquillity,—
> Fresh as if Day again were born,
> Again upon the lap of Morn!"[1]

The dying away of the winds, the melting off of the clouds, the bright tranquillity of land and sea, all contribute to produce in the mind of the reader the impression actually made by "the stilly hour when storms are gone." So, how perfectly one can see the ship in which Arthur Hallam's remains are being wafted home;—

> "A favorable speed
> Ruffle thy mirror'd mast, and lead
> Thro' prosperous floods his holy urn.
>
> "All night no ruder air perplex
> Thy sliding keel, till Phospor, bright
> As our pure love, thro' early light
> Shall glimmer on the dewy decks.
>
> "Sphere all your lights around, above;
> Sleep, gentle heavens, before the prow;
> Sleep, gentle winds, as he sleeps now,
> My friend, the brother of my love."[2]

337. The question how far a prose writer may avail himself of the rhythmic movement of language has already been answered by implication.[3] That the best Prose has a rhythm of its own, and that exceptional Prose may come quite near the domain of verse,— perhaps, may trespass upon it,—has been seen. But a prudent writer will always prefer an unmistakable prose rhythm, and will rarely or never *choose* a rhythm of any other kind. If his subject, the feelings it naturally arouses, any sufficient causes, lead him into a verse-like rhythm, he must be able to find the fullest justification for

---

[1] Moore, *Lalla Rookh* (*The Fire Worshippers*).
[2] *In Memoriam*, ix.
[3] §§ 40 ff, 158 (2) ff, *above*.

that rhythm in those causes. Inadvertencies in this matter, especially the unconscious joining of rhyme with an unmistakable verse-rhythm, produce the most ludicrous effects. The examples cited above[1] show the truth of the first part of this statement; the following evidently accidental structures of sentences establish the other part;—

"A view closely analogous to the *belief that good shall fall at last to all.*"[2]

"When parallel rays come contrary ways, and fall upon opposite sides."[3]

(3) Variety.

338. Variety implies a judicious interchange of the many forms of expression, modes of composition, all the characteristics of discourse. Monotony is not only displeasing to the taste; it imperils the success of the work, both by diverting the attention that a judicious exchange of forms, *etc.*, excites and retains, and by failing to stimulate the mind of the reader to its best exertions. Feeble as the itching for "something new" undoubtedly is, when it is only the idle desire of a gossip, there is, nevertheless, a legitimate craving for something new, a craving with which man has been endowed by nature. Besides, Variety implies only something different—new, not in itself, but only so far as it is in contrast with its immediate surroundings. Many examples showing this quality of style have already been quoted; and, hence, no special citations seem necessary here.

(4) Elegance.

339. Elegance is the Quality of Style by which discourse commends itself to the Taste of the hearer or reader. By Taste is meant either "artistic sensibility,—as Blair defines it, 'the power of receiving pleasure from the beauties of nature and of art,—'" or "artistic judg-

---

[1] §§ 40 ff, 158 (2) ff, *above.*
[2] Quoted from Canon Farrar in *The Churchman*, February 16, 1878.
[3] Quoted by Day, § 262.

ment," *correctness* of Taste. Bain thinks it may also mean "the kind of artistic excellence that gives the greatest amount of pleasure to cultivated minds;" and, hence, he accepts it as the name of the quality; but to say the least, the word is unfamiliar in this meaning, and the term *Elegance* is now so well established, that it would seem unfortunate to substitute for it an unfamiliar name. As used here, Taste means *artistic judgment*, and Elegance the quality of Style that disposes this judgment favorably. A few examples of the Elegant in composition may be added;—

"They walked out hand-in-hand, through the court, and to the terrace-walk, where the grass was glistening with dew, and the birds in the green woods above were singing their delicious choruses under the blushing morning sky. How well all things were remembered! The ancient towers and gables of the hall darkling against the east, the purple shadows on the green slopes, the quaint devices and carvings of the dial, the forest-crowned heights, the fair yellow plain cheerful with crops and corn, the shining river rolling through it towards the pearly hills beyond; all these were before us, along with a thousand beautiful memories of our youth, beautiful and sad, but as real and vivid in our minds as that fair and always remembered scene our eyes beheld once more. We forget nothing. The memory sleeps, but wakens again; I often think how it shall be when, after the last sleep of death, the *réveille* shall rouse us forever, and the past in one flash of self-consciousness rush back, like the soul revivified."[1]

> " My soul is an enchanted boat
> Which, like a sleeping swan, doth float
> Upon the silver waves of thy sweet singing;
> And thine doth like an angel sit
> Beside the helm conducting it,
> While all the winds with melody are ringing.
> It seems to float ever, forever,
> Upon that many-winding river,
> Between mountains, woods, abysses,
> A paradise of wildernesses!
> Till, like one in slumber bound,
> Borne to the ocean, I float down, around,
> Into a sea profound of ever spreading sound."[2]

[1] Thackeray, *Henry Esmond*. [2] Shelly, *Prometheus Unbound*.

340. Bain has aptly defined two elements of Taste, one *permanent*, and one *variable*. Certain questions of taste though men should dispute about them forever, do not admit of discussion. The points at issue have been decided by an appeal to fundamental and unchallengeable truths: the questions are closed. Many rules of Rhetoric are of this kind, —the doctrine of judicious Brevity, the necessity of Clearness, the evil effect of incessantly recurring mannerisms, the excellence of an idiomatic style, the importance of being oneself in composition, *etc.* But on other questions, tastes vary in different ages and in individuals. Neither the drama of the Greeks nor the "license of personal vituperation" they allowed their orators are in taste to-day. English literature of the Classic Period—loosely 1660 to 1789—accepted many rules of composition which the common sense reaction of the succeeding period abrogated. Lessing gave form as well as life to German literature, till his time almost a wilderness. So, "the emotional constitution, the intellectual tendencies, and the education of each individual" cause divergencies of taste. Poetry appeals to many minds that music fails to touch, and *vice versa*. Men "of wider literary knowledge and superior discernment groan inwardly, some of them outwardly, at the judgment of the multitude in the matter of sublimity, pathos, and humour." Further, there are schools of writers, each with its own admirers and its own clamorous defenders. In a word, as there are "many men," so there are "many minds;" and, provided the disagreement turns solely on matters of a personal, individual character, "there is no disputing about tastes." Perhaps the whole case for both elements of Taste may be summed up in a single law;—Men differ most when their sensibilities are engaged; their intellectual judgments are more nearly at one.

PART SECOND.

INVENTION.

SUB-DIVISIONS.

341. INVENTION *states the Rules that direct and control the Discovery of Matter for the Composition.*[1] These rules concern either the subject about which one writes, the *Theme*,[2] or else the composition itself, what one writes about the Theme, the *Discussion*. Hence, two sub-divisions of Part Second,—(A) THE THEME, (B) THE DISCUSSION.

342. The word *Discussion* is used here in a slightly broader sense than in § 280, *above*. There it meant the *body* of the composition, as opposed to the Proposition, the Introduction, and the Conclusion: here it includes these parts as well as the Discussion properly so called. But, all told, these parts add but little, in proportion, to the Discussion Proper; and the extension of the term to include everything but the Theme is, hence, not a material variation of its meaning. Besides, although the parts named must be considered as belonging to the Discussion in this broader sense of the term, yet the rules to be stated for the Discussion apply to it most particularly in its narrower meaning. The Introduction and the Conclusion have already been characterized as *non-essential;* and the Proposition itself is in a certain sense *outside* the composition, since, in any case, it is determined rather as a part of the development of the Theme than as a part of the Discussion properly so called.

[1] § 23, *above*.
[2] Greek τιθέναι, to put (forward as the subject of a composition).

(A) THE THEME.

343. The Theme may be (1) *given*, (2) *suggested* (or, at least, *limited*) by the *occasion* for which the composition is intended, (3) *left* wholly to the *choice* of the writer. For example;—

(1) The lawyer has his "case" brought to him; and it is to *that* case, and no other, that he must address himself, whether in the papers filed as preliminaries to the trial, or in what he may say before judge or jury. His theme is chosen for him: should he for any reason speak on a subject not fairly raised by the case, the judge but discharges a plain duty in demanding that he shall keep to his subject. So, the legislator must speak on the bill before the house. A "Duluth" Knott or a "Sunset" Cox may spend his store of humor or wit on his colleagues; but there is no pretence that in this sort of talk the house is occupied with the debate.

(2) The sacred preacher has, indeed, a wide range of subjects for his sermons; but, nevertheless, he meets much adverse criticism, if he steps far beyond the limits of the religious or the moral. Important public questions that affect these sides of man's nature,—even the political life of the people considered as one means of their education by Divine Providence,—may (perhaps, should) receive his attention; but merely secular topics, topics not even remotely his, are justly objected to in the pulpit. Besides, the many special occasions that arise in the year, even in the churches that do not observe a fixed order of services, often limit the preacher in his choice of subject; while many occurrences are not unusual that render one subject more fit than another. The preacher's subject is, of course, not set; but in many ways his choice is biassed.

(3) The public lecture, the magazine article, the *opus magnum* of a scholarlike Casaubon, have their subjects at the will of their authors. Circumstances, to be sure, may influence even these cases; but, so far as any subject of composition is at will, the subjects of these and other such works are so.

344. In all three instances, however, ample room is left the writer to exercise his judgment.

(1) In the suit at law, not a little depends upon how a case is put before the court. The question that presents itself on the surface is not always the real point at issue; and the lawyer may therefore abundantly employ his ingenuity in finding this real question: in fact, by thus "making" his case, he all but chooses his subject. For example, John Hampden, sued in the time of King Charles the First for non-payment of taxes, showed the magistrate that the real question was whether the King should be allowed to usurp unconstitutional powers. Many a proposed act of legislature has been successfully represented or misrepresented by a re-reading of its title or by an open or covert sneer. The repeal of the Corn Laws in England was, on different views of the bill, either an act to put bread into the mouths of starving women and children or a measure to ruin the English farmer. A certain "bill for the Relief of the Surviving Officers of the Revolution"[1] was kindly mentioned by Mr. Webster as proposing "an annuity:" a senator from Georgia had sneered at its beneficiaries as willing to accept "a pension."

(2) The clergyman, more than any other public speaker, will find room for a wise judgment in selecting his theme. The pro's and con's are often nicely balanced in regard to a subject; and a mistake on his part is commonly fatal. When Slavery was still a factor in American politics, a famous clergyman preaching on the Psalms in course, found himself face to face with the story of Doeg the Edomite who betrayed to Saul the hiding-place of David. A general discourse on Doeg's treachery would have avoided the "burning question" of the day, the Fugitive Slave Law. But the preacher held decided Anti-Slavery views, and he considered his meeting thus incidentally a text that allowed him to free his soul of a long undischarged weight of responsibility, a call from Heaven. Till then, had he introduced the subject, he must have gone out of his way to bring it into his pulpit; and his conscience had hitherto absolved him. But now the question had presented itself to him: to evade it would be cowardice. His sermon broke some old friendships, might have rent his church asunder; but the topic was not of his choosing, and consequences, he felt, might wisely be left to Him in whose name he stood before the people.

(3) Even the writer whose choice seems wholly unbiassed can not be absolutely indifferent to circumstances. A number of

[1] U. S. Senate, April 1828.

considerations determine him,—considerations that must be detailed in full. The same considerations are often of value, too, in the second case.

345. Whenever the subject is not definitely given,— cases (2) and (3), § 343, *above*,—the writer must determine, before attempting a selection, (*a*) the occasion for which he intends his composition, (*b*) the character of the persons he may reasonably expect to address, and (*c*) the end he has in view in writing. His selection will then be made in accordance with his determinations upon these three points. In case (2), condition (*a*) will be in some measure satisfied; but there will still remain to be settled the *particular* circumstances under which the discourse is to be delivered. Of course, a writer may work in ignorance of points (*a*) and (*b*) or in indifference to them; but what he writes will then be addressed to minds of a certain order only, and be suited to occasions of only a certain sort. When brought into use, it will either prove adapted as if by chance, or else have to be recast.

346. Further, (*d*) the theme must be one that the writer is *capable of handling*. Not that he must know beforehand all that can be said about it: on the contrary, the strongest incentive a writer can have, is the interest that his subject has for his own mind; and this interest is never greater than when it is prompted by the discovery of something new. All that is meant by the rule is that the writer must be prepared by previous studies, *etc.*, to understand his subject, to learn what he will need to know of it, and, hence, to be able to express worthy thought about it.

347. (*e*) "Fertile" subjects are especially to be avoided. They are commonly hackneyed and, hence, difficult to make interesting. They involve, too, a great body of details, for the definition and classification of which a vigorous mental grasp is needed, and the presentation

of which to the reader requires a commanding use of method. If such a subject *must* be written on, the writer will find his powers tested to their utmost: he will need to call to his aid every help that Nature or Art can render him.

348. The theme obtained, it must be developed: (*a*) its exact meaning must be determined; and (*b*) the particular form it is to take in the work in hand must be selected. This selection may have to be postponed until the student has read on the subject proposed, and has collected at least a part of his material; but in actual literary work, the purpose in writing is always known, and the material to be used is selected in accordance with this purpose, not the purpose determined in accordance with the material used. The Proposition may then be distinctly written out; and now the writer is ready to outline his Discussion, to set down its several heads and sub-divisions, and to arrange for necessary introductory or concluding matter. Of course, formality in this process is fatal: the finished work must show as slight traces of the mechanical part of composition as may be. *Ars est celare artem.* Yet, consciously or unconsciously, the writer does take each of these steps, and must take them.

Thus, suppose the subject selected to be *Self-Preservation.* The first question must be, What does the term mean? Is self-preservation only an instinct that keeps men from unnecessarily endangering life or limb, that makes them avoid danger and suffering when nothing is to be gained by incurring either; or is it a cowardly self-love that, indulged freely, would render deeds of heroism or self-sacrifice impossible? Or, again, does the word mean only the judicious care of one's life and health and the promotion by every wise means of bodily vigor to old age? On the definition accepted will turn, of course, the form the work is to take,—the Proposition, the matter proper for the Discussion, every part of the composition from its first word to its last. In the first case, the Proposition might be, *Self-Preservation is a Law of Nature;* the Discussion, an illustration of the law and a definition of the privileges it confers and the duties it imposes. In the second case, the paradox might be affirmed that, although self-preservation has its root in selfishness, yet, because a genuine sympathy comes only through suffering, and self-preservation inclines a man to avoid suffering for himself, the instinct of self-preservation will irresistibly draw him through his sympathies to deeds of self-sacrifice and even heroism in behalf of others. If the third definition were accepted, the essay might consist of such a series of hygienic suggestions, and such moral applications of them, as the occasion and other circumstances would warrant.

349. Thus, out of a single theme, (stated most broadly, to be sure,) three distinct compositions suggest themselves. Nor was the subject at first glance most promising. A young writer, working without the directions here given, would in all probability have set down the disjointed thoughts that occurred to him, as they occurred to him, without defined purpose in writing, and without consistency with either this purpose or one another. He would have achieved such a result as "young Mr. Brown" achieved, when he refused "to be put into the leading strings" of a proposition, and tried to write on *Fortune* instead of on the thesis *Fortune Helps the Brave*.[1] He would ignominiously have failed; while the experience of every teacher of Composition proves that reasonably good work can be done by even young writers, if they are taught the subject in this systematic way.[2]

[1] J. H. Newman, *Lectures on University Subjects*, p. 150.—Dr. Newman's idea, however, that a young writer should always have a proposition *stated* for him, —that (in the University tutor's words in the Brown case) "it would have been very cruel to have told a boy to write on 'fortune'; it would have been like asking his opinion of 'things in general,'"—loses sight of the valuable discipline a student receives in stating his own proposition. Besides—supposing always that idle jottings about *Fortune* or any other subject are rigorously forbidden by the instructor—why not allow the young writer the freedom that a choice of propositions gives him? Few subjects of thought, few themes forced on a man by his experience, come in the shape of a sentence. Does not every one, sooner or later, formulate *for himself* judgments about Life and Death and numberless other topics? Since Whately, Rhetoric has too often taught Logic, and not the Art of Discourse.

[2] Among the many thousand compositions read by the author as professor of Rhetoric, only a mere handful have been like young Mr. Brown's.

(B) THE DISCUSSION.

350. The collection of matter for a composition on any theme is guided chiefly by the *purpose* of the writer; for it is this purpose, in the main, that determines *the mode of discussion* proper to the given work.[1] At the same time, certain general rules can be stated; though, of course, no special directions can be given to meet each theme. Hence, two chief heads of this sub-division of Invention—I. *General Rules*, II. *The Modes of Discussion*.

350 a. To give specific directions for the discussion of separate themes, Rhetoric would have to teach men universal knowledge;[2] whereas what a writer needs to know on a given subject he must learn from the authorities on that subject. Earnest writing presupposes earnest reading—and not this alone, but earnest thought and an earnest effort to make what is read one's own, or even to be stimulated by it to truly original thought. Simply to appropriate another man's work, even if one expresses it in one's own words, is the flagitious act called by the hard name *plagiarism*, or *literary theft:* to "assimilate" what one reads, making it the source of new life and power, is work worthy of the highest intellectual and moral powers in man. The best work on important subjects must be grounded on the work of one's predecessors;[3] and, hence, whatever has been written on a subject *must* be considered as at a later writer's disposal. But this principle gives no license to literary theft, nor does it warrant the transferring from another writer's pages to one's own his matter bodily.[4]

---

[1] § 355, *below.*

[2] Appendix, p. 331.

[3] § 351, *below.*

[4] Except, of course, in quotation-marks.

I.

GENERAL RULES.

351. (1) *Exhaustive* treatment of a subject requires on the writer's part a complete knowledge of that subject,—especially, a wide acquaintance with the views of all previous writers. In this way, not only will completeness be secured, and the repetition as original of opinions tried and found false or inadequate, be prevented; but, and especially, will the stimulus that knowledge broad and deep always applies to thought, most surely be felt by the writer. It is only when the mind is heavily charged with truth, that the finest display of power in writing is possible. For example, Mr. Dowden, in *Shakspere: His Mind and Art*, says that, although he was writing from a new point of view, yet, "in order to get substantial ground to go upon," he had "thought it necessary to form acquaintance with a considerable body of recent Shakspere scholarship;" and that, although he was avoiding "purely scholastic questions," and was aiming "to approach Shakspere on the human side," yet he believed "that Shakspere is not to be approached on any side through dilettantism." So, Motley and Macaulay—doubtless every great writer—spent years of patient, pains-taking toil, often among musty, worm-eaten state or private papers, before a single volume of their works was possible.[1]

352. (2) *Within limited portions of a subject* very good work can be done without an exhaustive knowledge of the subject as a whole. But constant watchfulness will then be necessary, lest an essential relation between the department under treatment and those left out of sight

---

[1] See Dr. Holmes's *Memoir of Motley* and Trevelyan's *Macaulay*.

escape attention. De Quincey's and Herbert Spencer's essays on Style are examples of work good as far as it goes, but misleading because it is incomplete.

353. (3) *For certain specific purposes*, partial knowledge is often sufficient. For example, to show that Phonetic Spelling will or will not overthrow the etymological basis of the English language, one need not have as much knowledge of the proposed "Reform" as would be requisite, were the question that of the merits or the demerits of the system as a substitute for the received spelling.

354. In all cases, however, there must be at least as much knowledge of a subject as is necessary to bring that subject, in the form in which its treatment is proposed, fully before the writer's mind. Preparation less than this is superficial: more may actually be a hindrance; for the mind, like the eye, may read itself blind. Thus, a study of Shakspere's *Hamlet* for the purpose of illustrating the state of the English language at a certain epoch, must include whatever is necessary to accomplish this purpose: but anything more would be out of unity. The author not only may be a specialist: he often must be. On the other hand, comparatively defined questions may require painfully extended work. The text of Chaucer's *Canterbury Tales* offers a diligent scholar work for many years.

II.

THE MODES OF DISCUSSION.

355. The second factor in determining the matter of a composition is the *purpose* of the writer;[1] and this, as it is always to communicate thought, must be to address primarily and chiefly either the *Understanding*, the *Feelings*, or the *Will*.[2] An address to the understanding, however, may present either an *intuition*, a *perception*, a *conception*—in other words, a *term*—or else a *judgment*, a comparison of terms.[2] Hence, four Modes of Discussion;—(I.) EXPLANATION, which sets forth the nature of *Terms;* (II.) ARGUMENT, which deals with *Judgments;* (III.) EXCITATION, which seeks to arouse the *Feelings;* and (IV.) PERSUASION, which aims at influencing the *Will*.[3]

356. Moreover, these four Modes of Discussion are related to each other in the order stated; and, when two or more of them occur in the same composition, they must stand in this order, except in certain cases to be noted below. A very little reflection will prove the truth of this; for terms can not be compared, until they are understood, and appeals to the feelings or the will can be successful, in minds that are properly constituted, only after the judgment is convinced. Moreover, the will is most commonly to be reached only through the feelings; and even in those cases in which the feelings are appealed to, before the judgment is convinced, or contrary to conviction, the understanding must be at least so far touched as to bring the object of the feeling (or something that is falsely affirmed to be that object) clearly before the mind addressed.

357. The positive processes just described include, also, their opposites, or negatives,—the replacement of a false notion or judgment by the truth, the allaying of feelings already excited, and the changing of a determination already reached.

358. In practice, the processes of Explanation, Argument, *etc.*, can never be carried on strictly alone. Even when the

---

[1] § 350, *above*.   [2] §§ 5, 6, *above*.   [3] § 75, *above*.

purpose of the composition is only one or another of the four possible, the others may be more or less involved. Thus, Explanation often brings on Argument; nothing (or but little) is ever accomplished with uninterested or inattentive hearers; and neither powerful arguments nor seductive motives suffice to enlighten the ignorant or to remove prejudices.

(I.) EXPLANATION.

359. Explanation—from the Latin *planus*, level, plain —is the process of making *intelligible* the nature or the meaning of an object or a word. It includes, also, the converse process of removing obscurity from objects or words. Another term for the same thing is *Exposition;* but this word is more formal and technical than Explanation, and therefore less available for use here. In this use, Explanation has the same sense as that which it has in everyday life—the setting out of what a thing is, or what a word means.

360. The Theme in Explanation is always a *noun*, the *name* of an object of thought. It is presented intelligibly to another mind, only when it is shown 1. *clearly*, and 2. *distinctly;* that is, 1. when it is separated from all *other* objects, (as *man* from *horse*, *dog*, *etc.*,) and 2. when its *own separate parts* are plainly set forth, (as *man* in his *essential attributes—rationality, mortality, etc.;* in his *component parts—head, trunk, limbs, etc.;* or in other such details.)

361. The difference between *clear* and *distinct* presentation is aptly illustrated by a familiar occurrence at dusk. On a lawn planted with trees and bushes, and ornamented, perhaps, with statuary, a distant object is seen that resembles a man, but which may be a bush or a statue. On closer inspection it proves to be a bush, The object is then *clear*, for it is entirely separated from all other objects. But a yet narrower examination shows the bush to be a closely trimmed evergreen, easily mistaken, at a distance and in the dark, for a statue or a man. Now the object is *distinct:* not only its class, but its essential features as of that class, are fully made out. Similarly, the

traveller in the Tyrol spies at a distance an object perched on the highest point of a rock. At first it seems to be but the topmost crag of a ragged mass of hill; but, as the road comes nearer, the object is plainly an animal. Next, it is a chamois; and the delighted tourist thinks he has seen a real example of the now rare, if not extinct, mountain goat. Alas! on coming closer, his chamois is indeed a chamois, but one carved from the solid stone, and set by some clever hands on an almost inaccessible pinnacle of rock.

362. The intelligible presentation of an object of thought proceeds by two means,—1. DEFINITION, 2. EXPLANATION PROPER. Definition (from the Latin *de*, from, and *finis*, a limit, or *boundary*) presents the object *clearly*, separating it from all other objects, and setting its limits or boundaries. Explanation Proper presents an object *distinctly*, exhibiting it in its several parts, and giving a full account of these parts by one or more of several subordinate processes to be described below.

1. DEFINITION.

363. The most exact DEFINITION is that of a *species* by its *genus* and *differentia*,[1] the so-called "logical definition." For example;—

Species.		Differentia.	Genus.
A whale	} is a {	mutilate[2]	mammal.
Man		rational	animal.

364. But logical definition is often impossible. Either the genus to which an object belongs or its differentia is not known, and the definition is thus left incomplete. Many simple ideas, *color, beauty, goodness,*[3] *life, etc.*, defy definition. So, no one has ever told the world what *electricity* is. In such cases, other modes of definition must be used;—

(1) *Division* or *Partition*[4]; as, The animal kingdom consists of Radiates, Mollusks, Articulates, and Vertebrates; The

---

[1] § 370, *below*. [2] Having fins instead of legs.
[3] Atwater, *Logic*, p. 76. [4] § 366, *below*.

prismatic colors are red, orange, yellow, green, blue, indigo, violet; (2) *Colligation*, the reverse of (1); (3) *Substitution* of narrative or descriptive phrases or of symbols or names; as, Wisdom leads to virtue and happiness; Religion is piety;[1] (4) *The Method for Individual Objects;* as, Abraham Lincoln was the president of the United States who issued the Emancipation Proclamation.—By the last method, the individual is assigned to its *species*, as if this were a *genus*, and some *distinguishing mark* is taken as *differentia*. Such definitions are most like logical definitions.

365. Definition is controlled by certain general principles, of the first importance in composition;[2]—

(1) A definition should be co-extensive with the objects included in the term defined: otherwise it is too broad or too narrow. For example, to define a *horse* as an *animal* implies that *all animals are horses;* to define an *animal* as a *horse* implies that *nothing not a horse is an animal*. Of course, exposition by exemplification,—setting forward the horse as a type in certain respects of all animals,—is perfectly legitimate;[3] but it is not definition. (2) Negative definitions, except of negative words and conceptions, are useless. Thus, *Men are not birds* is perfectly useless as a *definition*. (3) Definitions "in a circle," or "in vague, ambiguous, or senseless language," should be avoided; as, Life is the vital force; Poetry is the stuff of which our life is made. (4) A single surplus word in a definition may imply a falsehood. For example, The opposite sides of a parallelogram are parallel *and equal*.[4]

2. EXPLANATION PROPER.

366. Explanation Proper involves one or more of *six* processes;—[5]

(1) *Narration*, "the relation of the *particulars* of any *transaction* or *event*, or of any *series* of transactions or events;"[6] as, the story of a battle, a campaign, *etc.;*

(2) *Description*, the enumeration of the *essential qualities* of a thing or species; as, a sketch (in language) of a battle-field, an account of a chemical substance, *etc.;*

---

[1] Atwater, p. 79.   [2] Atwater, pp. 73 ff.   [3] § 366 (5), *below*.
[4] Appendix, p. 329.   [5] Day, § 73.   [6] *Webster's Dictionary*, 1864.

(3) *Division*, the separation of a *class* into its *specific* parts; as, *animals* into *radiates, mollusks, etc.* ;[1]

(4) *Partition*, the separation of an *individual* into its *component* parts ; as, a ship into *sails, masts, hull, etc.* ;

(5) *Exemplification*, the exhibiting of a *member* or of certain *members* of a *class* as *representing* the *whole* class; for example, the *horse* as representing *all animals;*

(6) *Comparison and Contrast*, the exhibiting of an object by citing the *resemblances* or the *differences* between it and another object or other objects of the same class ; as, Christ's parable of the *sown seed* and the *spoken word;* St. Paul's antithesis between *faith* and *works.*

367. The distinction between Division and Partition is most clearly made by Dr. Atwater.[2] The *divisum* (the class divided) can always be predicated of each of its subordinate classes; as, All *radiates* are *animals:* the *partitum* (the individual separated into its component parts) can not be predicated of one of these parts. *Sails* are not a *ship:* only the sum total of the component parts makes the *partitum.*[3]

368. Of the six processes defined in § 366, Narration and Description, though they present the object *through its parts*, present it *as a whole;* Division and Partition, on the other hand, exhibit the parts *as parts;* while Exemplification and Comparison and Contrast set forth a *characteristic* part (or parts) *as a means* to desired knowledge. The six processes, therefore, are in one view three *pairs* of processes, and will first be so discussed. Further remarks on them as single processes will follow.

369. (1) Narration and Description are (to borrow a Greek word) *antistrophic:* where each is weakest, the other is most strong. (*a*) A narrative details at length a *course* of events, shows a series of *dissolving* views; presents ever *changing* scenery;—functions that language is especially fitted to perform. A description, on the other hand, exhibits a *state* of things, photographs

---

[1] § 364 (1), above. [2] *Logic*, pp. 71 ff.

[3] On this point Day is wrong, and is not followed here.

its object at a *definite* moment of time and in a *fixed* expression, offers to view scenery that is always *the same;*—functions fulfilled by language only with difficulty and when used by a master; for the picture that a description would call up can be only suggested in words, can not be fully exhibited. (*b*) The historian, however, has *a multitude* of details to set forth, details that are often *complicated* to a high degree and *perplexing* to both writer and reader; while *the necessary length* of a narrative, (for it must tell everything, and that completely,) often endangers its success. In a connected story, subsequent details, intelligible only in the light of those that have preceded them, fail to produce their desired effect, if the preceding details have been forgotten; while, if the narrative repeats itself at these critical points, it becomes prolix. The "word-painter," on the other hand, has *fewer details* to exhibit; these details are commonly *less complicated*, and therefore, *less perplexing;* while *the necessary* (certainly, *the desirable*) *brevity* of a description enables even a hearer to keep it well in hand. Words, it has been said, can only suggest a picture: hence, in a description, they need never be many, if well-chosen. (*c*) For this reason, Narration is especially the work of the writer; Description, of the painter or the sculptor. Language has its limitations, just as painting and sculpture have theirs.[1] But it is important not to infer too much. Just as a picture may suggest a long story, if a critical point in the tale be taken for representation, so description may be effected in words, if the words are aptly chosen. On the other hand, the phrases "word-painting" and "historical picture," unless understood in a very moderate sense, are actual contradictions in terms,—too often the cant of men who forget that the chief excellence of a composition is its expressing worthy thought, not its bearing tawdry

[1] § 8, *above.*

ornaments, and who believe (or affect to believe) that a page may glow like the canvas of a Tintoretto, a canvas read like a page from Macaulay.

370. (2) Division and Partition must be carefully distinguished. The one is applied to *classes* of objects; the other, to *individual* objects. Classes are either *genera* (higher classes) or *species* (lower classes); the essential difference or differences between any species and its nearest genus constituting its *differentia*. Of course, the same class may be at once *genus* to a species below it and *species* to a genus above it. Natural historians, philologists, many writers on subjects that require and admit of systematic classifications, have used other terms, *Kingdom, Class, Order, Variety, Family, Group, etc.;* but these are nothing more than *genera* or *species*, according to the relationships in which they stand.

371. (3) Exemplification and Comparison and Contrast agree in always presenting *single* parts of objects. Further, Contrast is only Comparison *by negatives;* so that the double process of Comparison and Contrast is, in fact, but one process,—a double mode of Explanation, not two separate modes. Of course, in all cases, objects compared must be also different, objects contrasted must be also alike. Otherwise, the objects in the one case would be the same, in the other case utterly without relationship. The ground of the process is in the part or parts that the objects have *in common*.

(1.) NARRATION.

372. A narrative may follow (*a*) the strict order of *time*, (*b*) the order of *change in the subject* (*c*) that of *cause and effect;* and, though the several forms may be united in the same composition, one or another will predominate and give character to the narrative. History of the first form is *Chronicles* or *Annals;* of the second form, *Proper History;* of the third form, *Philosophical History*. Proper

History (*b*) rests upon (*a*), and both it and (*a*) are presupposed in (*c*). Further, as (*a*) is the form natural to the narratives of children, so it is the form of the earliest histories; and as (*b*) and (*c*) correspond to a proportionate mental development, so they are the forms of later and the latest histories. As examples, Prof. Day cites Herodotus, Gibbon, and Guizot: other examples, and all of histories of Greece, are Thucydides, Grote, and Curtius.

373. In any form, Narration obeys the following laws, extensions of Canon (2) of the Whole Composition;[1]—

374. (*a*) The events narrated must commonly be set forth in the order chosen, whether of time, of change, or of cause and effect.

375. But (*a*) "A recent state of things more familiar to the persons addressed," may be first exhibited, and then "the previous steps by which that state was arrived at." The history of Language is a notable example of this law. The philologist begins with what is about him, and, from this present, by a careful comparison of its several parts with one another, constructs the past. So, Morley introduces his *First Sketch of English Literature* with the following significant words;—"As soon as we can feel that *we belong to a free country* with a noble past, let us begin to learn *through what endeavours and to what end it is free*."[2]

376. (β) The complication of details is often best unraveled by following each stream of events as if it were a separate narrative; care being taken, however, to keep the several streams united by bringing on each, in its turn, to the great epochs of the story. This plan is especially useful, when the narrative exhibits "a principal action with subordinates," several "concurring streams of nearly equal importance," the state of parties, or a "plurality of departments." For example, the history of England is necessarily complicated by the entangling of the nation in foreign affairs; and the reader's attention must often be diverted from England to the foreign

---

[1] § 289, *above*.—As stated here, the laws are condensed from Bain's extended account of the process (Am. Ed., pp. 166 ff.) Fresh examples, however, have been taken in nearly all cases.

[2] Page 1.—The italics are inserted here.

lands concerned. In each case, the points of divergence and of return must be clearly indicated, and every other means be taken to notify the reader of the exact relation held by the subordinate story to its principal.—The history of the United States before 1789 must trace thirteen streams of colonial history flowing side by side.—Either English or American political history is largely a story of the struggles of two great bodies of the people (or of their leaders in or out of the national legislature) each to secure the adoption of its policy by the national administration.—The Departments of Foreign Affairs, of the Interior, of the Treasury, *etc.*, are convenient heads under which to group the history of an administration.

377. (*b*) A brief summary (*résumé*, recapitulation,) of antecedent events often forms a proper introduction to a narrative, and is sometimes necessary. Thus, Macaulay's first two chapters contain a summary of English history from the Roman conquest of Britain to the Death of Charles II. in 1685; Froude's Chapter II. is concerned with "the Last Years of the Administration of Wolsey." In like manner, the writer may stop at certain points in his story to resurvey the ground passed over. Each chapter of Freeman's *General Sketch of History* closes with a brief *résumé* of its contents.

378. (*c*) A narrative may consist of a series of *cross-sections* of the theme, made at different epochs of its existence, connected by a thread of story, and each delineated as a *status quo* rather than as a part of a movement or action. Or, in ordinary narrative, such a cross-section may now and then be introduced, in order to keep the reader aware of the state of affairs to which the story has brought him, and from which he must make a new start. Froude and Macaulay again furnish examples;[1] and, nearer home, Prof. McMaster's account of "the State of America in 1784" is a brilliant specimen.[2] A short extract from this account will show even more clearly the method referred to :—

"The Americans who, toward the close of 1783, celebrated with bonfires, with cannon, and with bell-ringing, the acknowledgement of independence and the return of peace, lived in a very different country from that with which their descendants are familiar. Indeed, could we, under the potent influence of some magician's drugs, be carried back through one hundred

[1] Froude, ch. i.; Macaulay, ch. iii.
[2] John Bach McMaster, *A History of the People of the United States*, ch. i.

years, we should find ourselves in a country utterly new to us. Rip Van Winkle, who fell asleep when his townsmen were throwing up their hats and drinking their bumpers to good King George, and awoke when a generation that knew him not was shouting the names of men and parties unknown to him, did not find himself in a land more strange. The area of the republic would shrink to less than half its present extent. The number of the States would diminish to thirteen, nor would many of them be contained in their present limits or exhibit their present appearance. Vast stretches of upland, which are now an endless succession of wheat fields and corn fields and orchards, would appear overgrown with dense forests abandoned to savage beasts and yet more savage men. The hamlets of a few fishermen would mark the sites of wealthy havens now bristling with innumerable masts, and the great cities themselves would dwindle to dimensions scarce exceeding those of some rude settlement far to the west of the Colorado river. Of the inventions and discoveries which abridge distance, which annihilate time, which extend commerce, which aid agriculture, which save labor, which transmit speech, which turn the darkness of the night into the brilliancy of the day, which alleviate pain, which destroy disease, which lighten even the infirmities of age, not one existed. Fulton was still a portrait painter, Fitch and Rumsey had not yet begun to study the steam-engine, Whitney had not yet gone up to college. Howe and Morse, McCormick and Fairbanks, Goodyear and Colt, Dr. Morton and Dr. Bell, were yet to be born."[1]

(2.) DESCRIPTION.

379. Description, like Narration, has three forms : it may exhibit (*a*) strictly the spacial parts, (*b*) the parts of a substance,—especially, its attributes,—as representing that substance, (*c*) the substance itself in its relations to its parts or attributes. Further, all three forms may concur in a single composition ; and they are related to each other as are the corresponding forms of Narration.[2]

380. The Canon of Method has here the following applications ;—

---

[1] Vol. i. p. 2.   [2] § 372, above.

381. (*a*) When addressed only to the *understanding*, when intended simply to present intelligible and (as far as possible) complete ideas, without regard to the vividness of the picture as a whole, Description may proceed by *a mere enumeration* of the parts or attributes. In this way a text-book of natural history describes animals or plants, an inventory or a catalogue describes the objects it names, and even the didactic poet,— Virgil, for instance,—describes a fine cow or a handsome colt.[1]

382. (*b*) When addressed to the *imagination*, Description must produce *illusion;* that is, it must call up a vivid picture of the object described, and thus enable the reader, in his absorbing consciousness of the presence of this picture, to forget the words employed to summon it. Hence, such a description will always be brief and suggestive, never enumerative; for language, ill-fitted to description,[2] embarrasses rather than promotes illusion, imprisons rather than sets free the imagination. Homer, for example, portraying the divinely beautiful Helen, for whose sake two Greek worlds were convulsed with strife, speaks only of her coming to the walls of Troy to see the battle, and of the impressions her beauty made on the old men who sat there. Imagination does the rest.[3]

> "Small blame is theirs if both the Trojan knights
> And brazen-mailed Achaians have endured
> So long so many evils for the sake
> Of that one woman. She is wholly like
> In feature to the deathless goddesses."[4]

"What can give a more vivid idea of her beauty," adds Lessing, "than that that cold-blooded age should deem it well worth the war which had cost so much blood and so many tears." "Constantinus Manasses," on the other hand, who "sought to adorn his bald chronicle with a picture of Helen," enumerates the points of her beauty as might a colorer of photographs;—"She was a woman right beautiful, with fine eyebrows, of clearest complexion, beautiful cheeks; comely, with large, full eyes, with snow-white skin, quick-glancing, graceful; a grove filled with graces, fair-armed, voluptuous, breathing beauty undisguised. The complexion fair, the cheek rosy, the countenance pleasing, the eye blooming, a beauty

---

[1] *Georgics*, iii. 51, 79. [2] § 369, *above*.
[3] Barring "a passing mention that she had white arms and beautiful hair." (Lessing.)
[4] Iliad, iii. 156, translated by Bryant. (Lessing, xxi.)

unartificial, untinted, of its natural color, adding brightness to the brightest cherry, as if one should dye ivory with resplendent purple. Her neck long, of dazzling whiteness; whence she was called the swan-born, beautiful Helen."[1] The passage fills eleven fifteen syllabled lines; and reading it, says Lessing, "is like seeing stones rolled up a mountain, on whose summit they are to be built into a gorgeous edifice; but which all roll down of themselves on the other side. What picture does this crowd of words leave behind? How did Helen look? No two readers out of a thousand would receive the same impression of her."

383. (c) *Illusion* is produced by mentioning certain *individualizing* or *associated circumstances, thoughts* or *feelings*, and then *leaving the reader to himself.* Thus (as has been seen) Homer describes Helen; thus Shakspere leaves his readers to construct his characters. Of Portia, for instance, he says ;—

> "In Belmont is a lady richly left;
> And she is *fair* and, fairer than that word,
> Of wondrous virtues:
> Her name is Portia, *nothing undervalued
> To Cato's daughter, Brutus' Portia:*
> Nor is the wide world ignorant of her worth,
> For the four winds blow in from every coast
> Renowned suitors, and *her sunny locks
> Hang on her temples like a golden fleece;*
> Which makes her seat of Belmont Colchos' strand,
> And many Jasons come in quest of her."[2]

Nothing more: the curious reader must draw his lady of Belmont from these hints. Even Portia's character is thus delineated ;—

> "nothing undervalued
> To Cato's daughter, Brutus' Portia;"

> "the full *sum* of me
> Is *sum of something*, which, to term in gross,
> Is an *unlesson'd* girl, *unschool'd, unpractised.*"[3]

So Bassanio's ambassador is pictured ;—

> "A day in April never came so sweet,
> To show how costly summer was at hand."[4]

And so Edmund is described in *King Lear.*[5] Gloucester, Edmund's father having said, "I have often blushed to acknowledge

---

[1] Cited by Lessing, *Laocoön,* xx.
[2] *The Merchant of Venice,* I. i. 161.—Portia elsewhere adds of herself, "By my troth, Nerissa, my *little* body is aweary of this great world."
[3] III. ii. 159.   [4] II. ix. 93.   [5] I. l. 10.

him," Kent replies,—"I can not wish the fault undone, the issue of it being *so proper.*" Later, Edmund claims for himself as compact dimensions, as generous a mind, as true a shape, as his brother's, and even "more composition and fierce quality than go to the making of a whole tribe of fops."[1] One conceives a handsome, strong, intellectually able, high-spirited villain; but Shakspere only starts the reader, the imagination does the rest.

384. (*d*) In such passages, Illusion is dispelled almost by a touch. Add but a word, and the effect is spoiled; many additional words veil the picture in a cloud that even the most vivid imagination can not penetrate. Indeed, when the conception desired by the writer is offensive or horrible, such additions are made aforethought, in order to temper the otherwise unendurable effect.[2] Thus, the crook-backed Earl of Gloucester paints his own portrait;—

> "But I, that am not *shaped for sportive tricks*,
> Nor *made to court an amorous looking-glass;*
> I that am rudely stamp'd, and *want love's majesty*
> *To strut before a wanton ambling nymph;*
> I, that am curtail'd of this fair proportion,
> Cheated of feature by dissembling nature,
> Deform'd, unfinish'd, sent before my time
> Into this breathing world, scarce half made up
> And that so lamely and unfashionable,
> That *dogs bark at me as I halt by them;*
> Why, I, in this weak piping time of peace,
> Have no delight to pass away the time
> Unless to *spy my shadow in the sun*
> And *descant on mine own deformity.*"[3]

The words in italics alone help the reader to conjure up the monster whose crimes form the story of the play: the rest serve only to break the otherwise offensive impression.

385. (*e*) Hence, the failure of many descriptions in novels and poems. At best they are but faithful copies of their originals, interesting enough as such, but destitute of the picturesque. At other times, they fall as flat as a handbill announcing the personal details of a lost child or a stray horse. Most readers skip them, impatient of the delay they cause; and this, although a wide-spread opinion of their excellence inclines these readers to believe themselves guilty in so doing. Mr. R. D. Blackmore, for example, is famed for his descriptions both of forest and of sea-shore scenery. Yet even with really suggestive descriptions he mixes dreary inventories. Nowelhurst Hall, as a house "too

[1] *King Lear*, I. ii. 7.   [2] Lessing, xxiii.   [3] Richard III., I. i. 14.

respectable for any loose doings of any sort," or as the prospective home of the retired seaman, sets the reader's imagination to work; but what of the rest of this paragraph?

"Nowelhurst Hall looks too respectable for any loose doings of any sort. It stands well away from the weeping of trees, like virtue shy of sentiment, and therefore has all the wealth of foliage shed, just where it pleases, around it. From a rising ground the house has sweet view of all the forest changes, and has seen three hundred springs wake in glory, and three hundred autumns waning. Spreading away from it wider, wider slopes 'the chase,' as they call it, with great trees stretching paternal arms in the vain attempt to hold it. For two months of the twelve, when the heather is in blossom, all that chase is a glowing reach of amaranth and purple. Then it fades away to pale orange, dim olive, and a rusty-brown when Christmas shudders over it; and so throughout young green and russet, till the July tint comes back again. Sometimes in the spring morning the black cocks—'heathpoults,' as they call them—lift their necks in the livening heather, swell their ruffling breasts, and crow for their rivals to spar with them. Below the chase the whiskers of the curling wood converge into a giant beard, tufted here and there with views of a varying richness; but for the main of it, swelling and waving, crisping, fronding, feathering, coying, and darkening here and there, until it reach the silver mirror of the spreading sea. And the seaman, looking upwards from the war-ship bound for India, looking back at his native land, for the last of all times it may be, over brushwood waves, and billows of trees, and the long heavé of the gorse-land: 'Now, that's the sort of place,' he says, as the distant gables listen: 'the right sort of berth for our jolly old admiral, and me for his butler, please God, when we've licked them Crappos as they desarves.'"[1]

So, writers of a far higher reputation err in the same way;—

"The Faun is the marble image of a young man, leaning his right arm on the trunk or stump of a tree; one hand hangs carelessly by his side; in the other he holds the fragment of a pipe, or some such sylvan instrument of music. His only garment—a lion's skin, with the claws upon his shoulder—falls half way down his back, leaving the limbs and entire front of the figure nude. The form, thus displayed, is marvellously graceful, but has a fuller and more rounded outline, more flesh,

[1] *Cradock Nowell*, ch. i.

and less of heroic muscle than the old sculptors were wont to assign to their types of masculine beauty. The character of the face corresponds with the figure; it is most agreeable in outline and features, but rounded and somewhat voluptuously developed, especially about the throat and chin; the nose is almost straight, but very slightly curves inward, thereby acquiring an indescribable charm of geniality and humor. The mouth, with its full yet delicate lips, seems so nearly to smile outright, that it calls forth a responsive smile. The whole statue—unlike anything else that ever was wrought in that severe material of marble—conveys the idea of an amiable and sensual creature, easy, mirthful, apt for jollity, yet not incapable of being touched by pathos. It is impossible to gaze long at this stone image without conceiving a kindly sentiment towards it, as if its substance were warm to the touch, and imbued with actual life. It comes very close to some of our pleasantest sympathies."[1]

What idea does one who has never heard of a faun get of this statue? And does not each man who has heard of and conceived a faun simply replace the printed words with his own previously imagined idea? Such descriptions may sometimes be necessary;[2] but they add nothing to the novel as a work of art.

386. Even though most strongly tempted to inventory-description, one writer[3] has set a good example in resisting the temptation;—

"But, after all, the great wonder, the glory, of these Pompeian houses is in their frescoes. If I tried to give an idea of the luxury of color in Pompeii, the most gorgeous adjectives would be as poorly able to reproduce a vivid and glowing sense of those hues as the photography which now copies the drawing of the decorations; so I do not try."

387. (*f*) Descriptions of the "inventory" kind, however, are useful in many subjects, and often necessary. They properly begin with an outline, (comprehensive statement, general plan,) the details of which are to be filled in afterwards. This outline may even rise to the picturesque; for it may serve, as does the plate that accompanies and illustrates the text, to present the description as a whole. For example, Hawthorne, in the passage quoted above, doubtless believed a detailed picture of

---

[1] Hawthorne, *The Marble Faun*, ch. i.   [2] § 387, *below.*
[3] W. D. Howells, *Italian Journeys*, p. 99.

the Faun necessary; as, equally without doubt, he believed the many descriptions of his romance essential to its local coloring. But, to lighten the reader's task, he sets out the object fully in his first sentence,—"the marble image of a young man . . . figure nude,"—and then fills in the details. Indeed, it is only these first sentences that aid the imagination: the rest may address the understanding, but they add nothing, perhaps, to the picture. So, in the following description of a portrait of Edmund Spenser,[1] the writer possibly had no alternative; but it may be questioned how far an artist painting from this description would reproduce the original;—

"Short curling hair, a full moustache, cut after the pattern of Lord Leicester's, close-clipped beard, heavy eyebrows, and under them thoughtful brown eyes, whose upper eyelids weigh them dreamily down; a long and straight nose, strongly developed, answering to a long and somewhat spare face, with a well-formed sensible-looking forehead; a mouth almost obscured by the moustache, but still showing rather full lips, denoting feeling, well set together, so that the warmth of feeling shall not run riot, with a touch of sadness in them."

388. (*g*) Where a picture is too extended for presentation *on a single canvas*, a succession of views may be brought forward, a sort of panorama or series of dissolving views. This method of description has been aptly called "*the traveller's point of view,*" and is much used. Its advantage is in its combining the vividness of picturesque description with the special fitness of language to narrate. The plan has been successfully pursued by M. Taine in his *Tour through the Pyrenees;*—

"The carriage leaves Eaux-Bonnes at dawn. The sun is scarcely yet risen, and is still hidden by the mountains. Pale rays begin to color the mosses on the western declivity. These mosses, bathed in dew, seem as if awakening under the first caress of the day. Rosy hues, of an inexpressible softness, rest on the summits, then steal down along the slopes. One could never have believed that these gaunt old creatures were capable of an expression so timid and so tender. The light broadens, heaven expands, the air is filled with joy and life. A bald peak in the midst of the rest, and darker than they, stands out in an aureole of flame. All at once, between two serrate points, like a dazzling arrow, streams the first ray of the sun."

[1] G. W. Kitchin, Clarendon Press Edition of Spenser's *Faëry Queene.*

Subsequent sections describe the country beyond Pau, and the towns of Coarraze, Lestelle with its chapel, Saint Pé, and Lourdes. Here and there appears a thread of narrative, like the first sentence in the paragraph quoted ; but oftener the mere mention of a new place keeps up the sense of movement.

389. (*h*) Description is often involved in other kinds of composition. A narrative may be simply a string of bead-like descriptions upon a slender thread of story ; an argument may be rendered more convincing by a vivid presentation of the scenes to which reference is made; while, in appeals to the feelings or efforts to arouse the will, descriptions of the objects of feeling or of the ends proposed often constitute the whole work. Examples are Taine's *Pyrenees*, just cited ; Webster's well-known description of the murder of Mr. White, at Salem, Mass. ; and his notable (but less known) picture of the "few old, gray-headed, poor, and broken warriors of the Revolution" who appealed to Congress in 1828 for relief in their decrepitude.

(3) Division.

390. Division is governed by the following laws,[1] applications of Canons (1), (2) and (4), § 289 ;—

(*a*) It must proceed from the given genus to the species immediately below,—from *proximate* genus to *proximate* species. For example, *animals* are properly divided into *vertebrates, articulates, etc.;* each of these *sub-kingdoms* into its *classes;* each *class* into its *orders;* and so on. A division into *men, fishes, reptiles, etc.*, would be scientifically useless.

(*b*) There must be but one *principle of division;* though the same *divisum* may often be classified *successively* upon several different principles. Thus, a library cannot be arranged at once by *subject, size,* and *cost;* though all the books it contains may be successively arranged by each of these distinctions.

(*c*) The classes obtained must be *mutually exclusive*, and, of course, will be, if rule (*b*) is strictly applied. Otherwise, they overlap, and the mind is puzzled rather than aided by the attempt at explanation. Thus to classify men as *Jews, Mohammedans*, and *Believers in God* would be faulty, since both Jews and Mohammedans are also believers in the true God.

---

[1] Atwater, *Logic*.

(*d*) The sum of all the parts should exactly equal the *divisum*. For example, the sum of the classes *organic* and *inorganic substances* exactly equals the divisum *chemicals*.—This rule is simply an extension of rule (*b*).

(*e*) Division *a priori*, (into one class and its inevitable contradictory; e. g., *partridges* and *not-partridges*,) is "a completely useless division." A useful division presents all the classes needed to exhibit the theme. At the same time, a convenient designation for a number of objects or even a number of classes often results from an *a priori* division. Thus, the terms *non-metals, invertebrates, etc.* are valuable designations, however useless as heads of a classification.

(4) Partition.

391. The laws of Partition are the same as those of Division except rule (*a*). For example, to distribute the component parts of *Man* into *head, limbs,* and *mental* or *moral faculties;* to assign his *liver* and his *heart* to the class *entrails*, but his *kidneys* to another class, *members;* to omit any of his component parts; or to describe him as made up of *feet* or *hands* and *all his other parts;*—Each would be an invalid partition.

(5) Exemplification.

392. As a means to Explanation, examples must be,—

(*a*) *Intelligible* or even *familiar* to the persons addressed; as, *the immediate neighborhood* of a child's home by way of teaching him Geography, political or physical;

(*b*) *Enough in number* to relieve all difficulties, and to cover every point of the subject to be explained; as a mere *handful* of words to show how the addition of *s* forms the usual English plural; but *many* and *carefully chosen* sentences to exhibit the nature of English syntax;

(*c*) *Simple at first*, if possible; *more complicated afterwards,* if necessary; as, the ordinary *suction-pump* by way of preliminary description of the steam-engine; many and more intricate examples by way of detailed illustration of its construction;

(*d*) *Free* from all *distracting circumstances;* as, wholesome, natural stories in illustration of right living, not sentimental or even sensational love-tales that debauch the intellect while they fail either to arouse the feelings or to stimulate the will.[1]

393. In systematic treatises, examples must usually follow the rules or principles they explain; but they may often and with advantage stand first, arousing the reader's curiosity and stimulating his mind to unwonted effort. Thus, long before a child can conceive the idea *noun*, he can be made familiar with the office of *nouns* in a sentence. Then to teach him that *nouns are the names of objects* is an easy task; whereas the reverse of this process has perhaps never been successful. The child has learned the required definition by heart, has committed the examples in the same useless fashion, and, after all, has learned both definition and function of the part of speech (if, indeed, he has learned them at all) in the exercise of *parsing*. Many recent and most approved modes of teaching the objective sciences, Botany, Mineralogy, *etc.*, proceed on this plan.

6. Comparison and Contrast.

394. Comparison and Contrast includes not only the *direct* methods of exhibiting objects in the light of their resemblances and their differences, but also the *indirect* methods of *Repetition, Obverse Repetition, Illustration*, and *the Presentation of Difficulties*. Repetition and Illustration are indirect methods of Comparison; Obverse Repetition and the Presentation of Difficulties, indirect methods of Contrast. Repetition adds to a statement already complete another or others like it in thought but different in expression. For example;—

"Rugged furrows, seamed with yawning gashes; reddish wounds, torn and crossed by pallid wounds; scar upon scar."[2]

Illustration compares examples under the rule or principle with similar cases not under the rule or principle. For example;—

"Could knights in armor pursue the herdsman into his bog? What could they have taken as prisoners, except a few half-starved goats? The daring climbers, hunters of the bear and

---

[1] The rules are condensed from Bain.   [2] Taine, *Pyrenees*, p. 170.

[the] wolf, would willingly have played at this game, sure of winning at it warm clothes, arms, and horses. It is *thus*[1] that independence has lasted in Switzerland."

Obverse Repetition adds to a statement its contradictory denied. For example ;—

"Beside him sat an English girl and her mother. The young woman had not succeeded in extinguishing herself, she was frozen at her birth."

The Presentation of Difficulties is the method of stating objections *etc.* to truth, only in order to contrast them when refuted with the truth itself. Thus, Paley's *Moral Philosophy* "proceeds in the *disquisition*" only after the reader's "own *doubts* and solicitude about" the question to be discussed have been excited. In other subjects than Moral Philosophy, a capital incentive to *hard work* is a humiliating sense of one's own *ignorance*.

(II.) ARGUMENT.

395. The theme in Argument is always a *judgment*, the assertion of the agreement or the non-agreement of two terms; for example, *The whale is not a fish; The Constitution of the United States ought to be amended.* The Discussion establishes the truth or falsity of this judgment;—in other words, *convinces* the reader that the judgment is true or false.

396. This judgment, however, is not always given as *the subject of composition*. In actual work, subjects are rarely so presented: they rather come in a shape not prepared for discussion ; for example, the case at law, the fact of a crime—a fact that demands explanation—that is, tracing to a criminal as its author ; *etc.* In the usual school or college exercises, it is, therefore, an excellent plan, in order to allow the writer the greatest freedom

---

[1] So far the case referred to is that of the people of Bigorre : now the *similar* case of Switzerland is cited.—The words *illustration* and *example*, however are often exchanged.

in choosing his proposition, to state subjects as broadly as possible: then the particular judgment that it is proposed to establish,—the judgment, in other words, that is selected as proposition,—must often be determined with great care.

Thus, suppose a writer had a subject assigned him as Cowper had when Lady Austen bade him write her a poem on *The Sofa*. He might do as Cowper did, string on this slender thread many and diverse pearls of thought, bringing all modes of discussion, perhaps, under contribution in the course of his work; or, reaching more or less immediately one of Cowper's propositions,—

> "Like a coy maiden, Ease, when courted most,
> Farthest retires,"—

he might make this judgment his proposition, developing and establishing the moral truths contained in it. Even when the subject admits of only argumentative treatment, no little skill may be used in stating the proposition. A certain sermon on the text, "And Jesus stood before the governor: and the governor asked him, saying, Art thou the King of the Jews? And Jesus said unto him, Thou sayest," argued the dilemma, "Either Jesus was what he claimed to be, the long-expected Messiah, or he was an out and out impostor."

397. The work of determining exactly what is the question involved in a given subject, is materially promoted by a knowledge of the meaning of the following terms;—(*a*) the *subject* of discussion, (*b*) the *question raised*, (*c*) the *point at issue*. The subject of discussion is the theme stated in its most general terms; for example, *Liberty*. The question raised is the particular question proposed for argument under this subject; for example, Is liberty an inalienable right of man's? The point at issue is the special question on the answer to which the question raised must turn; for example, Ought the power to control (govern) oneself to be a condition to the enjoyment of liberty? The theme in Argument then will be, The power to control (govern) oneself ought (or ought not) to be a condition to the enjoyment

of liberty. So, the resistance of the American colonies in the last century was ungrateful rebellion, if the point at issue between them and the home government was the refusal of the colonies to pay a mere pittance begged of them to relieve the burdens of the motherland; but, if that point was the right of the home government to impose taxes on British subjects without the consent of their representatives in Parliament, then the resistance was lawful opposition to tyranny.

398. The judgment thus obtained as the point at issue in any argument, may be (*a*) "known both in its matter and in its truth" or (*b*) "unknown either as to its truth or as to both its matter and its truth."[1] In (*b*) it is an *Hypothesis*, a *tentative* judgment held only for the purposes of *Investigation:* in (*a*) it is a *Theory*, an *established* principle exhibited for the purposes of *Conviction*. Thus, when Galileo, first suspected the motion of the earth, his proposed judgment, the earth moves, simply was an hypothesis. Kepler and Newton, who established the truth of Galileo's suspicion, placed the judgment in the category of theories. To-day a widely received hypothesis of electricity regards it as a subtle force possessing certain attributes and qualities: as yet no theory of electricity has been evolved.

399. In all cases, Argument proceeds by the exhibition of PROOFS,—"the conceptions or judgments on which the proposition to be confirmed depends."[2] The general nature of this process is set forth in Logic, and does not properly belong to Rhetoric; but certain truths of Logic essential to the due comprehension of the rhetorical laws, must be briefly stated.

400. (*a*) Reasoning is (*a*) *Immediate*, from one judgment directly to another; (*β*) *Mediate*, from one judgment to another through a third. For example, (*a*) All men are mortal; No man is immortal. (*β*) All M is P; All S is M; All S is P.

[1] Day, § 119.   [2] Day, §§ 125 ff.

401. (*b*) Proof is (*a*) *Direct*, "when applied immediately to the establishment of the proposition;" (*β*) *Indirect*, "when applied to the overthrow of objections."[1] (*β*) is known as *Refutation*. For example, (*a*) Daniel Webster,[2] defending the life-tenure of office for the Massachusetts judges by asserting that only with it could they be independent, cites the venality of the English judges before 1688, the noticeable change after the establishment of life-tenure for them, the illegal forfeiting of the colonial charter of Massachusetts by judges dependent on the Crown, and the complaint of the Declaration of Independence itself that the British King had made colonial judges venial by limiting their tenure of office. (*β*) In his famous speech on the Knapp trial, before he says one word on the direct evidence against the prisoner, he refutes certain objections on which the counsel for the defense had made no small part of their stand; *viz.*, that he had been brought into the case "to hurry" the jurymen "against the law and beyond the evidence," that unusual means had been taken to discover the perpetrators of the crime, *etc.* His replies to these objections are made, not as proving the guilt of the prisoner, but simply in order to free the minds of the jurymen from everything that might deprive the direct evidence of its full weight.

402. (*c*) Proofs have been classified and sub-classified as follows;—All proofs are either *Analytic* or *Synthetic;* Synthetic proofs are either *Intuitive* or *Empirical;* and Empirical proofs are *A priori*, *A posteriori*, and *Examples*.

Analytic proofs *are given in the terms of the judgment itself;* Synthetic proofs *come from outside the judgment.* Thus, the assertion, God did not create man a two-legged animal, and leave it to Aristotle to make him rational, carries with it its own proof, for the definition of *man* is *rational animal;* but the assertion, Man is mortal, contains nothing in either term by way of proof of the judgment

Intuitive proofs *are furnished by the mind itself;* Empirical proofs, *by experience.* Thus, one's own existence is proved by one's own consciousness.[3] That water freezes at a certain temperature, or that heat expands iron, can be known only from observation.

A priori proofs, or proofs from *Antecedent Probability*, are arguments from *whole* to *part*,—either from *substance* to *attribute*

---

[1] Day, §§ 125 ff. [2] Remarks in the Mass. State Constitutional Convention.
[3] "*Cogito, ergo sum*," said Descartes: "I think, therefore I exist."

or from *cause* to *effect*. *A posteriori* proofs, or *Signs*, are exactly the reverse of *a priori* proofs; they are arguments from *part* to *whole*,—either from *attribute* to *substance* or from *effect* to *cause*. *Examples* rest on "the common property or relation that exists between parts of the same whole."[1] They are arguments either by *Induction* or by *Analogy*. Thus, the facts that a certain substance is gold, and that a certain man, having swallowed a certain dose of arsenic, died shortly afterwards, are respectively *a priori* proofs that the substance is malleable, and that the dose of arsenic killed the man. *Vice versa*, the facts that gold has been dissolved by a single acid, and that water has frozen, are respectively *a posteriori* proofs that the acid was *selenic acid*, and that the temperature of the water had fallen to the freezing point or below it. The arguments by Induction and by Analogy can be exemplified by formulæ;— A, B, C, *etc.*, cases observed, all show a common property X: therefore, D, E, F, *etc.*,—all other like cases,—will show the same property; A and B resemble each other in having the common relation X: therefore, they will resemble each other in having the relation Y.

403. The words *cause* and *effect*, as used here, mean more than *physical cause* and *physical effect*. They intend anything that, in the loosest sense of the phrase, *accounts for* the effect, or which *is accounted for* by the cause. The inclusion of *substance* and *attribute*, too, in the definitions of *a priori* and *a posteriori* proofs seems just. Inferences from either to the other are certainly not examples; yet both are known by experience, and, therefore, proofs of them are empirical.

404. (*d*) Arguments of the several classes differ in value from apodictic certainty (a) to the lowest degree of mere probability. (ω) Analytic and intuitive arguments are of class (a); empirical arguments never rise to apodictic certainty, but may reach the highest degree of probability. The weakest argument is that by Analogy: its chief use is to *refute objections* by showing that like objections in similar cases have no weight. Concurrent arguments, if drawn from wholly independent sources, are cumulative in force, but, otherwise, are of no greater value than each would be alone. This truth needs especially to be remembered in weighing Testimony or Authority, (*a posteriori* arguments respecting matters of *fact* or matters of *opinion*.)

[1] Day, § 147.

Either is truly cumulative, only when the several witnesses are undeniably independent.

405. The successful presentation of a new judgment may depend quite as much on (*a*) the state of the mind addressed, (*b*) the mode of presenting the proposition, or (*c*) the arrangement of the several proofs, as on the intrinsic value of these proofs. Each of these points, which are strictly *rhetorical*, needs elaboration.

406. (*a*) The mind addressed may be "without any belief;" "in weak faith," or "in positive disbelief;" and belief may vary in degree, "from a faint probability to absolute [*apodictic*] certainty."[1] In each case, the method of argumentation is in some respects different.

First, to a man who professes strict impartiality because he has as yet reached no conclusion on the subject of discussion, the method of Investigation may properly be proposed. For example, the value of the study of modern languages for discipline is both affirmed and denied: a discussion of the subject may, therefore, properly open with the question, Is the study of modern languages as conducive to mental discipline as the study of the ancient classics? *Secondly*, to one who believes, indeed, but is seeking further and stronger grounds for his weak faith, only supporting evidence should be presented; as to one whom it is proposed to rob of even his weak faith, only destructive argument should be addressed. "If a man will know of the doctrine whether it be of God," said the Saviour, "let him do the will of my Father which is in heaven;" that is, let him assume it true, and test its truth by practising it. On the other hand, modern Scepticism says, "Miracles are scientifically impossible; and the whole Christian system rests on the story of the Resurrection of Christ." *Thirdly*, when positive disbelief is to be met, two methods are possible;—either sudden, bold attack, in supreme confidence that one is right, or else wary approach through principles generally conceded, but which lead ultimately to the truths in dispute. For example, the public improvements that a certain city needs are refused by a state legislature the majority of which really believes that no necessity exists for the im-

[1] Day, §§ 120 ff.

provements. In this case, argument may proceed either from a bold assumption that the buildings or water-works or apparatus for lighting or other such public arrangement is shabby or old-fashioned or long since insufficient, or else from a conciliatory setting out of the many beauties of the city, its advantageous situation, the natural pride every citizen of the state has in it as the metropolis of *his* state, and so on, until the point of safety has been reached at which the suggestion may be ventured that this really noteworthy city would be even more an object of everyone's affection and pride, were its buildings only newer, its main streets lighted by electricity, *etc.*

407. Compositions intended to be delivered can, of course, be the more easily accommodated in this respect; for the speaker is able, in many cases, to estimate fairly well his probable audience, while the writer is far less able to judge what readers his argument will reach. Hence, argument intended to be read must either be specifically addressed to one class of minds, or else cover ground enough to enable it to reach one class of readers after another. Thus, the argument by dilemma mentioned above[1] would have no weight with a man who denied the authenticity of the New Testament; Mr. Morrison's *Proofs of Christ's Resurrection*, a summary of the evidences to the Resurrection *as an historical event*, would have no weight with one who denied the possibility of such an event. A *complete* defence of Christianity must refute *all* the objections brought against it or likely to be brought against it.

408. (*b*) The Proposition must commonly be stated at the outset;[2] but, (*a*) if it is complex, it may be set forth *seriatim;* (*β*) if the subject is likely to be unpleasant, certain general considerations calculated to excite interest may be stated first; while (*γ*) if prejudices exist, only the general subject must be distinctly stated, and the proposition be brought in later, as if by way of necessary conclusion from conceded premises; or (*δ*) the question raised

[1] § 396.   [2] § 285, *above*.

may be proposed for investigation, and every care be taken to preserve absolute impartiality in the discussion. The last three cases need exemplification.

(a) In *Ad Fidem*, the Rev. Dr. Burr proposes, not only to present some of the evidences of Christianity, but to bring his hearers into a particular "*moral state* in which alone [he believes] they can fairly use the evidences." He therefore unfolds his plan little by little ; his first eight lectures "prepare the ground" for his house; the rest "build it." (β) In the same work, (a volume of Parish Lectures, and addressed, therefore, not to believers only,) Dr. Burr evidently takes especial pains to make his subject attractive, and to postpone arguments that might prove unpleasant, until an interest in the general subject has been aroused. (γ) In another work, *Pater Mundi*, Lectures addressed to the students of Amherst College, his plan is evidently that of allaying prejudices by proposing, in the extreme of fairness, to test Christianity by experience.

409. (c) The arrangement of the several proofs in an argument is also a matter of the first importance. It depends on the following principles ;—

(a) The state of the mind addressed may influence the order. (a') If the hearer is without belief, or if there is "weak faith" to be strengthened, the less powerful arguments naturally stand first, so that the strongest impression may be made last. But to this rule circumstances may indicate exceptions. (a'') If there is "positive disbelief" to be overcome, this opposition must be borne down at once, and that by unmasking the "heaviest guns."[1] This done, the order of what follows is of secondary importance, except that the argument must not close so weakly as to leave an impression that damaging concessions have been made to the other side. Two methods of avoiding this unfortunate result have been suggested ;—a capable reserve may be kept up to give "the finishing stroke ;" or the arguments, exhibited from strong to weak, may be recapitulated in inverse order. The danger of tediousness, however, is always great in recapitulations.

[1] Cf. § 406, *Thirdly, above.*—The two rules are not contradictory ; for this rule refers only to the order of presenting the proofs, that to the whole process of argument.

(β) Proofs depend upon each other. "Some are explained by others; some presuppose others; some have great weight if preceded by certain others, and are of little moment unless so preceded." These principles determine the following rules;—(β′) "*Analytic* proofs precede all others." The terms of the proposition must be explained; and proof that comes out during this process will clearly be of primary importance. (β″) *A priori* proofs precede both *signs* and *examples*. A sufficient cause once shown, (*e.g.*, a motive to the commission of crime,) proofs from the effects of that cause back to the cause itself, or from examples of the action of such a cause back to the cause, acquire double weight: no amount of *a posteriori* proof or examples can make an allegation of crime seem probable, when no motive can be found for its commission.

410. The process of Argumentation varies further as the speaker has or has not on his side the *Burden of Proof* (*onus probandi*.) In the former case, he must make the attack, must act on the offensive: in the latter, (when he is said to have the *Presumption* in his favor,) he may simply stand on the defensive. The Greek word *apology* (ἀπολογία, a pleading off,) was once commonly used, and is still used occasionally, to denote an argument of this sort; though it may mean an argument, which, though really intended to enforce belief, takes the form of a reply to possible or actual objections. Thus, even in the early Christian centuries, when the *onus* was upon Christianity to establish its truth, and to convince men of its superiority to all other systems of religion, it nevertheless carried on its struggle with error, as it now does, chiefly by apologies.

411. The importance of determining on which side the Burden of Proof rests, lies, not only in the fact that thereby the labor of proving one's thesis may often be saved, but also (and still more) in the fact that to undertake to prove what may fairly be *presumed* is to endanger one's own position. It would be arrant folly to *volunteer* a defence of the veracity of a witness, till this had been impugned: the very offer to do so would arouse suspicion.

412. The Presumption is always on the side (*a*) of *the negative of every issue*,[1] (*b*) of *what exists*, as opposed to a change, (*c*) of the *innocence* of a person accused, and (*d*) of *what promotes the well being of men*, as opposed to what is restrictive and injurious. Thus;—

He who maintains that Anglo-Saxon *is* the same language as modern English, or that Shakspere did *not* write the plays received as his, must show reasons for his thesis; the advocates of the substitution of modern languages for the classics in the college curriculum, or of the admission of women to colleges for men, certainly *had* the burden of proof, whether this has more recently shifted or not. So, charges against a man in politics, simply because he is in politics, on the assumption that all politicians are dishonorable men, fall of their own weight; as the reactionary policy of a Julian or a James the Second was censurable as tending to impair the prosperity of his realm.

413. Presumptions may be *opposed to each other;* or they may shift from one side to the other, even in the course of a single argument.

Thus, the presumption that once existed against the admission of scientific and modern language studies to the college curriculum has been borne down by the opposing presumption in favor of what will benefit mankind; the allegation that the education of women should be as thorough and as advanced as that of men finds few disputants, however much men (and women, too) may question the propriety of admitting women to men's colleges. So, Luther nailed theses to the church-door at Wittemberg; while to-day, in Luther's and all the other protestant churches, the burden of proof rests on a *non*-protestant theology. In a single suit at law the presumption raised by a charge in a "book of original entry" may be shifted to the defendant's side by a showing of fraudulent book-keeping or of a receipt for the amount claimed.

In the first case a balance must be struck, and a decision be reached by this means; while, in all the cases specified,—espe-

---

[1] That is, on the side *that does not make the affirmation*. This affirmation may be a negative judgment, or the negative side of the issue may be expressed in an affirmative judgment. For example, *The earth does not move*, or *The sun does move* (if *now* opposed to the established truth that the earth moves round the sun).

cially when the argument is by way of refutation,—it is politic as well as right to concede whatever the other side can fairly claim.

414. Argument is often joined in the same discourse with Explanation,—as, of the terms employed, the attendant circumstances, *etc.*[1] Such explanations may commonly be placed in the introduction; but they may sometimes be better inserted between the parts of the argument. The self-evident rule on this point is to place such helps to the proofs where they will help most,—especially where they will best serve to render the argument intelligible and convincing.

415. Further, certain personal relations,—for example, between the speaker and his opponent, the speaker and his audience, *etc.*,—as well as certain relations between the audience and the proposition advanced, the mode of discussion, and the occasion of speaking, may also demand attention in an argumentative composition. Such matter will commonly stand in the introduction; or, if it must be admitted into the body of the discourse, should always be distinctly marked as constituting a digression. An introduction of this kind has been called the Introduction Conciliatory. Thus, Mr. Webster, in a speech on the Panama mission,[2] defends his own *consistency* in opposing a certain amendment, and in the same speech, describes as follows the special relations he and his fellow public men held to the questions before them as representatives of a great people;—

"Mr. Chairman : it is our fortune to be called upon to act our part, as public men, at a most interesting era in human affairs. The short period of your life, and of mine, has been thick and crowded with the most important events. Not only new interests and new relations have sprung up among States, but new societies, new nations, and families of nations, have risen to take their places, and perform their parts, in the order

---

[1] A notable, and very familiar, example is Webster's description (in the Knapp murder case) of the death of old Mr. White.
[2] U. S. House of Representatives, April, 1826.

and the intercourse of the world. Every man, aspiring to the character of a statesman, must endeavor to enlarge his views to meet this new state of things. He must aim at adequate comprehension, and instead of being satisfied with that narrow political sagacity, which, like the power of minute vision, sees small things accurately, but can see nothing else, he must look to the far horizon, and embrace, in his broad survey, whatever the series of recent events has brought into connexion, near or remote, with the country whose interests he studies to serve."

416. The Conclusion of an argumentative composition is generally occupied with a summary of the argument presented. The full force of an argument is more or less dissipated, of course, by the necessity the writer—much more the speaker—is under of presenting it part by part: the summary serves to bring these parts into their smallest compass, and thus to show their relations. But the conclusion may also be either explanatory or further confirmatory; and it is frequently occupied with an appeal to the feelings or the will. In the latter cases, it will be guided by rules to be stated below.

(III.) EXCITATION.

417. The theme in Excitation is always an object of thought towards which the feelings may be called out. Hence, it will always be expressed by a noun or noun-clause; as, "The Sufferings of the Poor," or "That the poor are suffering."

418. Passion is aroused either by *Pathetic Explanation*, the proper setting forth of the object of feeling, or by the *Employment of Sympathy*. The latter alone will excite blind, unintelligent feeling, for "passion" (as Antony says) "is catching;" but both fairness and good policy urge the laying of a sufficient ground for the feeling appealed to. *Vice versa*, while explanation alone may suffice to evoke feeling, an unsympathetic speaker or one who is plainly "acting his part" will inevitably fail of

his end: dispassion, too, is catching; and discovered hypocrisy only disgusts. Pathetic Explanation is effected by the processes set forth under the head of Explanation above; but these processes will be modified according to principles to be stated presently. The Employment of Sympathy is governed by rules entirely its own.

419. Regard for the persons addressed is nowhere more imperative than here: "ignorance or mistake may occasion an entire failure."[1] Three states of mind are, of course, possible,—favorable disposition, indifference, and unfavorable disposition. A mind favorably disposed or indifferent may be approached directly; but a mind that is in a position of unqualified antagonism must be addressed with great caution. In this case, the unfavorable feeling must first be allayed; or "other feelings, in their nature incompatible with those to be allayed, and yet not directly opposed to them, may be awakened, and thus the unfavorable feelings be displaced."[2] Prof. Day cites an apt example of these two methods;—

Brutus, who finds the people disposed to demand rather grimly the reasons why their favorite, Cæsar, was murdered, appeals to their love of country, and so displaces their love for Cæsar; Antony most craftily hides his real feeling, "appears, at first, as the friend of Brutus, disclaims all intentions of praising Cæsar, gets the attention of the crowd, fixes it on Cæsar, and then, though at first he speaks of Cæsar's faults, gradually passes to defend his character." The effect is just what Antony intended. The rage of his hearers at Cæsar's usurpations and tyranny gradually subsides; Brutus's warnings are forgotten; the feelings of the mob are turned in the opposite direction; and they leave Antony, clamoring furiously for the blood of Cæsar's enemies."

420. The place of the Proposition in Excitatory Discourse has been much debated. Whately thinks that an appeal to the feelings should never "be introduced as

[1] Day, § 189.
[2] Day, § 191.—Day's whole passage, §§ 185-208, is worth careful study.

such, and plainly avowed;" for, if the purpose is to suggest motives that the hearer ought not to act on, then plainly cautious approach is necessary; whereas, even if the motives are such as he may rightly act on, the hearer will nevertheless resent "the apparent assumption of superiority in a speaker who seems to say, 'Now I will exhort you to feel as you ought on this occasion;' 'I will endeavor to inspire you with such noble, and generous, and amiable sentiments as you ought to entertain;' which is, in effect, the tone of him who avows the purpose of Exhortation."[1] But, as Day points out,[2] bad as "*such* avowals of intention are on every principle of correct taste," it is their form, rather than their being avowals of intention that is objectionable; and they are as objectionable in one sort of discourse as in another. "In pronouncing a eulogy," for instance, "in endeavoring to inspire sentiments of confidence and courage," or "in seeking to strengthen the sentiment of Christian gratitude for the blessings of the gospel," there surely can be no impropriety in setting the Proposition at or near the beginning of the work; or, if there is, the Thanksgiving Day preacher blunders who proposes "the timely fruits of the earth" as a reason for gratitude to God, and Demosthenes was no orator when he told the Athenians that, if Philip's growing power had not made them afraid, he would briefly give them reasons for entertaining such a fear.[2] Whately's statement is by far too sweeping: the truth is, that, in Excitation,—and, indeed, in discourse of all kinds,—the Proposition *must* stand wherever it will *contribute most* to the end in view in writing. Doubtless, reasons will often exist for postponing its introduction; but, *vice versa*, good reasons often determine its bold presentation at the start. *Other things being equal*, Variety may be allowed to control a writer in this particular.

[1] II. ii. § 1. [2] ¶ 194.

421. When, however, opposition is reasonably to be expected, or when known prejudices are to be met, a gradual approach to the subject is judicious. Obscurity as to what the speaker "is coming to" will excite curiosity and secure attention; adroit management will also engage the interest; and thus the most resolute opponent will be outgeneralled.

For example, a famous living preacher, who has loosened more purse-strings, and led the way to more true charity, perhaps, than any other one man, always approaches his theme gradually. Perhaps without intention, though apparently by intention, he announces a text that does not even suggest a "begging" sermon. The flood of his eloquence is irresistible. Before they know it, his listeners are committed to principles the logical consequences of which they little suspect; and then a sudden turn in the sermon applies one or more of these principles to the charity, the church-work, the toiling and suffering missionaries. The generous response of the audience is secured; and the indirect approach has accomplished infinitely more than a direct appeal could have achieved. A feeling of agreeable surprise is felt, almost epigrammatic in its power, and resistance is disarmed. On the other hand, the case of another preacher is doubtless typical. He was famous for sermons of this class that were simple presentations of the "object," supported by the most irresistible logic. They were always announced on the previous Sunday, they always occupied the whole hour, (Dr. —— never preached short sermons,) and they always presented a distinctly avowed proposition, "This object demands your unqualified sympathy and support." The preacher was not eloquent, except as worthy thought is always eloquent; his manner was quiet, but deeply charged with sincere sympathy with his subject; yet his congregations were never smaller on one Sunday than on another; and it was actually said of him that men who went to church resolved not to give, always gave liberally before they came away.

422. The presentation of the *object* of feeling—the process already called Pathetic Explanation—is governed by certain special rules. These, as stated by Prof. Day, are four; but Day's first and third rules may conveniently be combined;—

423. (*a*) The Canon of Selection must have wide scope in Pathetic Explanation. Only those points or features in the object that are especially *adapted to the feelings or sentiments to be awakened*, and only the most *prominent* and *striking* features and outlines of the object should be presented. More will only obscure the reader's view, and so tend to defeat the writer's aim. In the passage already cited from Shakspere's *Julius Cæsar*, Brutus speaks mainly of Cæsar's usurpations, Antony mainly of his love for the people ; and each selects the details especially suited to his own purpose.

424. (*b*) Particular rather than general views of the object must be taken. Examples under this law, too, will be found in the extract from the *Julius Cæsar*. So, Sheridan's Invective against Warren Hastings describes "the paroxysm, fever, and delirium," the natives hastening their own death by tearing open their wounds, and their prayers to God that their blood might cry aloud for vengeance.

425. (*c*) Clearness and distinctness are not *necessary:* something may wisely be left to the imagination. Thus, Antony does not tell the Roman mob *how much* Cæsar had left each citizen in his will; and, in fact, he did not dare to, the amount was so small.—In the motto, "Not one cent for tribute, millions for defence," the accurate "one cent" expresses the conclusion the American people had reached, not to yield to tyranny, while the vague "millions" was an appeal to patriotism.

426. The emotion that controls the speaker's mind, and into sympathy with which he would bring his hearer, may be expressed either directly or indirectly. By the first method it appears naturally : rein is given to his feeling. By the second method, the feeling appears only "by glimpses." A sob that *will* break through one's self-control,—the "One, two, three, fire ; he's dead !" of the maniac duellist,—and Antony's cunning disclosure of his love for Cæsar,—are apt examples of the second method cited by Prof. Day.

(IV.) Persuasion.

427. The object in Persuasion is always to move the will, to urge it to a resolve to do or not to do a certain

act, to adopt or to refuse to adopt a certain course of conduct. This act or course of action is the theme of the composition, and is, of course, expressed by a noun or a noun-clause. For example, *Repentance; I will arise and go to my father; Your man shan't stand; Not one cent for tribute, millions for defence.*

428. Persuasion proceeds (*a*) by *explaining* the decision urged, (*b*) by assigning *motives*. Hence, fair and judicious Persuasion involves Explanation, Argument, and Excitation.

Thus, Edmund Burke, endeavoring to dissuade the British parliament from levying taxes on America, first explains that the whole scheme was a going "out of the plain high road of finance," a giving "up of most certain revenues and the clearest interests, merely for the sake of insulting the Colonies;" then agues that, while tea could readily "bear an imposition of three-pence, no commodity will bear three-pence, or will bear a penny, when the general feelings of men are irritated, and two millions of men are resolved not to pay;" and finally appeals to the interest of England itself in favor of a conciliatory policy towards America.

At the same time, the will, like the feelings, may be influenced unintelligently, and then but too often wrongly.

429. A motive is anything that "occasions or induces free action in man." By a minute classification, moral philosophers have distinguished motives according to several principles; but these the writer will learn best from the books of Moral Philosophy. However interesting a summary of these principles might be, and great as their value undoubtedly is to the writer, their discussion except at a length that would be out of all proportion to the necessary limits of the present work, is dangerous. The following general truths, however, may be at least stated;—

(*a*) Motives differ in strength, and, hence, consummate skill is often required in their presentation.

(*b*) Motives high "in their own purity and excellence are ever to be preferred;" and such as are lower in character should always be exhibited as subordinate to the higher, or as reinforcing them. The good of mankind, the promotion of public ends, the reasonableness of considering others' rights as well as one's own,—these and other such motives are superior to feelings of narrow selfishness or of a brutal intrusion upon the rights or privileges of others. Honor, the doctrine of *noblesse oblige*, *etc.*, are other examples.

(γ) Motives must be chosen by "the specific tendencies of the minds addressed." For example, a notably selfish man can not *at first* be reached by an appeal to his consideration of others, a coarse man by feelings of delicacy, a bigoted man by the beauty of toleration.

(δ) The larger the audience, "the more freely may the higher motives be urged, since the higher are the more universal." Doubtful as this statement may seem, it is unquestionable. The race as a whole, whatever may be true of individuals, is most susceptible to the noblest influences. Pessimistic views on this topic are as untrue as they are depressing.

430. The state of the mind addressed is a vital question: success in persuasion requires prudence, tact, high intelligence, and remarkable powers of other sorts. The mind addressed may be in any of three states;— (*a*) Indecision, (*b*) Indifference, (*c*) Adverse decision. In each case great care, sometimes extreme strategy, will be required in one's approach. Many a failure to persuade is doubtless explained by the unwariness, the awkwardness, sometimes the downright brutality, with which the attempt was begun. It is far easier to talk a man into stubborn resistance than to bring him into intelligent compliance. Especially, when efforts are made to induce a victim of some evil habit to abandon that habit, caution, deep sympathy, the avoidance of everything that may even seem like self-assertion or self-sufficiency, are absolutely necessary. It was the remark of a most pious woman, deeply stirred by the sight of the sin and misery around her, that, in her opinion, the first lesson a minister of the gospel needed to learn, was a knowledge of his fellow men and of human nature.

431. The rule for the Proposition is the same as in Excitation: it may safely be announced whenever the needs of the discourse shall demand it. To spring the proposition on a prejudiced listener is, indeed, unwise; but there is surely as great imprudence in arousing his suspicion by evidently talking "all round" the subject, because one is afraid to declare it.

432. The Arrangement of a persuasive discourse will be determined mainly by the laws thus laid down. Of course, regard must also be had to the purpose in writing; and the student must remember that, in all kinds of composition, any principle of Rhetoric may for the nonce be of superior weight to the special rule for the particular subject in hand. But, other things being equal, a knowledge of the persons addressed, and a careful estimate of the real character of the motives to be presented, will give method to persuasion. One truth, however, should never be forgotten, that, although it may sometimes be necessary to approach men through an unworthy appeal to their lower natures, yet the work of persuasion can not rightly be looked upon as ended, till action has been secured based on the higher, and, therefore, sufficient, grounds. Otherwise, the writer may fail of his end, or even find that he has only induced a stubborn continuance in regretted courses of action or a stubborn refusal to move from the ground first taken.

APPENDIX.

I. The Definition of Rhetoric.

Two objections have been brought against Prof. Day's definition of Rhetoric, accepted in the text;—(1) That it is equally true of Grammar; (2) That it characterizes Rhetoric only as an art. Each of these objections demands attention.

First, According to the objectors, Grammar as well as Rhetoric teaches the laws of speech and writing : Rhetoric seeks to make discourse effective; it teaches men, not only how to convey intelligence to other minds, but how to obtain over these other minds a mastery. The time-honored definition of Grammar describes it as teaching men how to speak and write. Surely Rhetoric is something more than this ; and in what, if not in adapting discourse to its purpose, or end in view?

But all this proceeds upon a time-honored misconception of the office of Grammar, which has not necessarily anything to do with speaking and writing. Grammar seeks only to discover and establish in a system the theory of the sentence : Rhetoric deals with the whole composition, and with the sentence as only one part of this whole. Grammar is not an art, but a science : it aims at knowledge, not at skill.[1] The ancient definition of Grammar simply confused it with Composition ; for, the moment Grammar gives lessons in composition, that moment it becomes Rhetoric, on however low a plane. Campbell long ago commented on the close-lying border lands of Grammar and Rhetoric ; and, but for his faulty definition of Rhetoric, he might have commented, also, on the erroneous definition of Grammar. Further, the words *effective, etc.* add nothing to Prof. Day's definition of Rhetoric ; the qualification they express is already in the word *art;* for all arts aim at efficiency; and the only possible results of adding a qualifying term to the definition are to set up a tautology and to give color to the unjust aspersion of Rhetoric as an art that teaches an *unusual, bookish,* or *fussily ornamented* style of writing—the very mode

[1] See p. 331, *below.*

of expression that a true Rhetoric pillories as mere "jewelry and rouge,"—the acme of the unrhetorical, because it is unnatural and displeasing to every cultivated mind.

Secondly, Rhetoric is often defined as a science as well as an art; but in no true sense is Rhetoric a science. It discovers nothing; it simply states laws that are true in the nature of man, and grounded on principles furnished by its nomothetical sciences.[1] To argue this question fully needs the light of certain distinctions to be set out in the next section of this Appendix. Before passing to these distinctions, however, a glance must be thrown at several other definitions of Rhetoric anciently or even still adopted by many writers.

(1) The Ancients, whose only means of addressing large bodies was speech, and who had only written books and but few of them, naturally thought of Rhetoric as the art of *Oratory, or Spoken Discourse*. (2) Many writers, both ancient and modern, have limited the art to *Prose Composition*,[2] excluding Poetry (or both Romance and Poetry) as fine arts. The end of Poetry (and Romance), they say, is to please; while Rhetoric strives after an outward end, "that mastery over other minds which it does not quietly wait for, but obtains by a struggle."[3] (3) Whately, accepting Aristotle's dictum, "Rhetoric is an offshoot [$\dot{\alpha}\nu\tau i\sigma\tau\rho o\phi o\varsigma$] from Logic," still further limits Rhetoric to *Argument*, and practically considers *Persuasion* as the end of the art. (4) On the other hand, Quintilian extended the province of the art. In his view, Rhetoric was "more like an encyclopædia of all arts and sciences, than a limited and specific branch of knowledge."[4] It included "everything that could conduce to the attainment of the object proposed—Law, Morals, Politics, *etc.*, on the ground that a knowledge of these subjects is requisite to enable a man to speak well on them."[5]

On these definitions, the following criticisms seem just. (1) The Ancients' definition of Rhetoric was due solely to their circumstances. Had they known printed books, or had even the manuscript copies of their books been many in number, they would doubtless have extended the scope of their art. As things were, they were by no means ignorant that much of their teaching applied equally to writing.[6] (2) The restriction of Rhetoric to Prose Composition is often useful by way of limiting the scope

---

[1] § 16, *above*. [2] § 73, *above*. [3] Theremin, *Eloquence A Virtue*, I. ii.
[4] Shedd, *Literary Essays*, p. 106. [5] Whately, § 1.

APPENDIX. 331

of a text-book or a course of study; but it can not be maintained in a definition of the art. Many rules apply equally well in all kinds of compositions; and any restriction would be unscientific. (3) So, too, with regard to the proposed limiting of Rhetoric to Argument or Persuasion: the full definition of the art is squarely against the advocates of restriction; and nothing would be gained by it, but much lost. (4) Quintilian's extension of the art is equally unwise. Rhetoric is no more under obligation to supply the knowledge needed by a writer than is Architecture to supply bricks or mortar or other materials for building. One might almost as well insist upon its furnishing men with mental faculties. At the same time, Quintilian's notion that only a well-informed man can write well,—that, in this art, as everywhere in nature, nothing comes out of nothing, —is an important truth. Dr. Shedd's maxim, printed on the title-page of this volume, is even more binding on the writer, who addresses his thousands, than on the speaker, who has comparatively a small audience.

II. THE SCIENCES THAT GIVE LAWS TO RHETORIC.

The relations of Rhetoric to its nomothetical sciences will be better understood, perhaps, in a careful consideration of the following distinctions.

1. SCIENCE, ART, CRITICISM.—Science analyzes the finished art-product or other fact presented to it, in order to discover the laws of its being. By way of preparation, it observes and classifies all the related facts and processes. Its work, therefore, is one of *discovery*, and tends to *knowledge*. Art teaches the rules by which this finished product is constructed; either grounding these rules upon the related science or sciences, or stating them arbitrarily. Its work, therefore, is essentially *constructive*, and tends to *skill*. "It uses knowledge, not as knowledge, but as power."[1] Criticism examines the product, in order to pronounce upon its merits or demerits, basing itself upon knowledge of both the art-rules and the scientific principles. Its work, therefore, is *judgment*, and tends to *the improvement of the art-product*.

2. PURE AND APPLIED SCIENCE.—Science is either Pure or Applied;—Pure, when it teaches necessary truths as abstract

[1] A. S. Hill, p. iii.

propositions; Applied, when it adapts these truths to particular concrete cases. "Applied Science is a knowledge of facts, events, or phenomena, as explained, accounted for, or produced by means of powers, causes, or laws. Pure Science is the knowledge of these powers, causes, or laws, considered apart, or as pure from all applications." Hence, the principles of pure science are always true, true in themselves and in all possible cases: the principles of applied science are true only as applied, and in the special cases.

3. THEORY.—Theory is a body of scientific principles underlying and explaining or justifying the rules of an art; or it is the study of these rules viewed in the light of their underlying principles. Hence, it is properly opposed to Practice,—a sense, says Sir William Hamilton,[1] in which it both was known to the Ancients and is now commonly used on the continent of Europe.

Hence, (1) Art is more than Applied Science; for the latter is content to *know* the truth in the special case, while the former is dissatisfied until it has *done* the work that the application of the truth enables it to do. Art promotes *skill;* Applied Science teaches special *truths*. For example, Surveying may be taught either as an applied science or as an art. As the one, it seeks only knowledge for its own sake; as the other, it seeks to make skilled surveyors. (2) Science and Art are incompatible terms,—terms, that is, which are not affirmable of the same object at the same time. The same name, indeed, may be given to both science and art;—for example, to Mechanics, which is either "the science of the action of forces on bodies" or the art of constructing machines and other mechanical contrivances;—but, unless the two things so named are only one and the same thing, it is no more true that they are at once a science and an art, than it is that two men, both named John Smith, are only one man. Confusion is often created by this loose way of speaking, and serious errors have been inculcated by it. (3) Science and Theory, though often interchanged, are, in fact, essentially different terms, and should not be confused. The scientific principles on which an art is based are often drawn (as is the case in Rhetoric) from several nomothetical sciences; and, in this case, though they constitute a *theory*, they can not be said to constitute a *science:* they are only excerpts from *several* sciences. Even when they all come from a sin-

[1] *Metaphysics*, Edited by Bowen, p. 113.

gle science, they are, with reference to the art, plainly not *a* science but only a body of scientific principles underlying the rules of an art,—that is, a *theory*. This error has led to erroneous definitions, as well as to false, and, therefore, misleading, conceptions of the nature of art.

In order of *time*, the art-product is always evolved first; then come rules; and finally, the underlying theory is made out, and both rules and theory are arranged in a system. (1) Practice necessarily precedes theory; for neither scientific principles nor rules for work can be discovered except through experience, and this experience "can have no foundation, other than previous practice. Such must obviously be the case with all the arts. Many a house must have been built, before a system of architecture could be formed; many a poem composed, before an art of poetry could be written."[1] (2) Rules are always suggested by the work already done, and are inferred from it. At first, they are but "rules of thumb,"—mere *dicta* of experience, liable to revision, correction, and even retractation; but later, when brought to the bar of Criticism and carefully tested, they become more accurate and more trustworthy.[2] This criticism, it is true, is at first uncertain, because without a sufficient foundation in knowledge; but, the underlying art-theory being once detected,—knowledge exists abundantly, and Criticism has a fair field. (3) Finally, guesses are made at the "why" of the rules; scientific principles are brought forward to explain or justify them;—that is, a theory of the art is constructed; while the rules themselves are more and more revised, till they are perfected into a system. Thenceforward, the art, its theory, and intelligent criticism of the art-work are mutually dependent; each throws light upon the others; each helps to make the others perfect.

In the light of all this, Rhetoric is plainly not a science, but an art. Its end is to construct the composition, not to discover knowledge. Its rules are the *dicta* of experience; its underlying principles, truths drawn from four nomothetical sciences; and the phrase *science of Rhetoric* is simply a blunder for *theory of Rhetoric*.

---

[1] John Quincy Adams, *Lectures*, I. pp. 73, 74.

[2] In Pope's trite couplet,—

"Those rules, of old discovered, not devis'd,
Are Nature still, but Nature methodiz'd."

III. THE TRUE METHOD OF STUDYING RHETORIC.

The principles thus established would seem to determine, also, beyond dispute, the correct method of studying Rhetoric. (1) The goal before the student should be skill in writing and speaking; (2) the order of study should be the order of development, and no one of the three elements, *Practice, Rules, Principles,* should be omitted; (3) the study should rest on *all* the nomothetical sciences—not on any number less than all.

And yet the study of Rhetoric has constantly proceeded in violation of one or more of these principles.

(1) Rhetoric has been treated as if its chief end were to make *critics,* not *writers.* It has tended to skill in judging, not in constructing. Hence, not only has undue importance been attached to the form of discourse, and too little attention been paid to the thought expressed, but the course has been narrowed to a theoretical discussion of rules and principles, while practice in composition has been wholly or in great part omitted.

(2) The natural order of teaching the art has been inverted, and one or more of its three elements been omitted or else unduly emphasized.[1] Hence, three mistakes in the methods of teaching;—(*a*) Rules and principles are put before practice in writing, although it is practice that in the highest degree makes rules and principles intelligible. Earlier practice in composition, (such as is, or certainly was, common in the preparatory schools,) is confined to the writing of themes; and the student, who is ill-prepared for such work, gains but little benefit from it. Simple exercises in sentence-building or in the recasting of work that is more or less defective,— exercises that tell most powerfully on all subsequent practice, and which need only the briefest rules by way of suggestion to guide the student,—such exercises are rarely employed.[2] (*b*) A second blunder results from the error already noted, the error of treating Rhetoric as the art of Criticism. Men whose end in teaching is only to make competent judges of discourse, can not be expected to value highly either

---

[1] In all arts, the *greatest* amount of attention must, of course, be given to practice; but this greatest amount is not necessarily an undue amount.

[2] *How to Write Clearly* is a capital book for the purpose.

rules for composition or practice in it. Hence, their instruction omits both rules and practice, while it gives at length abstract discussions of the scientific truths (especially, the truths of Æsthetics) that underlie the art. Rhetoric with them becomes a philosophical study, both interesting and profitable in itself, but contributing as little as may be towards the making of competent writers. (*c*) Still more serious, because (if possible) more misleading, is the error of teaching Rhetoric by practice alone,—practice guided only by "rules of thumb" and the study of worthy models. Whatever value an empirical study of Rhetoric may have, formal Rhetoric has also its place in the course; for, had not practice needed the guidance of underlying truths, only one element of art would in all probability have been developed. The very men who quarrel most bitterly with formal Rhetoric are often the men who, unconsciously, to be sure, seek its aid. Macaulay is a notable example.[1]

(3) Rhetoric has not been based on all its nomothetical sciences, but now on one of them, now upon two. Campbell starts from his famous dictum, "It is by the sense that Rhetoric holds of Logic, and by the expression that she holds of Grammar." Blair grounds his work on Æsthetics Theremin thinks Eloquence a virtue. Whately says Rhetoric is an offshoot of Logic. Day seems to have been the first to state formally the truth that Rhetoric rests on four nomothetical sciences. The opposite belief has enfeebled and belittled the art, and disgusted many really sensible persons, who have (unfairly, no doubt, but not unnaturally) charged the vices of "fine writing," puerility, desultoriness, *etc.*, on the art that professed to teach something better, but failed. As a result, "Rhetoric has become extremely superficial in its character and influence, so that the term 'rhetorical' has become the synonym of shallow and showy."[2] "Considered as jewelry and *rouge*," says another author, "Rhetoric is sufficiently contemptible."[3]

[1] Compare the parallel cases of Engineering and other scientific professions. The civil engineer was once trained in the field, the geologist in the bowels of the earth. To-day they are instructed—some say over-instructed—in colleges, and in nothing more than in the underlying truths of their arts. Who would think of showing a raw country boy a finished bridge or a "crack" coal-mine?

[2] W. G. T. Shedd, *Preface to Theremin*, p. x.

[3] T. Starr King, in Whipple's Introduction to *Substance and Show*, p. xii.

IV. Certain Technical Terms of Rhetoric.

The following table will help the student as he reads the older modern or the ancient writers on Rhetoric ;—

Greek.	Latin.	English.
Ἡ (τέχνη) ῥητορική.	(Ars) Rhetorica.	Rhetoric.[1]
Ἄσκησις.	Exercitatio.	{ Composition.[2] { Oratory.[2]
Εὕρεσις.	Inventio.	Invention.[8]
Λόγος.	Oratio, Eloquentia.	{ Composition.[4] { Discourse.[1] { Eloquence.[5]
Λογιότης.	Eloquentia.	Eloquence.[6]
Λέξις.	Elocutio.	{ Elocution.[5] { Style.[8]
Ῥητορεία.	Oratoria.	{ Oratory. { Elocution.

Certain terms—*oratory, eloquence* (in the sense of the Greek λογιότης), and *elocution*—refer wholly to spoken discourse. The other terms have the double reference to either speech or writing.

V. The Latin Word Tropus.

What did *tropus*—Greek τρόπος and τρόπη—mean? Cicero (Brutus, xvii.) defines τρόπος as *verborum immutationes*, and says that the Greeks called *sententiarum orationisque formas* σχήματα. But Quintilian says, "Tropus est *verbi vel sermonis* ... mutatio," and, "vertique formas non *verborum* modo, sed et *sensuum* et *compositionis*. Quare mihi videntur errasse, qui *non alios* crediderunt *tropos*, quam *in quibus verbum pro verbo poneretur*."[7] Curiously enough, no Greek writer now extant seems to have used τρόπος in its rhetorical sense, and Lucianus alone of Greek writers (A. D. 160?) has τρόπη in this meaning. [See Liddell and Scott's *Lexicon, s. vv.*] More than this, the confusion of *trope* and *figure*—especially the modern use of *figure* as genus—had begun in Quintilian's time.[8]

---

[1] § 1, *above*.   [2] § 10 ff, *above*.   [3] § 23, *above*.   [4] § 3, *above*.

[5] Obsolete in this sense.—Eloquence seems to be used sometimes by Campbell to mean as much as Rhetoric. (See. I. i.)

[6] Theremin defines Eloquence as "thought in a flood."

[7] VIII. vi. 1-3. Cf. IX. i. 4.   [8] IX. i. 2.

INDEX.

ABBREVIATIONS, 92.
Abstruseness, 252.
Æsthetics, 14.
Alienisms, 76.
Ambiguity, 254; in pronouns, 258; in negatives, 260.
Anglo-Saxon words, 139.
Antithesis, 237.
Anticipation, 170.
Archaisms, 85.
Arrangement, 19; grammatical, 94; of words and clauses, 160; unusual for emphasis, 163; in persuasion, 327.
Argument, 309; proposition in, 315.
Art, 331.

BALANCED sentence, 184.
Barbarisms, 86.
Bathos, 220.
Brevity, 149; exceptions to, 154; violations of from excess, 152; from deficiency, 156; means to, 158.
Burden of proof, the, 317.

CANONS for divided use, 127; of the whole composition, 232.
Choice of words, 133.
Circumlocution, 152.
Clauses, order of in sentence, 160; modifying, 166.
Clearness, 254.
Climax, 220.
Colloquialisms, 124.
Composition, 9, 12; the whole, 223; parts of, 223; canons of, 232.
Compositions with respect to form, 23; to intrinsic character, 30; to purpose, 49.
Completeness, 234.
Comparison and contrast, 294, 308.
Compounds, 89.
Condensed sentence, 188.
Connectives, 175, 200.
Conjunctions, initial, 203.

Conclusion, the, 223.
Continuousness, 250.
Contrast, 294, 308.
Criticism, 331.

DARTMOUTH College case, 30.
Definition, 292; of Rhetoric, 9, 329.
Departments of Rhetoric, 19.
Description, 294, 299.
Dicta, 16.
Diction, 51; varieties of, 114; of poetry, 116; figures of, 236.
Discourse, 9; matter, or content, of, 14; form of, 14, 50; kinds of, 23; representative, 36.
Discussion, the, 223, 287; general rules for, 288; modes of, 290.
Divided use, 125; canons for, 127.
Division, 294, 306.
Due proportion in sentence, 194; in paragraph, 219.

ELEGANCE, 278.
Elements of style, 52, 132.
Emphasis, 162.
Ethics, 14.
Excitation, 320; proposition in, 321.
Exceptions to purity, 114; to brevity, 154.
Exemplification, 294, 307.
Explanation, 291; proper, 293; pathetic, 320.
Explicit reference in sentence, 174; by repetition, 178; in paragraph, 198.

FIGURES of speech, 235; of diction, 236; of thought, 236; rules for, 243.
Force, 262.
Form of Discourse, 14, 50.
Fundamental maxims, 16.

GOOD use, 55; characteristics of, 64.
Grammar, 14.
Grammatical purity, 53; propriety, 87; precision, 95.

INDEX.

Harmony, 275.
Humor, 271.
Hybridism, 91.
Hypothesis, 311.

Idiotisms, 69.
Illustration, 308.
Improprieties, 86, 111.
Impassioned prose, 119.
Initial topic sentence, 197; conjunctions, 203.
Introduction, the, 223.
Invention, 19, 281.
Issue, the point at, 310.

Kinds of discourse, 23.

Language, 10.
Letter, the, 35.
Literature and Rhetoric, 22.
Logic, 14.
Long and short words, 146; sentences, 179.
Loose sentence, 179.
Ludicrous, the, 271.

Maxims, fundamental, 16.
Matter, or content, of discourse, 14.
Means to brevity, 158.
Melody, 275.
Metre, 23.
Method of paragraph, 214; of whole composition, 233; of studying Rhetoric, 334.
Metric prose, 26, 119.
Modes of discussion, 290.
Modifiers, 162.
Modifying clauses, 166.
Motives, 325.

Narration, 294, 296.
National use, 65.
Naturalness, 250.
Negatives, ambiguous, 260.
Neologisms, 85.
Nomothetical sciences, 14, 331.
Nonsensical, the, 248.
Novel, the, 42.
Number of words, 149.

Obverse repetition, 308.
Offenses against purity, 69.
Oratory, 30; spurious, 248.
Order of words and clauses in sentence, 160.

Paragraph, 196; initial topic sentence, 197; parallel construction, 209; method, 214; unity, 216; due proportion in, 219.
Parallel construction in paragraph, 209.
Parentheses, 192.
Paraphrase, 152.
Partition, 294, 307.
Pathetic explanation, 320.
Pathos, 268.
Periphrasis, 152.
Perspicuity, 254.
Periodic sentence, 170.
Persuasion, 324; proposition in, 327.
Phraseology, 51.
Pleonasm, 152.
Poetry, 44.
Point at issue, the, 310.
Precision, grammatical, 95; rhetorical, 254.
Present use, 67.
Presumption, the, 317.
Prolixity, 152.
Pronouns, relative, as connectives, 177, 202; ambiguous, 258.
Properties of language, 51.
Propriety, rhetorical, 87; grammatical, 95.
Proportion, due, in sentence, 194; in paragraph, 219.
Proposition, the, 223; in argument, 315; in excitation, 321; in persuasion, 327.
Proofs, 311.
Prose, 24; metric, 26, 119; rhythmic, 27; impassioned, 119.
Prose rhythm, 25.
Provincialisms, 76.
Purity, grammatical, 53; standard of, 55; offenses against, 69; exceptions to, 114.

Qualities of style, 52, 247.
Question raised, the, 310.

Redundancy, 152.
Relative pronoun as connective, 177, 202.
Repetition, tautological, 152; justifiable, 154; for emphasis, 163; for explicit reference, 178, 200; obverse, 308.
Reputable use, 64.
Representative discourse, 36.
Rhetoric defined, 9, 329; proper, 12; departments of, 19; sciences that give

INDEX. 339

laws to, 14, 331 ; true method of studying, 334 ; certain technical terms of, 336.
Rhetoric and Literature, 22.
Rhetorical propriety, 87 ; precision, 254.
Rhythm, 23 ; of prose, 25.
Rhythmic prose, 27.
Romance, 42.

SATIRE, 271."
Schemata, 236.
Sciences nomothetical to Rhetoric, 14, 331.
Science, 331 ; pure and applied, 331.
Selection, 233.
Sentence, the, 160; order of words and clauses in, 160; periodic, 170; loose, 170; explicit reference, 174; long and short, 179; balanced, 184; condensed, 188 ; unity of, 188 ; due proportion in, 194 ; initial topic, 197.
Shall and *will*, 108.
Short and long words, 146; sentences, 179.
Significance, 248.
Simplicity, 252.
Solecisms, 86, 94.
Spurious oratory, 248.
Standard of purity, 55.
Style, 19, 50; elements of, 52, 132; qualities of, 52, 247.
Suspense, 170.

TASTE, 278.
Tautology, 152.

Technicalities, 76.
Terms, 10 ; technical, of Rhetoric, 336.
That, *who* and *which*, 106.
Theory, 311, 332.
Theme, 282.
Thought, 9 ; figures of, 236.
Tropes, 236.
Tropus, the Latin word, 336.

UNITY, of sentence, 188 ; Blair's rules for, 190; of paragraph, 216; of whole composition, 232.
Use, 55 ; reputable, 64; national, 65 ; present, 67 ; divided, 125.

VARIETY, 278.
Verbosity, 152.
Verse, 23.
Violations of purity, 69 ; of brevity, 152, 156.
Vocabulary, 133.
Vulgarisms, 69.

WEBSTER, Dartmouth College case, 30.
Who, *which* and *that*, 106.
Whole composition, the, 223 ; canons of, 232.
Will and *shall*, 108.
Wit, 271.
Words, choice of, 133 ; Anglo-Saxon, 139 ; short and long, 146; number of, 149 ; order of in sentence, 160; emphatic,162; ambiguous, 256.

www.ingramcontent.com/pod-product-compliance
Lightning Source LLC
Chambersburg PA
CBHW020242240426
43672CB00006B/609